THE EU AND ITS NEIGHBOURS

Manchester University Press

 SERIES EDITORS: *THOMAS CHRISTIANSEN AND EMIL KIRCHNER*

The formation of Croatian national identity ALEX J. BELLAMY
The European Union and the accommodation of Basque difference in Spain
ANGELA K. BOURNE
Theory and reform in the European Union, 2nd edition
DIMITRIS N. CHRYSSOCHOOU, MICHAEL J. TSINISIZELIS, STELIOS STAVRIDIS AND KOSTAS IFANTIS
From integration to integrity: administrative ethics and reform in the European Commission
MICHELLE CINI
The transatlantic divide OSVALDO CROCI AND AMY VERDUN
Germany, pacifism and peace enforcement ANJA DALGAARD-NIELSEN
The changing European Commission DIONYSSIS DIMITRAKOPOULOS (ED.)
Supranational citizenship LYNN DOBSON
Reshaping Economic and Monetary Union SHAWN DONNELLY
The time of European governance MAGNUS EKENGREN
Adapting to European integration? Kaliningrad, Russia and the European Union
STEFAN GÄNZLE, GUIDO MÜNTEL, EVGENY VINOKUROV (EDS)
An introduction to post-Communist Bulgaria EMIL GIATZIDIS
Non-state actors in international relations: the case of Germany
ANNE-MARIE LE GLOANNEC
Globalisation, integration and the future of European welfare states
THEODORA ISMENE-GIZELIS
Habermas and European integration: Social and cultural modernity beyond the nation-state
SHIVDEEP GREWAL
Mothering the Union ROBERTA GUERRINA
European internal security: towards supranational governance in the area of freedom, security and justice CHRISTIAN KAUNERT
Turkey: facing a new millennium AMIKAM NACHMANI
Europolis: constitutional patriotism beyond the nation state
PATRIZIA NANZ
A political sociology of the European Union: reassessing constructivism
MICHEL MANGENOT AND JAY ROWELL (EDS)
The changing faces of federalism SERGIO ORTINO, MITJA ŽAGAR AND VOJTECH MASTNY (EDS)
The road to the European Union
    Volume 1 The Czech and Slovak Republics JACQUES RUPNIK AND JAN ZIELONKA (EDS)
    Volume 2 Estonia, Latvia and Lithuania VELLO PETTAI AND JAN ZIELONKA (EDS)
A political sociology of the European Union: reassessing constructivism
MICHEL MANGENOT AND JAY ROWELL (EDS)
The activation of citizenship in Europe THOMAS PFISTER
Democratising capitalism? The political economy of post-Communist transformations in Romania, 1989–2001 LILIANA POP
Europe and civil society: movement coalitions and European governance
CARLO RUZZA
Constructing the path to eastern enlargement ULRICH SEDELMEIER
Governing Europe's new neighbourhood: Partners or periphery?
MICHAEL SMITH, KATJA WEBER AND MICHAEL BAUN (EDS)
Two tiers or two speeds? The European security order and the enlargement of the European Union and NATO JAMES SPERLING (ED.)
Recasting the European order JAMES SPERLING AND EMIL KIRCHNER
The Europeanisation of conflict resolution: regional integration and conflicts in Europe from the 1950s to the twenty-first century BOYKA STEFANOVA
Political symbolism and European integration TOBIAS THEILER
Rethinking European Union foreign policy BEN TONRA AND THOMAS CHRISTIANSEN (EDS)
The Europeanisation of the western Balkans: EU justice and home affairs in Croatia and Macedonia FLORIAN TRAUNER
The European Union in the wake of Eastern enlargement
AMY VERDUN AND OSVALDO CROCI (EDS)
Democratic citizenship and the European Union ALBERT WEALE
Inclusion, exclusion and the governance of European security MARK WEBBER

Gergana Noutcheva, Karolina Pomorska and Giselle Bosse
EDITORS

THE EU AND ITS NEIGHBOURS

Values versus security in European foreign policy

MANCHESTER UNIVERSITY PRESS

Copyright © Manchester University Press 2013

While copyright in the volume as a whole is vested in Manchester University Press, copyright in individual chapters belongs to their respective authors, and no chapter may be reproduced wholly or in part without the express permission in writing of both author and publisher.

Published by Manchester University Press
Altrincham Street, Manchester M1 7JA, UK
www.manchesteruniversitypress.co.uk

British Library Cataloguing-in-Publication Data is available

Library of Congress Cataloging-in-Publication Data is available

ISBN 978 1 7849 9106 7   paperback

First published by Manchester University Press in hardback 2013

This edition first published 2016

The publisher has no responsibility for the persistence or accuracy of URLs for any external or third-party internet websites referred to in this book, and does not guarantee that any content on such websites is, or will remain, accurate or appropriate.

Printed by Lightning Source

Contents

List of tables and figures	*page* vii
List of contributors	ix
Acknowledgements	xi

1 Values versus security? The choice for the EU and its neighbours   1
Gergana Noutcheva, Karolina Pomorska, Giselle Bosse

I Power and values in the EU's relations with its neighbours

2 The EU as a regional hegemon? From enlargement to ENP   25
Dimitar Bechev

3 The re-bordering of values through the European neighbourhood   46
Bohdana Dimitrovova

II Democracy and good governance

4 EU political dilemmas in North Africa and the Middle East: the logic of diversity and the limits to foreign policy   67
Rosa Balfour

5 Values and security: the EU's dilemma of democracy promotion in the Middle East   84
Bezen Balamir Coskun

6 Forging a wider European security community? Dilemmas of ENP in the South Caucasus   103
Licínia Simão

7 Values versus security? Assessing the EU's pragmatic engagement with Belarus in the Eastern Partnership policy   122
Giselle Bosse

III Hard and soft security challenges

8 The EU and ethno-political conflicts: a secure Europe in a more peaceful neighbourhood? 139
Elena Baracani

9 Deeds not declarations: Ukraine's convergence with the EU's foreign and security policies until 2010 157
Michal Natorski

10 Conducting relations with a difficult neighbour: the EU's struggle to influence Russian domestic politics 175
Anke Schmidt-Felzmann

11 Values versus security in the external dimension of EU migration policy: a case study on the readmission agreement with Russia 201
Florian Trauner, Imke Kruse and Bernhard Zeilinger

12 Conclusion: conceptualising the EU's role in the European neighbourhood 218
Karolina Pomorska and Gergana Noutcheva

Bibliography 234
Index 263

List of tables and figures

Tables *page*
5.1   EIDHR allocations 2005–9 (€)   89
5.2   MEDA/ENPI allocations 2002–10 (million €)   89
5.3   The EMP partners' Freedom House survey results, 1995 (the
      beginning of the Barcelona Process) and 2010   90
5.4   GCC states' Freedom House survey results (1988 and 2010)   92
8.1   Main ethno-political conflicts in the EU's neighbourhood   142
9.1   Ukraine's alignment with CFSP declarations   166

Figures
8.1   Total aid to Georgia by all donors, net disbursements,
      1994–2004   151
8.2   Total, EC, US, EU member states and EC plus EU member states
      ODA to Georgia, net disbursements, 1994–2004   152
8.3   Total, EC, US, EU member states and EC plus EU member states
      ODA to Israel, net disbursements, 1994–2004   152
8.4   Total, EC, US, EU member states, UNRWA and EC plus EU
      member states ODA to PAA, net disbursements, 1994–2004   153
10.1 The development of Russian GDP volumes   186
10.2 The growth of Russian GDP in the post-Cold War period   186
10.3 Russian energy in member states' electricity generation (2006)   188
10.4 Russian energy in member states' total consumption (2006)   189
10.5 Russian gas supplies and the effects of the January 2009
      disruptions   190

List of Contributors

Rosa Balfour is Senior Policy Analyst at the European Policy Centre (EPC), Brussels, Belgium.

Elena Baracani is Senior Researcher and Lecturer at the University of Florence, Italy.

Dimitar Bechev is Senior Policy Fellow and Head of the European Council on Foreign Relations (ECFR) office in Sofia, Bulgaria.

Giselle Bosse is Assistant Professor at the Political Science Department of Maastricht University, The Netherlands.

Bezen Balamir Coskun is Assistant Professor at Zirve University, Turkey.

Bohdana Dimitrovova is Research and Academic Assistant at the College of Europe, Bruges and Associate Research Fellow at the Centre for European Policy Studies, Brussels, Belgium.

Imke Kruse is Researcher at the Max Planck Institute for Human Development, Berlin, Germany.

Michal Natorski is Senior Research Fellow at the European Neighbourhood Policy Chair of the College of Europe, Natolin Campus, Warsaw, Poland.

Gergana Noutcheva is Assistant Professor at the Political Science Department of Maastricht University, The Netherlands.

Karolina Pomorska is Marie Curie Fellow at the University of Cambridge and Assistant Professor at the Political Science Department of Maastricht University, The Netherlands.

Anke Schmidt-Felzmann is Postdoctoral Fellow at Statsvetenskapliga Institutionen, Stockholm University, Sweden.

Licínia Simão is Assistant Professor at the University of Beira Interior, Covilhã and Postdoctoral Fellow at the Centre for Social Studies, University of Coimbra, Portugal.

Florian Trauner is Assistant Professor at the Institute for European Integration Research of the University of Vienna, Austria.

Bernhard Zeilinger is Lecturer in Political Science and EU Politics at the University of Applied Sciences BFI, Vienna, Austria.

Acknowledgements

This book evolved from a workshop on the European Neighbourhood Policy held at Maastricht University in June 2008, and from a successive follow-up meeting held in Brussels in May 2009. We are thankful to the Riksbankens Jubileumsfond, Stockholm, for its sponsorship of these events and to Fredrik Lundmark for his support of this project. We appreciate the financial assistance of the Research Stimulation Fund of the Faculty of Arts and Social Sciences (FASoS) of Maastricht University, which helped cover the costs of editing this volume. Gergana Noutcheva would also like to acknowledge the financial support of the European Commission through a Marie Curie Intra European Fellowship N 219597, which gave her time to work on the project. We are grateful to the editor of the 'Europe in Change' series of Manchester University Press, Thomas Christiansen, for his valuable feedback on the first draft of the manuscript. We are also grateful to Geoffrey Edwards at Cambridge University for his comments and suggestions regarding the book's conceptual framework. We would also like to thank Paul Stephenson for his excellent work on proofreading the text, and Dorina Baltag and Sophie Behrmann, who together provided invaluable editorial assistance in putting the manuscript together. We extend our sincere thanks to everyone who offered support and helped us develop the volume to its present shape.

GERGANA NOUTCHEVA, KAROLINA POMORSKA,
GISELLE BOSSE

1

Values versus security? The choice for the EU and its neighbours

Is there a tension between the normative fundamentals and strategic objectives of European Neighbourhood Policy (ENP)? While both values and security are present in the official discourse on ENP, the conceptual literature has frequently juxtaposed them as mutually exclusive paradigms, raising questions about the compatibility of the EU's norm export in the wider neighbourhood and the EU's interests in ensuring the cooperation of neighbouring states on hard and soft security matters. Can the EU pursue these two objectives simultaneously? What are the implications for its influence on the neighbourhood and its status as an international actor in the global context? Is 'values versus security' an unavoidable choice to be made by the EU and its neighbours or, rather, a false dichotomy?

This book argues that what is often considered a fundamental dilemma of EU foreign policy – a choice between the EU's values and its quest for security – misrepresents a much more complex reality in which values and security interplay to shape the EU's external positions. There is more than one way of looking at the relationship between values and security. While there may be a tension between the two, clashes in EU foreign policy-making can also result where it is difficult to reconcile the different values that underpin the EU's normative stance. They might also arise owing to differences in security approaches, both among EU member states, within the EU, and between the EU and its neighbours. There are also scenarios in which values and security can be seen as complementary paradigms rather than opposing principles, creating dilemmas in foreign policy-making.

The debate about values and security as driving forces of EU foreign policy has often been oversimplified by reducing it to a simple opposition between normative and rational motivations in choosing policy options. The objective of this book is threefold: 1) to draw attention to the complexity of the relationship between values and security in European Neighbourhood

Policy; 2) to conceptualise the various facets of the interplay between the two paradigms; and 3) to examine that interplay in a number of case studies. The book situates ENP in the broader conceptual debate about European Foreign Policy and draws upon its theoretical insights to shed light on the relationship between the normative dynamics and security rationale of the EU's evolving relations with its immediate neighbours in areas such as democratisation, good governance and security cooperation.

This introductory chapter first presents a brief overview of the policy dilemmas facing ENP since its inception and how these have been presented in the existing literature. It then turns to the theoretical and methodological discussion of the concepts of values and security and their complex interplay with regards to the broader academic debates about European Foreign Policy. Finally, it situates the arguments of the individual chapters in this conceptual framework and introduces the empirical findings of the chapters.

The dilemmas of European Neighbourhood Policy

It is no secret that ENP faces several dilemmas, which arguably limit its ability to influence political and economic developments in its immediate neighbourhood. The existing literature has engaged with some of these dilemmas, including: the 'one-size-fits-all' approach of ENP; the contradictions between the mechanisms of conditionality and equal partnership; and the tensions between regionalism and bilateralism in ENP (Bechev and Nicolaidis 2010). These key dilemmas and corresponding arguments are presented below.

One-size-fits-all policy?
Launched at the time of the EU's enlargement to Central and Eastern Europe in 2004, ENP was designed to avoid new dividing lines on the continent and to offset the costs of exclusion for the EU's 'new' eastern neighbours (Commission 2003b). Short of consensus on further enlargement eastwards, a new policy formula had to be invented, on the one hand to replicate the success of enlargement in transforming the neighbourhood, but on the other, to silence any further demands for accession to the EU from some eastern neighbours, in particular Ukraine and Moldova.

The geopolitical realities of the EU's southern and eastern frontiers, however, led to inclusion of both the southern[1] and the eastern[2] EU neighbours in ENP. The southern EU member states insisted on closer ties with the Mediterranean partners, while the northern and eastern EU member states supported more intensive cooperation with the former Soviet republics (Del Sarto and Schumacher 2005; Joffé 2008). A neighbourhood policy of sorts was thus proposed to the two groups of neighbouring states, which were, it should be acknowledged, very different in terms of their domestic conditions, even if they shared a common geographical proximity to the EU. The eastern neighbours are newly independent states that (re-)gained sovereignty after the dissolution of the Soviet Union in the early 1990s. They have been undergoing a transition from centrally planned to market economies and are experiencing different degrees of political pluralism, even if the record of political reform in many of them has been unimpressive. Above all, the societal sense of crisis that accompanied the collapse of the Communist system in the early 1990s, and the democratic aspirations of the societies expressed through the political mobilisation leading to regime change in some of them (such as in Georgia in 2003 and Ukraine in 2004), have both given a popular mandate to the new elites of the former Soviet republics to put in place a functioning model of governance. The results to date have nevertheless been mixed, with many of the countries reversing on earlier democratisation gains, and others consolidating autocratic rule under market conditions.

With a few exceptions (Israel, Lebanon, Palestinian Authority), the EU's southern neighbours have until recently been stable regimes, skilful at suppressing political dissent. Their economies have been part of the global economy for years, while their societies did not feel the same urge to see domestic change as the EU's eastern neighbours did in the 1990s and the 2000s. The events of the Arab Spring of 2011 (discussed at length in the Conclusion) have however shaken the myth that Arab societies are immune to democracy, showing that Arab citizens are determined to challenge their regimes and demand political change, as demonstrated by the political upheavals in countries such as Libya, Egypt, Tunisia and Syria. Expecting the EU to enjoy similar successes in promoting its values of political and economic governance and/or in achieving its security goals in domestic settings as diverse as those in Palestine, Ukraine, Algeria and Armenia would be highly unlikely. However, through ENP, the EU has set itself the objective of raising the governance standards of the two neighbourhoods, though analysts have doubted the seriousness of its intentions with regard to democracy promotion (Youngs 2004). First evaluations of the EU's impact on its neighbours reveal that the EU is 'punching below its weight' in both regional groups (Whitman and Wolff 2010).

Conditionality versus equal partnership?
One of the key policy questions weighing on the minds of policy-makers concerning the EU's approach to its neighbourhood, is how much conditionality it is willing and able to apply in order to reach its goals. With Enlargement Policy being the conceptual reference for policy instruments used in the ENP context, conditionality and socialisation have been the main tools for managing relations with neighbours (Kelley 2006). Yet the neighbourhood is different, not only because the partner states have diverse backgrounds but also because the *finalité* of their relationship with the EU is not defined by the prospect of accession. Hence, it is difficult to justify

applying conditionality in quite the same way that the EU practised it previously with the countries of Central and Eastern Europe. The incentives the EU has offered to the neighbouring states exclude political integration and are limited to stronger trade relations and participation in the internal market, although ideas about the selective inclusion of partners in the EU's dense institutional environment have also been floated around in official documents (Commission 2006a). ENP incentives are thus much weaker compared to the 'carrot' of membership in the enlargement context (Smith 2005a; Weber, Smith and Baun 2007; Emerson, Noutcheva and Popescu 2007). The EU has also been vague in articulating them, further undermining its leverage vis-à-vis its neighbours. This has led Sasse (2008) to conceptualise the incentive model of ENP as 'conditionality-lite' characterised by open-endedness and non-commitment on both sides of the relationship – the EU and ENP country. Arguably, the weaknesses of ENP conditionality may provide opportunities for socialisation to prove its worth as a mechanism of promoting domestic change, by socialising local elites (Sasse 2008), even if strong supporting evidence for such a claim has yet to be provided in the literature.

In the neighbourhood context, the EU has emphasised the domestic ownership of a process of *rapprochement* with the EU, leaving the door open for socialisation practices to influence patterns of change in the neighbouring countries. Partner states are invited to choose their own degree and pace of convergence with the EU on political and economic governance standards. The reform priorities are jointly decided upon and the monitoring of reform implementation is jointly conducted, under the so-called principle of 'joint ownership'. In other words, the partnership component is given great importance in ENP tools, often prioritised over a more robust line on divergences in political values with some neighbouring governments. In reality, however, the EU has been rather reluctant to apply the principle of partnership and to make reciprocal concessions vis-à-vis its neighbours (Bosse 2010). Conditionality, whenever it is applied, is more the positive than negative type, stressing rewards and inducements ('carrots') rather than sanctions ('sticks'). For example, the EU has set up a Governance Facility to support top performers from the neighbourhood on governance reform with an annual budget of €50 million. Similarly, the European Neighbourhood Investment Facility allocates additional funds (a budget of €700 million for 2007–13) for infrastructure investment in the neighbourhood, meant to top up lending from international financial institutions for pre-approved projects in priority sectors (Commission 2007b). Supplementary financial stimuli to encourage domestic transformation have been devised and monies can, in theory, be disbursed on evidence of reform.

Since its inception, ENP has been heavily criticised for its mismatch between the incentives for reform it provides and the goals it seeks to achieve (Emerson 2004a; Zagorski 2004; Kubicek 2005). The ambition of its objectives embodied in the European values of democracy, good governance, rule of law, peaceful management of disputes and so on, has not been matched by a clear vision of how exactly the EU sees the integration of its neighbours in its common policy space and how much inclusion the EU is really willing to offer to outsiders from the East and the South. If a neighbouring state, for example, grows to become a viable democracy and adopts the EU *acquis*, how would the EU reward the progress made? Alternatively, if a neighbour co-operates half-heartedly and adopts some of the governance rules but not all, how much access to the common market is the EU going to allow? Inherent in these questions is the essential difference between Mediterranean partners who are 'neighbours of Europe' and the eastern partners who are 'European neighbours', as aptly described by Polish Foreign Minister Sikorski.[3] ENP does not resolve the 'exclusion/inclusion dilemma' of the EU's relations with the countries in its immediate vicinity, as Karen Smith (2005a) has noted. The lack of clarity on these matters among member states, and the divergent messages emanating from national capitals, together have a negative effect on the credibility of ENP, and perception of the EU's intentions in the eyes of its neighbours.

Ambiguity has decreased the EU's potential leverage and ultimately meant exerting less impact on the neighbours than anticipated (Smith 2005a; Whitman and Wolff 2010). The new pledge to apply strict conditionality on those neighbouring states wishing to strengthen their ties with the EU, as contained in the strategic review of ENP of May 2011 (Commission 2011b), so far remains little more than a good intention.

Regionalism versus bilateralism?
Another significant dilemma facing ENP has been how best to strike the right balance between the regional and bilateral components of the EU's initiatives vis-à-vis the neighbours. Bilateral policy instruments allow the EU to hone in on specific shortcomings in the domestic governance arrangements of partner states. They also provide for differentiation among the neighbours, which is key when it comes to playing symbolic politics in the group by praising or criticising the progress of specific countries. The demonstration effects aimed through these public appraisals are meant to set in motion a learning dynamic between partners, who can inspire each other for further reform, as observed by scholars of EU enlargement (Grabbe 2001). The bilateral Action Plans that the EU negotiates with each country separately, along with the progress reports that evaluate the implementation of the reform commitments undertaken, are the main ENP instruments for influencing the domestic governance arrangements of each partner.

Encouraging partners to work together on common problems in regions marred by 'frozen' conflicts and inter-state disputes is also just as important if not more pressing, and calls for a regional approach. The EU's regional initiatives in the Mediterranean and in Eastern Europe have mushroomed in the last 15 years, leaving outsiders confused about the purpose and usefulness of the various EU-sponsored multilateral undertakings. The Euro-Mediterranean Partnership (EMP) was launched in 1995, with the intention of bringing peace, prosperity and democracy to the southern shores of the Mediterranean through a multilateral forum of dialogue among the countries from the region. It was also meant to indirectly contribute to the resolution of the Israel–Palestine conflict, which had long overshadowed regional politics and blocked potential regional cooperation. Analyses of the EMP's achievements tend to conclude that it failed to deliver on its ambitious promises (Del Sarto and Schumacher 2005). It was subsequently succeeded by the Union for the Mediterranean (UfM) in 2008, a new French initiative intended to invigorate exchanges across the Mediterranean Sea by promoting a more pragmatic approach to regional cooperation, one focusing on supposedly low-politics sectors such as transport, environment, energy, etc (Emerson 2008). The Union for the Mediterranean was also meant to increase the ownership of the process by the southern neighbours, being co-presided by the EU and a Mediterranean state (European Commission 2008b). First analysis of its potential to reinvigorate the regional agenda in the region has shown its structural predisposition to strengthen the bilateral components of the EU–Mediterranean partnership at the expense of regionalism (Bicchi 2011: 9). Notable as well was its move away from the normative agenda of democracy promotion in the regional context when it was launched (Kausch and Youngs 2009). The Arab–Israeli conflict has marred its functioning since inception, while the Arab Spring has questioned its very relevance as an appropriate policy tool.

For some time, nothing existed for Eastern Europe similar to the institutionalised framework of the Barcelona Process in the Mediterranean. The EU was reluctant to engage the countries in the East in a multilateral fashion, not least because 'the region' in that part of the continent is not easy to define, being situated in the interest sphere of a range of actors such as Russia, Turkey, the republics in the South Caucasus, Ukraine, Bulgaria and Romania (the latter two became EU members in 2007). The Black Sea proved the geographical reference for launching a regional cooperative platform called the Black Sea Synergy in 2007 (Commission 2007c) which was the EU's first more pronounced attempt to become involved as a bloc in the regional context (Tassinari 2006). The idea behind the Black Sea Synergy is similar to that of the Northern Dimension – practical cooperation in areas of common interest such as transport, environment, energy, the fight against organised crime, etc. Yet the question of Russia and how to deal with it both bilaterally and within the region has divided EU member states and prevented them from coming up with a clear vision of how to build a partnership with the former Soviet republics in Eastern Europe (Popescu and Wilson 2009).

The events of August 2008, when relations between Russia and Georgia escalated to a full-scale military conflict, provoked a thorough rethink of the

EU's engagement in the region. The short war in South Ossetia in August 2008 demonstrated unequivocally the differences in the EU's and Russia's approaches to their common neighbourhood. The EU's reaction in the aftermath was to step up its involvement in the region through ENP's soft instruments, in order to anchor the countries more firmly in the European liberal space. This took the form of a new initiative called Eastern Partnership (EaP) which Poland and Sweden had already campaigned for, and which the European Commission was already working on prior to the August 2008 violence in the Caucasus (Copsey and Pomorska 2010). Launched officially in May 2009, the Eastern Partnership strengthens both the bilateral and the multilateral dimensions of the EU's relations with the eastern neighbours. Unlike any of the previous initiatives it also encourages multilateral dialogue between the EU and the region on integration issues. An institutionalised framework of contacts between the EU and the region is developed at all levels – from heads of state to experts in various sectors – which complements more concrete ideas about economic integration, visa liberalisation and cooperation in areas of energy, transport, environment, etc (Commission 2008c). Notable, too, is the involvement of civil society in eastern partner countries through the establishment of the Civil Society Forum, engaging the third sector in a structured multilateral dialogue on governance issues dominating the bilateral ENP agenda with eastern governments.

Some have seen the Union for the Mediterranean and the Eastern Partnership as comparable initiatives in the South and the East, respectively, and whose launch signals ENP splitting into two regional tracks in recognition of regional differences. It should be acknowledged, however, that from an EU point of view the goals, nature of relations and means of engagement remain similar in both neighbourhoods, oscillating, sometimes uncomfortably, between bilateralism and regionalism. In the South, the launch of ENP has been viewed as a step away from the regional agenda and a move towards greater bilateralism in dealings with the Mediterranean partners (Del Sarto and Schumacher 2005; Pace 2007; Bicchi 2011). In the East, the regional approach adds a new dimension to the bilateralism preferred by the EU in its relations with the newly independent states of the former Soviet Union since the 1990s.

Since its inception, ENP has gone through several rounds of strengthening those policy instruments available, largely on the initiative of the European Commission in reaction to external events or criticism (Commission 2004b, 2006a, 2007b, 2008a, 2011a, 2011b). Its shape and substance have thus become more concrete and concerned with operational aspects, though its real impact on the neighbourhood is yet to be seen. So far, ENP has raised more questions on the governance problems of the neighbouring states than it has given answers. It has nevertheless generated hope that the 'European neighbourhood' can become a more orderly and better-governed space than at present.

Even though the existing academic literature has engaged with the various dilemmas underpinning ENP, the relationship between the EU's normative and security agendas in its policy towards its neighbours has not been analysed in a systematic manner. Many scholars focus on the 'dilemmas' described above and simply assume an inevitable dichotomy between values and security in ENP. The existing academic contributions have not made an attempt to conceptualise this dichotomy, or to place the two concepts into the wider context of EU foreign policy; nor have they presented any sound empirical evidence to show the complex interplay between the two paradigms and their varied impacts on ENP partners.

Conceptual underpinnings

Values versus security? Does a trade-off exist between the two concepts in the literature on EU foreign policy? Scholars of EU foreign policy often juxtapose them, suggesting an inherent incompatibility between a values-based and an interest-based foreign policy. Manners (2002) was among the first to articulate the normative vision of EU foreign policy, attributing to the EU a certain normative predisposition in its external relations and describing it as a different type of actor on the international scene, a normative one. In contrast, Hyde-Price (2006) has staunchly defended the opposing view, insisting that there is nothing new or different about the EU as an international player, one whose policy is determined by the rational interests of its member states, the biggest of which weigh more heavily on the common line (if it exists). This contrast in the conception of foreign policy motives reflects the rationalism–constructivism debate in International Relations theory (see for example the anniversary issue of *International Organization* in 1998, Vol. 52, Issue 4, devoted entirely to this problem or, for a more recent critique of such a dichotomous approach Barkin 2010). Whereas most constructivists subscribing to a positivist methodology tend to credit norms as determining factors of foreign policy behaviour (Checkel 1998), rationalists see material or other interests as primary drivers of international exchanges, with realists putting an emphasis on 'hard security' (Morgenthau 1973) and liberals stressing 'soft security' (Keohane and Nye 1977).

The official discourse of EU foreign policy is not so clear-cut about the motives behind EU foreign policy actions. Official documents on ENP abound in references to 'shared values' as a basis for the EU's relations with its neighbours (Commission 2003b) as well as to the 'European interest' in being surrounded by a 'ring of well-governed states' (European Security Strategy 2003). The value-driven and the interest-driven logics thus co-exist in ENP rhetoric, with the latter often being equated with EU security. To achieve security for the EU, security on its outer periphery is deemed to be necessary and the way to achieve this is essentially the normative expansion of its internal space, or so the official line seems to suggest. But do values and security complement each other as EU policy-makers may imply?

It is important to move beyond the simple dichotomy between 'values' versus 'security' in the debate on EU foreign policy, and to narrow down the methodological divide between rationalism and constructivism in order to grasp the complex interplay between the two paradigms in ENP. There are different ways to conceptualise the relationship between values and security; looking at the two concepts as dichotomous or complementary categories are only two possibilities. The following section develops five typologies that theorise possible constellations to perceive the relationship between 'values' and 'security' in international relations and EU foreign policy: (i) 'security as a value'; (ii) 'values as part of security'; (iii) 'values versus security'; (iv) 'values versus values'; and (v) 'security versus security'. Researching these typologies requires a variety of methodological tools that draw on both rationalist and social constructivist approaches.

Security as a value

Many traditional treatments of security equate it with a rational process of interest-calculation, but security can be viewed as a value in itself when defined in broader terms – as the opposite of instability and chaos, a guarantee of people's peaceful existence or as building a community of like-minded states that stand for peaceful relations and renounce military means as a way of settling disagreements among themselves. The human security literature, for example, focuses on conceptualising security in normative terms by placing the security of human beings rather than states at the centre of analysis (United Nations Development Programme 1994; Kaldor, Martin and Selchow 2007; Ellner 2008). This conceptual shift not only challenges traditional state-centric approaches to security, linked to both the realist and liberal schools of thought, but also expands the discussion of security to areas such as human rights, human development, environmental security, etc. It also redirects the debate about the means for enhancing security away from the strictly military domain and towards more civilian approaches to addressing threats to security such as humanitarian aid, development assistance, conflict prevention, poverty reduction, institution-building, civil society empowerment, strengthening the rule of law, etc.

Some scholars have argued that the EU's approach to security is strongly influenced by the human security doctrine even though it is not endorsed as such at the official level (Kaldor, Martin and Selchow 2007; Ellner 2008). Not only does the EU engage in building a security community internally, based on common values and shared aspirations for peace and stability (Deutsch 1957), but it also does so externally, by trying to act as a 'peacebuilder', keen to transpose its own security experience to other parts of the world (Aggestam 2008). Security is a normative category in the EU's own security discourse with the European Security Strategy (2003) reflecting quite remarkably the absence of any zero-sum logic in the EU's own conception of its role in the world as a 'force for good'.

If security is approached as a value worth pursing internally as well as externally, then no clash emerges between the EU's pursuit of security and its normative approach to international politics (see Licínia Simão's chapter in this volume). Security and values converge in this scenario, suggesting a policy that is not only normative in its goals but one that is also pursued through normative means such as engagement, partnership, dialogue and positive inducements (see Elena Baracani's chapter in this volume). Tensions may still arise between different values the EU espouses, such as the need to reach out to political opposition in autocratic societies for the sake of encouraging political pluralism, while at the same time engaging and talking to authoritarian leaders in order to prevent closing off communication channels and forgoing opportunities for persuasion and socialisation. These tensions, however, do not undermine the normative nature of EU foreign policy in this conceptual setting, which involves foreign policy dilemmas not captured by a narrow 'values versus security' lens. Rather, they would result in a dilemma as to how best to prioritise certain values over others, an issue we discuss below under 'Values versus values'.

Values as part of security

Constructivist claims about the primacy of values in foreign policy formulation (Checkel 1998) can be countered by the possibility of norm diffusion for the sake of achieving strategic objectives. In other words, certain values may well be promoted out of a strategic choice or on the basis of a justification that they will advance one's material (or other) interests, which raises the question of whether a values-based foreign policy is truly normative in character (Youngs 2004; Laïdi 2008). This conceptualisation is reminiscent of Wolfers' pursuit of *milieu goals* by foreign policy actors seeking to normatively shape to their own benefit the external environment within which they operate (Wolfers 1962). It also relates to Laïdi's pursuing 'geopolitics with norms' – of which, he asserts, ENP is a good example (Laïdi 2008). If the EU is instrumental both in its conception of security and in the pursuit of its values, no clash arises in its normative and strategic orientations (see Dimitar Bechev's chapter in this volume). This is a distinct and unambiguous opportunity for the EU to pursue its external relations without having to make a choice between values and security, nor choose between ways of achieving security, be they normative or otherwise. And although the EU's foreign policy behaviour may not follow the classical realist paradigm (military power is not a feature of the EU's international position), a self-interested foreign policy advancing the EU's security and the EU's values as a strategic goal provides a distinct angle, and a purely rational one, for examining the values-security nexus.

Related to this discussion is the question of what means the EU is using to advance its foreign policy objectives. The debate has evolved around civilian instruments such as trade and diplomacy traditionally relied upon by the EU in its foreign policy exchanges, as opposed to military means (Duchêne 1972; Whitman 1998). Yet even soft instruments such as sanctions can be seen as coercive, if they try to impose ways of doing things on other actors, while disregarding their own preferences (Sjursen 2006). The use of conditionality in foreign policy is an example of such a soft yet forceful method of inducing behavioural change in third parties by offering rewards and threatening punishments (Schimmelfennig and Sedelmeier 2004). Positive types of conditionality that emphasise positive inducements rather than sanctions can be viewed as less coercive and better aligned with normative conceptions of foreign policy means. On the opposite side of the spectrum are softer methods of persuasion, social learning and lessons-drawing based on social interaction and non-hierarchical communication (Checkel 2001), all of which seem to support claims that the EU is a normative actor (Tocci 2008). In reality, the EU's preference to deliver rewards conditional on third countries' compliance with its normative principles – whether in the fields of democracy promotion and human rights, or rules governing various sectors of the single market – has become common practice in its foreign policy, enlargement policy, ENP and its development policy. There has been considerable criticism about the way the conditionality mechanism has been applied, with accusations of double standards in its application. This would seem to confirm rather than dismiss the possibility for the instrumental promotion of values, hence the conceptual rationale for examining values and security as complementary strategic objectives of the EU's foreign policy.

Values versus security
A clash between values and security might arise when the EU's views on achieving security are seen to be at loggerheads with its values, implying the need for a choice. A classical example of this foreign policy dilemma is the question of how to deal with authoritarian governments whose cooperation is needed for addressing security issues such as counter-terrorism, illegal migration or stable energy supplies (see Giselle Bosse's chapter in this volume). Another example might be the EU's visa regime which is deliberately very restrictive for reasons of internal security, yet the liberalisation of the movement of people is considered conducive to the promotion of political pluralism in partner states and societal socialisation in general (see Trauner, Kruse and Zeilinger's chapter in this volume). Similarly, the opening up of the EU's market is considered conducive to spreading liberal norms and creating wealth. However, the EU's frequent reluctance to allow greater market access to neighbouring states in sectors particularly sensitive for individual EU member states is seen to reflect the EU's primary concern with its own economic security and well-being. These situations, however, do not

exhaust the variety of exchanges the EU maintains with partner countries. To argue that the tension between the EU's security and its values lies at the very heart of EU foreign policy-making overlooks alternative ways of seeing security and values.

The alleged clash between values and security in the EU's external relations is usually presented as a clash between normative and strategic (rational) approaches to foreign policy. What is, however, often disregarded is the divergence among the member states over definitions of values and security (see Rosa Balfour's and Anke Schmidt-Felzmann's chapters in this volume). Notwithstanding the degree of Europeanisation reached among the EU member states through common institution-building and common policy-formulation in the framework of the Common Foreign and Security Policy (CFSP) (Tonra 2001; Wong 2005), national representatives still often lack a common vision as to which values should be prioritised in the EU's external relations or what threats to security are more pressing than others. This was only too clearly demonstrated in the divisions over the United States' invasion of Iraq, over EU policy towards Russia, or the EU's policy towards Belarus after the eastern enlargement. In fact, what appears to be a dilemma between norms and rationality in EU foreign policy decision-taking often conceals a more complex reality of divergent views among member states on the type of values or type of security that the EU as a whole should stand up for in its foreign policy.

The EU's political values, encoded in its treaties, are well known and widely cited in the EU's official discourse on foreign policy issues. Democracy, good governance, rule of law, human rights and the protection of minorities, reflect a normative consensus among the member states about what is right and fair in relation to domestic governance (Lisbon Treaty, art. 2).[4] The EU has also publicly declared its commitment to such normative principles as multilateralism, the respect for international law and institutions, and the promotion of peace and international security (Manners 2002). In reality, the pursuit of these different values may at times be contradictory, bringing to the fore the question of which values should have a higher priority in guiding the EU's external policies. Is it better to engage autocrats regardless of the normative divergence with respect to democratic governance, or to isolate them by taking a position of the moral high ground? Is it right to insist on political pluralism in autocracies when the initial steps of democratisation are known to bring about instability and even violence in some cases? Is it good to preach free and fair elections when the forces with popular legitimacy are in certain cases the ones espousing extreme nationalist views or radical ideologies? These are difficult questions that often divide public opinion across the political spectrum in any state, let alone an entity comprised of 27 member states needing to reach consensus before it embarks on any policy towards external partners. Similar issues involving normative choices often make it onto the agenda of EU foreign ministers; they require concrete answers not always easy to produce in a club of 27 nations with different understandings of what is appropriate from a normative standpoint in specific situations. The different initial reactions of the member states to the popular uprisings against the autocratic regimes in Northern Africa in spring 2011 present a good illustration of the dilemma discussed here.

With regard to security, the European Security Strategy reflects the tentative consensus among member states on the basic security challenges facing the EU as a bloc, such as terrorism, proliferation of weapons of mass destruction, regional conflicts, state failure or organised crime (European Security Strategy 2003). Concerns about other types of security have also dominated the EU's security agenda at times, such as the security of energy supply and how to deal with supplier and transit countries, the security of borders and how to ensure the efficient management of migration flows, or with regard to environmental security and how to tackle the adverse effects of climate change, etc. There are different perceptions among the member states about the type of security that merits greater attention and more resources at the EU level. Some see the threat of terrorism as paramount whereas others consider the need to address the influx of immigrants arriving on the Mediterranean shores as more urgent. In the same vein, some member states from Central and Eastern Europe view Russia's assertive energy policies in the Eastern neighbourhood as a direct threat to their energy security whereas some older member states such as Germany and Italy perceive Russia as a major trading partner (Leonard and Popescu 2007).

The divergent views about the hierarchy of security challenges extend to the means of tackling those challenges too. For example, some see diversifying energy sources as the appropriate strategy to ensure energy security whereas others prefer bilateral deals with energy supplying countries. Some favour a more robust EU involvement in handling illegal migration whereas others give priority to national solutions. Even on questions of hard security, differences of opinion persist. Some member states, especially the UK, the Netherlands and Portugal, as well as those from Central and Eastern Europe, see NATO and the US as the main security provider in Europe while others are more lukewarm with regard to NATO and would like to see, in parallel, a more independent role for the EU in security matters (Howorth 2005). Similarly, some member states are more willing than others to deploy troops abroad in peacekeeping operations and police missions in order to boost stability in conflict zones. It is difficult to speak of a common approach to security among member states, even if there is a basic agreement on the major threats to European security.

Values versus values
The EU's values can be seen as contested not only internally but also externally. The EU may think of its values as universally applicable (see Bohdana Dimitrovova's chapter in this volume) but there remain different conceptions

of what is acceptable from a normative point of view (Wagnsson 2010). The concept of democracy and its applicability in all cultural contexts has stirred considerable debate, in particular its compatibility with Islam (Diamond 2010). Arab societies, some argue, because of their different historical development, political philosophy and cultural practices, have developed distinct views about domestic governance which are not wholly compatible with European conceptions of democracy (see Bezen Balamir Coskun's chapter in this volume). The Arab Spring has questioned that interpretation, at the same time showing that domestic understandings of what political pluralism and accountability entail are context-bound and critical for an endogenous process of democratisation. The point here is that non-EU countries may sense a strategic agenda behind a seemingly benign emphasis on 'common values' in the EU's rhetoric. For example, the promotion of political liberalism, free and fair elections or women's rights may be justified on the grounds of human rights, individual empowerment or equality of men and women but it does little to appeal to authoritarian regimes, who may see it as a direct threat to their power basis. The way in which values are pursued and disseminated may leave others doubting the EU's good intentions, instead suspecting an interest in expanding its influence, if not securing some kind of direct gain.

Those who have debated the normative power of the EU have alluded to different normative benchmarks. For Manners (2002), the EU's internal normative standard is enough to designate the EU a normative actor whereas Sjursen (2006) considers international law the ultimate yardstick for 'normativity' in foreign policy. To ensure that norms are not being used as cover for advancing strategic interests, a foreign policy action needs to lean on internationally sanctioned rules and principles codified in the international legal order (Sjursen 2006; Tocci 2008). A tension nevertheless exists, given that the present-day international legal system provides stronger protection for the rights of states than for the rights of individuals. As such, the system provides a weak basis for the safeguard of norms enjoying universal appeal to human beings across state borders, such as human rights, equality of men and women, children's rights, etc. The possibility for different interpretations of what is normative remains strong and, with it, the likelihood of clashes between the EU's definition of norms and those definitions by agents on the receiving end of its foreign policy actions. Without a degree of reflexivity, the EU can easily assume the position of self-righteousness, if it attempts to project its own norms as being universally valid categories (Diez 2005; Bicchi 2006). The extent to which such differences in normative standards create foreign policy dilemmas for the EU needs to be conceptually explored and empirically tested in concrete situations before assigning 'normativity' to the EU's foreign policy actions.

Security versus security
Finally, the EU's notion of security may differ from that of its neighbours, in so doing affecting the likelihood of its policies being effective. It is not always clear whose security the EU has in mind when it claims to act in the name of security – its own security or that of its neighbours, or both? And even if the EU's intentions genuinely mean security for all, its ideas about what is appropriate to do in order to obtain security may clash with those of its neighbours in specific situations. For example, some of the protagonists in the so-called 'frozen' conflicts in the Eastern neighbourhood have been keen for the EU to become more involved in the settlement of a conflict, but the EU has kept a low profile, opting for long-term structural solutions rather than quick fixes, not least because of a fear of provoking Russia and exacerbating the conflict rather than resolving it (German 2007; Popescu 2007). This has led to criticisms that the EU is more interested in its own security (energy and other) than in bringing security to conflict-torn societies. Others have maintained that the EU not only places a higher importance on its own security, but also views its neighbours as a source of insecurity (see Michal Natorski's chapter in this volume). External actors looking on at EU policies aimed at enhancing security may perceive a certain self-interest in the EU's actions or non-actions, irrespective of its rhetoric of pursing international security for the sake of global safety and stability.

Inherent in this discussion is a series of ethical questions pertaining to the exertion of power externally, which involves making choices or balancing one's own interests and those of the third party concerned (Aggestam 2008). An altruistic foreign policy that takes into consideration the well-being of 'the other' is a theoretical possibility, but scholars have also asserted that the 'combination of self-regarding and other-regarding motives' is a win-win solution that lives up to ethical standards (Barbé and Johansson-Nogués 2008). The various motives perceived by both sides add another layer of complexity to the already difficult balancing act between potentially diverging interests of all parties concerned. Given that the EU publicly aspires to be a 'force for good' in the world, such situations presenting ethical dilemmas happen to constitute a central challenge to the EU's foreign policy-makers, a challenge not directly captured by a 'values versus security' approach.

Researching the five typologies: towards ontological openness and methodological pluralism

The role of 'values' or normative issues in foreign policy has been the subject of a long-standing debate in International Relations as a discipline, as much as the place of ethics and principles in states' behaviour in international politics. Some schools of thought, such as neo-realism, perceive values merely as 'smokescreens' that conceal the true strategic interests of states

(Waltz 1979).⁵ Others, such as those linked to the liberal school of thought, including Keohane, link its sources directly to values and principles (Jørgensen 2006: 44) and attach more importance to normative aspects of state behaviour even if they consider it to be rationally motivated (Axelrode and Keohane 1985; Keohane 1989). Many of the later critics of these rational choice approaches have pointed out the necessity of including normatively motivated aspects of behaviour into the explanatory paradigms. The English School in particular has drawn attention to the role of shared norms and values in the functioning of the international society of states (Bull 1966, 1977; and Jackson 2000, who made a call to 'bring the values back' into the analysis). Constructivist approaches focusing explicitly on these issues have only recently appeared on the agenda (e.g. Wendt 1999), gearing research towards the role of ideas, culture and discourses in foreign policy. Such approaches are less concerned with the objective of *explaining* foreign policy outcomes or 'interests', more so in *understanding* their origins through an examination of their discursive and social construction – one that explores the interplay between individuals, states and institutions (*agency*) and values, norms and institutions (*structures*).

The research on European Foreign Policy has for a long time been dominated by the dichotomous approaches of scholars who have either studied norms and values, or mainly focused on interests and rationality (see above). The debate so far has reinforced the dichotomous understanding of EU foreign policy. This is not surprising and directly mirrors the broader debate in political science and International Relations between rational choice and constructivist approaches in explaining individual or state behaviour. Our conceptual framework treating values and security in both rationalist and constructivist terms suggests that a direct juxtaposition between constructivist and rationalist explanations and the privileging of one over the other (values/security) is not informative of how EU foreign policy is made. Our analysis questions the IR dualisms of calculation versus internalisation, interests versus norms, rational choice versus identity. By suggesting that the two notions of values and security can be complementary categories (security as a value, and values as part of security), our conceptual framework argues in favour of overcoming ontological rigidities. By suggesting that conflicts about foreign policy issues among the EU member states may occur because of a different prioritisation of values or different sensitivities to security threats (values versus values and security versus security), our analysis also demonstrates that the constructivist-rationalist opposition does not reflect political reality, hence the question is not so much whether actors follow a 'logic of consequence' or a 'logic of appropriateness' but under what conditions certain values would be preferred over others and/or certain conceptions of security would be favoured over others.

It has already been observed in the literature that while some deep-rooted values underline actions, other values may be developed more consciously (so that interests take precedence). Chong (1996), for example, has argued that both normative and rational choice theories have ignored possible explanations for the motivations behind actions. Rational choice (economic) models underestimate the power of values when conceptualising the calculation by agents of opportunity costs (Chong 1996: 2132). Sociological or normative models have arguably not attached enough importance to interests when explaining value formation; this is why some scholars in IR but also in the domain of EU studies, have recently acknowledged the need to reconcile the two approaches, calling for research in that direction (Saurugger 2009: 937; Youngs 2010: 11).

This volume does not aspire to outline a new theoretical framework, but it proposes a new method of approaching the dilemmas of European Foreign Policy, using the example of ENP. The contributions to this book show that it is not helpful to label any findings as supporting either purely normative or rational explanations of foreign policy processes. Contributors were encouraged to explore the possibilities outlined in our five typologies above. It is clear that there are some ontological differences between the paradigms, reflected in their varied views of the world and their understandings of how it should be studied. For those that prefer constructivist approaches, including security as a value and/or considering self-regarding motives in norm formation and norm diffusion, may offer a way forward. For the more rational-choice-oriented approaches, the inclusion of certain norms in the calculations of actors (values as part of security) may point to a new avenue to explore. Only by finding a middle ground and engaging both strands of research in a dialogue may we be able to search for a meaningful answer to the foreign policy dilemmas presented by real life.

Researching the interplay between 'values' and 'security' in ENP also requires some methodological openness. First, both values and security are relevant objects of analysis, as all of the contributions in this volume demonstrate. Second, values and interests can be analysed as 'fixed parameters', which the EU defines *a priori* (see the chapters by Bechev and Schmidt-Felzmann), but also as social constructs subject to constant reinterpretation and reconstruction (see the chapter by Dimitrovova). Third, the interplay between values and security can be researched with reference to clashes and contradictions between different 'fixed' values or security interests of the EU (see the chapters by Trauner, Kruse and Zeilinger, and Bosse). But the interplay can also be understood as a constant process of different actors within the EU and the recipient neighbouring states socially constructing the meanings of 'values' and 'security' (the chapters by Natorski and Balfour). Fourth, the impact of the complex interplay between values and security in ENP is analysed both in terms of a cause–effect chain (i.e. the interplay causes a particular impact of the EU) (see the chapter by Baracani) and as a process in which the EU's impact is inextricably linked to diverging or converging perceptions of values and security both within the EU and among its member states and ENP partners (see the chapters by Coskun and Simão respectively). Fifth, the contributions in this volume employ a variety of research methodologies, ranging from rational choice analysis, including quantitative data analysis, to more constructivist-inspired content and discourse analysis.

Mapping of the book: the empirical reality of 'values' and 'security' in ENP

The contributions in this volume cover a range of empirical case studies that run the gamut of the EU's external policies vis-à-vis neighbouring countries, from democracy promotion (Part II), Common Foreign and Security Policy, conflict management and resolution and soft security issues such as energy or immigration policy (Part III). Some policy areas are traditionally associated with EU security interests (such as the CFSP) whereas others immediately evoke the EU's normative agenda (democracy promotion). By covering the whole range of EU external policies, the contributions provide a unique opportunity to compare the complex interplay between values and security and its impacts across the wide policy spectrum of ENP. The contributions also cover the geographical space of ENP in its entirety, including the Mediterranean, Middle East, Eastern Europe and the Southern Caucasus. Taking into account the variety of other international actors with interests in the EU's 'neighbourhood', two case studies focus specifically on the EU's relations with the Russian Federation, and other case studies pay close attention to the role of the US, Turkey, China and other regional and global players of relevance to ENP.

The contributions demonstrate the ontological and methodological openness necessary for examining the complex relationship between values and security in EU's foreign policy-making, taking the example of the EU's policies vis-à-vis its neighbours. In so doing, the book questions the predominant view in the literature that the two concepts necessarily clash as drivers of EU foreign policy, i.e. that studying EU foreign policy-making has to follow the strict rationalism/social constructivism divide. The individual contributions challenge the dichotomy of the values–security relationship through the pluralist conceptual treatment of the two concepts and the empirical material of their case studies, in so doing providing a more nuanced account of what is often presented as an either/or proposition – a value-driven or a security-driven foreign policy. The arguments of the chapters are illustrative of the different typologies of the values–security relationship discussed above.

The traditional clash between the normative and security dimensions of the EU's external policies is demonstrated by Anke Schmidt-Felzmann in her chapter on EU–Russia relations. Arguing from a realist perspective, she claims that security interests, particularly those related to energy, take priority over value-driven considerations. Further empirical evidence is provided by Trauner, Kruse and Zeilinger who examine the dynamic relationship between the security-focused logic and the values-based logic in EU migration policy. With a particular focus on the EC re-admission agreement with Russia, they analyse the extent to which this type of agreement violates the values of the EU (democracy, the rule of law, human rights and fundamental freedoms) and those enshrined in international law. They argue that there is a clear tension between values and security and re-admission agreements are a clear expression of the 'security logic' in the EU's external relations. Giselle Bosse also focuses on the dichotomy between values and security by juxtaposing the notions of '*realpolitik*' and 'idealist values' in recent EU–Belarus relations. She analyses the significant 'sea-change' in the Union's policy from a 'principled' approach based on the conditionality of values, such as democracy and human security, towards a more 'realpolitical' engagement, based on mutual interests and the premise to secure EU citizens exclusively. The Eastern Partnership, she argues, can be seen as a formalisation of *realpolitik* in the Union's relations with Belarus.

In contrast, Bohdana Dimitrovova's contribution looks at the external promotion of EU values as a purely normative matter, one which may still provoke resistance. She deconstructs the 'common values' dimension of European Neighbourhood Policy. She focuses on the discourses of EU-level elites (representations of 'neighbouring') in order to trace the nuances in the 'social construction' of the values in ENP by reference to processes of cultural re-bordering. She argues that common values are central to ENP, which is designed to export the EU's common values to its neighbourhood through two strategies: re-bordering via a 'repertoire of integration' and re-bordering via a 'repertoire of differences'.

The idea that values and security can be seen as complementary categories is discussed from two conceptual standpoints: 'security as a value' and 'values as part of security'. Licínia Simão and Elena Baracani make the case for the former typology, providing empirical support for it from the South Caucasus and the Middle East, whereas Dimitar Bechev makes the case for the latter typology, using the example of the EU's relationship with its periphery. Licínia Simão argues in her chapter that security can be viewed in normative terms: it is a value in itself and should not be automatically equated with a rational agenda of interest calculation. She then explores the EU's normative attempt to expand its security community to the South Caucasus and discusses the challenges this project faces in bringing security to both the EU and the South Caucasus. In a similar vein, Elena Baracani examines the EU's conflict resolution policies vis-à-vis Israel and Palestine, and vis-à-vis Georgia with its secessionist regions Abkhazia and South Ossetia, as simultaneously norms-driven and security-enhancing. She contends that the EU can have a transformative impact on these conflicts through its normative means and discusses the factors that determine the EU's varied performance in contributing to the resolution of the two conflicts.

The reinforcing role of values for the EU's strategic goals is captured by

Dimitar Bechev's examination of the role of the European hegemonic order in determining the relations between the EU and the regions and countries in its proximity. In contrast to viewing the EU's foreign policy through the lenses of 'civilian' or 'ethical' power, Bechev returns to the language of power politics in order to critically reflect upon the EU's relations with its neighbours through the notions of hegemony, order and hierarchy. He contends that 'thinking about Europe cannot be divorced from the issue of power and power politics'.

The issue of diversity among EU member states on conceptions of values and security ('values versus values' and 'security versus security') is taken up by Rosa Balfour who points to the contested nature of these categories even within the EU, let alone outside it. She also shows that the reluctance of some EU member states to support more firmly the EU's values of human rights, rule of law and democracy in its external relations can be normative in nature too, reflecting a preference for dialogue, engagement, partnership – values which are also at the core of the EU's identity. Anke Schmidt-Felzmann, in turn, shows not only the considerable differences in the interests of EU member states vis-à-vis Russia, but also the differences in the conception of values between the EU and Russia.

The possibility of a clash between the EU and its neighbours on perceptions of values and security ('values versus values' and 'security versus security') is demonstrated in the contributions of Coskun and Natorski. In her chapter, Bezen Balamir Coskun examines how societies in Western Europe and the Middle East have ended up with different understandings of what democracy means and how society should be organised politically. She concentrates on the different conceptions of values that exist in Europe and the Middle East, highlighting the dilemmas the EU faces in pushing for its political values in the Middle East, a region it identifies with some of the sources of its own insecurity. Michal Natorski, in turn, shows in his chapter the different perceptions of security between the EU and Ukraine. He maintains that the EU has quite an instrumental view of security and tends to treat Ukraine (as well as other neighbours) as a security threat, whereas Ukraine confronts the EU's attitude with a normative understanding of what the EU is as a security community and how it (Ukraine) should behave in order to become part of this community. The empirical confirmation is an impressive convergence between Ukraine and the EU on CFSP issues, on Ukraine's own initiative, notwithstanding the Ukrainian short-term deviations from the EU line which may be justified on rational grounds.

It is beyond the scope of this book to analyse the conditions under which these typologies affect the EU's impact in different policy areas linked to external action – from trade and aid to hard and soft security cooperation. Further research is nevertheless needed to clarify this aspect. The preliminary findings from the functional domains included in this study suggest that the dilemmas discussed in the conceptual framework are neither policy-specific nor geography-contingent. They can occur in policy areas as different as energy policy, democracy promotion or conflict resolution, and in geographical areas as different as the Middle East, Eastern Europe or Russia. Carefully constructed impact studies can reveal how these dilemmas inhibit or enhance the EU's influence in different areas of external action and we encourage further research in this direction.

Concluding remarks

The academic debate about the driving forces of the EU's foreign policy has focused narrowly on juxtaposing normative and rational factors overlooking the conceptual diversity of defining the concepts of values and security and the relationship between them. It has also overlooked the diversity among EU member states on the relevance of the two concepts for explaining their positions on foreign policy questions. The unpacking of the two concepts has revealed a plethora of different ways in which values relate to security, and opened up a variety of research themes and methodologies to explain and understand their complex relationship in ENP. Values and security may complement each other if both concepts are approached and operationalised in normative or rational ways (values as part of security and security as a value). Equally important are the conceptual opportunities and real-life situations where different types of values oppose each other, or different types of security are set against one other, in turn calling for different uses of what are essentially rather limited foreign policy instruments and resources (values versus values and security versus security). The EU is often confronted with choices in its relations with its neighbours but the choice between values and security may not be the fundamental issue determining the potential impact of its policies, its credibility as a foreign policy actor and its international identity.

The empirical evidence from all policy domains examined in this book – democracy promotion, CFSP, the external dimension of justice and have affairs (JHA) policies – and in all geographical areas covered – the Mediterranean, the Middle East, Eastern Europe and the South Caucasus – shows that the EU faces challenges in exporting its values and addressing security problems. However, these challenges may be the result of normative tensions within the EU, or between the EU and its neighbours, as much as the outcome of differences in the perception of threats within the EU, or in approaches to security between the EU and its neighbours. The contributions to this volume demonstrate that such divergent views may limit the EU's impact in the neighbourhood and its external leverage, but that they can also open up new opportunities for political dialogue and the construction of common understandings of values and security between the EU and its neighbours.

The book places ENP in the broader debate about European foreign policy and goes beyond the early scholarship on ENP, which largely focuses on analysing the applicability of EU conditionality and socialisation as drivers of change in the European Neighbourhood. The analysis in the volume suggests that the ENP debate has so far focused narrowly on secondary questions concerning the instruments for influencing neighbouring states (conditionality versus ownership, regionalism versus bilateralism, East versus South). At the same time it has avoided key questions of grand strategy and design involving discussions about the EU's views on security and values in the neighbourhood (security for whom? whose values?) and the ways of achieving agreed priorities in security and promoting common values in the neighbourhood. Notwithstanding the number of official communications on ENP, the EU lacks a clear vision about its relationships with neighbouring states, which a strategy for the neighbourhood would otherwise imply. In its current shape, ENP does not answer key policy questions, such as what to do about authoritarian governments, how to treat energy-rich countries, how to get involved in the resolution of territorial conflicts, etc. The answers to these practical questions necessitate a different kind of debate than that so far engendered by ENP. In the absence of strategic thinking about the neighbourhood, ENP has appeared more like a bureaucratic framework for structuring relations with the neighbouring countries than a strategy with clear objectives, instruments and resources for achieving desired ends. It has also remained disconnected from the macro-political dynamics in many of the neighbouring states, rendering its impact to date marginal and below expectations even though opportunities for increasing the EU's influence clearly exist. In the concluding chapter of the volume, Karolina Pomorska and Gergana Noutcheva further consider the policy implications of the conceptual analysis presented in this introduction, including recent policy reviews, and examine how they have been influenced by the events in North Africa in early 2011.

Notes

1. Algeria, Morocco, Tunisia, Libya, Egypt, Jordan, Israel, Palestinian Authority, Syria and Lebanon.
2. Ukraine, Moldova, Belarus, Georgia, Armenia and Azerbaijan.
3. Quoted from Radio Free Europe, 'Poland, Sweden Breathe New Life into Eastern Neighbourhood', 26 May 2008, available at www.rferl.org/content/article/1144495.html (accessed 20 October 2011).
4. The full text of the Lisbon Treaty is available at http://europa.eu/lisbon_treaty/full_text/index_en.htm (accessed 20 October 2011).
5. Even though some argue that the neo-realism represented by Waltz has normative concepts 'intrinsic to his arguments, not as its extremities but at its foundations' (Jackson quoted in Jørgensen 2006: 51).

PART I

Power and values in the EU's relation with its neighbours

DIMITAR BECHEV

2

The EU as a regional hegemon? From enlargement to ENP

Is the European Union a hegemon in denial? How does the often-heard talk of values, norms and higher principles relate to the daily realities of exclusion and disempowerment for people on the Union's periphery – largely absent from the EU citizens' radar screen? This chapter investigates the sources and dynamics of power that the EU wields in relation to its next-door neighbours. The exploration is informed by familiar concerns about power and hegemony in international politics set against the backdrop of the Union's dealings with its vast and diverse peripheries. These include the new members in Central and Eastern Europe (CEE), especially pre-2004, as well as the Union's present-day borderlands: the western Balkans and Turkey, now in the membership queue, as well as the countries of North Africa and the Middle East ('Southern Mediterranean') and the former Soviet Union covered by European Neighbourhood Policy (ENP). The quick overview of these case studies sheds light on the centre-periphery structures that underpin the EU's presence beyond its geographical core in Western Europe. The chapter investigates the hypothesis that the Union has emerged as the centre of a layered economic space with various circles of inclusion. This finding is hardly original *per se* but where the chapter differs from the bulk of the academic literature is in the conceptual labels it attaches to the empirical material. The central proposition is that the regional order in a wider Europe exhibits certain hegemonic features which manifest themselves in the EU's policies, most recently ENP. On a more theoretical level, the recourse to hegemony as a perspective, rather than a finely tuned concept derived from the Realist, Institutionalist or Gramscian tradition, implies that the dichotomy between values and security should be opened up to serious questioning, rather than being taken for granted. Indeed, as the introductory chapter asserts, the projection of values could be seen as an integral part of the security order, constructed around the economic behemoth that is the EU.

The paradox of power without politics

The EU has been experiencing an existential crisis, triggered by the turmoil in the Eurozone, while continuing with its own expansion project (Croatia being the last addition), and at the same time grappling with some old questions dating as far back as the Maastricht Treaty. The terrain trodden by the failed Constitutional Treaty and now its successor, the Treaty of Lisbon, is replete with points of contestation: the very nature and directions of the European construct; the proper balance between member states and supranational institutions; the perennial anxieties about efficiency, subsidiarity, and democratic accountability underwriting integration; the capacity of the Union to deliver growth, jobs, sustainable environment and security to its citizens. These internal conundrums are inextricably linked with concerns over the EU's engagement with the wider world. Back in 2005, the would-be Constitution was defeated at the French and Dutch referendums by voters apprehensive of the perceived ills of globalisation, uncontrolled immigration and the resulting (perceived) erosion of the venerated welfare state. The tremendous challenges but also, let us not forget, the opportunities stemming from the Union's global exposure explain why the conversation about 'Europe in the world' has been deepening and widening over the past decade, so much so that this heading ranks high amongst the priorities of the Seventh Framework Programme financed by the European Commission (2007–13). An ever-growing cohort of scholars and policy analysts continue to probe the Union's role in global governance, its interactions with powerful states and institutions, and its impact on global issues such as financial regulation or climate change, etc.

It is hardly an exaggeration that collective thinking about the external dimension of the EU is more often than not conducted in the language of values and norms, irrespective of certain notable counter-examples (Hyde-Price 2006). Flashy but certainly testing and complex concepts such as 'civilian power' (Duchêne 1973), 'normative power' (Manners 2002; Diez 2005) or 'ethical power' (Mayer and Vogt 2006) are the point of departure in most treatises on the subject, and this chapter makes no exception. The grand debates about the nature and moral foundations of the EU's presence and 'actorness' in global affairs has left its mark on the scholarship investigating the nitty-gritty aspects of the Common Foreign and Security Policy (CFSP) and external relations, which is broadly speaking tantamount to the interplay between national foreign policies and the various policy positions adopted in assorted global arenas (Hill and Smith 2005). However, to fully appreciate the salience of this reading of the EU as a torchbearer of values, one should start from the regional level. There is now a voluminous literature on enlargement towards post-Communist CEE and the western Balkans, on EU–Turkey, on the relations with North Africa and the Middle East ('the Southern Mediterranean'), on Russia and the former Soviet republics. It is on the

Union's fringes that 'normative power' has undergone several reincarnations, both as 'transformative power' (Youngs 2004; Leonard 2005; Grabbe 2006) and as 'soft power' (Vachudova 2005). Former Enlargement Commissioner Ollie Rehn has also spoken of 'smart power', the latest reincarnation of an already familiar and generally well-received idea.

All these much-circulated EU-isms are suggestive of inclusion and benign projection. They are all aspects of 'external governance', a term coined to describe the extension of regimes in specific issue-areas such as the environment or migration beyond the current borders of the Union (Lavenex 2004; Weber, Smith and Baun 2007; Lavenex and Schimmelfennig 2009). The use of 'governance' is not fortuitous as it is a markedly horizontal and non-hierarchical – but also arguably depoliticised – concept. The implication is that the fuzzier and more permeable the external borders of the EU as a polity-in-the-making, the more these borders will 'nudge' the integration process towards what Jan Zielonka qualifies as neo-medievalism, an arrangement where jurisdictions overlap and authority is shared by national, subnational and supranational institutions, in ways reminiscent of the pre-Westphalian Europe (Zielonka 2006). Seen from this perspective, the EU is reshaping, transforming and 'unbundling' established notions of territoriality and order based on a conceptual distinction between 'inside' and 'outside' (Ruggie 1993) on at least two fronts. First, it entangles nation-states in a supranational legal and political order through the process of pooling sovereignty. Second, the immediate neighbours are increasingly drawn into the Union's institutions and policies. To grasp this trend one needs to look no further than the European Commission's communications on ENP (Commission 2006a). Among other things, they foresee the inclusion of neighbours in the declarations and joint actions undertaken in the context of what is now called Common Security and Defence Policy (CSDP), as well as their participation in specialised agencies such as FRONTEX, in charge of policing the EU's external boundaries.[1] Integration, even without the prospect of accession, is becoming *de rigueur* in the current discussions (Bechev and Nicolaidis 2010).

The transformative, post-national directions of the EU project are what really feeds the values versus security dilemma. The presumed transcendence of the inside–outside matrix is nothing less than a radical departure from what Hans Morgenthau once called 'politics among nations' (Morgenthau 1948). EU practices such as the pooling of sovereignty, delegation of authority to supranational bodies, multilayered governance, and the inclusion of non-members in the decision-making process, are all arguments suggesting that the European construct is essentially about recasting or reinventing *the* core norms, institutions and habits of the (Westphalian) world of self-seeking nation-states. A particularly noteworthy example to that effect is furnished by the shifting meaning of 'power' in the language that frames integration in Europe. The EU institutions, as well as their policy-making elites, seem to have taken on board the whole lexicon of normative, transformative, soft or civilian power originating from the ivory towers of academia. At the same time, notions once closely interwoven with the practice and discourse of power from Machiavelli onwards, such as hegemony or order – and to a lesser extent, security – have been swept aside together with large chunks of IR's existing conceptual toolkit. Power, usually preceded by a qualifier such as 'civilian', 'transformative' or 'soft', has been domesticated, a theme which is no doubt close to the heart of seasoned Euro-watchers from across the Atlantic such as Robert Kagan.

Why use 'power' but not refer to the familiar conceptual apparatus of power politics? The answer has to do, in part, with the cosmopolitan reading of European integration that gained momentum in the post-Cold War era and reached its climax roughly in the mid-2000s with the completion of the enlargement of Central and Eastern Europe and the ill-fated war in Iraq. The Union's agency in international affairs is rooted in a moral consensus distinctive from that within the nation-state. While *raison d'état* builds on the interests and particularist identities which constitute the national body politic, EU power is animated by the universalist credo of liberal democracy and human rights, as shared by a community of states but also citizens (Linklater 2005). This understanding resonates in the writings of the continent's foremost literati such as Jürgen Habermas, Jacques Derrida or the German sociologist Ulrich Beck, and is 'married' to a distinctive set of aspirations and goals. Europe sees itself as a force for good in the world, spreading the 'gospel' of conflict resolution through functional integration. Finally, it is a power by means other than those we are accustomed to: not the military muscle favoured by the 'apostles' of neo-conservatism in the Bush administration, but rather by attraction; by the projection of standards, laws and institutions; and by persuasion and reward. By contrast, the pursuit and maintenance of hegemony is a pattern of action emanating from the very 'genetic code' of the state, from classical Athens to post-Cold War America. It is an extension of (narrowly defined) self-interest and backed up by the ability and willingness to use (military) coercion to impose order and provide security for those *inside* the boundaries of the polity. What matters from the vantage point of the central questions raised in this volume is that such a clear distinction between anachronistic power politics and cosmopolitan post-nationalism renders the choice between security and (universal) values a very stark one. Normative principles such as individual rights, democratic institutions, functional cooperation among governments and transnational actors are assumed to be incompatible, if not the direct opposite, with interest-driven foreign policy underpinned by a parochial conception of moral obligation (vis-à-vis 'our own' rather than *erga omnes*). This allows the EU to claim a moral higher ground in relation to other players in global politics and even its closest partners, such as the US, still 'stuck' in the twentieth, if not nineteenth, century.

To be sure, the claim that Europe is an altogether different animal with an enlightened mission in world politics is not accompanied by a sense of triumphalism. On the contrary, it is fraught with frustration. Received wisdom has it that the Union cannot live up to its promise: the proverbial 'capabilities–expectations' gap (Hill 1993). The usual culprits are the member states themselves with their clashing visions or unwillingness to forego national myopia in the name of the greater good for Europe and of internationalism. In addition, there is the realisation that 'soft power', understood as the power of attraction, might just not be enough. As in the US case there is a heated discussion about whether the effective wielding of 'soft power' ultimately depends on 'hard power' resources or whether, on the contrary, there is a clear trade-off between attractiveness and military might. Yet what those anxieties and frustrations do is to reconfirm, yet again, the near-consensus that the EU has a transformative mission, both in the wider world but even more so in its immediate neighbourhood.

This rejection of power politics, in the name of 'normative power', narrows and indeed hampers our understanding about the external aspects and consequences of European integration and, *mutatis mutandis*, of the EU's presence or actions in the world.[2] To make full sense of power, one has to take notions such as hegemony, order and hierarchy seriously. In other words, rather than operating in its comfortable microcosm, EU studies should re-engage in a much more genuine way with the sort of questions posed in the academic discipline of IR. First, this *ouverture* is essential for de-provincialising the study of Europe. Second, it will allow the Union to touch base with Europe's own multifaceted history and internal diversity. Third, the concept of hegemony shows the interrelatedness between values and the pursuit of security, even if it may fail to reconcile entirely.

The main argument I would like to explore is that regional order created in the process of European integration and unification, though underpinned by liberal values and institutions, operates in hierarchical ways and exhibits elements of hegemony (cf. Ikenberry 2001). Thus, values are a fundamental part of the (quasi-)hegemonic edifice comprised of a centre and of layered peripheries. However, a disclaimer is due here: the intention is not to make a normative point or indeed expose the duplicity of the EU institutions or leaders. Rather it is to understand how structures of power operate in the Union's environs, how they shape its economic space and the political institutions of what could be labelled, following the European Commission, 'Wider Europe'. I take power and hegemony as heuristic and analytical devices rather than a political slogan. Hegemony reflects a deeply entrenched structural logic and, in the main, is not a policy choice by certain actors (states, governments, supranational institutions) aimed at subjugation and/or political control.

Features of hegemonic order

Before we proceed to the chapter's empirical backbone it is worthwhile listing several features of the EU's hegemonic presence beyond its boundaries, whether past or present. Certainly this is a condition that differs in important ways from other hegemonies, notably America's global preponderance or, indeed, Soviet hegemony in Eastern Europe during the Cold War. Much of its dynamics is structural rather than reflecting the collective action on the part of the complex animal that is the EU. Put simply, the sheer size of the internal market – a product of the integration process under way since the 1950s – has made the EU an economic hub attracting the exports of virtually all neighbours, as well as a principal destination for labour and other types of migration from the peripheries. The central position of the EU in various networks of production, exchange and mobility, in turn, has enabled its institutions to shape, define and export rules; it is therefore a source of structural power. In cases where democratisation processes have taken root, notably in Central and Eastern Europe in the 1990s, the EU has also assumed the role of external anchor, source of political legitimacy and model, which gave a normative layer to its hegemonic presence. Here is the list:

Asymmetry

What one observes across the edges of Europe is economic interdependence skewed in favour of the EU. As a rule, neighbours, past and present, account for a minuscule share of the EU's trade while the Union is the main partner for all of them. Access to the EU market is generally linked to the conditions extended by Brussels through association or first-generation agreements and/or unilateral trade preferences. However, the EU is empowered to put forward rules of engagement to larger countries such as Turkey, Ukraine or Egypt, or prosperous relatives such as the European Economic Area (EEA) members, Norway, Liechtenstein and Iceland (recently upgraded to a membership candidate), as well as to Switzerland. Access to the EU's massive internal market, completed in the early 1990s, is also conditional on compliance with the *acquis communautaire*. The Union has consistently shielded sensitive sectors such as agriculture, engaging only in piecemeal liberalisation. The EU's advantage in bargaining over trade relations is, in many cases, also significant because of its agents' largely superior expertise on multiple technical aspects relative to the expertise of most interlocutors in the periphery. Improved access to the EU marketplace, but also territory (through the liberalisation of visa regimes as implemented in the western Balkans in 2009–10), and decision-making has been conditioned, especially with respect to post-Communist countries in CEE and the former USSR, on commitment to democratic reforms. The relationship is at its most asymmetrical in cases such as Kosovo or Bosnia where the EU has engaged, alongside other international actors, in a broad range of state-building activities that also involve the deployment of military and police contingents. The relationship is much more equal in the case of oil and gas exporting countries (Russia, Algeria, Libya, Azerbaijan), partly because of their stronger bargaining position and partly because of the circumscribed community competences in the energy sector. As a rule these countries have largely avoided the ready-made institutional templates put forward by Brussels, such as ENP.

Hub-and-spoke structures

The EU's 'pull' effect creates a hub-and-spoke dynamic in its periphery. On average, third countries have much larger trade volumes with the EU trade compared to their immediate neighbours, with Russian energy exports being the one significant exception. The reasons for this are complex and well beyond the scope of this chapter. One of the key determinants of this pattern has been the similar product structures of the economies in question exporting labour-intensive, low value-added manufacturing and services, natural resources and agricultural produce. It is hardly surprising, for instance, that the bulk of trade in the 'Southern Mediterranean' occurs between Turkey and Israel, two of the most developed and diversified economies on the EU periphery.

On the diplomatic front, peripheral countries also tend to prioritise their relations with Brussels or with key members (e.g. the Maghrebi countries with former colonial master France and/or southern European states). There is little evidence of joint strategies aimed at improving neighbours' bargaining positions vis-à-vis the Union. Collective action has been constrained by historical conflicts which are common in the EU's periphery, but also by the very structure of incentives. Prior to their accession, the states of Central and Eastern Europe raced towards membership while the EU itself made ample use of the 'regatta principle', both in the 1990s and in the western Balkans, encouraging convergence with entry standards through competition. The EU's power of attraction inhibits regional cooperation. States prefer integrating with the Union rather than focusing on schemes involving their neighbours – most recently the multilateral dimension of the so-called Eastern Partnership (EaP) but also the Agadir Process in the 'Southern Mediterranean', the plethora of institutions operating in south-east Europe (Bechev 2011) or the Visegrad Cooperation in Central Europe (prior to 2004).[3]

The primacy of stability

The third feature has to do with agency rather than structure. Interdependence results in a demand for the EU to devise strategies to tackle potential soft- and hard-security threats originating in the neighbouring regions. What is important to note in light of this volume's key theme is that in most cases, the pursuit of stability has gone hand in hand with the push from Brussels for political transformation. The European Security Strategy of

December 2003 speaks of 'a ring of well-governed countries' around the Union. As shown in some detail below, the encouragement of political and market reforms in Central and Eastern Europe and now in the western Balkans has been aimed at preventing negative knock-on effects inside the Union. However, where stability and democratisation clash, as in the 'Southern Mediterranean' (see Rosa Balfour's chapter in this volume), the former invariably prevails. Of course, this is a broad-brush portrayal of the EU's policies and objectives in that it blurs the important differences and nuances across the member states. Some of them, especially in the North, have taken a much more normative stance on issues of democracy-promotion and invested heavily in civil society. Nevertheless, the strong emphasis on soft-security issues, energy and infrastructure development, as well as managed market integration, suggest that strategic considerations, not least those of the EU countries located at, or close to, the respective frontier, tend to top the agenda. This does not mean that the EU has abdicated from spreading its norms and values, which are the ultimate guarantee for long-term stability. Rather, it sees diffusion as a gradual and largely technocratic process. It is also sequenced; authoritarian regimes are expected first to converge with the EU's liberalisation and good-governance norms applicable to the economy, which might then subsequently spill over into the political sphere.

Let us now move to the empirical evidence and consider the cases of pre-2004/7 Central and Eastern Europe, the western Balkans, Turkey and the so-called 'neighbourhood'.

A wider Europe of layered peripheries

Central and Eastern Europe

The main vehicle for the Union's engagement with Central and Eastern Europe was the enlargement process, which kicked off in earnest with the inauguration of the famous Copenhagen Criteria in 1993. The criteria linked membership with the fulfilment of a set of political and economic reforms as well as the transposition of the body of legal and technical standards developed by the Union (the *acquis communautaire*). Another critical stage was marked by the opening of membership negotiations with the 'best performers' in the region at the December 1997 Luxembourg Council, and with the rest of the group two years later, at the 1999 summit in Helsinki. The process wound up with the formal closure of the negotiations, the signature of accession agreements in 2002 (2005 for Bulgaria and Romania), and the admission as formal members on 1 May 2004 (1 January 2007 for Bulgaria and Romania).

There is a very lively debate in the literature about the reasons why the EU chose to enlarge. On the one hand, authors such as Frank Schimmelfennig

(2003) argue that the process reflected the logic of 'rhetorical entrapment'. Back in the early 1990s, the EU12 had to respond to repeated calls by the eastern *demandeurs* applicants appealing to provisions such as Article 49 of the Treaty Establishing the EU (TEU) enabling any European democracy to seek membership, as well as to the ideological discourse of the Cold War highlighting the preservation and, potentially, proliferation of democracy across the continent. The Westerners found themselves 'entrapped' by their own words in the course of the 1990s and receptive to the CEE leaders' rhetorical action. An alternative position treats enlargement as a proactive policy undertaken by the EU in the interest of securing stability in countries undergoing rapid political and socio-economic changes, which were moreover haunted by a myriad of long-standing disputes over borders and minorities. Critical decisions coincided with the upheavals such as the failed coup against Mikhail Gorbachev (August 1991), the outbreak of ethnic conflicts in former Yugoslavia and parts of the Soviet Union, and the 1999 intervention in Kosovo.

Notably, all these theories and accounts of enlargement are principally about the EU's motivation rather than the motivation of the candidate countries. Their choice for membership is, more or less, taken for granted. Beyond the oft-repeated adage about the 'return to Europe', the pursuit of EU accession can be explained by turning to the growing economic interdependence between the two parts of Europe. The Moscow-dominated Council for Mutual Economic Assistance (COMECON) which was largely defunct by the late 1980s was officially disbanded in June 1991. Trade within the post-Communist countries of Central and Eastern Europe underwent a major westwards shift, a process which, for some, dated back to the two previous decades. The countries in question only stood to gain by entering the EU and integrating on equal terms as this would lead to access to the internal market, the Union's budget, and, not least, decision-making. Moreover, democratically elected governments stood to benefit domestically as integration into the club of prosperous countries was a popular cause with the voters. Finally, similar to NATO, the orientation towards the EU was a guarantee for the democratic consolidation and maximisation of security vis-à-vis third countries, such as hostile neighbours and/or a resurgent Russia. In other words, even prior to the formal commencement of the accession process these states were already inexorably drawn into the EU's orbit.

In that sense, EU enlargement could be interpreted as a process in which 'old' Europe secured its new frontiers vis-à-vis the 'externalities' originating from the East, such as the spread of inter-state and civil conflicts and illegal migration through gradual co-optation. The key instrument at the Union's disposal was its membership 'conditionality' linked with the three Copenhagen criteria. It worked through the logic of 'gate-keeping' in the pre-negotiation and the negotiation period. Political, economic and institutional reforms were rewarded with progress on the membership 'path', increased financial allocations via EU aid programmes, trade concessions, the removal of visa regimes preventing travel or even (illegal) work in the member states. The candidates could not negotiate the nature and scope of adjustment as they were expected to meet the EU demands and prescriptions in full, even in areas where there were no agreed common standards at the EU level, such as minority rights or judicial reform. The most that applicants could hope for, even in cases of bigger countries like Poland, was to obtain longer transition periods for the introduction of particularly costly elements of the *acquis*.

One can argue that elements of conditionality remain even after accession, perpetuating the centre–periphery relationship. A particularly important area is Economic and Monetary Union (EMU) since new members do not have a right to opt out, and some of them who have pegged their currency to the euro have an incentive to switch to it, especially in the longer term (Slovakia, Slovenia and Estonia are the only ones who have made it past that hurdle). In the case of Romania and Bulgaria, the two most problematic entrants, there is the so-called 'Cooperation and Verification Mechanism', a monitoring progress in the fields of anti-corruption and judicial reform. The Commission issues regular reports, much as it did in the period before the 2007 accession. Bulgaria and Romania have still to meet a number of conditions and benchmarks in order to be admitted into the Schengen Space like the rest of the enlargement countries that joined in late 2007.

The peripheral position of the new member states in the Union stems not from any 'second-class' status within the institutions, but from the stark disparity in wealth levels. While the countries of Central and Eastern Europe enjoy full rights in the Union at present, some of them like Poland making their voice heard on a number of issues, on average they are much poorer than the EU15, even if the 'Club Med' countries (Portugal, Greece, Spain, Italy) have suffered tremendously in the ongoing Eurozone crisis, and are now facing a decade of austerity. That is not remedied in the short to medium term by the growth rates in the region that are relatively higher than those in Western Europe. At present, only Slovenia has managed to 'leapfrog' the poorest member of the EU15, Portugal, in terms of GDP per capita. Furthermore, according to EUROSTAT data for 2004, GDP per capita in the richest region of the EU, Frankfurt, is at €68,751 while in Romania's northeast, the corresponding figure is €5,070 (€21,503 being the average). The bottom of the table is occupied by 15 regions in Romania, Poland and Bulgaria. Aggregate figures might also skew the picture since they do not register pockets of poverty commeasurable with those in the developing world e.g. concerning the Roma population. While the current trend is towards narrowing the wealth gap it is clear that convergence with 'core' Europe or even the 'old peripheries' in southern Europe is a long-term project.

The western Balkans

Starting in early 1991 with the disintegration of Yugoslavia and escalation of full-blown war, the EU's policy towards 'the western Balkans' has aimed at resolving conflict and stabilising the region. The stakes were particularly high due to the negative fallout on EU member states given former Yugoslavia's immediate geographical proximity to the then European Community (EC). It is worth remembering that in the summer of 1991 hostilities broke out on what is today the border between Slovenia and Italy. The prospect of migration waves and the further spread of violence to neighbouring countries loomed large in the minds of EU policy-makers and there were several particularly sensitive 'sticking points': the recognition of Croatia and Slovenia in 1991; the proper response to the war in Bosnia in 1992–95; how to handle Slobodan Milošević's regime in Belgrade; and how to react to the economic embargo imposed by Greece against the former Yugoslav Republic of Macedonia in 1994. The Yugoslav crisis was ultimately settled with the intervention of NATO under US leadership in 1994–95 and the conclusion of the Dayton Peace Accords in November 1995. US action also played a critical role in the Kosovo conflict, climaxing with the air campaign against Serbia in the spring of 1999.

Once the 'hard security' challenges had been checked, the EU gradually assumed the lead from the US. Slowly but surely, the western Balkans were drawn into the Union's orbit and inserted into the institutional webs centred on Brussels. Slovenia was much ahead of the group. As early as 1996, it had signed its own Europe Agreement and was invited to start membership negotiations at the 1997 Luxembourg Summit. For the rest of former Yugoslavia and Albania, the EU devised the so-called Stabilisation and Association Process (SAP). SAP is based on association agreements closely resembling those previously signed with the candidate countries. Even prior to the conclusion of those treaties, Brussels liberalised its trade regime vis-à-vis the individual western Balkan countries, which contributed to their further integration into the internal market. As early as 2002, EU leaders labelled the SAP countries as 'potential candidates' and a year later, in Thessaloniki, resolved that the process was geared towards eventual membership. In 2005, Croatia qualified to open membership negotiations with the EU, negotiations that had been wrapped up six years later leading to an accession treaty being signed on 9 December 2011.

In the western Balkans, the EU has been as much a 'pull' as a 'push' force, thanks to CSDP machinery deployed in post-conflict areas. In Bosnia-Herzegovina, the Union deployed a police mission and later, in 2004, took over responsibilities for peacekeeping from NATO via the EUFOR contingent. In Macedonia it ran the police missions Concordia and Proxima, dealing with the fallout of the 2001 conflict, solved through joint EU–US diplomatic intervention. Finally, as of late 2008, the Union has been in charge of a task force of police and magistrates in Kosovo (EULEX), the largest civilian mission launched under CSDP. This is a novel type of intervention that distinguishes the EU's presence in the western Balkans from the relationship established with the candidate countries of Central and Eastern Europe in the 1990s. Still, as in the latter group, the main facet of the EU's policy relates to gate-keeping and staged inclusion into the EU institutions, in exchange for compliance with political, economic and *acquis*-related standards. What is more, the Union's conditionality has been expanded with demands reflecting the region's past marked by turmoil and violence; these include full cooperation with the International Criminal Tribunal for Former Yugoslavia (ICTY), the return of refugees and the creation of a single police force in Bosnia, etc.

Similarly to Central and Eastern Europe, the EU has become a factor in the domestic politics of the western Balkan membership hopefuls, thanks to its conditionality. In countries such as Croatia (post-2000), Macedonia and Albania, opposing political forces from the post-Communist left and right have established consensus on accession, and been competing to move their countries closer to the EU by trying to legitimise domestic policies with Brussels' demands. This has also been the case in Montenegro, independent since 2006, where the political system has been controlled by a relatively small elite around Milo Djukanović. Granted candidacy in 2010, Montenegro is at the time of writing on the verge of opening membership negotiations with the EU. Serbia and Bosnia-Herzegovina have diverged from this trend as the demands put forward by Brussels, such as ICTY extraditions, constitutional reform, or cooperation over Kosovo, have exacerbated communal and political cleavages, making it more costly for leaders and parties to comply. Even here, important steps have been taken, with Serbia submitting a membership application in 2009 and being granted candidacy status in March 2012.

In sum, the western Balkans has been gradually drawn into the sphere of influence of the EU. On the one hand, the region is integrated more deeply into the 'core' European market thanks to the liberalisation of the trade and investment regimes. On the other, the EU member states have agreed to engage proactively and allocate resources for managing security in hotspots such as Bosnia and Kosovo. This has prompted high-profile observers such as Robert Cooper (2004), the European External Action Service (EEAS) official in charge of the ongoing Belgrade–Prishtina talks, to coin the term a 'postmodern empire', to describe the state-building agenda carried forward by EU peacekeepers and civilian administrators deployed in the region. Finally, political actors in domestic arenas have appealed to a sense of belonging and unjust exclusion from 'Europe' in order to mobilise domestic support. However, in cases where EU conditionality has deepened cleavages and therefore increased compliance costs, the legitimising power of Europe as a model has been undermined. All in all, with the exception of Croatia, the western Balkans are expected to accede to the EU at the earliest by the end of the present decade, meaning that, although surrounded at present by EU territory, those countries constitute a separate peripheral cluster by virtue of the level of their trade relations with the EU and policy relations with its institutions.

Turkey

In political, institutional and economic terms, Turkey is also part of wider Europe. The country has been an associated member of the EC since 1963 and in 1995 formed a customs union with the EU. The Helsinki Summit in 1999 recognised Turkey as an EU candidate, some 12 years after it had submitted a membership application. After a positive assessment by the European Commission, the European Council resolved to open negotiations with Turkey in October 2005. This came after a wave of political reforms in areas such as civil–military relations and human and minority rights, pursued by two successive governments: the secularist coalition led by Bülent Ecevit; and then the government of the 'soft Islamist' Justice and Development Party (AKP), which swept to power in the parliamentary elections in November 2002, July 2007 and June 2011.

Since the autumn of 2005 the negotiations process for membership has not developed smoothly. The reasons are manifold: opposition towards Turkey's membership by leading political actors inside the EU, notably the Christian Democratic Union in Germany or the French President, Nicolas Sarkozy; the nationalist backlash inside Turkey fuelled by the Kemalist opposition against both the AKP and the liberalisation reforms required by Brussels; the fallout from the war in Iraq and resurgence of Kurdish separatism in the south-eastern provinces; and the AKP increasingly shifting the focus of its policies to its neighbours in the Middle East, particularly as the Arab Spring bloomed in the course of 2011. Finally, one should not forget the Greco-Turkish disputes in the Aegean and the Cyprus issue. While Greece has pushed for Turkey's membership, Cyprus has teamed up with France in blocking negotiations on a number of chapters. As of 2011, negotiations have effectively ground to a halt with no new chapter opened since the first half of 2010 – and yet neither of the parties has openly called for a termination of the process.

Observers have argued that EU membership is becoming a lesser incentive for Turkey and the power of EU conditionality is decreasing. However, even if negotiations derail, or if membership is vetoed by a referendum in France or another member state, this will do little to alter the hard facts concerning the deep-running interdependence between EU and Turkey. The Union is the destination of 52 per cent of Turkey's exports, while EU imports account for slightly under half of the total volume, even as the country's trade has shifted to other regions such as the Middle East and the former Soviet Union. As with Central and Eastern Europe and the western Balkans, Turkey is a recipient of billions of euro of EU foreign direct investment (FDI), accounting for 80 per cent of the overall volume. The exposure to the Single Market, thanks to the Customs Union concluded in 1995, has made the Turkish economy globally competitive and driven the manufacturing sector up the 'value-added ladder'. This means that political closure towards the EU is not an option for policy- makers in Ankara, regardless of their political orientations. The rhetoric of Turkey considering other strategic directions such as Central Asia, as employed by politicians like Mesut Yilmaz in the 1990s, has proved to be little more than wishful thinking. True, Turkey is a 'double gravity' country, in the apt phrase of Philip Robins (2006), embedded in (at least) two regions at the same time, Europe and the Middle East. However, the EU vector dominates the country's economy and it is 'locked in' to a web of institutions. The customs union involves a considerable level of harmonisation with the EU *acquis*, thus already providing an advanced framework for integration. Even if the negotiations process is derailed, the privileged partnership offered by the opponents of Turkey's membership is likely to be a very comprehensive type of arrangement, akin to the EEA.

This counter-factual exercise suggests that, in the final analysis, EU power derives from the structural position of the internal market rather than the capacity to deploy political conditionality. As everyone studying enlargement knows, conditionality's effectiveness diminishes as the prospect of accession becomes more distant. While political liberalisation in Turkey has slowed down or even reversed, its interdependence with the trade policy 'core' of the EU will keep Turkey in the Union's ambit. Admittedly, this relationship is less asymmetric than the one with the western Balkans on account of Turkey's political and economic weight. Yet as long as the EU controls the access to its market and decision-making process, it remains the privileged partner in this interdependent relationship.

The new and old neighbours in Eastern Europe and the 'Southern Mediterranean'

The outer circle of the EU's periphery encompasses those countries covered by the so-called European Neighbourhood Policy (ENP): the new neighbours, Ukraine, Moldova and Belarus; Georgia, Armenia and Azerbaijan in the Southern Caucasus; and the littoral states in the Middle East and North Africa.[4] ENP was launched in 2003–4 as the 'new' member states acceded to EU. With its principal characteristic being open-endedness, ENP assists partners in implementing EU-compatible reforms, as spelled out in the so-called Action Plans, bilateral political documents that are somewhat reminiscent of the Accession Partnerships used in the pre-enlargement process. At the same time, the process does not offer an accession perspective but uses incentives such as improved market access, financial aid and, more recently, inclusion in specialised EU agencies. ENP also builds upon the existing association agreements signed since the mid-1990s with the Mediterranean countries, as well as the Partnership and Cooperation Agreements in force with the Eastern European neighbours. Ukraine (since

2008), Moldova, Georgia, Azerbaijan and Armenia (since 2010) are furthermore negotiating a new generation of Association Agreements including 'deep and comprehensive trade components' geared to bringing about advanced alignment with EU legislation, the removal of non-tariff barriers and integration of service sectors. Such functional instruments are complemented by CSDP missions operating in the countries and regions in question, such as the EUBAM deployed between Ukraine and the breakaway republic of Transnistria, nominally part of Moldova, or the border task-force at the Refah crossing point in Gaza.

ENP's rationale is to ensure that those not taking part in the enlargement exercise are not completely left out either. The concern of new members such as Poland has been that the EU external borders would jeopardise traditional economic and political ties with ex-Soviet republics further east. For reasons of internal and external balance, the EU has also had to bring the Mediterranean partners into the new policy format. Through ENP, the Union has attempted to project stability beyond its current borders, tackle cross-boundary challenges and secure a steady supply of energy to meet its growing demands. In that sense, ENP is designed to address the externalities related to the eastwards expansion. It reassures neighbours such as Ukraine or Moldova that they would not be abandoned and provides the EU institutions and member states with tools to deal with the challenges originating in the periphery.

Though the launch of ENP was accompanied by lofty words about the EU's transformative power, the modest incentives it extends somewhat limit its effectiveness. Even in countries such as Ukraine, Georgia and Moldova, where important political actors and constituencies have been calling for closer integration and ultimately accession, EU conditionality does not play as prominent a role as in the western Balkans. That might change to some degree with the EaP unveiled in May 2009 now that the Eastern European partners have been effectively 'decoupled' from those in the southern tier with no prospect of membership and where the EU's power is least pronounced. Though notionally part of both the EMP and ENP, political conditionality is used much more sparingly in North Africa and the Middle East. The stability of the existing political regimes which are key allies on issues such as migration, energy and the fight against terrorism is still the common denominator of the Union's policies. The implementation of the Action Plan reforms is rewarded with additional financial aid but democratic shortcomings are rarely criticised let alone punished by the cancellation of funding (Youngs 2006). In the East, this state of affairs is mirrored by the EU's approach to Azerbaijan, an important ally of the West and energy producer but hardly a beacon of liberal democracy.

The limited scope for proactive engagement does not rule out the notion of the EU as a hegemonic centre. As in the case of Turkey, the critical variable is the extent of economic interdependence. The EU is by far the largest trading partner of all neighbourhood states. Even in relatively remote places such as Egypt the Union accounts for about 43 per cent of the imports and 31 per cent of exports. This is an outcome of the duty-free regime regarding industrial goods established with the Association Agreement signed in 2001. However, proximity to core EU markets matters too. Even in pariah states, which are excluded from ENP and have no association agreements (or were even removed from the EU Generalised System of Preferences, as in the case of Belarus), the EU is respectively the first and second trade partner with 40 per cent / 33 per cent of the total turnover. Since the early 2000s, Belarus's trade with the EU has tripled in size and the Union is the principal destination for the country's exports.

The key to ENP, therefore, is the EU's capacity to manage interdependence. Typically the countries of the 'neighbourhood' demand improved access to the EU markets, including for their agricultural products, the removal of non-tariff barriers, and the relaxation of the visa regimes for travel to the Union's territory through the visa liberalisation roadmaps that are currently being extended to countries such as Ukraine and Moldova. However, internal constraints and protectionist moods within the old member states have prevented the EU from opening up in exchange for greater convergence with its political norms and economic governance standards. The selective liberalisation of trade at present has deepened interdependence with the EU while protecting sensitive sectors and groups such as agricultural producers in the southern member states or the steel manufacturers. The real test case of functional integration is the new generation of Association Agreements (AAs), to be concluded with the eastern partners and starting with Ukraine,[5] as well as the regimes on free movement of people, which are set to be altered to facilitate labour migration from the neighbourhood countries into the EU.

The limits of hegemony

The key contention thus far is that ENP should be examined in the wider context of the EU's presence in its peripheries from the early 1990s onwards. One straightforward critique to using hegemony as a way to describe this presence is the Union's mixed record in projecting its influence. A regional hegemon would be expected to underwrite political and economic order in its sphere of influence by leveraging various power resources, not least military capabilities. In the early 1990s, the wars in ex-Yugoslavia dealt a major blow to the nascent CFSP. Later in Kosovo, the EU stepped in only after the US-led NATO was able to contain the conflict by defeating one of the warring parties. The CSDP mission was deployed in Bosnia only after the situation on the ground was relatively settled, following almost a decade of international presence backed up by NATO. The interventions in other conflicts around the periphery – including Israel/Palestine, Western Sahara, Lebanon, Transnistria, the breakaway Georgian territories of Abkhazia and South Ossetia – have been, in the main, ineffective. The Franco-British military operation in Libya that helped topple the Gaddafi regime was carried out outside CSDP, and later put under the NATO 'umbrella', depended nonetheless on US support. Short of its promise of membership, the EU has few tools to deal with conflicts. The cases of Cyprus or Serbia/Kosovo present a warning that even the prospect of accession might not be sufficient. All these failures of the EU to live up to its rhetoric of promoting conflict resolution and stability invite us to reflect on the concept and on manifestations of hegemony; one needs to go a bit further in unpacking it to draw out several distinctions.

Traction versus intervention
The EU's hegemonic power emanates, ultimately, from the structural effects of functional integration. The creation of the Single Market and its institutional framework around it has led to knock-on effects on the territories, and fosters asymmetric interdependence. This does not necessarily predict that the actors within – states or supranational institutions – will be able to harness this condition effectively in order to wield influence. As we very well know, constraints include colliding national interests and visions as regards enlargement and neighbourhood policies. Since EU hegemony rests on structural facts rather than agency, it is exercised through the control of access to those resources (in exchange for various forms of institutional convergence) and not through their active deployment and projection (e.g. through military or civilian operations, the disbursement of aid to the neighbours etc).

One hegemon or several?
The EU's capacity to shape its periphery does not imply that its power is unchallenged. The resurgence of Russia in the 2000s, as well as the presence of the US in a number of regions surrounding the EU, are all facts to be reckoned with since these two actors are highly influential in matters of hard security and 'high politics'. Russia's assertive role in the East has prompted some of the local governments such as those in Georgia and Ukraine (prior to the presidential elections in early 2010) to seek closer diplomatic and military ties with the US and NATO. Others, like Moldova, at least until the most recent parliamentary elections, seek to strike a balance between the EU and Russia. Meanwhile, the Maghreb countries, such as Morocco or Algeria, previously closely aligned with West European states such as France, have pursued links with the US amid the 'war on terror'.

The relationship with these alternative hegemons is complex as it involves both elements of cooperation and competition. On the one hand, both the US and Russia have challenged the Euro-centric mapping of the neighbourhood by promoting their own concepts of 'near abroad' or the Greater Middle East.

In the eastern flank, ENP faces the neighbourhood policy projected by Moscow, while in the Middle East and even the Caucasus, Turkey is becoming a regional hub in its own right (Krastev and Leonard 2010). On the other had, the EU and Russia have been drawn together by the forces of economic and functional interdependence, again skewed in favour of the Union. This is becoming visible as prices of gas and oil are plummeting amid the economic crisis unleashed in late 2008, with the pursuit of a 'modernisation partnership' with the EU, or at least, with major stakeholders such as Germany, becoming a core objective for the Kremlin. Europe and the US share the objectives of building stability and liberal democracy in Eastern Europe and the Middle East, though they might differ in their definitions and the relative priority that they give to each of those goals.

The hegemony of Europeanness

Perhaps the most important aspect of hegemony is how it is legitimised within societies on the 'receiving end'. Eastern enlargement has shown us that the EU's power of attraction, though grounded in the economic realities of the late twentieth century, is very tightly linked with narratives of 'belonging to Europe'. The political momentum for adjustment to the EU's demands and the social legitimacy of costs sustained in the process were related to the ideology of a 'return to Europe'. It is here that values and the maintenance of order intersect. A purely rational-choice account of how centre–periphery dynamics function in a wider Europe is, therefore, insufficient since it tells us only part of the story. What has mattered for those countries, beyond direct gains, is obtaining recognition as being part of a club of wealthy liberal democracies. The EU has been empowered to shape the meaning and contents of the notion of 'Europeanness', deeply embedded in national discourses in all countries, from the Baltics down to the Balkans. As in previous periods, in the 1990s 'core' Europe acted as a source of social, political and cultural 'inspiration', to be shadowed and emulated (Bechev 2006).

While material interdependence is a relatively invariable condition across Europe's fringes, the strength of the EU's appeal varies. For instance, in North Africa, Europe is associated with the legacy of colonial empires. In countries like Algeria or Egypt, the struggle against foreign domination is a key reference point in the construction of mass political identities. The drive for recognition by 'Europe' has been minimal and limited to certain strata such as the French-speaking middle classes in the Maghreb. Being recognised as truly European, in the cultural as opposed to the geographical sense, has been much more salient in the East where significant constituencies in countries such as Georgia and Ukraine embrace historical discourses projecting links with 'European civilisation'. These constructs have been opposed to an orientalised Russian 'Other'. Even there, however, the 'return to Europe' narrative is not as dominant as it was in the Central and Eastern Europe of the 1990s, which constrains the 'enlargement-lite' policies of the EU (Popescu and Wilson 2009). In Turkey, Europe has been synonymous with the ideals of modernity ('contemporary civilisation') to which the Kemalist nation-building vision aspired. Though republican ideology is fundamentally about national sovereignty, as demonstrated by the dogged opposition to some of the EU conditions, the models it draws upon originate from Western Europe. This explains the dual logic of attraction and resentment which defines societal attitudes towards the EU in Turkey (Fisher Onar 2009).

The ideological sway of Europeanness and its constitutive values, though shifting in meaning, empowers the EU to act beyond its boundaries. However, it also sets the limits of the EU's power. Recognition ultimately depends on the willingness of EU citizens to underwrite enlargement by supporting or, at the minimum, not punishing elites driving forward the process. As the constitutional referendums and the phenomenon of enlargement fatigue show, this is not the case. Being a functional initiative, ENP exports EU rules and regimes outside its borders, but does little in the way of making grand political gestures to convey the sense of inclusion into the very political institutions constitutive of Europeanness today. The EU's ideological hegemony is ultimately inhibited because it is vulnerable to democratic pressure from the inside the Union.

Concluding thoughts: the emerging order in a wider Europe

Thinking about Europe's presence in global and regional affairs is intimately linked to the dilemmas of power and power politics. At the structural level, the order which emerged in the wake of the Cold War is inherently hegemonic since it is founded on a basis of a core–periphery relationship. Some facets of the latter hark back to what historians call 'the long nineteenth century', a time when (Western) Europe provided models of socio-economic and political organisation for the societies located on its fringes, as well as for the colonial possessions some of which now form part of the EU's neighbourhood. The attraction of the EU cannot be comprehended without a reference to the historical experience of 'catch-up', modernisation and institutional borrowing.

However there are important discontinuities. Nowadays, the EU is a pole of attraction because of its accumulated economic might. Paradoxically, economic integration from the times of the European Coal and Steel Community (ECSC) in the 1950s was aimed at domesticating power politics and moving away from hegemonic politics in the heartlands of the European continent. Externally the long-term effect of unification has been to create webs of asymmetric interdependence gravitating towards the single market and the Brussels institutions. This structural logic results in hegemony by default rather than a conscious policy geared towards the maintenance of power hierarchies. By implication, if the present Eurocrisis results in much tighter and deeper fiscal integration, linked to more power being transferred to supranational institutions, this would inevitably strengthen the EU's hand in dealing with its neighbours. On the contrary, if the Eurozone is destroyed and disintegration spreads to the single market this would certainly sweep aside the EU's hegemonic position in a wider Europe.

When we shift our focus from structure to agency, that is, the EU institutions and member states, we see that hegemony is exercised mainly through differentiated integration and reciprocity rather than by coercive action. It is based on access to the EU market and institutions, in exchange for convergence with the Union's laws and standards. Like any hegemon, the EU is providing certain public goods: rules on the free flow of industrial goods and capital. In the closest regions, such as the western Balkans, the Union is also a provider of security. These policies have contributed to the emergence of concentric circles around the core of the EU: the new member states; the candidate countries (Turkey, Croatia, Macedonia; Montenegro); the potential candidates; the neighbours (themselves divided into membership hopefuls in the East, and those in the South aspiring at best for an advanced institutional relationship) (Bechev and Nicolaidis 2010). The EU does make borders fuzzier through the export of its policies and templates, but it is important to acknowledge that its external policies are nonetheless about gate-keeping, with selective opening and, ultimately, closing and exclusion.

This discussion brings us back to the question of labels. Why characterise this hierarchical order as hegemony and not empire (cf. Dimitrovova's contribution to the volume)? Beyond Robert Cooper's views, there is an important body of literature arguing that practices such as the management of peripheries and the projection of models and values are all attributes of an imperial set-up. To quote the diehard Marxist historian, Perry Anderson (2007), 'from ancient to modern times, imperial power has been required to stabilise adjacent power vacuums or turbulent border zones, holding barbarians or terrorists at bay'. Surely, there are elements of imperial governance: interventionism (e.g. in the context of state-building in the western Balkans), the EU's version of *mission civilisatrice* (normative power?), or indeed, the distinction between core polity and external dependencies.

What this view fails to appreciate is that the EU is a supranational construct based on functional integration through law, distinctive from European empires of the nineteenth century, or indeed, their pre-modern antecedents. For the most part, the EU's influence is extended through bargains with sovereign states in conditions of asymmetric interdependence, and not through the despatch of administrators, military and police personnel working in concert with co-opted local elites. Finally, the EU projects values, templates and rules that are binding for itself too, just as they are an extension of its own institutional make-up. Hierarchical in nature, hegemonic order in a wider Europe accommodates certain notions of reciprocity. It also goes a long way in bridging the (perceived) gap between security interests and values.

Notes

1 See the chapter by Michal Natorski in this volume, dealing with Ukraine's contribution to CSDP and its institutional predecessors.
2 Although I consciously leave aside the question whether the EU is a regional hegemon or an aspiring global one.
3 On the travails of regional cooperation in the Southern Caucasus, see Licínia Simão's chapter in the volume.
4 This cluster is also covered by the Euro-Mediterranean Partnership (EMP) recently upgraded into 'the Union for the Mediterranean'. The EMP was launched in November 1995 at a summit held in Barcelona by the 15 EU members and 12 countries from the southern and eastern Mediterranean (Algeria, Cyprus, Egypt, Israel, Jordan, Lebanon, Malta, Morocco, Palestinian Authority, Syria, Tunisia and Turkey). Since the 2004 and 2007 enlargements of the Union, Central and Eastern European countries have been part of the process, while Libya has had observer status since 1999. The EMP aims at the promotion of stability, economic integration and cultural dialogue across the two sides of the Mediterranean. The Union of Mediterranean, originally a French initiative, was inaugurated in July 2008.
5 As of December 2011, the signature of the AA with Ukraine, containing provisions on establishing a Deep and Comprehensive Free Trade Area (DCFTA), has been postponed because of the sentencing imposed on the opposition leader Yulia Tymoshenko.

BOHDANA DIMITROVOVA

3

The re-bordering of values through the European neighbourhood

Debates on European Neighbourhood Policy (ENP) largely surround questions about the transcendence of cultural boundaries of Europe.[1] Indeed, with this new ambitious yet ambiguous policy, cultural re-bordering is on the increase, expanding the EU's functions beyond its institutional boundaries from a purely economic to a cultural entity, defined by a set of common values. Cultural boundaries are defined here in terms of notions of democracy, the respect of the rule of law, human rights and the development of civil society, notions which are, at the same time, presented as fundamentals of the European political community. But they also refer to notions of a common European heritage, history and culture.

This chapter explores the ways in which the EU is managing its cultural and political boundaries vis-à-vis its neighbours while seeking to 'escape' a trap of simplistic dichotomies that have occupied much of the mainstream writing on security and values.[2] This contribution attempts to avoid this juxtaposition of values and security (the third typology) by introducing the concept of borders, albeit in a limited way, and by applying a discursive analysis of spoken and written discourses. Furthermore, to argue that values can be securitised, and that security can become a value, is to undermine important ethical values in the name of security. For these reasons this chapter is placed within the third typology 'values versus values' of the conceptual framework of this book. The methodological approach applied in this chapter starts from the assumption that borders are not simply lines on the ground, but also manifestations of social practice and discourse (Paasi 2005). The phenomenon of cultural re-bordering is therefore understood as a contested political process surrounded by many ambiguities and contradictions. Instead of searching for a true or false picture, the primary concern of this analysis is to seek to understand the kind of meanings, symbols and representations that different actors attach to 'neighbouring'.

Cultural re-bordering is characterised by two competing processes, each with different implications for the development of a European political community. The first emphasises the need to transcend borders. This opening is however determined by compliance with prescribed norms and the adoption of European rules (or 'repertoire of integration'). The second ('repertoire of differences') is about confirming where the differences are recognised and reproduced, and where 'others' can be seen with a certain anxiety.

The first section discusses the complexities and ambiguities surrounding the dialogue on common values, where the EU, on the premise of promoting democracy and the rule of law, and strengthening of civil society, seeks to export or share its system of norms and values to its neighbours. The second section will explore how differences between Europeanness and non-Europeanness are represented and debated at the core of the EU vis-à-vis ENP countries, and how the criterion of difference is used to determine the EU's re-bordering strategies. Overall, this chapter will demonstrate how the negotiations over cultural boundaries remain the most contradictory and a problematic aspect of the re-bordering processes in the neighbourhood.[3]

A dialogue of common values: towards homogeneity and uniformity

Much ENP debate is centred on common values or the sharing of European experiences and the Union's model with its neighbours. In this sense, ENP is represented as a platform for the articulation of a shared identity and common interests between the EU and ENP countries or, to put it differently, cultural borders are defined by a level of commonality or series of similarities and shared values with the Union's neighbours. The rationale behind the approach of common values is to diminish the existing differences and to integrate ENP countries into the Union's spaces of governance. However, in a closer scrutiny of ENP documents and speeches, both spoken and written discourses reveal that this formation of a common European future and common values is a highly contested phenomenon.

The European Neighbourhood Strategy Paper from May 2004 ranks common values of respect of human dignity, liberty, democracy, equality, the rule of law and respect for human rights as the first priority of the Action Plans:

> The ENP's vision involves a ring of countries, sharing the EU fundamental values and objectives, drawn into an increasingly close relationship, going beyond co-operation to involve a significant measure of economic and political integration. (Comission 2004b: 5)

The ENP strategy paper from 2004 identifies those values fundamental to the Union's foundation and to its member states that should be promoted to the wider world. In other words, ENP seeks to establish a 'ring of friends' that will be gradually connected and integrated into the Union space of governance. This concept of a ring of friends extending EU influence to neighbouring states resonates with expansionist tendencies of empires ranging from those that traditionally seek to establish indirect rule over variably dependent clientalist states, to looser, more indirect forms of hegemony (see the chapter by Bechev).

In this context, the EU wants to convey that borders are geographically wider than those defined by the territorial border of the EU, and are even politically and economically inclusive. To financially support the objectives of integration – greater inclusion and more open borders – the EU has put aside specific funds (in the form of the European Neighbourhood and Partnership Instrument (ENPI)) to provide certain integration mechanisms, such as making EU programmes and agencies open to 'outsiders' who are, in exchange, willing to cooperate and to accept the Union's rules. Examples of such practice are educational and youth exchanges where some level of convergence with EU education policies, such as the Bologna Process, is encouraged and financially supported by different ENP mechanisms. ENP envisions different modes of participation for neighbours in the EU's agencies and programmes if certain conditions are met, thus reflecting the hierarchy of potential friends and neighbours inscribed within ENP. We may speak of diffuse patterns of centres with power fading out beyond its space into its peripheries, in a more concentric pattern (Waever 1997), increasing indirect control beyond the 'frontiers of empire' without any sharp inside/outside dichotomy.

The importance of legitimacy is another feature of ENP, which is created and sustained by voluntary processes. The EU is extremely careful in legitimising its interventions and pursuit of policies in foreign countries through the notions of partnership and ownership, but also careful at 'home' through the use of public surveys and opinion polls.[4] Furthermore, this self-legitimatisation stems from the Union's domestic democratic institutions and its self-perception as a well-governed entity based on values and democratic principles, which gives an impression of moral superiority similar to empires.

At the same time, it is declared that such reforms cannot be imposed from outside. They must be generated from within: 'the EU does not seek to impose priorities or conditions on its partner. There can be no question of asking partners to accept a predetermined set of priorities. These will be defined by common consent' (Commission 2004b: 8). The operational tools of declared partnerships are ENP Action Plans – 'fully negotiated and mutually agreed at political level. It is not an imposition by either side, but an agreed agenda for common work' (Commission 2006a: 3).

ENP countries are, therefore, expected to 'voluntarily' adopt the reforms and to modernise themselves. On many occasions Benita Ferrero-Waldner presented ENP as an offer to the EU partners, particularly in her speeches to

ENP countries and Russia. In her speech to the Brussels Economic Forum in April 2005, she referred to a 'ring of friends', an affectionate term missing from her later speeches:

> Our neighbours are not just citizens of 'third countries', they are our close partners and friends. We share practical interests, ideals and aspirations, and we face common challenges to our security. Our first priority is thus to share the enlarged EU peace, stability and prosperity with our neighbours. So last year, through European Neighbourhood Policy, we offered this 'ring of friends' a new, special relationship. (Ferrero-Waldner 2005c; emphasis in original)

These statements give the impression that re-bordering in the neighbourhood is determined by 'commonality', shared values, and joint partnerships. Likewise, EU documents place a lot of emphasis on mutual benefits, solidarity and joint ownership. However, the closer scrutiny of interviews reveals the rationale and logic behind this friendly and voluntary tone of the mutual exchange, dialogue and assistance that underpins common values or repertoire of integration. Furthermore, studying spoken discourses allows one to pay specific attention to the argumentative aspects of how 'common values' are constructed and managed through ENP.

The respondents from Directorate-General (DG) RELEX, primarily responsible for the implementation of ENP, frequently stressed the voluntary character of ENP. Also, officials were very careful to use the language of partnership and to stress that the Action Plans were negotiated on a bilateral basis and not imposed; thus, describing ENP countries as partners. This strong rhetoric of the voluntary character of ENP can be interpreted in following ways. Firstly, there is a widespread belief among the respondents from the EU institutions that the Union's model is admired around the world and, therefore, provides a model for ENP countries aspiring to EU standards and norms. In other words, ENP is about encouraging and not imposing reforms on neighbours:

> If you look world-wide, you see that the EU example is seen positively, if not admired by countries everywhere. Our model is convincing for others. We do not need to impose our model because you see efforts around us to create the same model inspired by European integration.[5]

This quotation reveals to a great extent the logic behind the common values dialogue. The EU's self-presentation in the neighbourhood is very much about exporting and sharing its values with the outsiders; hence ENP can be read as a carrier of the values of modernity. It creates an image of a 'core Europe' that shares a set of cultural values based on pluralistic and secular political systems, social solidarity and a respect for individual rights. The EU is presented as an ideal model of prosperity, stability and wealth that undoubtedly attracts the others and therefore there is no need to impose its norms and values. It is true that this self-modelling of the Union has found resonance in countries with European aspirations (e.g. Ukraine and

Moldova) who wish to become part of the EU in order to confirm their belonging to the 'European family'.

At the same time, these values are of European origin and of common inheritance or, as Ferrero-Waldner put it, 'common to the European home' (2005a). This European home is to be secure, known and familiar to its inhabitants. Therefore, the values are not negotiable with outsiders but should be simply accepted by the neighbours. They are defined *a priori* and inherited from the Western experiences. In this context, references to common history, a Christian inheritance and the enlightenment, generate a belief in common values and common ideas among the members of the European community:

> It is a European culture and tradition that is a basis for the EU. European civilisation has been elaborated in centuries based on values of Christianity, the understanding of individual values and the dignity of persons. Russia is more Asian than European because it lacks a real understanding of individual values and dignity.[6]

Values are at times presented as common issues which should unite members of the European Community. They give a sense of belonging and justification for the existence of the European Community whose members have much in common with each other but which is, at the same time, separated from those who are described as poorly governed, with poor records of human rights and individual freedom, and having a history of autocratic and non-democratic regimes. The processes of internal de-bordering and re-bordering are accompanied by a confirmation of cultural borders with others. In other words, this self-definition and self-limitation of European 'community' must be seen as a dual process taking place with reference to both inside and outside.

A civilising mission: spreading values in the neighbourhood

ENP is based on the assumption that gradual integration will diminish differences and hence prevent instability spilling over into the EU territory. In this sense, ENP is attempting to create a sense of generosity, sharing and solidarity beyond the Union's borders, which should tie together the neighbours to the Union naturally. While doing so it reinforces the inferiority of the 'other' less developed, badly governed and generally backward ENP countries on the cultural periphery of the EU.

The objective of ENP is to project its political and economic influence across the borders, even to the extent of advancing a 'civilising' mission – a desire to connect Europe to the rest of the world. Some scholars have rejected this 'civilisation' discourse by arguing that EU policy does not involve the spread of a people or a civilisation across a continent: 'The EU expansion might diffuse certain norms, values and practices, but it leaves many others in place' (Anderson and Bort 1998: 143). Similarly, Walters (2004) points out that EU norms are no longer associated with notions of civilisation but, instead, are more neutral, technical and universal norms of political and economic governance. Nevertheless, while the EU may not be about spreading people across different countries, it does seek to export its value system outside its borders.

This civilisation mission of spreading values and norms has undoubtedly a strong security rationale. In this sense, the creation and maintenance of a common values dialogue serves the purposes of peace and order. In the same way, ENP can also be understood as a 'peace project' with a similar mission to develop a zone of peace and stability with which the EU can enjoy close, peaceful and cooperative relations. As Böröcz (2002) further observes, the 'naïve good intentions' in Western Europe reflect an imperial-colonial teleology. The logic derives from the Union's own experiences, the history of imperialism of the core members, and the expansionist nature of the European Community.

The discourse of common values is about the transformation of governments and societies in the neighbourhood in line with European standards, norms and values. In this context, ENP builds on the enlargement instruments for achieving stability, that is to say, on what has been described in EU studies as Europeanisation, social learning or external governance (Lavenex 2004; Schimmelfennig and Sedelmeier 2004; Lavenex and Schimmelfennig, 2007). From their point of view, ENP can be seen as a test of the Union's transformative or soft power (Whitman 2005), or an example of 'soft geopolitics' working through different means to spread European values, without offering the prospect of EU membership and without having any real military power at its disposal. This conceptualisation of the EU's external governance does not pose any problems for the dynamics of Europe's re-bordering project. Moreover, its external governance fails to critically question the intentions and rationales of its own foreign policy agenda which, perhaps for normative reasons, tends not to engage with the questions of geopolitics, unequal exchanges and domination.

Exerting 'transformative power' in the neighbourhood space of very different cultures, traditions and histories, but also different European aspirations, is undoubtedly more problematic. In its conclusions from June 2007, the Council referred to utilising 'Europe's great modernising (transformative) power even more efficiently to avoid the spill over effects of political instability and weak governance to the EU'. It went on to state that, 'Fleshing out this positive conditionality and applying the arsenal of measures ... is, therefore, essential, especially when considering the potentially high long-term costs of failing to support our neighbours' (General Affairs and External Relations Council 2007).

Conditionality was applied by the EU to the new member states, which claimed to aspire to European values and to be willing to fully adopt the Union's model in exchange for their integration into its structures. Inherited from the enlargement process, the 'carrot and stick' approach of 'conditionality' remains one of the key principles of ENP. The degree of proximity of relations and degree of integration are offered on a differential basis, as clearly stated in one of ENP communications: 'the level of ambition of the EU's relationships with its neighbours will take into account the extent to which these values are effectively shared' (Commission 2004b: 3).

In my view this notion of the gradual integration and incorporation of the 'neighbours' into the EU under strict conditionality and supervision seems closer to more neo-imperial practices of highly differentiated and unequal power distribution (Böröcz 2002). In that context, Pace (2006) and Browning (2003) have argued that the EU needs to change its practice of treating its neighbours as objects to be 'saved'.

Despite a variety of calls for a more effective usage of conditionality, it is not clear how or under what circumstances it should be applied to ENP countries, particularly in the case of those reluctant to subscribe to European values in the areas of democracy, the rule of law and governance. Here, the principle of conditionality becomes more problematic and contested among different actors in Brussels. Instead, we can find a spectrum of views on whether and how conditionality should be applied. Some doubt the effectiveness of conditionality in the neighbourhood, arguing that the EU is not offering enough incentives, or 'carrots', for the neighbouring countries to seriously undertake their commitments to reform. In this context, a sense of a shared commitment to common values may merely sound like wishful thinking. There is a certain degree of scepticism about establishing a common values dialogue with neighbours who are not interested in transcending cultural borders.

It is no surprise that we can find more critical voices among representatives of European civil society in Brussels who question this self-representation of the EU as a model to the 'others', and criticise the motives behind the Union's use of conditionality. In essence, the EU uses conditionality as a strategic tool to impose certain modes of governance for reasons of self-interest rather than for the creation of dialogue, joint ownership and learning from other cultures, themes which are often missing from the local or regional contexts (Joenniemi 2005). The problem is that European regulations and laws have been largely imposed from the outside with little consideration of local settings and available resources; they are top-down. A similar situation may be observed in the neighbourhood where asymmetric neighbourhood relations are a strong source of European power politics, allowing the EU to establish its rule through what Emerson (2002) calls 'ordering policies' in particular zones of influence or interest. To sustain its attraction, core Europe (the EU) diffuses its power towards the peripheries through reward mechanisms, persuasion, and the projection of standards and norms.

At the same time, European values are rarely questioned by respondents from the EU institutions. It is not difficult to detect a strong and distinctive sense of superiority on the part of EU officials when it comes to their understanding of how to define and diffuse European values. Some EC officials even spoke about a teaching exercise in a sense that the EU is offering its knowledge and expertise:

> Our negotiations with these countries are part of a pedagogic exercise. We promote reforms by dealing with these governments and it is part of a learning process. So, that is one exercise we need to conduct if we want the system to change one day. Little by little we see their adaptation to our values and to our language of communication.[7]

The discourse is about giving 'them' a chance to learn from the Europeans and to adopt the Union's model. The tone of the discourse is often mentoring and patronising. It is a teacher–pupil relationship that emphasises the process of adaptation and integration of values rather than the declared values of partnerships; the 'Others' are considered as 'an underdeveloped' part of the centre's (Western Europe's) past, while the EU is a good teacher that knows best how to export knowledge to its neighbours (Holm 2005).

In the process of establishing an asymmetric relationship, in which the EU assumes the right to define what is appropriate, borders acquire some features of 'soft imperialism' (Hettne and Soderbaum 2005). As we are reminded by Böröcz and Sarkar (2005: 162), this echoes the imperialist past of the core member states: 'The states that constituted the EU at the turn of the 21st century are the same states that had exercised imperial rule over half the inhabitable surface of the globe outside Europe just two or three generations ago.' The EU fears being labelled as a neo-colonial power that imposes its own rules and norms outside its territory and, therefore, insists on the voluntary character of ENP where the countries decide themselves which norms they wish to adopt. As suggested by Wallace (2003), former European colonies resent and suspect European motives as neo-colonial, as an attempt to re-impose Western values and economic interests. At the same time the export of EU legislation can be seen as a kind of intrusion into the domestic affairs of foreign countries, particularly when the security and political aspects of ENP are at stake. According to some respondents, the fear of a return to a form of colonial past is an important reason for the Union's cautious approach when cultural borders are addressed.

True, ENP was originally conceived in a very European political context as the strategic response to the enlargement. Today, the landscape of the Neighbourhood looks very different. It covers the Arab Neighbourhood, the Middle East and Sub-Saharan Africa, each presenting new challenges to the current European Neighbourhood framework. Despite this geographical and cultural broadening of the neighbourhood space, the EU-centric rhetoric still dominates in the official speeches. Though perhaps unintentionally, it conveys a message of the superiority of European values and might be regarded as some form of 'soft imperialism', particularly when addressed to the Arab countries. The EU's policies and attempts to re-establish control over domestic and foreign developments using a highly normative language of common values and democratisation can therefore often be viewed with suspicion by those with relatively recent experiences of occupation by colonial and imperial powers (Holm 2008).

A repertoire of differences

In this section, I will discuss cultural borders as dividing lines where the differences between European and non-European, 'us' and 'them', are confirmed mainly through spoken discourse. I am interested in exploring in which contexts and by whom such differences are either confirmed or neglected. The frontiers between European and non-European are rather blurred in the official documents and speeches; it is not clear who is to be European/non-European in the neighbourhood space. A critical inquiry into a 'repertoire of differences' is not only important to gain a better understanding of how the European political community is transformed, but also has practical implications for ENP countries.

The ambiguities in defining European borders
In spite of disagreements on where the final borders of the EU should be, the demarcation of these borders has become a burning issue within the Union and its member states. The territorial or geographical limits of Europe/the EU are influenced by different factors, including cultural and religious differences between Europeans and non-Europeans. Culture, history and religion are, however, only sporadically mentioned in the official ENP discourse. Similar to changing geographies, the cultural borders are subjected to personal views, historical links and experiences.

On the one hand, there is a desire to clearly define the geographical limits of Europe and to classify the countries eligible to become members of the Union. Such a desire or intention to confirm the territorial borders of the EU resembles the state-centric paradigm of borders according to which political community is circumscribed by common values. One of the key functions of state borders is to circumscribe territory and shape the identity of the political community within the border-confirming framework. As formulated by an EC official: 'Any political community has grown up in a defined territory. You have to somehow circumscribe the territory and within this territory you can build up a political community.'[8] The same idea can be applied to the EU in its efforts at building a political community: 'No boundary, no state – and by extension, no boundaries, no effective European institutions' (Wallace 2002: 83). Similar to the ways in which state borders come to define the very essence and identity of a political community, the nature and extent of its external borders is an important aspect for the EU as a polity.

On the other hand, however, the demands for a clearly demarcated territorial space clash with the Union's expansionist agenda, while a policy of harder exclusionary boundaries would risk destabilising the Union's surroundings. The state-centric paradigm for borders is therefore under pressure to shift towards a more inclusive border policy and to escape the logic of exclusion versus inclusion or the inside/outside dichotomy (Hassner 2002). The Commission itself acknowledges that the ultimate geographical limits of the Union are not settled yet and that 'any decision on further EU expansion awaits a debate on the ultimate geographic limits of the Union' (Commission 2003a: 5). The same communication recognises the right of any European state to apply for EU membership. The fact that the candidate countries (e.g. Turkey or the western Balkans) are explicitly excluded from ENP suggests that at least for now, the Union's borders are fixed.

The efforts of the Commission to promote fuzzy and fluid borders with no clear markers are not welcomed by those who prefer to be located in a clearly defined framework of European/non-European borders (e.g. Ukraine or Moldova). In other words, the blurring of the frontiers between 'them' and 'us', and between 'in' and 'out', might be beneficial for the Union's expansionist policies in the neighbourhood and in exerting its influence in the periphery, but are viewed, perhaps unsurprisingly, with great suspicion and mistrust by Moldovan and Ukrainian officials and civil society organisations (CSOs). These authors consider the EU to be a post-modern or neo-medieval empire, because, in their view, the EU is transcending state borders and the state system in order to develop a system of divided and overlapping sovereignties, where jurisdictions overlap, and with multiple identities in which the separation between the internal and external is no longer possible (J. Anderson 1996, 2007). As Hassner (1997: 41) argues, 'borders are becoming less territorial, less physical, more complex and less visible'.

The debate about Ukraine has crystallised this dilemma of fixing the EU's boundaries and defining the degree of Europeanness. In order to become a member of the EU, a country has to testify to its Europeanness. In other words, the lack of any prospect of EU membership puts in question and downgrades the Europeanness of countries which clearly see themselves as European. Ukraine, with clear European aspirations, expresses on every occasion its dissatisfaction with ENP, pointing out that Ukraine belongs to Europe. For Ukraine the ENP is an artificial construct of the Union that is deliberately ambiguous when it comes to the question of membership in the short term. There is a feeling among respondents from Ukraine and Moldova[9] that they are being downgraded by the current classifications; they are deeply dissatisfied with inclusion in the same policy framework as the EU southern neighbours. Therefore, on its eastern front in particular, the Union faces several challenges in sustaining ENP's rhetoric of 'everything but institutions'. It is expected that pressures on the EU to move Ukraine to the pre-accession stage may increase, thus jeopardising its relations with Russia.

Contrary to the Ukrainian position, Morocco has expressed satisfaction about inclusion in the ENP framework, acknowledging that it does not geographically belong to the European continent but wishes to get as close as possible to Europe. Morocco applied to join the EU in 1987 but its application was rejected because Morocco was not considered a European country and was therefore not eligible for membership. Despite this exclusion from the EU, Morocco is perceived by some interviewees as a European country with strong cultural links with Europe and as a country that is oriented towards Europe.

A criticism of including the European countries in the same framework as the Arab countries is shared by many respondents, particularly those from the new member states. Their own experience of exclusion from the Union's club of privileged members is an important factor, one that shapes their thinking of how cultural borders are not only physical lines but also imply mental and cultural differences or similarities.

These shifts, from clearly defined geographical boundaries to more complex and fluid borders encompassing a mix of factors, have created tensions among different actors in Brussels. Similarly, the European Parliament in its resolution of October 2007 expressed doubts about 'the meaningfulness of the ENP geographical scope, as it involves countries which are, geographically and culturally, European together with Mediterranean non-European countries'. At the same time, the resolution underlines that the lack of a European perspective 'should not transform southern ENP countries into second class partners' (European Parliament 2007). Despite these calls to differentiate between the neighbours, the European Parliament acknowledges that it would be impossible to split ENP into two separate policies for the Eastern European neighbours and the southern countries.

The official statements of the Commission, in response to this widespread criticism, are that ENP provides a framework for differentiation according to the progress and aspirations of the countries concerned. All ENP documents recognise differentiation as one of the key principles. Furthermore, on every occasion EC officials have stressed the bilateral character of ENP (Action Plans), which allows the EU to encounter the specificities of each individual country. Overall, the efforts of the Commission to synchronise the different approaches of the member states, and to act as a single entity with coherent approaches towards its neighbours, have proved problematic, if not impossible. Under such circumstances, the image of post-national (Diez 2004) or neo-medieval borders (Zielonka 2006) with multilevel and multicentred government, as increasingly promulgated by European scholars, remains rather limited.

The difficulty of accommodating differences
ENP uses the criterion of differences to recognise different degrees of permeability of cultural borders. More precisely, cultural borders are usually

confirmed when ENP countries are reluctant to subscribe to European values of democracy, human rights and civil society. Nonetheless, this acknowledgment of different standards for different ENP partners varies. There is no coherent strategy among the EU actors as to when a criterion of difference should be applied. This ad hoc approach of the Union indicates a heterogeneous mix of relationships with the neighbours involving power hierarchies.

The widespread view is that European values, as formulated in the Copenhagen criteria,[10] should be only applied to countries with European aspirations before their membership. Those aspiring to one day become members of the EU (Moldova and Ukraine) or wishing to have privileged relationships (Morocco) are expected to integrate and to overcome the existing differences, at least to a degree compatible with the EU rules. This rather pragmatic approach resonates with the state-centric paradigm of borders of the status quo. In other words, the EU should only be concerned with the affairs and events happening within its own territory. This is not to say that there should be no interaction with 'them' or that cultural borders are impermeable for those who are located in the framework of confirmed differences. Instead, they are allowed to cooperate within an inter-governmental framework based on 'common interests' rather than on common values. The promotion of democracy is, therefore, conducted primarily through institutional collaboration with governments and parliaments. Parliamentary twinning programmes and institution-building are just two examples of the cooperative practices promoted by ENP.

Russia illustrates the existing tensions between a common values approach based on the integration mechanism and an inter-cultural dialogue that refers to mutual learning and understanding of Russia's self-exclusion from ENP. Its 'big power' strategic influence underlines the EU difficulties in developing a uniform policy. Russia is aware of the advantages that EU membership could bring. However, it prefers to secure these advantages without any loss of sovereignty and within a clearly defined inter-governmental framework. Under the new slogan of 'sovereign democracy', the Russian government has been criticising the West for being interventionist and imposing its values beyond its territorial borders.

According to some respondents, the EU should not emphasise common values with Russia, whose strategic importance, but also cultural differences, are too big; hence, it is almost impossible to reach any consensus on European values. It is not only that Russia is not interested in a common values dialogue, but also that Russia's interpretations of values, particularly democracy and human rights, are markedly different.

Yet not all interviewees share these views. In particular, the respondents from new member states, with their recent experiences of Soviet occupation and their lack of colonising history, criticise the Union for its selective approach based on the strategic and domestic interests of its core members. This dissatisfaction and frustration with the current practices of the EU is clearly demonstrated by the following statement: 'Those countries who do not share fundamental values with the European community should not be included in the ENP framework only because, for instance, they are former French colonies. We should clearly recognise a common history with Eastern European countries – Ukraine and Moldova belong to Europe.'[11]

In other words, the EU should distinguish between European countries with European aspirations and common histories, with those unwilling to subscribe to European values excluded from the ENP framework. There is very little understanding and sympathy for a continuation of what can be labelled neo-colonial politics where member states pursue essentially national interests in their former colonies regardless of the latter's poor performance in democracy and human rights.

Others suggest that there should be a 'universal' application of values regardless of the cultural origins or strategic importance of the country. This universal approach favours a bordering strategy that would enable the EU to react and intervene beyond its borders of jurisdiction. In this context, borders acquire universal ethical or moral attributes which some scholars label as cosmopolitan (Delanty and Rumford 2005; Delanty 2006; Rumford 2008). These approaches of a cosmopolitan orientation downplay the distinction between European and non-European, claiming it to be inadequate and no longer fitting with the contemporary political environment. From this perspective, ENP may be challenging the modernist understanding of borders that distinguishes 'inside' from 'outside'. Such views about universal values are discussed only occasionally, particularly when the EU is facing criticism for being Euro-centric or when it is having difficulties in promoting its values in the neighbourhood (e.g. in Russia or Algeria). It is expected that these shifts of cultural borders from European values and norms to universal principles, as articulated in different UN conventions, will convince reluctant partners in the neighbourhood to cooperate. In other words, the identification of universal values seeks to provide a basic framework for cooperation and an exchange of views in order to accommodate cultural differences. The difficulty rests in the fact that while ENP claims a universality of values in both their origins and how they are pursued, these underpinning values and norms are, in fact, European. These claims of moral universality and global unity need to be viewed with suspicion, otherwise we risk underestimating the crusading logic hidden perhaps unintentionally behind cosmopolitan pretensions.

Inter-cultural dialogue
ENP applies the criterion of cultural differences to engage in inter-cultural dialogue, particularly with non-European neighbours in North Africa where such differences are enormous. Back in its first communication on a Wider Europe from March 2003 (Commission 2003b: 12), the Commission recognised the importance of cultural cooperation and enhanced mutual

understanding: 'the importance of dialogue between civilisations and free exchange of ideas between cultures, religions, traditions and human links cannot be overemphasised'. The communication from December 2006 (Commission 2006a: 6) calls for strengthening the human dimension of ENP: 'The ENP must have a human face, and the citizens of the EU and of the neighbouring countries should have more opportunities to interact, and to learn more about each other's society and understand better each other's cultures'. Many of these exchanges are predominately economic and social in character, but cultural exchanges and inter-cultural dialogue are also important here.

Despite these claims of engaging in mutual learning and fostering an understanding of different cultures, it is hard to imagine what and how the EU will learn from ENP countries. A certain level of scepticism can be found among some respondents. For instance, an official from the Council held a rather pessimistic view about the inter-cultural dialogue of ENP:

> There is a lack of understanding and knowledge of their societies. We think we know what is best for them because we believe our model is the best. Imagine if I come to my neighbour and tell him, *this is what you need to do*. It cannot work like this. These are very foreign lands and we need to learn how to engage with them. We can't accept them if we don't know who they are. ENP is not a solution for this. It is a unilateral EU policy.[12]

This general lack of acknowledgement of other cultures and a lack of respect for non-European values goes against the principles of inter-cultural dialogue, which require recognising differences and some degree of equality. Cultural differences are mainly described and represented in terms of the fearful unknown and potential threat to European values. This dark image of the 'other' gives an impression that cultural differences are recognised in order to avoid a 'clash of civilisations' and in order to manage potential risks associated with troublesome neighbours. Therefore, ENP can be seen as a tool to get closer to them, first, in order to know them better, and second, to be able to predict their behaviour. As one of the interviewees remarked, ideally they should 'become like us'. In other words, the differences are recognised and accepted as a necessity rather than as an opportunity for mutual learning. As suggested by Kovács (2001), in line with imperial logic, the accumulation of knowledge about 'others' allows the EU to better manage and control those who are outside of the Union's territorial borders. In her work on the EU's discursive strategies towards new member states, the colonisers (the EU) control and limit how the colonised can perceive them. Drawing on post-colonial theories, Manuela Boatca (2008) provides a historical analysis of East/West divisions showing how 'Eastern' European countries effectively assume an inferior status themselves by internally accepting the Western discourses of modernity and development. At first glance, this observation of 'colonising perceptions' may sound exaggerated when applied to the EU. It certainly does require a great level of imagination and a critical mind to understand the EU in these terms.

Religion is another criterion of repertoire of differences, although it is less visible in the official discourse. Generally, it is acknowledged that the EU can no longer ignore the question of Islam. There are, however, different views as to how far and in what ways Islam can be or should be part of any cultural re-bordering. Some insist that the borders should be confirmed between the two different worlds of Christian Europe and Islam, which coexist in a clearly defined framework. Here, Christianity plays an important role in confirming cultural borders. Others argue that different religions should not necessarily be an obstacle to deeper integration.

The criterion of religious differences was addressed in Ferrero-Waldner's speeches to the Euro-Mediterranean Parliamentary Assembly in March 2007 (Ferrero-Wadner 2006d) and during her first visit to Egypt in May 2006 when she spoke about the notorious Danish cartoons incident or the radicalisation of Muslims in Europe. The Mediterranean borderland is presented 'not as a barrier separating the people of its shores, but as a bridge for commercial, social and cultural exchange' (Ferrero-Waldner 2006c). Instead of a clash of civilisations, we witness what the Commissioner calls a 'clash of ignorance' which needs to be overcome by inter-cultural dialogue between the EU and Islam.

To further demonstrate its objectives of mutual learning and understanding, the EU declared 2008 'European Year of Intercultural Dialogue', aimed at promoting cultural exchanges, tolerance and mutual learning, in order to get to know one's neighbours better and respect their differences. Unlike cross-border practices formulated under the 'repertoire of integration' which aim at diminishing differences, such inter-cultural dialogue seeks to create a platform for dialogue and cooperation based on mutual respect and the explicit recognition of 'others'.

To conclude, ENP seeks to establish a framework for cooperation, laying down an 'order based on mutual respect, common interests'. Nevertheless, the cooperation framework requires the recognition of 'others' unlike traditional integration mechanisms. Transnational links of cooperation require more than a sharing of values through the types of institutional frameworks that have come to characterise the bilateral cooperation formulated in ENP Action Plans. Transnational (or post-national) borders depend on the recognition of shared values or common traditions and histories. It requires similar ways of acting, perceiving and understanding to properly transcend cultural borderlines; while differences are seen as a threat, they are at the same time acknowledged as a value.

Nevertheless, a brief look at neighbours in the East and the South suggests that the assessment and evaluation criteria are not solely based on democracy performance but also on energy geopolitics, the strategic importance of neighbours and the interests of member states in their former colonies (e.g.

Egypt, Tunisia or Azerbaijan).[13] Despite its good intentions, the rewarding principle of ENP may therefore lead to competition instead of to cooperation among neighbours, but may also in the long term undermine the credibility of the EU as normative international actor.

Conclusions

Promoting democracy, the rule of law, human rights and freedom, and supporting the efforts of countries aspiring to democracy are said to be central to ENP, and are used to define cultural re-bordering. The extensive use of the language of common values in the discourses of EU officials and in the documents examined reveals that normative changes are integral to ENP. In this sense, ENP is designed to export the Union's best practices and values to its neighbourhood through two re-bordering strategies.

The first re-bordering strategy ('repertoire of integration') seeks to integrate ENP countries through a dialogue of common values, determined by compliance with prescribed norms and the adoption of European rules. Because of their non-territorial character, values can be exported to the neighbourhood without the need for territorial expansion or the further enlargement of the Union. On the whole, the discourse of common values draws attention to the need to develop a common understanding and common language of values, as well as to build positive relationships with neighbours. As my empirical evidence shows, EU engagement in the rhetoric of common values with its neighbours is both problematic and contested.

Firstly, despite the emphasis on a 'friendly' tone of sharing values, the spoken discourses slip into what can be described as the civilising mission of the EU to project its own values in the neighbourhood, giving an impression of the superiority of European values, which are non-negotiable with 'outsiders' because they lie at the very foundations of the European community. From the EU's point of view, there is no doubt that its model is admired worldwide and therefore its values are to be adopted 'voluntarily'. On this reading, the EU is represented as a 'force of good' while teaching its neighbours how best to adopt value systems identical to those of Europe, yet this is done without considering the particularities of the individual neighbours. The discourse of common values is structured in such a way that the neighbours are the 'subjects' of ENP policy rather than 'partners'. This EU-centric character of cultural borders creates tensions in the largely non-European neighbourhood space. A common values dialogue may be appealing to Eastern European neighbours but, as a quick glance to the neighbourhood might suggest, is less so to the Arab world.

Secondly, while searching for unity among the members of the European Community, borders are re-confirmed with its neighbours. In other words, the process of internal and external re-bordering is mutually reinforcing. By strengthening its internal unity, the EU distances itself from the periphery.

Thirdly, the discourse of common values has introduced the principles of conditionality, according to which the EU draws closer those ENP countries willing to 'voluntarily' adopt its values and norms and give up their sovereignty in exchange for rewards. Those neighbours (e.g. Ukraine, Moldova and Morocco) who subscribe to these 'common values' have their status upgraded to new categories of 'privileged partner', 'friend' or 'semi-member' of the democratically governed European space.

According to the second scenario ('repertoire of differences'), cultural borders are conceptualised as dividing lines serving a variety of purposes – between European and non-European. The criterion of difference is used on different occasions, for instance, to determine the final borders of the EU, or to engage in inter-cultural dialogue with the neighbours. Sometimes, the repertoire of difference projects an inferiority complex (e.g. Moldova or Ukraine), while at other times it justifies a strategic choice (e.g. Russia).

Firstly, the question of the territorial and geographical limits of EU borders is only indirectly addressed in ENP documents by confirming the rights of European countries to apply for membership. The ENP strategy of blurring and creating fuzziness, however, gives the impression that any consideration of the question of where the Union's borders are ultimately demarcated is being postponed and thus viewed with suspicion by some, particularly those who find themselves presently excluded from the EU (e.g. Ukraine and Moldova). At the same time, certain voices among European actors desire a confirmation of where the Union's borders lie, and favour a clear demarcation of lines between domestic and foreign realms in order to clearly differentiate European and non-European neighbours. The process of fixing borders emphasises the territorial limits of the European community in line with state-centric thinking, whereas blurring or fuzziness reflects an imperial dimension to the notion of 'unlimited' borders.

Secondly, inter-cultural dialogue underlines the existence of a division between the EU and 'others'. According to this bordering strategy of ENP, the differences are recognised and should be confirmed by both sides on an equal footing. In this sense, ENP is about managing the existing cultural, political or religious differences through cross-border cooperation and exchanges in order that each side can learn and acquire knowledge about the other. The process of learning and entering into a exchange of views via inter-cultural dialogue, however, mostly reinforces, rather then challenges, the interpretation of 'others' as a dangerous aberration from the European norms of stability and order. As such, cultural borders are to be respected and tolerated; 'the other' has the right to coexist unless it becomes a threat to the EU. Though this logic of 'let it be' may sound promising, it should not be confused with genuine values of tolerance and respect of differences. As recent anti-Roma and anti-Muslim crusades in some of the old Western European democracies show, the boundaries of who is to be tolerated and who not are very thin.

In this chapter, I have demonstrated that values, which to a great extent underpin re-bordering processes, are not neutral. They are the expression of different interests prioritised at any given time by different actors, and are contingent on the geopolitical constellation. Put differently, the values can be applied to one situation but may be irrelevant or questionable in another situation. At times, European values are a flexible rather than fixed coherent system. At other times, we can observe less emphasis on common values and more on common interests when security or strategic interests are at stake (e.g. Russia).

And finally, what stems from my empirical research is that ENP is not about choosing between simplistic demarcations of security and values, 'us' and 'them', insiders and outsiders. Instead, the EU attempts to balance and reconcile these two otherwise opposing dimensions of ENP, but in so doing risks creating political destabilisation rather than stability, as well as deepening social and economic inequalities in the neighbourhood. All this suggests that there may be no set of principles that would resolve conflicts among values in ways acceptable to all parties concerned. Needless to say, a Europe that finds itself in an increasingly heterogeneous and unknown environment needs to do several things: to mobilise its internal creativity and flexibility to anticipate alternative narratives; to engage in dialogue with others beyond governmental elites; and to incorporate or reject differences based on listening to others. These options are still possible but require Europe to engage in much-needed self-reflection and a re-evaluation of its values, instead of merely taking them for granted.

Notes

1. The author would like to acknowledge the support for this research provided by the EU's 6th Framework Programme for the research project 'EUDIMENSIONS: Local Dimensions of a Wider European Neighbourhood' (CIT5–028804), as well as the research project, 'The External Image of the EU: Views from Morocco and Algeria' (financed by the Volkswagen Stiftung, within the European Foreign and Security Policy Studies (EFSPS) programme).
2. See for instance Bosse (2007); Jeandesbocz (2007); Tocci (2007a); Zaiotti (2007).
3. This chapter is based on the analysis of ENP documents, drawing on the selected speeches of the former ENP commissioner Benita Ferrero-Waldner and 40 face-to-face in-depth interviews conducted with EC officials, MEPs, EU diplomats and civil society organisations in Brussels from March–November 2007.
4. For instance, the EU regularly conducts surveys of public opinion in the member states which it uses to justify its policies towards neighbours.
5. Interview with an EC official, 12 June 2007, Brussels.
6. Interview with a Lithuanian MEP, 7 June 2007, Brussels.
7. Interview with an EC official, 19 June 2007, Brussels.
8. Interview with an EC official, 12 June 2007, Brussels.
9. Based on interviews with Moldovan and Ukrainian CSOs.
10. These criteria are the rule of law, human rights, respect of minority rights and

existence of market economy.
11 Interview with a Polish MEP, 8 June 2007, Brussels.
12 Interview with an official from the Council of the EU, 25 June 2007, Brussels.
13 These countries are known for the abuse of human rights and, in general, by very limited democratic practice.

PART II

Democracy and good governance

ROSA BALFOUR

4

EU political dilemmas in North Africa and the Middle East: the logic of diversity and the limits to foreign policy

Introduction

The political dimension of EU foreign policy towards North Africa and the Middle East has often been subject to three interconnected dilemmas concerning the ways in which 'values' and 'security' tend to condition relations between the two shores – dilemmas that were put under the spotlight with the outbreak of the Arab Spring in January 2011. The first refers to the aims of EU foreign policy, which revolve around apparent dichotomies that one might label 'values versus interests', 'transformation versus stability' and 'democracy versus security'. The second dilemma points to the universe of tools, strategies and methods that the EU can use to pursue its aims. Here the main dilemmas are between engaging or isolating partners, offering positive or negative conditionality, and promoting partnership and dialogue or sanctioning. The final dilemma has implications on EU identity-building as much as on concrete policy choices, for it regards the choice between applying degrees of flexibility in the treatment of partners and ensuring the consistency and coherence that the EU has established as a Treaty-based aim in its external relations. In other words, it concerns the aims of EU foreign policy: is the EU trying to be effective outside its borders, or is it seeking internal objectives of setting standards and principles around which its members and institutions can coalesce?

After analysing the nature of these foreign policy dilemmas (section 2), this chapter will highlight the ways in which these have manifested themselves in EU policy towards the South Mediterranean shore through strategies developed since 1995. The recent literature argues that the 'normative' agenda based on values developed in the 1990s was overshadowed by the conflicting security aims of the post-September 11 international and regional environment, as well as by a growing interest in contrasting irregular migration from the region towards EU member states. Only after the fall of the authoritarian presidents of Tunisia and Egypt did the EU return to more 'normative' positions which were, however, tested by the changing political developments in the region.

There is no doubt that many of the ways in which security is articulated are in contradiction with the 'values'-based dimension of the EU's declaratory policy towards the Mediterranean. At the same time, the degree of shift from a 'normative' agenda in the 1990s to more security-related aims in the 2000s is debatable. This chapter, through a brief historical overview of EU positions towards the region (section 3), questions the importance attributed to the consequences of September 11 as the key factor determining such a shift. It highlights certain continuities in EU foreign policy that may lead us to a different understanding of the 'values versus security' debate. It argues that since the inception of the EU's collective initiatives, the dichotomy between 'values' and 'security' has inhibited EU foreign policy towards the Mediterranean. In fact, the post-September 11 environment has seen more instances of EU rhetoric based on 'values', while the security agenda has been strengthening at the same time, with differentiated consequences on the concrete policies developed in the 2000s (discussed in section 4).

These continuities suggest that the changing international environment following September 11 is not the only factor determining the way in which the 'conflict' between 'values' and 'security' has been perceived, and, as such, the sources of this dichotomy may be found elsewhere (section 5). Using the theoretical tools provided by intergovernmentalism to conduct a historical 'macro'-level analysis from 1995 to the present, I show that these three dilemmas are not merely the consequence of conflicting or contradictory external aims in the Mediterranean but can, to a large extent, be traced back to the EU's own foreign policy-making processes. The 'logic of diversity' (Hoffman 2000) between the member states runs deeper than is often understood. Alongside the traditional bargain between northern and southern EU member states on finding a balance between the eastern and southern neighbourhoods, the member states do not share the same vision when it comes to the terms of the dilemmas related to 'values' and 'security'. This implies that there are different interpretations within the EU of what aims its 'normative agenda' should pursue, what means should be used to do so, and generally what the ultimate objectives of EU foreign policy are. The cacophony of political voices in the EU over how best to respond to the uprisings that spread throughout North Africa and the Middle East in 2011 reflected these dilemmas. Such diversity does not bode well for the EU in its attempts to renew relations with the countries of North Africa and the Middle East since the changes brought about by the Arab Spring.

The ways in which the member states and the institutions have debated these issues also reveal that the dilemmas are not captured by simply considering values and security as antithetical, but that there can be competing perceptions of different values. In turn, using intergovernmental approaches to understand the debate in the EU on the role of norms in foreign policy represents an attempt to bridge the traditional rationalist–constructivist divide of International Relations theory.

Before embarking on this exercise, a methodological clarification is necessary to delimit the field of investigation. The EU has developed a number of policies towards the South Mediterranean region since 1995: the Euro-Mediterranean Partnership (EMP, also known as the Barcelona Process) constituted the main format through which collective EU foreign policy was articulated towards the region as a whole through its multilateral dimension, and towards the individual countries. This was flanked by the European Neighbourhood Policy (ENP), developed from 2003–4 onwards, which placed a stronger emphasis on bilateral relations and on a differentiated approach towards individual countries. Unsatisfied with the state of relations between the two shores, in 2008 the EU launched the 'Union for the Mediterranean', a project led by the then French President Nicholas Sarkozy. Its aim was to strengthen the 'partnership' dimension of intergovernmental relations between two shores at the expense of the framework and the values of the EMP. The revision of existing policies in the aftermath of the Arab Spring has not (yet) led to rethinking the regional institutional architecture but, as we shall see, policies such as ENP have been revised in favour of greater differentiation between countries.

If these are the 'shapes' in which EU policy towards the region was created, the analysis of such initiatives does not exhaust EU foreign policy. These are considered here as 'instruments' of foreign policy. The assumption in this chapter is that a broader definition of EU foreign policy can shed light on how the values and security objectives are articulated. EU foreign policy is considered here as a 'system of external relations' (Hill 1993), with multiple interests, objectives, policy-making centres and decision-making structures. These relations include the role of member states central to Common Foreign and Security Policy (CFSP), European Community 'external relations', and the external dimension of EU policies (of all three pillars, before the Lisbon Treaty abolished them). Important elements of this approach include the regional and international environment, the identity and 'values' of the actors involved, and foreign policy output in terms of foreign policy production. These have been defined as constituting the contours of 'European foreign policy' (Ginsberg 1999, 2001; White 2001; Keukeleire 2002). However, for the purposes of this chapter, the analysis will focus on the decision-making process at the EU level, including member state input, but will exclude national foreign policies. Thus, it is more appropriate to speak of 'EU foreign policy' than 'European foreign policy'.

EU foreign policy dilemmas

Transformation or stability?

> The best protection for our security is a world of well-governed democratic states. Spreading good governance, supporting social and political reform, dealing with corruption and abuse of power, establishing the rule of law and protecting human rights are the best means of strengthening the international order (European Council 2003).

The European Security Strategy (2003) must be one of the most quoted EU documents to date. It effectively synthesises the liberal view whereby security and democracy are associated in such a way that they provide the best guarantee for the predictability of states' behaviour and for international stability. This view has been espoused by the EU in much of its rhetoric, and provided the logic underpinning successive rounds of enlargement to previously non-democratic states in the 1980s (Greece, Portugal, Spain) and in 2004–7 with the accession of 12 new members. It has also served to justify the transformative policies that the EU set up to support these countries' transition to democracy. Using simplistic definitions, this approach has been able to garner support within the EU because it links a supposedly 'altruistic' ideology with 'self-interested' aims of promoting stability in countries geographically close to the EU.

Particularly prevalent in the 1990s, the plentiful EU rhetoric espousing and justifying the combination of security and democracy, contained the 'normative' or 'principled ideas' which helped specify criteria for policy-makers to be able 'to distinguish between right and wrong' (Goldstein and Keohane 1993: 9).

Yet, as we shall see in the third section, there are many examples of EU action where the political values referred to in the above quotation clash most frequently with security aims – be they fighting terrorism, contrasting irregular migration, or maintaining friendly relations with states that do not embrace those same values. This raises the question of whether the conflict between such 'values' and 'security' is just a consequence of changing international challenges, or whether competing strategic priorities also reveal cognitive differences in what are otherwise assumed to be common 'principled ideas' (as will be examined in section 4).

Engagement or condemnation?

> Our task is to promote a ring of well-governed countries to the East of the European Union and on the borders of the Mediterranean with whom we can enjoy close and cooperative relations (European Council 2003).

European Neighbourhood Policy also speaks of a 'ring of friends'. Yet a ring of friends does not necessarily mean a ring of well-governed countries, as has been particularly evident in the Middle East and North Africa. How to achieve both aims?

The dilemma between engagement with non-democratic countries and the use of coercive measures to condemn or sanction a country which is breaching agreed values, of course, is not new to foreign policy, but has acquired new salience in the aftermath of the Cold War, in the context of the debate over justifications for military intervention in the name of democracy. The two paths are not incompatible: most EU policies do have 'strings attached' and focus strongly on engagement (Smith 2005b). In the 2000s, developments in the US have also given new twists to this conundrum, making the debate increasingly an issue for public opinion, from the neo-conservative 'regime change' of the first Bush Administration to the public debate in the 2008 presidential campaign on how to deal with Iran.

Leaving aside the military dimension of interventionism, the EU does have a fairly broad range of diplomatic and economic tools at hand to take sanctioning measures, ranging from the suspension of cooperation with a third country, boycotts of sport or cultural events and trade sanctions (general or specific trade sanctions, arms or oil embargoes), to financial sanctions (freezing of funds or economic resources, prohibition of financial transactions, restrictions on export credits or investment), flight bans, restrictions on admission and diplomatic sanctions (expulsion of diplomats, severing of diplomatic ties, suspension of official visits).

The pragmatic dilemma over which diplomatic routes to take in order to enter into political dialogue is relevant because it *does* frequently emerge in the practice of policy-making and, as we shall see, reveals the problems of practical choices and of striking the balance between 'values' and 'security'.

This internal debate illustrates what Goldstein and Keohane (1993) defined as 'causal beliefs'. The debate is about the most appropriate means to convey messages to EU partners, their potential impact on the country concerned and the consequences on the EU itself. The EU's condemnation of, for instance, repression of non-governmental organisations (NGOs) in a third country may not help improve the situation of NGOs and may lead to that third country cutting relations or retaliating against the EU. Externally, an instrumental and ad hoc use of engagement or condemnation could undermine the willingness of partners to comply with the political standards advocated by the EU, creating a problem of consistency and differential treatment, and potentially jeopardising the entire set-up of the EU's external transformative aims, as the next section will illustrate.

But alongside pragmatic considerations – which include a cost–benefit analysis weighing up the impact of condemnation on partners, and how that might affect further cooperation with the EU – the debates within the institutions and member states also highlight a diversity of views on the appropriateness of resorting to condemning partners, not just based on their 'causal beliefs', but also on 'principled ideas'.

What is hypothesised is that engagement and cooperation with partners is also understood as a 'value' *per se*, not just because it is instrumental in achieving external goals such as cooperation in migration control or counter-terrorism, but also because it reflects a belief in multilateralism as a process for addressing common concerns. Indeed, the European Security Strategy also refers to a need to support 'effective multilateralism' with 'a ring of friends'.

Consistency or flexibility?
Consistency represents an important issue in the EU's entire foreign policy set-up, and is a treaty-based requirement for EU external action. For the purposes of this chapter, consistency is addressed by examining the contrast between the principles the EU seeks to uphold and its general performance in practice. Overall consistency is complicated by the fact that the EU has framed relations (and the principles) in a pan-regional policy, but that the region is increasingly heterogeneous, especially since the Arab Spring.

Ensuring consistency would help legitimise the EU's foreign policies both inside and outside the EU. Of course, this would require EU member states to be the first to apply the principles they preach, in order to avoid any accusation of 'double standards'. By appealing to those universal principles codified in the international treaties and covenants signed by all UN members, the EU seeks to avoid accusations of trying to impose Western or European-based values at the expense of cultural diversity.

Dilemmas in EU foreign policy towards the Mediterranean: continuity and change

How have these dilemmas been evident in EU policies towards the Mediterranean? The literature has pointed to the fact that the consequences of September 11 have entailed a sharpening of the 'values versus security' dilemma in favour of the latter, with a special focus on combating transnational terrorism and on 'securitising' migration, but at the expense of promoting democracy and human rights (Jünneman 2003; Youngs 2006; Joffé 2008), while moving away from the 'normative agenda' of the Barcelona Process (Pace 2007).

These security priorities have undoubtedly challenged the 'values' dimension of those policies set up by the EU in the 1990s. However, beyond the fracture caused by the fight against terrorism, examining the continuities in EU policy reveals how the dilemmas regarding 'values versus security' were evident also before September 11. This raises a number of doubts: first of all, the extent to which the 'normative agenda' of the first years of the Barcelona Process was applied is questionable; secondly, the changes in the external environment alone are not sufficient to explain EU policies towards the Mediterranean; the 'values versus security' dichotomy might be more complex than is often assumed. Identifying the continuities in EU policy before and after September 11 may also offer some insights into evaluating the EU's potential for change after the Arab Spring. In turn, this suggests the need to search for further explanations of the challenges facing the EU's intended values-based policies.

An examination of both Euro-Mediterranean Partnership and ENP policy documents shows that the 'values' dimension continued to be pursued (in terms of declarations and intentions, if not in practice) alongside several other priorities relating to security. While the EU has sought to strengthen cooperation in migration control and in the fight against terrorism, it has also introduced the values of 'justice' and 'international accountability' by including the ratification of the Rome Statute of the International Criminal Court as one of the aims of the ENP Action Plans. These innovations reflect not only the changing international environment but also the integration at the EU level of the Justice and Home Affairs dossier, which has grown rapidly since the early 2000s, with a significant impact on external relations.

The content of the declaratory diplomacy carried out under the CFSP umbrella vis-à-vis the 'South Mediterranean' overwhelmingly regards upholding EU 'values'. An examination of the (few) CFSP declarations and démarches, of the discussions of 'values' held through the institutions of political dialogue, and of statements and support of resolutions at the United Nations and its bodies – as reported by the EU's Annual Reports on Human Rights – shows that, with few exceptions, CFSP is *not* used to coordinate EU positions on numerous political and security issues, such as fighting terrorism. Instead, it is used with regard to 'values', mostly the abolition of the death penalty, human rights issues, the respect of international law and justice (for instance support of the International Criminal Court) and peace. To 2011, there has been no significant departure statements and positions based on principles; if anything, there has been an increase in EU policy positions evoking 'values' since 11 September 2001.

Financial aid meant for promoting some EU 'values', such as human rights, good governance and the rule of law, has also increased in recent years. ENP has established a 'governance facility' to reward those countries making the most progress in reforming their system of government and aligning it to the objectives set out in the Action Plans. In 2011, the EU proposed strengthening its commitment towards the development of civil society and social media, and offering technological support to advance democracy, even encouraging political organisations and movements through the creation of a European Endowment for Democracy.

Even if declaratory diplomacy and aid allocation are not, *per se*, indicative of a genuine commitment to actually promoting these values – in the sense that they could be interpreted as 'window dressing' (Jørgensen 2006: 42) to hide 'real interests' pursued outside the CFSP framework – they are representative of a message that the EU is trying to convey to its neighbours.

Transformation or stability?

One of the main concerns with regard to political developments in the North Africa and the Middle East has been that political change and democratisation could, in the short term, produce instability and uncertain consequences. The EU has sought to foster partnerships with cooperative governments on the South Mediterranean shore for the pursuit of regional stability (the Middle East peace process, relations with Africa, with the Gulf, and with the Arab League), to try to contain irregular migration, ensure access to energy supplies, and fight terrorism. Until the Arab Spring, EU support of the status quo was also seen as a way to avoid the risk of a rise of Islamic fundamentalism. This helps explain the EU's initial support for Ben Ali and Mubarak, before they were ousted, and its dithering in the early days of the Arab Spring.

Indeed, where political change has entailed the rise of Islamist parties, the EU has been blatantly contradictory when it comes to its transformative and normative rhetoric and then its policy practice. This has occurred both before and after September 11. In Algeria, the military coup of January 1992 halted the electoral process that was leading to the rise of the Front Islamique de Salut (FIS), plunging the country into civil war. Throughout the 1990s the EU did not explicitly condemn the anti-Islamist regime, but limited its declarations to condemnations of terrorist activities, and invited the country to participate in the launch of the Euro-Mediterranean Partnership, a forum in which the two sides signed an agreement in 2002. France spearheaded the EU's support for the regime, blocking any European attempt to make financial support conditional on a process of democratisation (Bicchi 2004).

In 2006, the majority gained by Hamas in the elections to the Palestinian Legislative Authority – probably the most democratic elections conducted until then in the region – led the EU member states to sanction the Islamist forces in the Occupied Territories: Hamas was to stay on the terrorist list and its formal recognition was made conditional on its accepting three conditions (non-violence, the recognition of Israel and acceptance of previous agreements). In this case it was the member states closest to the US and/or Israel, such as the UK and Germany, who persuaded those EU member states that were more favourable to dialogue (including France) to adopt a strong sanctioning position, despite Hamas's performance in the elections (Balfour and Cugusi 2010). In 2011, when popular (and non-Islamist) uprisings shook the regimes throughout the Arab world, the EU took its time to distance itself from the leadership of these countries. It was only after President Ben Ali left Tunisia that the EU produced statements that went beyond neutral condemnations of the violence; in the Egyptian case the messages delivered over whether Mubarak should resign were contradictory.

EU institutional representatives have since recognised that past 'status quo policies' were misguided and ill-conceived. Post-electoral developments in the region will test whether the EU as a whole has shifted its position towards political pluralism in Muslim-majority countries. The electoral tests in 2011 have shown that power-sharing arrangements or co-habitation between secular and religious forces (such as in Tunisia and in Morocco) have so far been accepted by the EU as long as they ensure continuity in terms of regional security and stability. In Egypt the balance between the armed forces, the secular and revolutionary opposition, and the rising Islamist forces is leading to violence and destabilisation. Political developments will test the degree to which the EU will apply in practice the policy changes introduced after the Arab Spring. In this context, one preoccupation of officials in Brussels concerns the impact of democratically elected governments on relations between the Arab states and Israel.

Engagement or condemnation?
With regard to engagement or condemnation, the EU has fairly consistently privileged positive engagement. The Barcelona Process was set up with the aim of developing partnership and confidence-building measures between the two shores. ENP also strengthens the partnership dimension by using the jointly negotiated Action Plans as a tool to encourage closer relations. One of the aims of ENP was to strengthen a 'rewards-based conditionality', which would offer greater incentives and rewards (for instance extra funds through the 'governance facility') to those countries making most progress in implementing the objectives of the jointly negotiated Action Plan. The more recent Union for the Mediterranean project focuses too on strengthening partnership between the two shores of the Mediterranean by creating a co-presidency and introducing diplomatic summitry at the level of the heads of state or government, thus moving further away from using conditionality.

Conversely, until the war in Libya and the continued violent repression of the uprising in Syria, sanctioning measures had been used sparingly, despite the abundance of breaches of so-called EU 'values'. The 'essential element clause' included in all Association Agreements signed with the EMP countries contains the legal provisions and mechanisms to suspend a part or the entirety of the agreement in cases of a breach of its political principles. However, the EU has never invoked it or even threatened to do so. CFSP sanctions have been used only against Libya in the 1980s and 1990s, and then Palestine (Hamas) and Libya and Syria again in 2011. Nonetheless, CFSP declarations and confidential *démarches* show a modest increase in the attention paid by the EU to breaches of its values.

Yet the preference for engagement and the use of positive conditionality does not mean that a set of criteria is applied to a form of rewards-based conditionality. The examples of Israel and Tunisia both illustrate the disconnection between economic incentives and conformity towards EU values. Israel is occasionally criticised by the EU for its continued settlement activities and violations of international law (the respect of which is a 'value' of the EU), yet until Israel's December 2008–January 2009 war in Gaza this had not impinged on the contractual arrangements between the two; Tel Aviv was the Mediterranean frontrunner set to negotiate an advanced Association Agreement with the EU. The conduct of the war and Israel's continuation of its settlements policy has led the EU to put the upgrading of relations with Israel on hold, though the terms are not expressed as negative conditionality (Council of the EU 2009c). Until 2011, Tunisia's record on freedom remained abysmal while economic relations with the EU continued to be upgraded and, other than Israel, Tunisia was the closest of all Mediterranean countries to reaching the conditions to negotiate a Free Trade Area agreement with the EU.

Since the Arab Spring the EU has fine-tuned its use of positive and negative conditionality. It has introduced a new set of incentives ('more money, more market access, more mobility'), including the long-term possibility of negotiating Deep and Comprehensive Free Trade Areas (DCFTA), starting with Morocco, Tunisia, Egypt and Jordan. At the other end of the spectrum, a very broad range of negative tools has been used over the past months. While it is clear that NATO military intervention in Libya was an exception rather than a possible renewal of interventionism, the EU has tightened its position towards Syria incrementally, first by claiming to put the signing of the Association Agreement on hold (in reality, the EU had been waiting for Damascus to sign), and then by gradually imposing targeted sanctions, ranging from freezing financial assets and introducing visa bans, to imposing economic and trade sanctions and oil embargoes (agreed in September 2011 but implemented only in November 2011, once several contracts with European oil companies had been cleared). If at the two poles of the conditionality spectrum the tools and their use (be it at times clumsy) are discernable, grey areas remain with regard to the countries or situations that fall in the middle: the EU's positioning towards Algeria or Lebanon, with regard to stability and transformation, remains unclear, as do its reactions to ongoing changes in Egypt.

Consistency or flexibility?

The EU's external consistency has often been accused of double standards and of being contradictory, due to its differential treatment of countries. There have been plenty of occasions to raise concerns over breaches of values in all the countries of North Africa and the Middle East, yet the EU has addressed them differently. Initiatives prior to 2011 to engage Libya, which refused to participate in any regional EU-led policy which entailed subscribing to the values of the EMP or ENP, confirmed that not adhering to the principles was not an insurmountable obstacle to cooperation.

Notwithstanding the need for and merits of differentiation, the conception of broad frameworks addressing a whole region would benefit from the use of some common standards. Policies such as the EMP and ENP encourage the recipients to 'look over the shoulders of their neighbours'; indeed, the ENP was devised to stimulate competition between countries. Hence, the EU praised those countries performing 'best in class' (traditionally Morocco, now joined by Tunisia) in the hope that this would serve as an encouragement for reform. The creation in the late 2000s of subcommittees dealing with human rights issues illustrates the dynamic: Rabat led the way by agreeing to the subcommittees, followed by Jordan, keen to deepen relations with the EU, and Tunisia. However, Israel refused to enter into dialogue on human rights issues with the EU, and managed to negotiate the creation of a broader and vaguer subcommittee on 'political matters: human rights and democracy and international and regional issues'. This allowed Egypt to demand and obtain the same treatment.

The Arab Spring has led the EU to increase differentiation between countries. This reflects the fact that North Africa and the Middle East have become even more heterogeneous than before. It will take some time before the dust settles on the area, and countries on both shores are able to rethink frameworks for regional dialogue and integration. Differentiation also responds to the EU's new 'listening mode' intended to set the pace of bilateral relations, on the basis of requests from the 'countries of North Africa and the Middle East and not necessarily following any EU blueprint. This raises questions about whether, and if so how, conditionality will be applied in the changing context of North Africa and the Middle East.

The differential treatment of countries will also be an indicator of what priorities the EU and its member states develop after the Arab Spring, especially towards the transitional and new governments. One example tentatively suggests the priority accorded to Libya after the NATO military intervention there. All the Arab Spring transitional governments have been asking the EU to unblock the financial assets of the previous regimes which had been frozen during the upheavals. At time of writing, the EU had agreed to unfreeze Libyan assets (in December 2011) and began talks on this matter with Tunisia in September 2011, while for Egypt no conclusive decisions had been reached by the end of April 2012, raising questions about the treatment of partners south of the Mediterranean.

Double standards have also been evident in the EU. EU member states were held responsible for the mistreatment of irregular migrants and asylum seekers, and of the communities of South Mediterranean origin living in Europe. It is no surprise that whenever the EU tried to discuss human rights practices with its North African partners, the latter asserted that this should include a discussion of the rights of their citizens living in Europe (as well as the plight of the Palestinians). The practice of 'rendition', whereby some member states have allegedly breached the Geneva Conventions by returning terrorist suspects to countries where they might be subject to torture, made it hard for them to preach to those abroad.

The sources of the EU's foreign policy dilemmas

If external shocks such as September 11 and changing security priorities are themselves not sufficient to explain the dynamics of interaction between values and security, understanding the processes of foreign policy-making at the EU level may help.

Explanations of EU behaviour towards the Mediterranean have tended to focus on the outputs of EU foreign policy rather than on the processes that have created them. EU motivations for building the EMP have been explained broadly in terms of risk containment with security aims, or in terms of region-building, with varied emphases on institutionalisation, economic integration or on the normative dimension (Crawford 2004). In other words, in recent years the focus has been on examining the EU as a bloc, moving away from earlier interpretations that analysed the dynamics internal to the Union leading to the creation of the Barcelona Process.

EU policies towards the Mediterranean emerged as the result of compromises reached between member states, and as a reaction to external and structural changes. Mediterranean member states have pushed for the development of a shared agenda towards North Africa and the Middle East, firstly because alone they were unable to achieve their policy objectives, and secondly, to counterbalance the attention of the northern and eastern member states towards relations with Eastern Europe (Barbé 1998).

If Spain, France and Italy, supported by the Commission (Bicchi 2007), pushed North Africa and the Middle East up the EU agenda, the northern EU member states and the Commission pushed for the 'values' dimension in shaping the policy frameworks that have been successively developed. Have these diverse positions endured, or has cooperation in the Barcelona Process helped create a common vision within the EU as far as the dilemmas over 'values and security' are concerned?

These kinds of dynamics could be found when shaping the Barcelona agenda as well as the ENP agenda in 2002–3, with the southern EU member states pushing for the neighbourhood policy to include North Africa and the Middle East, initially excluded from proposals circulating in the Council and Commission. Controversy was raised during 2008 owing to French proposals for a Union for the Mediterranean, which was followed by Swedish-Polish proposals to strengthen the Eastern dimension; both confirm the diversity between member states as to the geographical priorities that should govern EU foreign policy.

The North–South 'divide' with regard to the priorities of the eastern and southern neighbourhood roughly extends to values. The northern EU member states are fairly consistent in pushing for the EU to adopt stronger values-based policies. This 'constituency' was strengthened with the accession of the new member states from Central Europe, whose position is rooted in their past experience of totalitarianism. Conversely, the southern EU member states tend to have a weaker tradition of values-based foreign policy, while they privilege maintaining their ties of dialogue with the Arab world. That said, member state positions vary according to the issue at stake.

The debates that occur behind closed doors within the Council on individual foreign policy choices illustrate the ways in which compromises are reached over the dilemmas. These debates concern 'principled' beliefs as well as 'causal' beliefs and their practical application, and reveal the different perceptions between European capitals on whether and how to promote the values enshrined in the EMP and ENP.

The story of the CFSP declaration issued towards Egypt in 2007 exemplifies in a nutshell the bargaining process behind many of the CFSP measures taken towards the countries of North Africa and the Middle East (Balfour, 2012). The declaration was about a constitutional reform package that the government in Cairo had approved and passed through a referendum, and which entailed, among other things, the replacement of the emergency law with a new anti-terrorist law, and the suppression of the role of the judiciary in supervising national elections. This clearly represented a strangling of the extremely limited freedoms enjoyed by Egyptians, as well as a clampdown on the judiciary, thus concerning two of the EU's 'values': human rights and the rule of law. More importantly, since the inception of ENP, the Commission had been searching for ways to encourage Cairo to abolish the emergency law. In 2005, the EU had praised Mubarak's decision to hold more pluralist elections, but the EU's response to the 2007 constitutional reform package reflected a step backwards.

The text of the EU's declaration was prepared following intense negotiations and wrangling between member states. The draft of the German presidency of the EU, keen to condemn the holding of the referendum, as well as the content of the reform package, faced opposition from a number of member states (in this case led by France, the UK and Portugal); a subsequent political bargain led to a 'soft' (in the words of one Commission official) and heavily watered-down declaration that 'noted the absence of a public debate on the terms of the referendum' and asserted that the EU expected 'any new legislation [on anti-terrorism] to abide by international standards' (Council of the EU 2007a).

In the case of constitutional reform in Egypt, Germany preferred to seek consensus among member states, but the subsequent elections to the *Shura* Council barely attracted any attention in the EU. The lack of any statement condemning the elections by those same member states that had watered down the previous declaration on constitutional reform, left the German head of the rotating EU Presidency to issue a reproachful statement that was *not* on behalf of the EU (Germany's Presidency of the EU 2007). However, Germany did not always stand by such principled a position. The previous year it was among those supporting the US position of isolating Hamas, despite the fact that Hamas had won the elections to the Palestinian

Legislative Council democratically (elections that the EU had 'welcomed' for their democratic conduct and voter participation) (Council of the EU 2006c). Nor did Britain consistently privilege maintaining good relations with Cairo: it had condemned the Egyptian government for its treatment of the country's secular opposition (without the backing of the entire EU). And France too had on occasion criticised Arab governments for the jailing of secular (but not Islamist) opposition leaders.

A first conclusion to be drawn from these examples is that EU foreign policy often remains hostage to the 'lowest common denominator' factor due to the bargaining process between the member states. CFSP action of this kind is often instigated by those member states most keen to promote 'values' in foreign policy – member states that find themselves in a strengthened position when acting as heads of the rotating presidency, but often opposed by those member states favouring a maintaining of friendly relations with the Arab governments.

To an extent, a degree of diversity among the member states is to be expected. But the justifications for these positions reveal that diversity is not limited to different 'interests', perceptions of security, or historical ties. The arguments used to justify 'softer' positions range from the pragmatic need to maintain friendly relations with partner governments, to a values-based reluctance to interfere in matters internal to other states (sovereignty versus legitimacy to intervene; cultural relativism versus internationalism). The arguments also reflect 'causal beliefs' about the tools of diplomacy, and the importance of dialogue in promoting values. Even if no member state is openly against the promotion of values that are controversial in Arab countries (such as political pluralism, political rights or gender equality), countries like France and Italy regularly object to issuing statements condemning the breach of those values, for the sake of cooperation, partnership and a need to keep channels of dialogue open. Against accusations of failing EU values, these positions are justified as the best means to maintain a dialogue through which informal processes of socialisation and norm diffusion are possible. In addition, dialogue is seen as a vehicle to strengthen multilateralism at the regional and international levels.

On the other hand, where public condemnation is preferred, it often responds to pressures within the EU – from the press and NGOs – reflecting the influence of internal political dynamics on foreign policy choices.

At one level, the debate among the member states and the institutions concerns the diplomatic tools used to convey messages about the 'values'. 'Causal' beliefs come into play when evaluating the potential impact on bilateral relations of a public statement, or of a confidential *démarche*, or by raising the issue more informally at the margin of a meeting. France has repeatedly argued that the condemnation of human rights abuses can be counterproductive to cooperation and dialogue, while dialogue can be used to channel concerns about values. These debates cut across the North–South cleavage within the EU. Even the Scandinavian states – the strongest supporters of some of the EU values – appreciate that informal dialogue can be more productive than public condemnation, especially where the expected reaction is a closure of communication channels.

Such a dilemma is not limited to the Council and the member states; the Commission too wrangles with difficult choices when it comes to the extent to which it is legitimate to engage with partners and the degree to which it should push for the respect of the values it espouses in its policy documents; it often prefers dialogue because it gives the Commission a greater role than in traditional diplomacy. Thanks to its position in negotiating the details of the Action Plan, the Commission was able to strengthen its role in informal diplomacy via its delegations in third countries.

On another level, these differences amount to cognitive perceptions and understandings on the role values should play in determining foreign policy choices. Alongside cost–benefit analyses on the potential impact of EU condemnation, EU member states hold different general assessments of the role of the country in question, and competing cognitive views on the importance of human rights and democracy vis-à-vis partnership, cooperation, non-interference in the internal affairs of other states and respect of cultural specificities.

In other words, engagement and partnership are understood as 'values' *per se*, not just because they are instrumental in achieving external goals such as cooperation in migration control or counter-terrorism, but also because they reflect a strong belief in multilateralism (another declared value of the EU) itself as a process for addressing common concerns.

After the Arab Spring it is unclear how the EU institutions and member states will address current foreign policy dilemmas in the region. The Commission and the High Representative have produced policy documents revising existing policies and placing a new emphasis on 'deep democracy' and on civil society support, giving more rounded definitions of the democratic expectations of the EU. As we have seen, positive and negative conditionality is also refined as a means to obtain such objectives. So far, however, it appears that such conditionality will be applied to countries that are committed to establishing democratic standards and closer relations with the EU, leaving out those whose intentions are less clear. Without a strong structure of incentives it will be hard to entice countries which have hitherto been reluctant to engage with the EU on the basis of ENP, such as Algeria, Libya before the ousting of Gaddafi, and Syria. Member states' positions are unclear; and it remains to be seen how the EU will react to further changes in the region, which may undermine regional stability or perceptions of it. These questions concern the dilemmas of transformation or stability, engagement or condemnation, consistency or flexibility.

Conclusions

The 'values versus security' dichotomy remains a viable lens through which to examine the performance and outcomes of EU policies towards North Africa and the Middle East, and the wider neighbourhood, and to understand EU foreign policy more generally. However, the picture is more complex than the dichotomy implies.

When the EU launched its collective policies towards North Africa and the Middle East in 1995, the policy documents upon which they were built had been framed in liberal values deriving from United Nations principles and from European post-Cold War optimism about the linkages and compatibility of democracy-related values with strategic security considerations. These ideas were the cornerstone of the rhetoric of the 1990s but were toned down in the 2000s. The consequences of September 11, and the challenges to the 'democracy agenda' posed by the 'regime change' rhetoric of Bush's first US administration, sharpened the perception of a conflict between the two values, though not necessarily the substance. Indeed, the Lisbon Treaty, with its description of EU foreign and security policy aims – which are supposedly to be strengthened in terms of their consistency and efficacy by creating the European External Action Service – further develops the range of values that should guide foreign policy (art. 21 TEU).

There was no 'golden age' of EU policies imbued in values that were shattered by the fight against terrorism. This chapter has tried to highlight the continuities in the challenges of the EU's values-based agenda before and after September 11, by scratching beneath the surface of the 'values *versus* security' dichotomy. The examples used in this chapter show that engagement with governments in North Africa and the Middle East has continued and in many cases been reinforced, such as through the Union for the Mediterranean. At the same time, the EU has expressed its concern repeatedly over the state of some of its 'values' in its diplomacy.

In short, the 2000s saw a simultaneous sharpening of the security agenda and a deepening of the 'values', even if the rhetoric was softened to lower expectations. But in substantive terms, neither development represented a significant break with the past: the gap between the EU's value-based 'good intentions' and its policy practices remained.

Therefore, additional explanations are necessary to understand the interaction between values and security. First of all, foreign policy processes and dynamics need to be taken into greater account when examining outcomes. How do member states interact with each other when it comes to deciding common EU responses to political developments in third countries? Behind the supposed unity of intent declared in the various policy frameworks that the EU has developed, the 'logic of diversity' between member states has led to foreign policy outcomes which are fragmented, disconnected from realities, and variously based on values, depending on the prevalent bargaining dynamics within the EU (for example, depending on the initiative of the rotating presidency).

Some 30 years of cooperation on the Middle East since the Venice Declaration, 20 years of action on the Common Foreign and Security Policy, years of work on the Barcelona Process and on the ENP, have together failed to produce sufficient incentives for EU member states to develop a collective 'vision'. Bilateral ties and national interests and values often override the drive towards a more substantive EU policy, compounded by the relatively high level of conflict and low level of integration in North Africa and the Middle East.

The dilemmas faced by policy-makers are the consequence of a 'logic of diversity' among the member states that runs deeper than is usually understood. Generally speaking, the member states that have pushed more strongly for the development of a collective EU policy towards North Africa and the Middle East are also those less keen on pursuing 'values'; France, Italy and Spain are among the least supportive of the principles outlined in the EMP and in ENP. Indeed, it comes as no surprise that the French-led Union for the Mediterranean hardly mentions the values of the Barcelona Process.

This diversity concerns not just the 'values versus security' dilemma. One can identify those member states more consistently in favour of supporting 'values' and those more sensitive to perceptions of 'security'. The dilemma also concerns the best means to secure outcomes and strike a balance between emphasising 'values' and pursuing more materially based interests, i.e. when the dilemma is clearest. The debates between the member states within the Council and national foreign ministries, and in the Commission, over how to respond to political developments in North Africa and the Middle East show that cost–benefit analyses of the potential impact of diplomatic initiatives of condemnation are also a matter for discussion.

This suggests that it would be useful to unpack the term 'values'. Alongside pursuing the principles of human rights, the rule of law, good governance and processes of political and economic liberalisation, the EU also favours partnership, engagement and multilateralism. These too can be ascribed to the category of 'values'; indeed, the analysis of debates between EU member states suggests that some consider these latter three 'values' more important than the former set. In other words, the 'logic of diversity' is not limited to the articulation of different interests and security perceptions in North Africa and the Middle East, determined among other things by geographical proximity, but also includes different understandings and perceptions of EU values *per se*.

BEZEN BALAMIR COSKUN

5

Values and security: the EU's dilemma of democracy promotion in the Middle East

The objective of this chapter is to assess the European Union's democracy promotion efforts in the Middle East. Cultural clashes between Western democratic values and the values of Middle Eastern states and societies ('values versus values') and the security implications of democracy promotion in the region ('values versus security') will be examined. It is argued that they can help explain the poor outcome of the EU's democracy promotion in the Middle East. In this vein, this chapter discusses the two typologies for understanding the interplay between values and security when it comes to the EU's relations with its neighbours. Europe was known as the cradle of democracy and human rights. The ideas of human rights and democracy flourished in Europe with the Renaissance and constituted our contemporary principles of democracy, human rights and freedom. At the core of Western political-philosophical development lies a universal principle concerning the construction of humanity as idea and fact. Hence, the global impetus for bringing about the universal jurisdiction of humanity was created.

The European Renaissance 'decisively and effectively prepared the global context for European engagement of the world's peoples' (Headley 2008: 1) and thus the emergence of European ideas of democracy and human rights. Two distinctive features of European civilisation evolved from the era of the European Renaissance and Reformation: the idea of common humanity that becomes a foundation for the programmes of human rights and the capacity for self-criticism and dissent entailed in constitutional democracy (Headley 2008: 1).

Throughout the seventeenth and eighteenth centuries, the principles of equality and universality had become the most prominent features of European civilisation:

> The growing practice on the part of contemporary thinkers and philosophers to invoke mankind posits the issue of an emerging sense of the expressly human, the human race, the nature of humanity and of the earth's common humanity. The pursuit of natural law itself necessarily commits one to a universalist perspective. (Headley 2008: 131–2)

John Locke's work in particular transformed the whole issue of natural law into the more immediate issue of natural rights. Locke understood law as an objective order of norms from which rights derived. Thanks to Locke, the concept of natural law transformed into a political theory, which led to dramatic changes in European politics. As discussed by Headley, the unconventional use of the notion of dissent became a contingency of European historical development and the second distinctive feature of European civilisation. Developments in the modern period contributed to the unique Western capacity for accommodating contentious division, diversity and dissent. As Headley pointed out, the religious fragmentation following the Reformation created the conditions of coexistence among confessional camps, which was a unique achievement (2008: 164).

Throughout its history, the ideas of democracy and human rights have become Europe's most precious exports. But at the same time the European tradition of universalising aspirations and projecting these values and aspirations as a means of securing Europeans' global dominance appears as a paradox of European civilisation. As experienced in the sixteenth and seventeenth centuries, the development of universal principles was driven by security, in the sense of overcoming the propensities for war and civil war in Europe, and of regulating competing European interests outside of Europe. The dilemma of 'security versus values' was particularly reflected in the tension over the European empires' colonial project.

Taking a more contemporary point of view, the establishment of the European Community (today's European Union) in 1992 and the Union's projection of soft power in international affairs can be viewed as another reflection of Europe's classical intention to dominate global affairs as a norm entrepreneur. Beginning with the second half of the twentieth century, besides being an economic and political project, the EU is also presented as a project for building a European community of values. In the post-Cold War period, in particular, the power of values has been influential in the evolution of the European Community into the European Union. The incorporation of the ideas embedded in the European civilisation project and the exercise of normative justification have become an intrinsic part of the EU's relations with the rest of the world, including enlargement, trade and development policies. In its relations with third parties, the EU positions itself as a civilising agent vis-à-vis those others who do not, in its view, inherently possess Europe's values and norms.

After the transition in Central and Eastern Europe, democracy has become an issue on the EU's agenda. Within this context, promoting democracy and good governance are defined as essential objectives for the EU. In 1991, the European Council declared that 'democracy, pluralism, respect for human rights ... are essential prerequisites of sustained social and economic development' (Commission 1991). Developing and consolidating democracy and the rule of law were also included in the Maastricht Treaty as an objective of the Common Foreign and Security Policy (CFSP). Furthermore, as declared in the European Union's statement on human rights in 1998, the promotion of pluralistic democracy and effective guarantees for the rule of law were declared as 'essential objectives for the European Union as a union of values and serve as a fundamental basis for action' (Commission 1998). In this regard the EU has implemented a number of measures to promote democracy, such as political conditionality, diplomatic instruments, international aid and election observation.

The promotion of democracy, good governance and human rights has become increasingly central to the European Union's presentation of its distinctive role as a global actor. Despite rhetorical commitments, in practice the EU is failing to meet the challenges of the complex international environment for democracy and human rights. The Middle East is chosen as a case study in this chapter since the region clearly reflects the paradoxes and contradictions within the EU's democracy promotion. What is striking in this case is the lack of any internal agreement on the substance of democracy promotion within the EU and a lack of reciprocity with Middle Eastern 'partners' as to whether they share in the EU's normative vision. The Arab Spring clearly shows that Arab societies are engaged in a process of establishing more plural and accountable regimes for themselves and that they may not want Western help in building home-grown democracies (Khalaf 2011). The 'values versus values' and 'security versus values' tensions discussed in this chapter are among the most relevant prisms for examining the EU's democracy promotion in the region.

The European Union's democracy promotion in the Middle East

As far as the EU's democracy promotion efforts are concerned, democracy promotion through enlargement has been its most successful strategy of democratisation. The use of conditionality has become the key element of the enlargement process to structure relations with candidate states. However, the EU's post-Cold War democracy promotion efforts did not remain limited to the EU candidate states. Gradually, the EU has extended its democracy promotion efforts beyond the candidate states and its enlargement policy. However, recent uprisings in the region – the Arab Spring – proved that the EU's democracy promotion efforts in the Middle East and North Africa were on shaky ground. Despite the EU's normative vision for the region, in practice European leaders had long backed the authoritarian regimes in the region in exchange for security (see Durac and Cavatora 2009). European support for the regional status quo was not sustainable, however, the EU ignored the changing internal dynamics of Arab political regimes. The uprisings in the Middle East and North Africa revealed the problems of engaging with autocrats who lack internal legitimacy and of ignoring the aspirations of Arab societies.

In 1995, the EU and its 12 Mediterranean partners (Morocco, Algeria, Tunisia, Egypt, Israel, Palestinian Territories, Jordan, Lebanon, Syria, Malta, Cyprus and Turkey) adopted the Barcelona Declaration and established the Euro-Mediterranean Partnership (EMP). According to Richard Youngs, the EMP was one of the EU's most high-profile commitments to democracy promotion (Youngs 2001: 47). With time, Cyprus and Malta became EU member states and Turkey an accession candidate, meaning that the shape of the EMP evolved around a strong Arab component. Arab partners of the EMP have been identified as the major recipient group of EU actions within the EMP framework in the field of human rights and democratisation (Commission 2003b). The EMP reflects the linkage between political and economic cooperation, promotion of democracy and the protection of human rights. In 2007, the EMP was included in the European Neighbourhood Policy. Besides its Mediterranean partners, the EU has also developed relations with other Middle Eastern states, particularly with the Gulf Cooperation Council (GCC) states (Saudi Arabia, Kuwait, Qatar, United Arab Emirates, Bahrain and Oman) and introduced elements of democracy promotion in its relations with the Gulf region's partners.

The Mediterranean

In 2003 the European Commission expressed its belief in the importance of human rights and democratisation regarding its relations with Mediterranean partners and proposed the inclusion of human rights and democracy in related policy documentation (Commission 2003b). It clearly underlined the linkage between security, economic development, human rights and democracy: 'The promotion of law and the respect for human rights and fundamental freedoms constitutes one of the core objectives of the EU's external policies' (Commission 2003b: 2).

All the documents adapted within the framework of the Barcelona Process (later Neighbourhood Policy) reaffirmed the EU's commitment to promote democracy in the region. Similarly, ENP established democracy as one of the values the EU wants to share with its neighbours. In each Action Plan a section entitled 'Democracy and Rule of Law' has been inserted to recall the EU's commitment to 'enhance the effectiveness of institutions entrusted with strengthening democracy and the rule of law', 'strengthen participation in political life, including the promotion of public awareness and participation in elections' (Commission 2007e) and 'promote the stability and effectiveness of institutions strengthening democracy and the rule of law including good governance and transparency' (Commission 2005b).

In order to promote democracy and human rights throughout its neighbourhood, the EU applies several instruments. Besides the European Neighbourhood Policy Instrument (ENPI) which supports the EU's commitments to support and strengthen democratic reform, there are funds available under the European Instrument for Democracy and Human Rights (EIDHR). A separate Governance Facility has begun distributing funds to neighbourhood partners to reward democratic progress (Youngs 2008: 1). Despite these intentions, the distribution of Mediterranean European Development Action (MEDA) assistance has demonstrated that political reform was not a priority. Between 2002 and 2006, the total amount of funds committed under MEDA was €2264 million, yet a very limited portion went to programmes related to political reform. Moreover, in the few cases where funds were allocated as political aid, they focused on administrative and technical issues, not on democratisation (see Table 5.1 and Table 5.2).

European Neighbourhood Policy put more explicit emphasis on democracy compared with MEDA. In accordance with its aims, ENP introduced a more targeted approach to political reform in North Africa. The financial support for ENP has been provided through the European Neighbourhood and Partnership Instrument (ENPI), which replaced the former programmes of EU funding. ENP has operationalised monitoring mechanisms and benchmarks for its objectives. Besides progress reports that evaluate the implementation of Action Plans, subcommittees have been created to assess the implementation of activities in the human rights, democracy and good governance sectors highlighted in each Action Plan.

The proposals regarding EU policy in the Mediterranean reaffirm the continuing difficulties in the 'ability and willingness of the EU to promote democracy' in the region (Vizoso 2008: 74). French President Nicholas Sarkozy's initiative to launch a Union of the Mediterranean shows that European leaders recognise the failure of the Barcelona Process to deliver on its promises. This new initiative highlights its shortcomings and underlines the lack of co-ownership by Mediterranean partners, as well as the lack of institutional balance between the EU and its Mediterranean partners, as the main reasons for the failure (Commission 2008a). The new initiative will seek to enhance co-ownership and 'make multilateral relations more concrete and visible through additional regional and sub-regional projects relevant to the citizens of the region' (Commission 2008a). But the projects proposed are very technical in nature and mainly focused on energy and energy security. The joint declaration includes a very brief mention of the commitment of governments to strengthen democracy.

The EU's record of promoting democracy in the Mediterranean is mixed, and stained by contradictions and inconsistencies. Since democratic principles and human rights have become part of both the Barcelona *acquis* and ENP Action Plans, Middle Eastern governments are not in a position to deny these principles officially. However, with more than a decade of cooperation within the EMP framework and four years within the ENP framework, the domestic implementation of democratic principles has failed to match official declarations of good intention by the regional governments. No significant improvement has been realised either in terms of political rights or civil liberties in the EU's Mediterranean partners since the launch of the Barcelona Process (Table 5.3). After 2007, in particular, many of the regional states

Table 5.1 EIDHR allocations 2005–9 (€)

	Fostering culture of human rights	Promoting the democratic process (2005)	Fostering culture of human rights (2006)	Promoting the democratic process (2006)	Stengthening the role of civil society in promoting human rights and democratic reform (2009)
Algeria	340,000	460,000	250,000	515,000	600,000
Egypt	340,000	460,000	250,000	515,000	900,000
Jordan	340,000	460,000	250,000	515,000	900,000
Lebanon	150,000	150,000	105,000	175,000	600,000
Morocco	465,000	560,000	300,000	650,000	1,200,000
Syria	340,000	0	250,000	0	–
Tunisia	150,000	150,000	100,000	175,000	–
West Bank & Gaza	575,000	700,000	380,000	800,000	900,000

Table 5.2 MEDA/ENPI allocations 2002–10 (million €)

	2002–6			2007–10		
	Total	Democratic governance and human rights	%	Total	Democratic governance and human rights	%
Algeria	256m	N/A	N/A	220	19	8
Egypt	594m	N/A	N/A	558	40	8
Jordan	197m	N/A	N/A	265	17	6
Lebanon	122	N/A	N/A	187	22	12
Morocco	701m	N/A	N/A	654	28	4
Palestinian Authority	–	N/A	N/A	632	–	–
Syria	–	N/A	N/A	130	30	23
Tunisia	394	N/A	N/A	300	–	–

Table 5.3. The EMP partners' Freedom House survey results, 1995 (the beginning of the Barcelona Process) and 2010

Country	Political rights 95–96	Civil liberties 95–96	Status 1995	Political rights 2010	Civil liberties 2010	Status 2010
Algeria	6	6	Not Free	6	5	Not Free
Egypt	6	6	Not Free	6	5	Not Free
Jordan	4	4	Partly Free	6	5	Not Free
Lebanon	6	5	Not Free	5	3	Partly Free
Morocco	5	5	Partly Free	5	4	Partly Free
Syria	7	7	Not Free	7	6	Not Free
Tunisia	6	5	Not Free	7	5	Not Free
Palestinian Authority	–	–	–	6	6	Not Free

moved backwards in terms of civil liberties and political freedom, as measured by Freedom House.[1] According to Freedom House's 2008 report, the year 2007 witnessed intensified efforts by authoritarian regimes like Egypt to consolidate power through the suppression of democratic opposition, civil society, and independent media in their own societies. In addition, not one of the countries that registered the lowest possible scores in the Freedom House index exhibited signs of improvement. According to the 2008 Freedom House index, 'countries that had made progress towards freedom in recent years took significant steps backwards ... In the Middle East, hopes for movement forward in Palestine and Lebanon were dampened by negative trends in the last year in both countries' (Freedom House 2008). The Palestinian Authority fell from Partly Free to Not Free. Moreover, three important countries of the Mediterranean – Egypt, Lebanon and Syria – showed a backward trend in 2007. Besides these three countries, Tunisia – one of the region's most repressive states – also experienced a further decline in political rights. As the Freedom House report shows, the period of modest democratic gains in the political landscape of the Middle East following the 9/11 events came to an end in 2007. Polity IV's Political Regime Characteristics and Transition Data[2] for the region support Freedom House's findings. According to Polity Survey, the regime types of the EU's Mediterranean partners range between 'anocracies' and 'autocracies', but are not established democracies.

The Gulf Cooperation Council (GCC)

Besides the Middle Eastern states located around the Mediterranean, the EU established contractual relations with the Gulf Cooperation Council (GCC) states with the signing of a Cooperation Agreement in 1988. As a result of its interest in securing energy resources, combating terrorism, and containing regional conflicts, the EU has been interested in securing greater involvement in the Gulf and enhancing cooperation with the Gulf States. Compared to its institutionalised value-oriented Euro-Med approach, its approach towards the Gulf States has been focused on trade and security. For example, the Cooperation Agreement does not include a single reference to democratic principles, good governance or human rights. Although there do exist references to the respect for human rights in EU–GCC documents, these were only introduced in the EU–GCC Joint Ministerial Meetings' agenda in 2004. Recently, at the 2007 EU–GCC Joint Ministerial Meeting held in Riyadh, both the EU and the GCC delegations reaffirmed their belief in democratic principles:

> The GCC and the EU reaffirmed that they share the universal values of respect for human rights and democratic principles, which form an essential element of their relations. They welcomed recent development relating to representative bodies in the region, including those related to Al-Shura ... The two sides expressed their commitment to promote the universal values which they share, while bearing in mind the significance of national and regional particularities and their various historical cultural and religious backgrounds. (Council of the EU 2007c: 6).

The GCC countries, with the exception of Bahrain, enjoy high levels of wealth from their oil and gas revenues. As a consequence, political activism in the region is more subdued compared to their regional neighbours. As power structures within the oil monarchies of the Gulf region determine the origins of reform, the ruling elite prefer to liberalise the economy rather than implement substantive reforms, in so doing retaining their traditional power in the long term (Nonneman 2006). In the Arab Gulf region, liberalisation is seen as an intermediate stage in political reform but any resulting power shifts to civil society and an emergent national bourgeoisie remains to be seen. As far as the EU's democracy promotion is concerned, the EU does not have a democracy promotion agenda in the Gulf as it does in the Mediterranean. EU–GCC relations have evolved around trade relations and energy security; there is no incentive or conditionally at stake. In this regard, Europeans have tended to support ruling regimes in the Gulf region in order to prevent further destabilisation in the region. The EU is largely absent in democracy promotion in the Gulf region, with the exception of its support in the reconstruction process in Iraq. Thus, there is hardly any tangible evidence to show any significant achievement in promoting democratic and human rights standards in the Arab Gulf (Table 5.4).

Table 5.4 GCC states' Freedom House survey results (1988 and 2010)

Country	Political rights 88–89	Civil liberties 88–89	Status 1988	Political rights 2010	Civil liberties 2010	Status 2010
Bahrain	5	5	Partly Free	6	5	Not Free
Kuwait	6	5	Partly Free	4	4	Partly Free
Oman	6	6	Not Free	6	5	Not Free
Qatar	5	5	Partly Free	6	5	Not Free
Saudi Arabia	6	7	Not Free	7	6	Not Free
UAE	5	5	Partly Free	6	5	Not Free

The European Union's scorecard in democracy promotion in the Middle East

As seen in Freedom House surveys and the Polity Project Database, in the end the EU's democracy promotion efforts were not able to bring about the intended domestic political reforms in the Middle East. Of course the EU has never played a key role in the region either in terms of democracy promotion or security. There exist a range of external actors including the US who have been actively involved in the region and contributed to the success and/or failure of attempts to establish democratic regimes. Therefore, the failure to promote democracy in the Middle East is not merely something that has happened as a result of the EU's failure to do it. However, there are particular reasons why the EU's democracy promotion in the Middle East has failed, such as lack of incentives, the clashing views of the EU institutions regarding the issue of non-compliance with EU standards, and a scarcity of funds, all of which are desperately needed in order to achieve its goals. The reasons accounting for the failure of the EU's democracy promotion in the Middle East have been discussed extensively by numerous scholars and practitioners; they will not be repeated here. However, it remains crucial to question the extent to which the EU has responded to the momentous changes of the Arab Spring in the region. ENP was under review well before the Arab uprisings of 2011, but such a political upheaval requires a new approach to the southern neighbourhood of the Union. In the next section, the ideas of democracy and good governance will be discussed within the context of the cultural and social realities of the Middle East. Here it is argued that the West's democracy promotion in general, and the EU's efforts in particular, are doomed to fail not just because of structural impediments and financial constraints, but also because of a cultural and social context that is not compatible with Western values and ideas of democracy.

Values versus values: democracy and the Middle East

In general, there is a tendency to explain the weakness of a democratic tradition in the region with the authoritarian character of Islam. While a range of different interpretations of the Islam–democracy nexus have been put forward, it has been the most conservative interpretations recognising a clash with the Western conception of human rights and democracy that were predominant in political debates in the West. In his earlier examination of the relations between political culture and democracy, Huntington agrees that Islamic principles are important impediments to the development of democracy but that 'Islamic doctrine ... contains elements that may be both congenial and uncongenial to democracy' (1992: 28–30).

Graham E. Fuller (2004) criticises this position of blaming Islam for the undemocratic nature of Middle Eastern regimes and discusses the following structural and geopolitical factors other than Islam's incompatibility with democracy, which affect democratisation in the Arab Middle East:

1. Large oil revenues inhibit the development of democracy because of the existence of rentier states that are reliant on externally generated revenues, or rents derived from oil.
2. A lack of taxation system in most of the oil-rich Arab monarchies limits constituents' demands from governments (no representation without taxation).
3. The arbitrary and artificial nature of the modern Arab state weakens the identity of individual Arab states.
4. The ideal of pan-Arabism weakens commitment to local autonomy.
5. The development of security-focused military regimes.
6. The geographical location of the Middle East on a central East–West axis and geopolitical reality of over half of the world's oil reserves has made the region a key focus of global powers.
7. Long-term Western support for pro-Western authoritarian regimes.

Moreover, it is a fact that the emergence of Islamist movements over the past few decades has been the primary source of opposition to Middle Eastern governments. Particularly, in the case of the moderate/pro-Western countries of the region, the threat of Islamist opposition often provides the pretext for a gradualist approach in promoting pluralism and democracy. Concerns about a possible resurgence of Islamist activity have affected the regional governments' democratisation agenda. For example, in Tunisia the government has faced vocal Islamist opposition and been fearful of a possible spill-over of neighbouring Algeria's internal strife between Islamist extremists and government forces (Zisenwine 2004: 113). Until very recently, Tunisians did not challenge the regime's uncompromising stance regarding democracy and pluralism in domestic politics, but in 2011 Tunisians were the first among the Arabs to challenge the decades-long authoritarian rule of Bin Ali. Elections that were held in October 2011 in Tunisia resulted in a clear victory for the Islamist Ennahda Party, which won the majority of seats and found partners in the liberal Congress for the Republic and the left-of-centre Ettakatol Party, to form a ruling coalition. Even though Tunisia is not as effective as Egypt in the region, in terms of leadership in the Arab world, it is the country that set off the wave of pro-democracy movements in the region; as such, Tunisia's efforts to build democracy are being closely watched by the regional actors (*Guardian* 2011).

In a similar vein, Egypt followed Tunisia. Protests in Tahrir Square in Cairo became the symbol of the Arab Spring in 2011. The first elections following the overthrow of Mobarak were held in November 2011. The Muslim Brotherhood's Freedom and Justice Party received 37 per cent of the nearly 10 million valid votes cast for party lists in the first of three electoral rounds for the Egyptian parliament (*USA Today* 2011). In both Tunisia and Egypt, free and accountable elections have resulted in the election of Islamist parties. The results show us that Islamist movements have been gaining popularity over the years, as opposed to secular authoritarian regimes which have been perceived to lack popular legitimacy in the region.

Apart from these structural and geopolitical explanations for the undemocratic nature of the region, here it is argued that the tensions between the important aspects of Arab and/or Islamic political values and Western principles of democratic practice may account for events. This brings us to the issue of cultural relativism in general, which refers to the idea that 'values are relative to circumstance, in this case culture, and that because it is only culture that validates values we can pass no judgment on them' (Dalacoura 1998: 23). Moreover, political culture is embodied in group identities, orientations towards authority and principles of equity and justice (Hudson 1995).

More recently, the question over the compatibility of Islam with democratic progress has been examined in several academic works (Dalacoura 1998; Roberson 1998; Norton 1999; Dorraj 2000). In *Islam, Liberalism and Human Rights*, Katerina Dalacoura (1998) argues that interpretations of Islamic approaches to the idea and practice of human rights should be seen in the socio-political contexts in which different interpretations of Islam have arisen.

Islam's emphasis on divine rather than popular sovereignty puts many of the most important issues of public policy outside the realm of public or participatory decision-making, hence hindering the consolidation of democratic regimes. Another factor that is key to the 'values versus values' discussion is the central position of the individual in Islam. In the Western tradition, the Enlightenment placed the individual at the centre. Natural law and Enlightenment's secular rationalism laid the foundations of Western values. However, unlike Western societies, many societies including Middle Eastern ones would place the collective higher than the sanctity of the individual. The idea that individuals have rights is absent from the Koran and Sharia (Islamic law). Only God has rights, not people, and only God has absolute freedom. Thus, human freedom is determined by the complete surrender to the divine will.

Submission to God is stressed as a cardinal value in the Koran. The individual's value depends on a man's behaviour and faith. Rather than rights, there are man's privileges in traditional Islam. The position of the individual and the centrality of duty in traditional Islam determine the relationship between authority and society. According to Islamic law the ruler holds a sacred trust. Because a divine authority is supposed to guarantee the welfare of all, the interest of the authority and the community, not that of the individual, becomes supreme (Dalacoura 1998: 43–5). In other words, Muslim Arab societies do not have any such precursor of the West's liberal idea of tolerance for pluralism and dissent.

Apart from the Islamic political culture, political values inherited in the Arab political culture also affect the prospects for democratisation. In most of the Arab societies, strong clan, tribal and sectarian loyalties inhibit the development of a sense of citizenship. Sometimes, the tribal system is thought to embody democratic principles of equality and consultation, but often it stands in the way of developing true democratic values, habits and institutions. In particular, the Gulf Arab culture has been determined by the tribal tradition, which is based on shared kinship and religious conviction.

The aforementioned issues embodied in the political values of the Arab Middle East have been further complicated by the political and intellectual consequences of colonialism. According to Said (1978), the Western concern with the authoritarian characteristics of Arab-Islamic political culture reflects Western ethnocentrism and a narrow ahistorical reading of Islam.

In fact, a careful study of Islam and Islamic culture shows elements of good governance and human rights embedded in Islamic tradition.[3] Prophet Mohamed's Last Sermon is considered as a good illustration of Islam's position on good governance. Prophet Mohamed delivered his Last Sermon before thousands of pilgrims during his last pilgrimage before he died, and it is recognised as a sort of political statement. In Arab academia there is a tendency to view Islam as a form of government, among other things, and democracy as one of its defining features. This position goes back to 1900s, to Muhammad Abduh, the founder of Islamic modernism. Abduh argued that the conceptual framework that defined democracy has its counterparts in Islamic terminology including *shura* (consultation), *ijma* (consensus) and *bay'a* (oath of allegiance) (Ismail 1995: 94). This line of thought has been influential in recent debates about the models of democracy in the Arab world. The puzzle of democracy is thought out at the heart of Arab world. As a consequence of this view, another model for democracy has been suggested, one that is constructed out of Arab-Islamic history, particularly the early period of the Prophet and the four Rightly Guided Caliphs. In particular, *shura* is understood as participation in governance (Imara in Ismail 1995: 96). Similarly, Khalid's reading of Islamic history claims that the political liberties defined in democracy had antecedents in the early forms of Islamic society. The right of the *umma* (Islamic community) to choose its leader following the death of the Prophet is shown as evidence for this claim (Khalid in Ismail 1995: 97). These attempts to trace the articulations of democracy within the Arab-Islamic model clearly reflect the desire to prove the possibility of coming up with indigenous models for democracy.

After the 1990s, in particular, the discourse of democracy and pluralism became widespread in the region, though Arab political scientists and commentators have pointed out the distinction between *dimuqratiyya* (democracy) and *ta'addudiya* (which can mean anything from multi-partyism to pluralism). In the Middle East, the latter has become more prevalent. In the Arab context, the debate over the nature of democracy reflects the tension between individual liberty, political rights and equality. Democracy in the region is understood as good government or the government that serves for the good of its people. Drawing on the Prophet and Rightly Guided Caliphs era (632–661), the central state is posited as the key institution in the region, the democratic nature of politics being associated with those elites who advise the ruler and who represent the national good. This notion is still relevant in the region today.

Regarding the Arab uprisings, the primary question that the EU must seek to answer is: what strategy would the EU follow were the democratisation process to be initiated by the people of the region? The Arab Spring refers to popular movements against authoritarian regimes of the region, and also against the roles given to those regimes by Western powers. As repeatedly underlined by Arab participants of the Abant Platform on 'The Future of the Middle East after the "Arab Spring" and Turkey', Arabs have taken their fate into their own hands, thus will decide themselves what kind of order they would like to establish for better governance and human rights.[4] At the end of the day the Arab people are now seeking a new order (*nizam* in Arabic) that can provide them with grounds for a better life. The Arab Spring has clearly emphasised that for Arabs the imposition of European (or Western) values is not acceptable, and that the values inherited in Islam and Arab societies *may* lead to democracy and/or good governance in the region.

Security versus values: democracy promotion in the Middle East and European security

In the European Security Strategy in 2003, five key threats to Europe were identified: terrorism, weapons of mass destruction, regional conflict, state failure and organised crime, all of which are firmly connected with the security and stability of the EU's neighbourhood regions. Consequently, the

Union has developed bilateral and interregional policy tools that aim at contributing to its neighbours' security and stability, and by extension, its own security. Within the context of the EU's wider foreign policy and security strategy framework, the Middle East is considered as the most important geographical region directly affecting the EU's well-being in economic and security terms. Ongoing turmoil and instability in the region, a lack of democratic tradition, and the continuous flow of arms into the region, accompanied by the existence of hostile regimes, have always been a major concern, as reflected in Brussels' strategy towards the Middle East. In terms of democracy promotion, the Middle East has become one of the regions where strategic interests and democracy promotion have been central to policy deliberations.

The EU's underlying rationale for getting involved in the Middle East through various political tools has been to ensure greater stability in the region. Besides the accumulation of arms, rapidly increasing flows of migrants from the southern shores of the Mediterranean are perceived as the main threat to the Union's s stability and security. The containment of organised crime and terrorism has also been acknowledged as one of the key elements in the EU's commitment towards the region. In particular, concerns over large migrant flows have given EU policy towards its Mediterranean partners its distinctive and defensive underpinning (Youngs 2001: 57). Flows from the region have been perceived as problematic since migrants from the Mediterranean are deemed by politicians to be hostile to, and uncomfortable with, European values (Aliboni 1997: 231).

The question is how these strategic security concerns relate to the EU's democracy promotion agenda. Would democratisation serve European interests? What if the EU's support for democracy were simply to assist anti-Western forces or militant groups in winning power? In this regard, the EU's commitment to democracy promotion was tested when the Palestinian Authority won free and fair democratic elections, resulting in the election of a Hamas-led government. The political wing of Hamas (Islamic Resistance Movement), which is on the EU's international terrorist organisations list, was declared the winner of the Palestinian elections on 27 January 2006. Immediately after the elections, the international community, including the EU, blocked international finance and aid to the Palestinian government and isolated it diplomatically. This situation undermined the democratically elected Hamas government and created a chasm between the internally legitimate government of the Palestinian Authority and the externally recognised presidency of Mahmoud Abbas. These tensions led to clashes between Hamas supporters and supporters of Abbas, and there followed a period of instability in the Palestinian territories. The election of the Hamas government in 2006, as well as the considerable number of seats that Hezbollah occupied in the Lebanese parliament, highlights the EU's policy dilemma when it comes to the Middle East.

Regarding democracy promotion in the Middle East, EU governments prefer to be 'on the safe side' and acknowledge that their main concern is to ensure that any political change in the region does not cause instability. Consequently, the EU's democracy promotion agenda has never aimed at undermining or changing incumbent regimes. Given the instabilities that occurred following the democratic elections in the region, the feasibility of democracy promotion raises the question: is democracy still perceived to be the most likely guarantor of stability in the region, and thus the best means to ease the EU's security concerns?

As far as the EU's Middle Eastern partners' non-compliance with their commitment to democratic principles is concerned, one of the main sticking points is that the EU has held back from taking any serious measures, arguably because of its dependence on the energy resources of the region. With external dependence on energy imports growing steadily, the EU has started to integrate energy aspects into its relations with third countries. As predicted in the 2006 Green Paper entitled 'A European Strategy for Sustainable, Competitive and Secure Energy', in the next 20 to 30 years, around 70 per cent of the EU's energy requirements will be met externally (Commission 2006c). The EU's rising import dependency on external suppliers has highlighted its vulnerability regarding energy supplies. Today 45 per cent of the EU's oil imports originate in the Middle East. Furthermore, in order to ease the Union's dependency on Russian natural gas resources, natural gas from across the Middle East, as well as Iran's natural gas reserves, has gained importance for the EU. Regardless of the anti-democratic regimes and acute human rights violations, for most EU member states, the possibility of cooperation with Iran regarding energy supplies is a far better alternative than cooperating with Russia. Simon Henderson, Director of the Gulf and Energy Policy Programme at the Washington Institute for Near East Policy, highlights Europe's increasing interdependence with Iran in the region through the trans-Turkey pipeline, bringing Iranian gas directly to Europe (Henderson 2007). Within this context, the EU has struggled to formulate a coherent policy that criticises Iran's authoritarian regime while at the same time maintaining an open political and strategic dialogue that does not isolate Iran and further escalate the tensions between the West and the Islamic Republic. The oil/natural gas-rich Middle Eastern states are well aware of their importance in the EU's energy security calculations.

Security seems to be the central concern for Europe's policy-makers in developing their Mediterranean policy. Stabilising Middle Eastern economies and politics, and avoiding spill-over effects for Europe have been the main considerations for the EU in its dealings with the Middle East. To stabilise the region, economic and political reform were seen as necessary. How serious the EU is about promoting democracy in the Middle East depends upon the position that democracy promotion holds in the ranking of European governments' strategic priorities and upon their wider interests in the region. In the

Mediterranean, the Middle East and the Gulf, the EU's scorecard regarding promoting democracy and human rights shows that democracy ranks far behind a number of security considerations. It is understandable that European leaders cannot prioritise the promotion of democracy and human rights over other foreign policy and security objectives. Indeed, in an international environment in which non-democratic regimes have been gaining strategic leverage over the EU, balancing a value-based approach with security objectives is becoming more and more difficult. However, if the EU wants to present itself as a different kind of global power – one which exerts soft power and which values democratic principles and human rights – it must toughen up on authoritarian/undemocratic regimes in the Middle East. Right now, the EU is giving mixed signals and this position in no way encourages democratisation in the region. Thus, the European vision of an international order based on the gradual expansion of democracy and human rights is losing credibility in the eyes of the Middle Eastern societies.

Last but not least, the most recent uprisings in the Arab world once more proved the vulnerability of the EU when it comes to political instability in the region. Migration flows to the EU through Lampedusa, a tiny Italian Island, triggered the feeling of insecurity within the European 'area of justice and freedom' following the Arab uprisings in 2011. In contrast to EU expectations, the democratisation process has been initiated by regional actors themselves, not due to any obvious European influence. The end of authoritarian rules and a bottom-up democratisation process in the Middle East and North Africa pose serious challenges to the security of the Union. In this regard, the EU has to consider balancing its security objectives with values, but not just with European ones – also with values 'indigenous' to the region.

For a more effective EU democracy promotion in the Middle East

In general, the role of third parties in democratisation is problematic since democratisation refers to a domestic regime transition process. Currently, democracy promotion has become a foreign policy goal for most of the international/regional organisations. Democracy has become a pre-condition for the enlargement of organisations such as NATO and the EU. External pressure from an international/regional organisation exerted on an authoritarian regime for democratic transition can be a force for democratisation (Pevehouse 2002: 522). In particular, the prospect of membership of an organisation pushes authoritarian regimes to democratise, as in the case of the democratisation of Central and Eastern European states prior to joining the EU. Membership or the prospect of membership of a particular international organisation can be based on conditionality. Yet, as the case of the EU's democracy promotion in the Middle East shows, this is not always the case. How does an external actor promote democracy without forcing regime change as the US did in Iraq? Why do regional actors simply accept a foreign governing system to rule their own states and societies? Is it simply interference in a certain state's internal affairs? What kind of incentives can be offered for compliance and what kind of measures can be taken in the case of non-compliance? All of these questions represent actual challenges for the EU's democracy promotion in the Middle East. Without conditionality, and without effective use of 'carrots' and 'sticks', the EU's efforts have failed. Last but not least, regarding the EU's role as democracy promoter in the Middle East, why should the EU be a value exporter? Are the EU's values and democratic model really the only alternative for good governance? As Hélène Flautre (2005: 1), Chair of the European Parliament's Subcommittee on Human Rights, points out, the Europeans 'must abandon the idea that the European Union is the teacher in matters of democracy and avoid what borders on a neo-colonialist attitude'. As discussed by Yesilyurt-Gunduz (2009), it is important to understand that the West in general, and the EU in particular, has to be modest about its ability to find the answers for other societies.

It is necessary to note that the challenges to democratisation in the Middle East are colossal. However, the EU can still serve as a positive force for democratisation in the region. Given the reluctance of the EU's Middle Eastern 'partners' to adopt Western values and the security–democracy promotion dilemma of the EU, it would seem that developing alternative modes of dialogue or alternative conceptualisations of democracy promotion might be better options for both sides. By imposing Western ideas on democracy, human rights and good governance the EU has not succeeded in securing democracy in the Middle East. It is true that the number of elections in the region has increased dramatically but these elections far from indicate the existence of consolidated democracies. The best option for the EU, if Europeans still wish to play a role in the democratisation of the region, is to discuss what democracy means with its partners, instead of automatically imposing Western concepts. It is important for the EU to recognise that its partners have their own ways and means of defining democracy and good governance, and may have different ideational priorities to the EU.

Since mutual commitments to promote democratic principles and good governance remain at the rhetorical level and do not translate into action, it might be better for the EU to concentrate on other aspects of political reform: developing political institutions to strengthen guarantees for fundamental freedoms and political rights; broadening public participation in governance; and pushing to overhaul the judiciary and security sector. In the case of both politically unstable and authoritarian regimes, the EU's efforts should link political reform with long-term stability.

Instead of making grand rhetorical gestures, the best option for the EU is to continue empowering the civil societies in the respective countries, so that they themselves may be one day equipped to trigger a democratisation process. An American neo-conservatist type of forceful regime change is not an option for the EU; as such it is preferable to operationalise technical assistance grants to regional NGOs. Within this context, there is increasing interest in civil society in the region, with issues such as social welfare and development becoming more popular. Particularly in Jordan and Egypt, there is a growing interest in Muslim social welfare organisations engaged in activities such as education, health care and financial assistance to the poor (Petersen 2008; Sparre 2008). These organisations are normally ignored by Western donors, who have tended to support secular civil society organisations in the region. The popular uprisings in some of the Middle Eastern and North African countries demonstrate that informal political groups can be extremely well organised and have the capacity to challenge the formal political structures in the region – note how quickly the popular uprising in Tunisia produced a domino effect in other Middle East and North African countries. The informal challenges to authoritarian formal political structures in the Middle East and North Africa have highlighted the role that civil society could play in demanding reforms in formal political structures. If these organisations prove they can serve as actors of political change in respective societies, the EU may then consider supporting these movements as a means of democratic reform in the Middle East.

Ultimately, the EU needs more detailed benchmarks on the Union's political reform priorities and commitments. There is also a need to revise mechanisms for political dialogue with its partners through the National Action Plans for Human Rights and Democracy. In this case, the EU must show its commitment to political reform in the region by adjusting its levels of aid allocated to political reform accordingly.

Conclusion

The ideas of human rights and democracy originated in Europe and developed to form the basis of contemporary principles of democracy, human rights and freedoms. Given the fact that Europe was the cradle of democracy, the European Union has adopted the ideas of democracy, freedom and human rights as foundation stones for the Union. Furthermore, the promotion of democracy, good governance and human rights has increasingly become central to the Union's presentation of its distinctive role as a global actor. However, as discussed in the EU–Middle East case, there is a growing tension between the rhetorical commitment of the EU to these values and the reality of what it does in practice. In this regard, the Middle East has become one of the regions where the strategic interests of the EU and its democracy promotion have created tension in the values–security nexus.

There are also tensions when it comes to what European and Middle Eastern societies understand by democracy, and how society should be organised politically. The discussion also highlights the EU's dilemmas in imposing its political values on the Middle East, given that the region is a source of its own insecurity.

To conclude, both a clash between Western democratic values and the values of Middle Eastern societies ('values versus values'), and the security implications of democracy promotion in the region ('values versus security'), have resulted in the failure of the EU's democracy promotion efforts – and to understand why this is so we must look to the popular uprisings of 2011 throughout the Middle East and North Africa. The developments show that the EU has struggled to influence its immediate neighbours in the Eastern Mediterranean. Unfortunately, the EU's uncertainty points to a loss of direction in its own policies in the region.

Notes

1   The Freedom House survey includes both analytical reports and numerical ratings for 193 countries and 15 select territories. Each country and territory is assigned a numerical rating on a scale of 1 to7 for political rights, and an analogous rating for civil liberties; a rating of 1 indicates the highest degree of freedom and 7 the least amount of freedom. These ratings determine whether a country is classified as Free Partly Free or Not Free by the survey.
2   The Polity conceptual scheme examines concomitant qualities of democratic and autocratic authority in governing institutions. This perspective envisions a spectrum of governing authority that spans from fully institutionalised autocracies through mixed, or incoherent, authority regimes (termed anocracies) to fully institutionalised democracies.
3   See August Bebel's *Prophet Mohamed and Arab-Islam Culture Period* (1883) and Ibn Rushd's *Basics of Political Thought* (*Ed-Daruri fi's-siyase: Muhtasaru Kitabi's Siyaseti li-Eflatun*) (1189–93).
4   The Abant Platform on 'The Future of the Middle East after the "Arab Spring" and Turkey' was one of the largest intellectual meetings on the subject. The Platform was held on 2–4 December 2011 at Gaziantep, Turkey with the participation of 150 intellectuals from Iraq, Jordan, Tunisia, Egypt, Morocco, Israel, Turkey, the EU and the US. A declaration was announced after the meeting which emphasises the complexities of the region and the futility of imposing models on the regional actors. Third parties' roles are defined in the declaration as supporting all democratically elected representatives of these countries and keeping communication channels open.

LICÍNIA SIMÃO

6

Forging a wider European security community? Dilemmas of ENP in the South Caucasus

Introduction

It is commonly acknowledged that the European Union comprises one of the best examples of what Karl Deutsch *et al.* (1957) termed a pluralistic security community. The historical process of economic and political integration, and the development of extensive interactions among sovereign states in Western Europe, led to the development of mutual expectations of peaceful change, based on shared values and particular views on how security could best be achieved. Security within this community became comprehensive and governance-oriented, resting on the ability of states to cooperate among each other and to provide citizens with public goods (Biscop and Arnould 2004; Biscop 2006). In this regard, the EU's approach to security fits a normative framework, seeking to strike a balance between state and human security. In an increasingly complex and unstable world, the European security community has been regarded as an island of peace and stability surrounded by a sea of chaos and threats (Cooper 2003). The prevalence of this conceptualisation of the periphery as a source of threats led to policy choices aimed both at protecting these domestic achievements and responding to the challenges of interdependence. Thus, the EU has taken on increased responsibilities and security functions, both through closer cooperation with the UN and NATO, and on its own. Over the last decade, the EU has developed extensive and overlapping instruments and approaches to security, including civilian and military capabilities, conflict prevention, crisis management and long-term stabilisation instruments. These security functions have arguably been most explicit in the successive enlargements of the EU (Stefanova 2005: 53), and in the development of policies of proximity, such as the European Neighbourhood Policy (ENP) (Charillon 2005; Browning and Joenniemi 2008), and the various stabilisation policies in the Balkans (Missiroli 2003).

The central objective of this chapter is to test the proactive nature of ENP in exporting security outside the EU's borders, through the analytical framework of security communities. The chapter takes EU relations with the three South Caucasus states – Armenia, Azerbaijan and Georgia – to enquire about the validity of this framework in complex geostrategic environments, and the consequences of its application in policy-making. It raises pertinent questions about the ability of the EU to position itself as a reliable and credible security option for the neighbours to the East and, inversely, about the ability of the neighbours to share a wider security community with the EU, building on ENP. The definition of a norms-based approach to security, visible in the discourse of the EU regarding ENP, raised expectations that the EU would devise the means to consolidate a shared political community with its neighbours. We can therefore argue that, at the rhetorical level, the EU has been presenting security as a value in itself, providing positive benefits for itself and its neighbours. Faced with shared security challenges derived from a context of interdependence, the EU proposed the creation of strong partnerships, based on integration and socialisation, as had been the case, to some extent, during previous enlargement processes.

In order to fully understand the variations in the EU's response to the dynamics taking place in the neighbourhood, not least in the South Caucasus, other typologies advanced in the introductory chapter of this volume can be insightful. The diverse nature of relations between the EU and the three states of the South Caucasus has demanded flexibility in the EU's foreign policy, and a lowering of expectations as regards the consolidation of either a regional South Caucasus community or the establishment of a shared political community between these states and the EU. Georgia's early demands for accession perspectives has challenged the EU's community-building approach and also demanded a more pragmatic answer, namely promoting its values as a part of security; the illustrative idea of doing 'geopolitics with norms' (Laïdi 2008). Furthermore, Georgia illustrates the competing understandings of security between the EU and its neighbours, especially when the civilian response to security challenges turns out to be insufficient to solve ongoing conflicts, as was patently demonstrated in the August 2008 war.

Another challenge to the conceptualisation of security as value is visible in EU relations with Azerbaijan. Despite the shared interests by both sides in developing a fruitful relationship, the EU's relations with this important energy-producing country have proved a challenge to its 'shared norms and values approach' to security. EU challenges regarding energy security are best developed elsewhere in this volume, but it suffices to say that neither conditionality, nor the promotion of a long-term prospect of building a common political community with the region (which could anchor their economic and political development), have provided the necessary incentives for long-term security in relations with Azerbaijan. This raises questions about the ability of the EU's political model to act as a transformational force for good in its vicinity, especially considering the conservative offers made by the EU and its constrained engagement with the neighbours in the Caucasus.

The first section of this chapter presents the nature of security understandings and policies developed by the EU: the historical context of the development of security functions inside the EU; the changing nature of security; and attempts to expand and export security models throughout the European continent. The second part analyses ENP and its potential to export a community-building approach to security in the geographical areas bordering the enlarged EU, with a special focus on its Eastern dimension. The final sections deal with the South Caucasus case studies, looking at how ENP has advanced three central elements for stability in the region: good governance; regional cooperation; and conflict resolution. It is argued that ENP has been prey to increasing mismatches in expectations, discourses and practices, affecting the ability of the EU to pursue both its values and its security, with profound consequences for the EU's strategic positioning in the wider European space, and the development of the EU's international identity.

The EU: a developing security actor

From the very beginning, the project of European integration has maintained a security rationale, aimed at establishing peace and security in Europe, in what Waever (1998: 76) called a 'non-war community', and according to whom, in the historical context of European integration, desecuritisation policies removed hard security from the European arena and moved it to the wider umbrella of NATO, proving to be a crucial factor in achieving peace. A pan-European security regime was further consolidated, building on four major normative and security-based institutional foundations: the EU, the Council of Europe, NATO and the Organisation for Security and Cooperation in Europe (OSCE). The founding treaty of the European Economic Community states in its preamble the wish for common action to 'eliminate the barriers which divide Europe' and to 'preserve and strengthen peace and liberty' in the continent (Treaty Establishing the EEC 1957: 2). Economic integration in Western Europe further consolidated a context of increased interdependence among European nation-states and, consequently, a commitment to a comprehensive understanding of security. It included freedom from fear, but also freedom from want, in a joint effort to prosper and develop a common European space, where people could fulfil their expectations as citizens and members of a wider European community. A governance-oriented approach to security developed, regarding state institutions as necessary vehicles to provide citizens with public goods (Biscop 2006: 89). Over the last fifty years, the EU has achieved the goals it set out to achieve, going further than it had hoped, and taking firm steps to overcome historical divisions in Europe between West and East.

However, it is partly due to its own successes that new challenges have emerged. The values inherent to the community of Western democracies became central elements in the process of defining 'friend' and 'foe'; 'us' and 'them' (Tunander 1997; Neumann 1998), implying a clear identity dimension, but also a security one. In the 1990s, EU relations with Central and Eastern European countries (CEECs) were part of a process of redefining the understanding of 'us' and 'them', juxtaposing conditionality and assistance and, ultimately, committing these states to the constitutive values and principles of the Union (Smith 2004: 138). In the conceptualisation of the EU as a security actor, we can say that the response of the EU to the challenges raised by the end of the Soviet Union was in line with its civilian nature (Duchêne 1972) and its normative character (Manners 2002); it derived as much from a rational assessment of the EU's interests and security concerns as it did from a normative view of a duty and legitimacy to act.

Security was understood as absence of war among states, following a liberal approach, which portrayed interstate relations among stable democracies as inherently pacific and focused on assuring common security through institutionalisation (Risse-Kappen 1994: 51–4). Functionalist integration, first developed in Western Europe and later extended to the CEECs, paved the way for the absence of war, but also for the development of a sense of shared destiny and identity, rooted in core values such as liberal democracy, human rights, free market, and peaceful settlement of international disputes. Security in Europe was assured by overcoming identity barriers and crafting a common political, economic, social and security space.

As defended by transactionalist theories, such as Karl Deutsch's security communities, states retain important functions in transnational community-building processes, including the promotion of transnational interactions, which are seen as the basis upon which shared meanings and common perceptions can develop. Security communities can be defined as transnational communities with a 'thick' body of interactions, by means of which a common identity arises, leading to the development of shared expectations for peaceful change (Deutsch *et al.* 1957: 7). Such transaction networks are at the core of the EU's security achievements, not only because they have altered the rational assessment that member states make of their interests, but also because they have promoted a redefinition of national identities, in the broader context of European integration; this was partly the rational underlying ENP.

The absence of war among EU member states has been the main achievement of the European security community – an achievement all the more outstanding if we consider that security understandings among EU member states today result from a multifaceted process. Peace has resulted from the interaction of national elites and the cultivation of rules, norms and principles embedded in European integration, eventually leading to institutional cooperation within the Common Foreign and Security Policy (CFSP) and the Common Security and Defence Policy (CSDP), as well as from the overall historical process of reconciling and securing the European continent. The outcome has been a diverse and complex set of processes contributing to a comprehensive understanding of security and a comprehensive security policy (Hauser 2006).

Thus, the EU has evolved from a security consumer – dependent on the presence of the United States in Europe – to a security provider. EU member states have taken increased operational responsibilities in stabilising regions around the EU, such as the Balkans and the South Caucasus, and in the process, the EU has also gained a more visible international political and security presence. Keukelaire (2001) has termed the EU's approach to international and regional challenges a 'structural foreign policy', arguing that the EU's foreign policy is more than the sum of its 'multipillar', 'multilevel' and 'multilocation' approaches (Keukeleire and MacNaughtan 2008: 25–34). This comprehensive view of security, with the development of coherent institutional capabilities to address policy challenges, has been a central contribution to security in Europe. As the EU's former High Representative for the CFSP, Javier Solana, stated, 'it is fair to say that no other region in the world has anything that comes close to our [European] security order: a sophisticated blend of rules and institutions. Its most important feature is its comprehensive character: cooperation in all three baskets of hard security, economics and human rights' (Solana 2009).

Taking the example of EU relations with the CEECs, where a shared identity was built by resorting to a mix of social learning and external incentives (Sedelmeier 2006: 150), ENP is also looking for the right balance between socialisation and conditionality, hinting at a strategic use of values as a way to assure security. As Checkel (2005) argues, shared beliefs develop either by a genuine compatibility of views and interests, or by the strategic calculation of an actor at a given moment. Therefore, in countries where the EU's power of attraction is greater, and where Euro-Atlantic structures are seen as the best option for stability (as is the case in Georgia and Ukraine), conditionality has been central. Socialisation, on the other hand, might prove to be a more long-term reliable strategy to deal with difficult neighbours, such as Azerbaijan or Armenia, where the incentives to comply and implement EU-led reforms are reduced. The weakness of incentives and the lack of a clear institutional perspective have limited ENP conditionality, while increased competition for influence, especially from Russia, has limited the EU's ability to resort to strict conditionality.

Moreover, creating the foundations for shared values of democracy, rule of law, good governance and structural security depends largely on the bility of state structures to take responsibility for, and be capable of, implementing decisions in the territory. Therefore, sovereignty and governance are preconditions for reforms to take root (Cornell and Jonsson, 2008: 248), whereas a regional consensus on stability and conflict transformation is necessary to strengthen the states' ability to provide its citizens with security. With ENP, the EU is aiming at expanding stability in the neighbourhood through a consistent engagement that deals with the root causes of instability. However, as Bechev argues in this volume, asymmetry and power politics are still part of the EU policy system, and particularly visible in economic terms. By withholding the incentive of full integration into the political structures of the Union, and with little EU proactivity in the South Caucasus in particular, the expansion of the European security community through ENP remains very much a long-term, governance-based approach that in the end fails to address the gap between the short-term needs of the region and the long-term goals set out in ENP. The focus on democratisation and economic reform has not been accompanied by increased engagement and support for the resolution of active conflicts and regional sources of instability.[1] Similarly, the EU has so far been unable to engage other actors such as Russia and Turkey, or the US, in a common approach that could benefit the region.

Conceptualising the neighbours in the framework of security and stability

The 'Wider Europe' communication (Commission 2003b) was drafted bearing in mind the impact of the EU 2004 enlargement in countries like Ukraine, Belarus and Moldova. The inclusion of the three South Caucasus countries – Armenia, Azerbaijan and Georgia – into this policy came later in the process, following a series of regional developments (Vieira and Simão 2008: 4) to which the EU felt compelled to respond. Thus, in 2004, the three former Soviet republics entered a 'new stage of relations with the EU' (Commission 2004b: 10–11), together with the participants of the Barcelona Process.[2] Although EU membership was a far-off prospect for these states, EU interest in the region's potential, both in terms of domestic reforms and energy and transport, was welcomed; ENP was received with enthusiasm in the three capitals.

The enlargement 'inheritance' of ENP proved complicated to manage, both due to ENP's exclusionary character (Rosamond 2000: 148), and the intrusive nature of its structural approach (Biscop 2006: 93). It was therefore necessary to fine-tune the 'carrots' and 'sticks' of ENP, since the EU was looking to match the expectations of the European neighbours with ambitious policy goals (Commission 2006a). Although there was a commitment to further integration with the EU, it was not clear how long it would take and in which areas it should first advance. Although the EU aimed at strengthening peace and stability at its borders, it was perceived as failing both to include its neighbours in the definition of security and to address their immediate concerns, such as visa issues, trade facilitation and conflict resolution. Dimitrovova's chapter in this volume approaches these mismatches, speaking of cultural re-bordering through integration and through difference to illustrate the difficulties inherent in the expansion of normative frameworks. Discrepancies in language and meaning became further crystallised with the establishment of the Eastern Partnership as a sub-policy of ENP (Commission 2008c). While for the EU it was a way to bolster relations with its Eastern neighbours, providing cooperation with new momentum and resources, for neighbours like Ukraine and Moldova, this was seen as a way to curtail their European aspirations, or even increase competition with Russia (RFE/RL 2009; Moldova.com 2009; Korduban 2009).

Perception has thus played a central role in the evolution of the political and institutional relations of the European institutions and of the EU member states with its neighbours. Discrepancies between perception, commitment and action have become part of the process of redefining actors' institutional identities, since identities are often deemed to be obstacles in the achievement of policy goals, whenever credibility is questioned. As Fierke and Wiener (2001: 131) argue: 'If one's identity and ability to act are understood to be fundamentally social and, therefore, dependent on the recognition of others, promise-keeping becomes extremely important. It is at the point that others recognise violation of normative expectations, or the failure to live up to previously stated ideals, that shame and disrespect are experienced.'

In this process, and as analysed by Natorski in this volume regarding Ukraine, identity becomes a disputed element often used for strategic and rhetorical purposes. This is a fundamental element in the process of including the European neighbours of the EU in a common security community, since security is perceived as a normative and values-based asset. Being perceived and accepted as 'European' is a fundamental step in assuring that ENP – beyond signalling EU acknowledgement of its interests in the neighbourhood and in the South Caucasus – will become a catalyst for action. It also illustrates a desire to rescue the EU from its 'border of order' (Fierke and Wiener 2001: 130), and to engage it in complex and unstable scenarios, with which the EU is increasingly interdependent.

Security is thus not only an output of specific policies, but also a core value, rooted in normative prescriptions of how states should relate to their citizens and to other states. The diversity of interpretations about what security should mean, not least between the EU and its neighbours, but also among and within its neighbours, has presented an obstacle to developing common meanings, common views and trust. As noticed by Coskun in this volume, a diversity of values and of interpretations is increasingly emerging as a factor to be acknowledged in the EU's relations with outside partners. The choice then rests on how to address diversity, and how the universalist claims of the European order can be 'replaced by a dialogue between different universes' (Tunander 1997: 28), to create an interaction that is more effective for building the basis for long-term security in the wider Europe.

The issue of membership provision to the Eastern neighbours of the EU rests as the element of uncertainty of ENP. If the EU attempts to forge a common security and identity with the European countries of the former Soviet Union, and if it is willing to export its governance system to these regions (or simply unable to find another option), then the question naturally emerges as to the validity of extending membership perspectives to ENP countries. Sjursen (2002: 508) speaks of a 'kinship-based duty' to enlarge, which shapes the pace and depth of EU choices for enlargement. But are these arguments valid in the context of ENP?

As we will see below, in the early stages of ENP, each of the South Caucasus countries sought to recreate a context of 'rhetorical entrapment' (Schimmelfennig 2001). Schimmelfennig's argument is that the strategic use of norms-based arguments, what he calls rhetorical action, managed to 'entrap' opponents to enlargement, by forcing them to move beyond the 'pursuit of egoistic, material interests' and instead focus on 'their collective interests and honour their obligations as community members' (Schimmelfennig 2001). Because of the lack of active supporters of membership perspectives for the South Caucasus among the EU member states (a notable exception are the three Baltic states), the South Caucasus states have taken it upon themselves to try to find ways of 'entrapping' member states. The first step is to pursue the acknowledgment of their European identity, after which accession to the EU, according to article 49 of the Treaty of the Union, becomes formally possible. From here on, it emerges as a moral duty of the EU to assist all European states to achieve stability and prosperity.

ENP is an attempt to forge a 'foreign policy of proximity', recognising the legitimate aspirations to membership of the South Caucasus and other European neighbours, but seeking to achieve positive results through limited engagement. Although ENP builds on the EU's fundamental values far more than other CFSP initiatives, and although the EU has acknowledged a direct security interest in engaging with these regions, it has been constrained in its actions and policy choices. While remaining the most attractive political and social project for the countries in Eastern Europe and the South Caucasus (not least due to its hegemonic action, as Bechev argues), the ambiguous nature of ENP and the open-ended process that it entails has left neighbours both free to manage the depth of integration sought and cynical about the EU's commitment to security issues directly affecting these regions.[3]

EU conditionality and socialisation measures are, thus, effective in varying degrees throughout the neighbourhood. The political, economic and financial support provided to the South Caucasus countries in the framework of ENP, for instance, has been designed to guarantee both the milieu goals of the EU's structural foreign policy and the necessary instruments to develop strategic capacity to influence events affecting regional stability. That is why strategic goals are severely affected when the EU is perceived as neglecting its values and norms, while its normative capital is weakened when the EU fails to address the strategic challenges of the neighbourhood.

Expanding the European security community to the South Caucasus

The expansion of the European security community to the South Caucasus is a complex and long-term endeavour. The EU has assumed the role of security provider, namely reinforcing the work of the Council of Europe and the OSCE by establishing a 'region of democratic security' in Europe (Adler 1998: 147), and by supporting the economic development of the region. However, it keeps its engagement in conflict resolution limited, seeking to build on multilateralism and local ownership to assist in building peace, but distancing itself from a more purposeful and proactive role. The reliance on the transformative potential of the EU, meaning the socialisation of local actors into EU ways of doing, norms and shared values, is puzzling since the South Caucasus is a highly disputed region, with a great number of external actors and overlapping historical, cultural and political affiliations. This chapter focuses on three aspects considered as structural points in the integration of the region into the European space of security: developing good governance structures at the domestic level; furthering regional cooperation among the three countries; and resolving active conflicts in the region. From the analysis of these three aspects it is possible to develop important insights as to the potential of ENP in expanding a European security community.

In the South Caucasus, post-Communist challenges and a rapidly globalising context overlap, adding complexity to processes of consolidating democracy, the rule of law and good governance. Problems are also visible in the relations of the society with the state. The Soviet inheritance bearing on these states is quite visible in the suspicion of the population towards state structures, while simultaneously revering the leaders of the nation. This makes the process of institution-building and good governance promotion much harder. As Adler and Barnett (1998: 36) underline, 'a security community's governance structure will depend both on the state's external identity and associated behaviour and its domestic characteristics and practices'. Domestic behaviour must also conform to the rules of the community of which a state is part, or seeks to be part. Sovereignty and authority are thus contingent on the security community, since the safeguarding of the community is understood as a primary goal of the member states, with the states' agency framed by the shared understandings of the community (Adler and Barnett 1998: 36–7). Post-Communist states, however, regard their sovereignty as a highly precious asset. It becomes difficult to imagine a short-term future where sovereignty will be constrained by a new overarching order, especially one that these states do not control. This is a primary illustration of how EU and post-Soviet neighbours' understandings of security diverge and of how values can be shared but still rank hierarchically in a contentious way.

Moreover, deep problems remain as regards the development of a common framework of action among the region. There are several obstacles to the development of a shared security community among the South Caucasus states, or between them and the EU member states. Although Armenia, Azerbaijan and Georgia form part of a Caucasus security complex (Coppieters 1996; Simão and Freire 2008), their views on security diverge profoundly since political relations are tense, and economic interdependence has been hampered by the persistence of incompatible national projects and active conflicts. At the regional level, therefore, there are no relations of trust, which remains the major obstacle for peace. Despite a common political 'inheritance', each South Caucasus state has recently pursued individual paths, and the differences among them have grown. Therefore, an overview of the specific dynamics affecting each state is necessary.

Looking inside Georgia, Armenia and Azerbaijan

The pro-Western Georgian administration that came to power in 2003 with the Rose Revolution made integration into the EU and NATO a top foreign policy priority. This was meant to strengthen Georgia's nation-building project, including control of the territory and of the informal networks developing across Georgia, but especially the resolution of the separatist conflicts within Georgia's territorial integrity (National Security Concept of Georgia 2006). This implied the reform of the state, granting it legitimacy as the central authority – an area where cooperation with the EU proved profitable. Georgia's economy grew considerably from 2004 onwards, and the World Bank ranked Georgia as a top reformer in 2006 (World Bank 2006). A crucial part of this growth, and of the regained stability in Georgia, was due to the completion of the Baku-Tbilisi-Ceyhan (BTC) pipeline, which provided the state budget with much-needed revenues, and simultaneously raised Georgia's international profile as an indispensable energy transit country. Engagement with Georgia became a fundamental interest for the EU's energy security and, simultaneously, a litmus test as to its ability to support the values of the EU, which the new Georgian leadership embraced with the Rose Revolution. The EU's role in Georgia has evolved considerably since the war in 2008, now with a clear hard security perspective.

Armenia's situation, although less dramatic than Georgia's, has remained harder for the EU in several aspects. Armenian national identity is closely linked to the conflict with Azerbaijan over Nagorno-Karabakh. This means that religious and ethnic elements are often underlined as the basis for political and strategic alliances (Simão 2010: 4–9). Armenia is a long-standing Moscow ally, perceiving itself to be surrounded by hostile nations and seeing in Europe its natural home. According to its 'complementarity' foreign policy, engagement with the EU would allow Armenia to advance its interests through a highly respected and powerful partner, as well as to gain much needed financial and economic incentives. Despite a good record of reforms in key areas of the ENP Action Plan, serious problems remain in Armenian domestic politics (Freire and Simão 2007). The best description is an 'imitation of democracy' where formal democratic institutions are in place and coexist with informal institutions through which power is exerted, largely following the Russian example.

Moreover, following the violent outcome of the presidential elections in February 2008 and the lack of tangible results in foreign policy, namely in the attempts to normalise relations with Turkey, the political situation is very fragile. The EU has faced great challenges to balance its policy between Armenia and Azerbaijan,[4] especially regarding Nagorno-Karabakh, and ultimately had limited achievements in consolidating the European choice for Armenia.

For Azerbaijan, EU engagement has meant increased autonomy from Moscow and support to become an energy and transportation hub between Asia and Europe. Baku has also sought to reinforce its position as a modern and secular regime in a Muslim country, capable of contributing to Europe's stability and security on several fronts. The EU has been accused of mild criticism as regards Azerbaijan's democracy and human rights record, due to its energy interests (Alieva 2006). However, Javier Solana has underlined that 'Azerbaijan is not only a producer of energy; it's an important country [in] an important region, with which we want to have a deep relationship' (quoted in Lobjakas 2006). Despite this statement, however, EU–Azerbaijani relations are complex and hard to manage. The sources of tension revolve around the Nagorno-Karabakh peace process, namely the EU's reluctance to openly support Azerbaijan's territorial integrity and Baku's intransigence in refusing to participate in regional cooperation with Armenia until the conflict is solved. Moreover, the EU has also been reluctant to support the development of the Nabucco pipeline – an alternative to Russian routes – politically or financially (Ria Novosti 2009b). Baku has responded to these hesitations by drawing economically closer to Russia (Ria Novosti 2009a).

Good governance: moving beyond electoral windows of opportunity

Underpinning the concept of governance is the idea of establishing positive cooperation among institutions and enhanced processes of coordination between the state and society, which make public intervention more effective and legitimate for citizens. At the international relations level, good governance procedures allow a reinforcement of peace among sovereign states, by developing the common norms and institutions from which political legitimacy is derived. The main rationale for governance is 'common interest' as a unifying element in international cooperation (Seminatore, 2006). This is a cross-cutting issue in the entire neighbourhood and a central one in measuring ENP partner countries' performance, as stated in the ENP Action Plans. Because the EU attaches great importance to governance issues, it has established specific funds to reward good performance in reforms, such as the Governance Facility (Commission 2006a), while its assistance and the pace of future relations are theoretically linked to progress in democratic reforms. Governance has been at the heart of Western donors' concerns, since it is directly relevant to making investments and partnerships more stable. The promotion of sound economic and political governance facilitates the development of a bureaucratic and institutional relationship between the EU and its partners, which in turn facilitates common understanding; this is the EU's promotion of structural security in action.

However, this is far from the case in the South Caucasus, where the transition to market economy and liberal democracy has been mixed with economic downturn and war, making the state and the shadow economy two of the few remaining places where prosperity can be pursued. An instrumental use of the state has been natural in this context. Thomas Carothers (2002) makes the point that transitions in the post-Soviet space might be over, but that we need to understand what other factors influence the path taken by authoritarian regimes – regimes which do not always yield to democracy – towards new forms of government. Moreover, after years of neglect on the part of the EU, the political situation in the South Caucasus has been neither one of complete transition to democracy, nor one of an absolute return to authoritarianism. The EU's focus has thus been kept to technical assistance and election monitoring as two important, albeit clearly insufficient, aspects of democratisation. However, it has appeared to be counterproductive to insist on electoral democracy and civil society development according to Western standards, when the state structures being legitimised were stripped of any real power and capabilities. Authors such as Fukuyama (2004) and Fareed Zakaria (1997) underline the risks of promoting electoral democracies when state-building is neglected. Without the necessary structures and constitutional constraints in place, political power could either be emptied of meaning in the hands of elected leaders, or could be exercised without restraints.

In the context of the Caucasus, these tendencies have prevailed amid a conjugation of weak sovereignty, governance and democracy. As Cornell and Starr (2006: 18) state: 'it is clear that the failure to build sovereignty in the Caucasus is related to the failure of governments to provide good governance and with the weakness of their democratic credentials. It is hence in Europe's long-term interest to work in tandem for the building of sovereignty, governance and democratic government in the Caucasus'.

These countries are members of the OSCE and the Council of Europe and, as such, are expected to deliver on their international commitments to democracy, fighting corruption, improving transparency and ensuring political accountability. The engagement of the EU in the region has confirmed the failure of current policies to deliver positive results and the importance of strengthening Western commitment to the region. Despite the reluctance of some EU member states to have the EU take a more active role in the region, there was an increasing awareness within the Council Secretariat and among some more active member states, namely Sweden and the United Kingdom, of the importance of using the window of opportunity offered by the electoral processes scheduled for 2003, in all the South Caucasus states (Lynch 2003: 185).[5] For the EU this represented an opportunity to assess the level of democratic commitment of the Caucasus states, which would be on the direct border of the EU after the 2004/07 enlargement, as well as at the heart of its energy and transport strategies.

The individual support of some EU member states such as Poland, Lithuania or the Czech Republic during events in Georgia in the autumn of 2003 and in Ukraine in the winter of 2004 were crucial, along with US support, in pushing the electoral revolutions through.[6] Taras Kuzio (2007) portrayed these events as a 'fourth wave of democratisation' and, according to Michael McFaul (2005: 7), these popular revolutions were successful both in Georgia and Ukraine due to a combination of specific factors and conditions.[7] Throughout the former Soviet space, however, there have been efforts to avoid the conjectural gathering of these factors (Krastev 2007: 243), as illustrated by a context of declining freedoms in all the Caucasus countries (Karlekar 2008). In 2007 and 2008, the scenario was different when again all the countries of the region held elections, the first since the drafting of the ENP Action Plans. The pressure both to retain strong governmental power to assure domestic stability in highly volatile contexts, and to maintain a multi-party competitive democratic political system, has been one of the strongest challenges in the entire post-Soviet space.

Overall, the EU has engaged in supporting democratic overtures in the region, as the Georgian case illustrates. In order to make elections an effective measure of democracy, it has strengthened its cooperation with government structures. It has focused on changing the legal frameworks for government action and, simultaneously, socialising political actors in European standards and procedures. So far, in the three countries there has been a selective engagement with EU-sponsored reforms, and an unbalanced EU relationship with local governments and civil society and economic agents. This has in part justified the failure of ENP to generate a domestic consensus as to the future of these countries and as to the steps felt necessary to bring them closer to Europe. The EU has failed to capitalise on the positive image it enjoys among the populations of the region, and increasingly risks being regarded as an incoherent actor, supporting governments that are corrupt and failing to improve the security of the populations.

Regional (lack of) cooperation

From a geographical point of view, the South Caucasus resembles a bridge stretching between the Black and the Caspian seas, between Europe and Asia. From the perspective of Brussels, and bearing in mind the international context of emerging Asian powers, this bridge is crucial for the EU's commercial and energy interests and, more widely, for its security. It is clear that, along with a values-based approach, ENP represents an attempt to address the EU's strategic interests on energy security and transportation corridors. However, as the EU enters the complex South Caucasus context of ethnical, religious and linguistic differences, can it really become a common pole of attraction, or will it focus on building on existing competitive regional dynamics? What results can be expected from the two approaches?

In the South Caucasus the EU has favoured regional cooperation among the three neighbours, in order to consolidate a common approach to European integration and, consequently, a 'normalisation' of relations. Regional cooperation within ENP serves strategic goals which, from the perspective of the EU, also bear a conflict transformation potential. The European Parliament recommended 'full utilisation of ENP to promote regional cooperation among countries of [the region] as an instrument for inter-state confidence-building' (European Parliament 2006a). In fact regional cooperation in the South Caucasus has been blocked mainly by the Nagorno-Karabakh conflict and the maintenance of closed borders throughout this land-locked region. Borders between Turkey and Armenia, and Armenia and Azerbaijan, as well as between Georgia and Russia, are not open and do not function normally, making economic integration, infrastructural development in transport and energy, the environment, and security issues related to transnational criminal activities, all unaddressed security challenges.

Although ENP seeks to increase differentiation through bilateral relations, a focus on the regional level is central, particularly from a security perspective. The EU has faced great difficulties in getting any regional cooperation going (Simão and Freire 2008: 55), and its attempt to link the progress in the ENP Action Plan negotiations of Armenia, Azerbaijan and Georgia (Freire and Simão, 2006: 139) was regarded as an outdated approach to a region that was rapidly growing apart.[8] For the EU, a regional approach was justified from a functional perspective,[9] but also out of fears of accusations of favouritism. Frequently, however, regional cooperation takes the form of three bilateral dialogues instead of one multilateral framework including everyone. Nevertheless, some non-political EU-sponsored initiatives have been developing at the regional level. The Regional Environmental Centre in Tbilisi is one of the few initiatives where all three South Caucasus neighbours participate. In 2007, the EU began to develop a Border Management Cooperation initiative, aimed at improving technical standards in the region.

Neither wider formats of regional cooperation, such as the Black Sea synergy (Commission 2007a), nor narrower ones, such as GUAM[10], have delivered positive results in terms of the development of inclusive projects, and in overcoming regional isolation. Regional cooperation must be preceded by meaningful advances in conflict resolution. As the Georgian case illustrates, any positive dynamics generated by the development of joint projects between the Georgians and the Abkhaz, with EU support, have been watered down by the military campaign of August 2008. This has left the EU's transformative approach in a fragile state.

Furthermore, regional cooperation should also reflect the realities on the ground. Economic integration among countries that have ties with each other could provide an important impulse for others to follow, and a more democratic process of defining regional priorities might reveal that average citizens find it more meaningful to develop links with their neighbours than to maintain the closure of borders.[11] Good neighbourly relations are a necessary condition for any level of integration to develop. In the case of the development of a security community, this acquires added importance, since it is through interaction among states that a common and legitimate framework of action emerges. The prospects for the EU's regional approach to the South Caucasus are thus not particularly favourable. However, one could argue that, along with increased differentiation in bilateral relations, the EU should keep a focus on regional cooperation, preferably with less politicised actors from civil society, including business, cultural and academic entrepreneurs. It should also seek to develop cooperation at the regional level wherever possible, and through that process, establish approaches that might be expanded, namely for conflict resolution.

Conflict resolution and the EU's transformative power

The development of EU instruments for conflict resolution has been slowly taking place at the institutional and political levels. Besides the important steps taken in the framework of the Lisbon Treaty, the creation of the post of High Representative for the CFSP in the Treaty of Amsterdam in 1997, and the establishment of the Helsinki Headline Goals in 1999,[12] are examples of the development of greater political and military capabilities. Furthermore, the Feira Headline Goals (Council of the EU, 2000a) and the Stability Pact for South East Europe predominantly underline a civilian perspective to conflict resolution. Moreover, the EU also pursues a structural conflict prevention approach through policies such as development and cooperation, enlargement and ENP. ENP, though not offering membership perspectives to partner countries, offers participation in the EU internal market and enhanced political dialogue, increasing coherence of the EU's regional approach. However, the impact in terms of altering conflict dynamics is far from clear.

The separatist conflicts of the South Caucasus, inherited from the collapse of the Soviet structures, have hindered the development of the region, in economic, political and social areas. State budgets have privileged the military, and governments and oppositions alike have used these conflicts as political banners, taking attention from reforms. At the level of foreign policy, the conflicts have led to the formation of political and military alliances that limit the options available for local governments and hamper regional cooperation. Despite these realities, incentives for regional and global actors to change the status quo and address these conflicts have been missing. The major change to the existing situation was brought about in Georgia. President Saakashvili's persistent attempts to alter the situation on the ground escalated into an open confrontation with Russia over South Ossetia in the summer of 2008. The outcome was Russian recognition of the declared independence of both South Ossetia and Abkhazia and an entrenchment of its interests in Georgia. However, from these events, limited positive dynamics have spilled over to the Nagorno-Karabakh conflict and a new dynamism was felt in the Karabakh peace process.

The current shifts in the regional context, following the South Ossetian war of 2008, led Turkey and Armenia to renew efforts to normalise relations and led Russia to engage proactively to mediate the Karabakh conflict. The possible implications of EU actions in conflict resolution in the region are not clear. In the South Caucasus, the EU's presence was felt mostly through assistance in reconstruction and rehabilitation to South Ossetia and the Gali district near Abkhazia (Popescu 2007). International assistance to Karabakh has been limited by the lack of conflict settlement, but also by the refusal of authorities in Baku to authorise such activities. The development of regional cooperation mechanisms supporting confidence-building, in the framework of the European Commission-supported Instrument for Stability, could also deliver some results, but overall the EU is ill-prepared to be engaged in conflict resolution. At best it can aim at 'conflict transformation', by supporting reforms in these countries and by engaging with non-governmental actors (Simão 2010).

The reluctance to deploy more visible CSDP instruments, and the low profile kept in the negotiation formats, has contributed to maintain an image of the EU as a weak political player in the region (Nodia 2008). The EU's transformative approach to conflicts and regional relations in the Caucasus region is by definition a long-term strategy aimed at changing the incentives and rationales for political action. The EU hopes to improve conditions in order to attract foreign investment – essential for economic and social development to take root. Moreover, it seeks to provide a new identity framework within which people from the Caucasus can see themselves sharing European credentials. Finally, it aims to strengthen those political institutions potentially capable of restoring the damaged social contract between leaders and citizens. This is an ambitious agenda, especially because it relies on local compliance to EU norms and values, on the basis of an argument that, in the end, stability will come.

Conclusion

This chapter has sought to evaluate the potential of ENP as a security community expansion tool in the South Caucasus context, taking into account the perceptions of the EU as a reliable security actor for the region, as well as the region's ability to integrate the EU's normative and security model. From this perspective, the chapter presented security as more than an interest-based process, but as a constitutive element of the European identity, and therefore closely linked to the values it sponsors. Security is thus understood as being more than the absence of war, and rather, to be perceived as the constitution of a shared community of principles through which states interact. As such, economic integration, interdependence, political consultation and the incorporation of the values and norms of the community in the domestic arena are all necessary elements to consolidate such a security community.

In the case of ENP, the EU's commitment to building closer relations with the neighbours based on shared values has meant trying to build on the EU's credibility and legitimacy as a balanced and normative actor. This has also raised hopes, among European neighbours at least, that the EU will maintain its commitment to expanding an area of security and prosperity in Europe, by eventually opening its institutions to new members. The EU's conditionality and socialisation processes, as well as the freedom to choose who can enter the European club and who cannot, make the process of European integration a highly intrusive and exclusionary one and, thus, also somewhat problematic for its normative image.

However, because the EU's approach to security provision relies more on normative alignment than on the deployment of means on the ground, it is becoming increasingly difficult to justify conditionality and socialisation strategies, without either a long-term commitment by the EU, or relevant policy instruments to address the short-term security needs of the neighbours. A first lesson for the EU is that 'constructive ambiguity' no longer provides a relevant incentive for reform. A further lesson, painfully raised with the 2008 war in the Caucasus, is that reliance alone on transformative norms-based approaches to security does not provide relevant answers in the context of active conflicts and competition for influence. This needs to be carefully balanced with conflict-prevention and conflict-resolution instruments, which can assure short-term visible incentives for transformative policies.

The inclusion of Armenia, Azerbaijan and Georgia into this framework has been quite challenging for the EU. The perception that the region can one day leave the 'former Soviet space' to fully integrate into an enlarged European security community is quite daunting, particularly at a time when Russia is reasserting itself on the international stage. Competition for influence over this strategic region has been a constant in the post-Cold War context, with dramatic effects on the region's foreign policy choices, including military alliances. Any expansion of the European security community must address such hard security issues, including conflict resolution. As the chapter has argued, the active conflicts in the South Caucasus represent the biggest obstacle to any meaningful and inclusive regional cooperation, and provide a context in which political reforms are not welcomed by regional elites.

ENP provides the EU with the right framework for action. It needs, however, to display flexibility and commitment to the values it sponsors, in order to be an effective tool for change. A common area of security and prosperity must address soft security challenges such as illegal migration and organised crime (mainly EU priorities), but equally the armed conflicts of the region. It must also balance the current focus on governmental structures with a democratisation of the political space. This would not only prepare the ground for sustainable conflict resolution, but also create new avenues for regional cooperation and for rooting democratic practices at the domestic level. These countries are today at a crossroads. Having survived the first years of independence in complete chaos and violence, they are now at the point where the future must be built. Europe represents this future in the form of prosperity, stability and peace. However, it must deliver results in the short term and open up clear and long-term perspectives if any meaningful shared political community is to be built.

The alternative might be for the EU to abandon the stated goal of establishing such a political community and focus more on pragmatic relations. This might even be welcomed in most of these countries, in a context where conditionality is deemed to lack legitimacy. Energy development is a key interest for Azerbaijan and Georgia, while keeping good relations with Russia is clearly in the interests of Armenia and Azerbaijan, and arguably even Georgia, despite the government's rhetoric otherwise. If the EU remains convinced that it has the power of 'attraction' and 'transformation' to sustain a structural shift in its neighbours' views of their own security, then it needs a coherent and principled approach, and renewed means for its foreign policy – only then will it be able to pursue a structural approach to security and remain an effective partner for the region, capable of delivering on its own interests and on those of its partners. The changes announced under the Lisbon Treaty are, in principle, favourable to more coherent EU action in terms of structural conflict prevention and crisis management. This would make the institutional and governance-based approach of ENP better complemented by a conflict prevention dimension that goes beyond political reforms to address the root causes of conflict.

Notes

1 The EU's engagement in Georgia's protracted conflicts increased considerably after 2008, albeit in a reactive and rather limited way.
2 Countries participating in the Barcelona Process (since 2008 called Union for the Mediterranean) include Algeria, Egypt, Israel, Jordan, Lebanon, Libya, Morocco, Occupied Palestinian Territory, Syria and Tunisia.
3 Due to the financial crisis and the lack of political leadership by European leaders, the European project has been perceived as losing its appeal, even to the EU's closest neighbours (see Lucas 2011).
4 Personal interviews with Azerbaijani officials: Brussels, 27 March 2007 and Baku, 2 May 2007.
5 In Armenia, both presidential and parliamentary elections were held in 2003; in Georgia there were parliamentary elections in November 2003 and in Azerbaijan there were presidential elections in October 2003.
6 Personal interviews with senior Armenian, Azerbaijani and Georgian officials, Brussels, 2007.
7 The factors of success referred to by the author are: 1) the presence of a semi-autocratic rather than fully autocratic regime; 2) an unpopular incumbent; 3) a united and organised opposition; 4) an ability to quickly drive home the point that voting results were falsified; 5) enough independent media to inform citizens about the falsified vote; 6) a political opposition capable of mobilising tens of thousands or more demonstrators to protest electoral fraud; and 7) divisions among the regime's coercive forces.
8 Personal interviews with Azerbaijani officials and senior Armenian, Azerbaijani and Georgian officials, Brussels and Baku 2007.
9 Personal interview with European Commision officials, Tblisi, May 2006.
10 GUAM Organisation for Democracy and Economic Development: a regional organisation that groups together Georgia, Ukraine, Azerbaijan and Moldova.
11 This much was illustrated by several initiatives on the Turkish–Armenian border, carried out by local business communities. For more on these processes see Tocci *et al.* (2007) and www.tabdc.org.
12 See the annex of the Helsinki European Council on 'Strengthening the Common European Policy on Security and Defence' and on 'non-military crisis management of the European Union'.

GISELLE BOSSE

7

Values versus security? Assessing the EU's pragmatic engagement with Belarus in the Eastern Partnership policy

Introduction

> ... new possibilities have opened up for dialogue and deepened cooperation between the EU and Belarus. (Council of the EU 2009a: 1)

Since its enlargement to Central and Eastern Europe in 2004 and 2007, the European Union has struggled to find an appropriate policy to address its new neighbours in the East. Its efforts to support political and economic reforms in Ukraine and Moldova have yielded little success, and hopes to repeat the Union's success-story of transforming post-Communist countries in Eastern Europe without offering the prospect of EU membership were quickly shattered. The EU has had to face an even more challenging situation vis-à-vis Belarus. The country has expressed no immediate preference for joining the Union and the regime led by President Lukashenko has made no visible moves towards democratisation. In fact, the regime has become more repressive in recent years. Following the rigged presidential elections in December 2010, the Lukashenko regime responded to political protests with unprecedented force, resulting in the arrest of over 800 individuals and the sentencing of several opposition activists to many years in prison and labour camps.

What to do with the 'last dictatorship on the European continent'? In this chapter, I argue that the EU has not found a clear answer to the question as it struggles to define a policy towards Belarus accommodating idealist values and security interests, in the absence of a clear strategy or vision for its relations with the autocratic regime both in the short and long term.

In the European Neighbourhood Policy (ENP) launched in 2003–4, the EU expressed its clear and unequivocal disapproval of the Lukashenko regime. An emphasis was placed on the supremacy and conditionality of adopting 'European values', with an explicit focus on 'winning the hearts and minds' of the Belarusian population:

> Unfortunately, at this stage, the policies pursued by President Lukashenko's authoritarian regime prevent us from offering Belarus full participation in our neighbourhood policy. The EU cannot offer to deepen its relations with a regime which denies its citizens their fundamental democratic rights. (Commission 2006h: 3)

Three years later, and following the launch of the Eastern Partnership (EaP) in 2009, however, the EU had revised its policy and announced a new 'pragmatic engagement' with Belarus, despite little indication that the Belarusian regime had significantly changed its repressive domestic policies. In its conclusions of October 2009, the Council noted that

> since October 2008 ... new possibilities have opened up for dialogue and deepened cooperation between the EU and Belarus. The Council welcomes the increased high-level EU-Belarus political dialogue ... and the participation of Belarus in the Eastern Partnership, as ways of building mutual understanding and creating opportunities to address issues of concern. (Council of the EU 2009a: 1)

In this chapter, I aim to analyse the EU's policies towards Belarus and to conceptualise and assess continuity and change in the policies over recent decades by distinguishing a policy approach based on 'values' from an approach based on 'security interests': when and how did the EU arrive at its values-based approach towards Belarus and when did the 'pragmatic engagement' paradigm based on security interests begin to dominate EU–Belarus relations? And what was the impact of the two policy paradigms on the Lukashenko regime and the wider political landscape in Belarus?

The rigged presidential election on 19 December 2010 and subsequent brutal crackdown of opposition protests and related activities in its aftermath have led many commentators to proclaim the failure of the EU's 'pragmatic engagement' with Belarus (Dempsey 2010; Marin 2011), but few systematic efforts have been made to analyse the concrete goals and implementation of the Union's 'pragmatic engagement' policy. In addition, many scholars continue to portray Belarus as an oddity of sorts, an ultimate 'outsider' (e.g. Dingley 1994; Marples 2005; Raik 2006), or to examine EU–Belarus relations with a focus on 'the regime' in Belarus and an 'indoctrinated' Belarusian public (Zagorski 2002; Møller 2005; Schimmelfennig 2005b; Portela 2008). Few efforts have been made to provide a nuanced and detailed analysis of EU–Belarus relations and to try to explain continuity and change in the EU's policy towards the country.

In the first part of this chapter, I develop the notions of 'EU idealist values' versus 'EU security interests' as conceptual frames through which to assess recent changes in the EU's policy towards Belarus. In the empirical sections which follow, I examine the interplay between idealist values and security interests in (i) the EU's policy towards Belarus immediately after the end of the Cold War, (ii) the European Neighbourhood Policy, and (iii) the Eastern Partnership and 'pragmatic engagement'. The future of the EU's 'pragmatic engagement' policy following the presidential elections in Belarus in December 2010 will be discussed in the concluding part of the chapter.

Conceptualising the aims of the EU's policy towards Belarus: the delicate coexistence of 'idealist values' and 'security interests'

The aim of promoting the values of democracy and human rights, as well as focusing explicitly on 'winning the hearts and minds' of the Belarusian population, features prominently in official documents and speeches addressed to Belarus (e.g. Commission 2006h). At the same time, the Commission has been keen to highlight the importance of EU interests, such as security threats emanating from Belarus, including cross-border crime, trafficking, illegal immigration and, above all, the security of gas transit through the country (e.g. Commission 2004b: 11–12). In other words, both 'values' and 'security interests' are central to the Union's approach towards Belarus. I broadly divide the EU's objectives in external relations into (i) the promotion of idealist values such as democracy, human rights and human security for citizens located outside the borders of the EU and (ii) the pursuit of security interests to ensure the security and prosperity of EU citizens exclusively.[1]

Idealist values and democracy promotion
In the Treaty of Maastricht the EU adopted democracy promotion as a goal for its own foreign policy, specifically with the aim of giving itself a 'new and special international profile' (Olsen 2000: 143). Since then, the democracy promotion activities of the EU have ranged from the monitoring of elections and the promotion of minimalist democratic standards to comprehensive measures aimed at creating the normative underpinnings of democracy through citizenship and participatory democracy (Lappin 2010: 193).

The promotion of democracy, human rights and human security abroad are essentially idealist values. The inclusion of 'ethical' values in foreign policy is generally seen as a reflection of a fundamental change in the principles of international legitimacy following the end of the Cold War: In a globalising and liberalising world, governments of liberal states could no longer derive their legitimacy solely by privileging the security and welfare of their own citizens within national borders but instead had to recognise and act upon their moral responsibilities towards all human beings within a borderless international society (Boulden 2002; Evans and Sahnoun 2002).

The values of democracy promotion and human rights are, however, not without internal dilemmas. In his work on the normative dynamics in the

EU's external identity, Richard Youngs (2004) has highlighted very authoritatively that the EU's human rights policies exhibit a gradualist philosophy because they are deployed with the aim of supporting gradual or 'controlled change' in third states. This particular approach tends to result in the support for 'top-heavy political structures to manage reform processes' and institution-building programmes (linked to the traditional value of 'state stability' underpinning democracy promotion efforts), often at the expense of developing bottom-up civil society initiatives (Youngs 2004: 421–2). In other words, different and potentially contradictory approaches or 'values' may underpin the EU's democracy promotion efforts. If democracy promotion is highlighted as a distinct value in one of the EU's policies towards Belarus, it is therefore essential to examine which *type* of democracy promotion (top-down or bottom-up) is meant and, more importantly, if the traditional type of democracy promotion contradicts the bottom-up efforts to promote democracy (in a 'values versus values' type of scenario).

Shared security interests *and* realpolitik

An early example of *realpolitik* was Machiavelli's *Il Principe* or *The Prince*, written to encourage the appearance of a political saviour who would unify corrupt Italian city states. The work advocated the notion that 'whatever was expedient was necessary' (Machiavelli, quoted in Skinner 2001: 56). In general terms, *realpolitik* depicts a policy of relations between nations based on pragmatic engagement and common interests, rather than on the basis of moral considerations or ethics. In contemporary scholarship of international relations, the concept stands for traditional realist approaches based on the assumption that security interests are deeply engrained in the structure of the European state system. More specifically, *realpolitik* incorporates the traditional statist value of privileging the security and welfare of one's own citizens within national borders over and above the security of human beings in other states (Hoffman 1995; Gelb and Rosenthal 2003).

Although the EU is often seen as a post-modern *sui generis* polity, beyond *realpolitik*, it is unreasonable to assume that the 27 member state governments will find it easy to privilege non-EU citizens over and above the security concerns of their own nationals (and electorates) at home. State-centred security interests underpin the EU's externalised border and immigration policies towards third countries (Lavenex 2001). EU border and immigration policies have focused on limiting access to the common EU territory through the strengthening of its external borders, tight visa policies and the allocation of exclusive responsibility for the expulsion of illegal immigrants (Guild and Niessen 1996). At the same time, and in the words of Hyde-Price, 'the EU as a collective actor seeks to shape its regional milieu in ways conducive to [its] economic, political and security interests' (Hyde-Price 2004: 12). These interests, and particular security interests, are likely to play a role in the EU's policy towards Belarus, in particular regarding the

Union's interest to secure its 'new' Eastern border and to ensure the security of energy supply.

Having outlined the conceptual distinction between 'idealist values' and 'security interests' in EU external policies, the following empirical analysis assesses continuity and change in the EU's policy towards Belarus, with a particular emphasis on the emergence, goals and impact of the new 'pragmatic engagement' paradigm.

From optimism to disillusion: EU–Belarus relations after the end of the Cold War

Relations between the Union and Belarus looked very promising just after the end of the Cold War. The EC recognised Belarus's independence in December 1991 and, until 1994, their relations were based on the Trade and Cooperation Agreement (TCA) concluded with the USSR in 1989. In 1995, the EC and Belarus signed a Partnership and Cooperation Agreement (PCA) as well as an Interim Trade Agreement to bridge the time until the PCA's final ratification by all member states. Between 1994 and 1997, however, the positive trend in EU–Belarus relations came to an end, following President Lukashenko's attempt to extend his presidential mandate in a referendum in 1996 by changing the constitution, as well as owing to increasing repression in Belarus of the opposition, independent media and judiciary. These developments prompted the European Council in 1997 to suspend the process of ratifying the PCA and to freeze the Interim Agreement. Since then, EU relations with Belarus remain covered by the 1989 TCA, which does not include any provisions for regulatory approximation to the EU's trade-related *acquis*. The 1997 Council decision also restricted all political contacts with Belarus to below ministerial level. At the time, the EU still lacked a single policy towards Belarus. The country was covered by a loose policy framework directed towards all ex-republics of the former Soviet Union and democracy promotion was not an integral part of the policy. Nevertheless, with the few tools available, the Union employed a fairly heavy negative conditionality towards Belarus with the aim of exerting pressure on Lukashenko to reinstate minimal democratic standards for free and fair elections. Therefore idealist values played a significant role in EU policy towards Belarus in the late 1990s, though EU policies and official rhetoric then were not explicitly aimed at exporting or ensuring respect for European values.

The isolation of Belarus: the priority of idealist values in ENP

In 2002–3 the EU began to develop what was called at the time the 'Wider Europe–New Neighbourhood Strategy', initially designed as a response to the challenges and opportunities arising from the Union's new Eastern border. The emphasis here was clearly placed on Ukraine, but Belarus was considered as a partner or 'subject' of a new neighbourhood policy right from the start. The Commission and High Representative initially highlighted an 'upgrading of PCA relations with Ukraine and Moldova', with Belarus being a 'different partner', yet still a central focus of the Union's efforts to 'engage more actively in resolving problems' on its 'doorstep' (Patten and Solana 2002: 3–4). In October 2002, the foreign ministers in the Council even underlined their intent to develop enhanced relations with 'Ukraine, Belarus and at a later stage Moldova' (General Affairs and External Relations Council 2002). The 2003 Commission communication on 'Wider Europe – Neighbourhood' did not, however, present a clear strategy for engagement with Belarus. It stated that:

> The EU faces a choice over Belarus: either to leave things to drift – a policy for which the people of Belarus my pay dear and one which prevents the EU from pursuing increased cooperation on issues of mutual interest – or to engage, and risk sending a signal of support for policies which do not conform to EU values. (Commission 2003b; p. 15).

Between 2004 and 2006, however, ENP towards Belarus began to involve a distinctly values-based approach, especially in the EU's official rhetoric. The Commission started drafting country reports as well as Action Plans for the implementation of ENP with most partner states, including the Mediterranean and South Caucasus, but excluding Belarus. The 2006 Commission communication on 'Strengthening ENP' makes no mention of Belarus (Commission 2006a). Instead, the Commission issued a 'non-paper' in December 2006, which essentially contained a list of democratisation measures to be implemented by the Belarusian government, 'reflecting a principled, non-compromising approach'. It stated that 'the EU cannot offer to deepen its relations with a regime which denies its citizens their fundamental democratic rights' and demands 'political, economic and administrative reforms' (Commission 2006h). The non-paper was, however, bound to have limited effects on the Lukashenko government, not least because the conditions set out in it threaten the very existence of Lukashenko. As George Dura (2008: 6) notes, 'Lukashenko would have to democratise Belarusian politics and society, thereby seriously jeopardising his future as Belarus' president'.

Besides the conditions set out in ENP for Lukashenko to establish a fully fledged democracy, the EU also placed much emphasis on 'winning the hearts and minds' of the Belarusian population. In its 2004 strategy paper, the Commission promises that:

> More can be done ... in particular to support civil society, democratisation, independent media, the alleviation of problems in the areas affected by the Chernobyl disaster, humanitarian assistance as well as regional cooperation. (Commission 2004b: 4, 12)

In its political rhetoric, the EU thus employed a rather value-laden approach vis-à-vis Belarus. Yet it is important to examine to what extent the EU has been able (and willing) to implement its values-based approach in practice.

EU democracy promotion in Belarus in practice: 'Values versus interests' and 'values versus values'?

Has the EU supported democratisation from 'below' and supported Belarusian citizens' political rights and human security? The Union's support for civil society and NGOs has been financed through the Neighbourhood Programmes (2005–6) and the European Neighbourhood and Partnership Instrument (ENPI) from 2007. Assistance in 2005–6 totalled €10m (€8m committed) and focused on: i) support for institutional, legal and administrative reform; and ii) support in addressing the social consequences of transition, including support to civil society and democratisation, education and training and support to the alignment with international conventions (Commission 2004d). Additional assistance was also provided via the European Instrument for Democracy and Human Rights (EIDHR) (€5m in total) (Commission 2004d). ENPI is a financial assistance tool to support ENP and comprises national, regional, cross-border and thematic components. Belarus receives assistance for projects under the thematic programmes 'Democracy and Human Rights' and 'Non-State Actors and Local Authorities development', of which the national component (€5m p/a) includes actions to alleviate the consequences of the Chernobyl catastrophe and support democratic development and good governance (Commission 2006i).

Whether and how this assistance translates into actual support for democracy on the ground is not clear. Most projects funded through the Technical Assistance to the Commonwealth of Independent States (TACIS) instrument since 2005 have aimed at improving border management. A mere €130,000 was allocated to micro projects (human rights/democracy). Some €2m went to awareness-raising TV/radio programmes for Belarus, but the funds only supported projects and project partners outside Belarus, e.g. a radio station for Belarus broadcasting from Poland (Commission 2008d). One specific problem with the funding of 'grass-roots' activity and NGOs is the lengthy registration process for projects, which has effectively given the Belarusian authorities a veto on proposed projects. According to a Commission official, projects under the annual programmes that had already been agreed in partnership with the relevant mid-level authorities often got rejected by the central authority which refused to register them.[2] The very strict auditing rules and regulations of the TACIS instrument were also to blame for the difficulties in allocating funding to unregistered NGOs. The rules within ENPI contained even stricter criteria that organisations participating in projects had to meet; this helps explain why, even within the European Commission, ENPI was not considered a useful tool to fund bottom-up/civil society projects, especially in countries that did not welcome such support.³

Because of their greater flexibility and direct funding channels (which do not require the prior agreement by national authorities), the EIDHR and the non-state actors programmes have been designed to finance the majority of civil society projects in the future (Bosse 2008b: 52–3). The suitability of ENP/ENPI as a tool in support of civil society and NGOs in Belarus is therefore questionable. The EU itself has appeared to hamper the effect of its own policy towards Belarus through its lack of direct financial commitment to the Belarusian population, and by having erected serious administrative obstacles to financing civil society initiatives through ENPI.

The EU's policy towards Belarus has clearly been further affected by the tensions between competing sets of values underpinning its democracy promotion strategy towards Belarus. Whereas support for the people of Belarus and support for civil society were paramount in the Commission's 2006 non-paper, ENPI was almost exclusively geared towards strengthening the capacity of the institutions of the Belarusian state, including support for border and customs institutions or the state capacity to deal with the long-term effects of the Chernobyl disaster on the environment and the health of the population. The mere fact that ENPI was no longer seen as a tool for supporting bottom-up civil society initiatives in Belarus by the majority of Commission officials signals that the traditional value of 'state stability' was not just institutionalised in ENPI but also in the mind-sets of those drafting the EU's official policy towards Belarus.

Security interests over values: the Commission's 'pragmatic engagement' with Belarus

Has the EU stuck to its principled stance vis-à-vis the Belarusian government? Despite the official rhetoric of ENP, technical or expert cooperation in areas of mutual interest to the EU and Belarus has been a relatively consistent feature of cross-border/regional cooperation under the TACIS instrument. Belarusian 'Oblast' (regions) participate in three of the EU's cross-border cooperation (CBC) programmes: Latvia–Lithuania–Belarus, Poland–Belarus–Ukraine and the Baltic Sea Programme. All three projects have continued to be financed under ENPI. Belarus has hosted several meetings of project selection committees, and cooperation in areas such as border crossing/service issues is generally regarded as very constructive.⁴ At the same time, and possibly as a side effect of shifting TACIS/ENPI finances towards projects focused on mutual interest rather than 'values', even meetings between the Commission and Belarusian line ministries on the indicative programmes have become less political.⁵

The Commission, in practice, has appeared to be moving towards an approach of technical engagement with Belarus in other policy areas too. The 2004 ENP strategy paper confirms that

> if significant positive developments take place in democratisation in Belarus, there is scope for more active engagement with the Belarusian authorities at political level. Contacts between officials at technical level could be intensified and meetings at senior level, such as the Regional Directors' Troika resumed. (Commission 2004b: 11)

Contrary to the 'principled' conditionality approach of its 12–point non-paper, the Commission's interpretation of 'significant positive development' in its 2004 communication appears to have been measured against fairly small political steps taken by the Belarusian authorities, such as the release of political prisoners. In January 2008, and following the release of three political prisoners, experts from the Commission met their Belarusian counterparts in Minsk to discuss 'technical matters relating to the energy and transport situation in the EU and Belarus' with an additional meeting taking place in early February on environmental issues (Commission 2008b: 1). The areas discussed in these technical meetings ranged from the identification of joint interests and possible projects, such as the improvement of safety of trucks, to investment plans or Russia's North and South Stream energy projects.[6] Usually officials from DG RELEX and the relevant line DGs participate on behalf of the Union, together with experts at or below the deputy ministerial level. According to one Commission official, the Belarusian side was always very well prepared, professional and committed not to exploit the meetings for media propaganda.[7] It is important to note that both the Commission as well as Belarusian officials saw these meetings as instances of cooperation based on shared interests (rather than values).

The Commission appeared to lack a clear strategy of how to link its engagement with the Belarusian regime with the strict conditionality of its values-based approach, while promising the Belarusian population that it would isolate the regime for as long as it refuses to implement the political reforms set out in the 2006 non-paper. According to one Commission official, democratic values were mentioned in technical meetings with Belarusian officials but only when requested by the Council, and then usually with the 'understanding' that 'we put our lines'.[8] In other words, the Commission did not recognise that its engagement with the Belarusian regime was part and parcel of one and the same EU policy so explicitly based on idealist values such as democracy and human rights.

Energy security in particular has been driving the European Commission to develop ever-closer ties to the Lukashenko regime. In the past couple of years the EU's growing dependence on Russian energy, coupled with Belarus's role as a major transit country for Russian oil and gas, has clearly alerted the Commission. In 2007, for example, the Russian state operator

Transneft cut off oil supplies transiting through Belarus via the Druzbha pipeline, which is one of Russia's principal oil arteries to Western Europe. Shortly afterwards, also in response to the Russia–Ukraine gas row in January 2006, the Commission published its proposals for the first comprehensive package of measures to establish a new Energy Policy for Europe with the aim of boosting the EU's energy security. In 2009, the Commission already anticipated the 'finalisation of a European Commission–Belarus declaration on energy, as a basis for further development of energy cooperation' (Commission, 200g: 9).

Belarusian experts were also included in technical meetings and training events to address issues of strengthening and reinforcing asylum, migration and border management standards and capacities within the framework of the 'Söderköping Process'. It comprised an annual senior-level review meeting and working-level cluster meetings for the migration service and border guard officials, as well as non-governmental organisations (Commission 2006i: 14–15).

In other words, despite the values-based rhetoric of ENP, the European Commission gradually began to implement a policy of engagement based on common security interests in its (informal) relations with Belarusian officials.

The Eastern Partnership: from idealist values to 'engagement' based on joint security interests?

The Eastern Partnership (EaP) was officially launched in Prague on 7 May 2009, at a joint summit between EU member states and the six partner countries in the East: Ukraine, Moldova and Belarus, as well as Georgia, Azerbaijan and Armenia in the South Caucasus. The Belarusian government, too, was invited to the summit. One year earlier, in May 2008, the Polish and Swedish governments had lobbied for the inclusion of Belarus into the EaP and held consultations on the initiative of Belarusian government officials. The Commission communication on the Eastern Partnership of December 2008 also confirmed the possible participation of Belarus in the EaP, albeit still in rather vague terms. The communication states that 'the level of Belarus' participation in the EaP will depend on the overall development of EU–Belarus relations' (Commission 2008c: 4). Later on in the document, the Commission, however, underlined that Belarus would be included in the annual spring meetings of Ministers of Foreign Affairs from the EU and the Eastern partners 'as appropriate' (Commission 2008c: 10). It also stressed the need to strengthen the EU's energy security under the EaP framework and mentioned the 'finalisation of a European Commission–Belarus declaration on energy as a basis for further development of energy cooperation', and as a bilateral measure to be taken under the EaP (Commission 2008c: 8–9).

It is clear from the above that the tone and proposed mode of engagement of the EU vis-à-vis Belarus has changed quite significantly compared to the Commission's non-paper issued in 2006. The joint declaration of the Prague Eastern Partnership summit, signed *inter alia* by the Belarusian government, no longer adopts the strong language based on a commitment to shared values. Instead, it highlights that the 'more ambitious partnership' between the EU and its Eastern European Partners is 'founded on mutual interests and commitments as well as on shared ownership and responsibility' (Council of the EU 2009b: 5). In November 2009, the External Relations Council reaffirmed the engagement with Belarus based on mutual interests within the framework of the EaP:

> The Council notes that since October 2008, as a result of the release of internationally recognised political prisoners, new possibilities have opened up for dialogue and deepened cooperation between the EU and Belarus. The Council welcomes the increased high-level political dialogue ... the intensified technical cooperation and the participation of Belarus in the Eastern Partnership, as ways of building mutual understanding and creating opportunities to address issues of concern. (Council of the EU 2009a: 1)

In practice, the EaP foresaw strengthened bilateral and multilateral cooperation between the EU and its Eastern partners. On the bilateral level, the foreign ministers in the External Relations Council agreed to extend the suspension of the application of travel restrictions, which had been imposed on certain officials in Belarus in November 2009 and again in October 2010. The Council also agreed to offer a visa-facilitation agreement to Belarus (in tandem with a re-admission agreement) and to 'take steps towards upgrading contractual relations with Belarus' (Council of the EU 2009a: 2). On the bilateral level then, the EU has significantly reduced the conditions under which it is willing to engage with Belarus, going from an idealist 'change of the regime' approach based on democratisation, to an engagement based on mutual interests and commitments.

Belarus was also included in the multilateral track of the EaP and its four platforms.[9] The State Border Committee of Belarus participated in a working session on the issue of integrated border management in Odessa in mid-October 2009 (with Ukraine, Lithuania and Poland), which is one of the so-called 'flagship initiatives' within the framework of the platform 'Democracy, good governance and stability'. The parties agreed to establish a permanent exchange of information between border management units and to improve the infrastructure at their common borders within the EaP (BelTA 2009b). At the end of November 2009, the foreign ministers of Belarus, Ukraine and Lithuania met in Kiev to discuss trilateral cooperation under the EaP, including a project for delivering electricity from Ukraine to Lithuania via Belarus, and improving the Vilnius–Minsk–Kiev highway (BelTa 2009a).

These concrete agreements and project plans under the EaP clearly point to the institutionalisation from 2009 of a more technical ad hoc type of engagement based on security interests.

Values still matter: internal challenges to the interest-based engagement with Belarus

Although the new form of pragmatic engagement clearly dominated the EaP towards Belarus prior to the presidential elections in December 2010, some elements of the 'idealist values approach' could still be found in the policy. Not all EU member states agreed with the new paradigm. The UK and Dutch governments fiercely opposed the lifting of travel restrictions against Belarusian officials and a broad majority of members of the European Parliament remained in favour of the dual-track approach of applying strict conditionality vis-à-vis the regime in combination with targeted support for civil society.

Part of the multilateral track of the EaP is the Civil Society Forum, in which civil society organisations from all Eastern partner states participate. The forum took place for the first time in Brussels on 16–17 November 2009. According to the Commission, 79 applications for participation were received from Belarusian NGOs, of which 27 were eventually admitted.[10] Many of these groups were part of the political opposition to President Lukashenko and, according to one observer, enthusiastically teamed up with like-minded NGOs present at the forum.[11] However, after several meetings of the Civil Society Forum in 2010 and 2011, it is still unclear what influence it can have on the EaP. According to one rather cynical participant, the forum seems to function as the 'kindergarten' for the government officials and experts discussing within the EaP's thematic platforms.[12] Civil society representatives were, for example, not invited to present their opinion in Platform 1 on 'Democracy, good governance and stability'.[13] Nevertheless, participation in the civil society forum has had fairly significant effects on civil society (mainly moderate reformers rather than the political opposition parties) in Belarus. According to one participant, civil society in Belarus has started to organise itself; groups and individuals now talk to one another, meet and agree common positions.[14] These developments are unprecedented in the country and have therefore underlined the importance of continuing the 'values-based approach' in EU policy and supporting bottom-up civil society in Belarus.

The EaP also established the Neighbourhood East Parliamentary Assembly (EURONEST PA) which aims to bring together members of parliament from the six partner states with members of the European Parliament. The majority of political factions in the European Parliament refused to accept members of the Belarusian parliament to the assembly and instead insisted on inviting representatives of the political opposition and civil society. That suggestion was instantly rejected by the Belarusian government and as a result, EURONEST was convened without a delegation from Belarus. Nevertheless, the intense discussions in the EP on the participation of the Belarusian parliamentarians in EURONEST showed that there was no clear majority in the EP for the pragmatic engagement approach with Belarus.

Conclusion: the 2010 presidential elections and the future of the 'pragmatic interest-based engagement' with Belarus

In this chapter, I have analysed if there has been a change in recent EU–Belarus relations, from an idealist values-based approach promoting democracy, human rights and human security to an approach based on security interests with the premise of securing EU citizens exclusively. I have developed and juxtaposed the notions of 'idealist values' and 'security interests' in order to better understand and highlight changes and continuity in the Union's policy.

During the early days of its relations with Belarus, the EU did use sanctions against the Belarusian regime, yet without the corresponding official rhetoric on the importance of European values. Between 2004 and 2006, the EU's approach started to take on more distinctly values-based contours. The Commission underlined the conditionality of relations under ENP and the need for the Belarusian government to introduce democratic reforms. At the same time, the Union stressed the dual-track nature of its approach towards Belarus and declared its support to the citizens of Belarus, their political rights and broader human security.

In practice, however, very little of the promised support to citizens materialised. The Commission also employed a rather relaxed conditionality in its direct cooperation with Belarusian officials on issues of mutual interest, such as border control, or energy- and transport-related issues, which serves as a clear indicator that interest-based considerations have prevailed in EU relations with Belarus in practice. The Eastern Partnership institutionalised the pragmatic engagement with Belarus but the interest-based approach did meet considerable opposition from the European Parliament and a number of member states wishing to return to a values-based policy.

The presidential elections in Belarus in December 2010 presented a serious test-case for the EU's engagement approach towards Lukashenko. Despite the politics of engagement, international observers agreed that the elections were anything but democratic. Moreover, the elections were accompanied by a violent crackdown on demonstrations organised by the political opposition, numerous arrests and beatings, and the closure of several websites run by political opponents of President Lukashenko. After the presidential elections, the EU did not respond with a clear message to the Belarusian regime; or in the words of one commentator, the response of the EU has been to 'look on helplessly' (Dempsey 2010: 1).

The EU member states have successfully pushed for new sanctions to reinforce the values-based approach vis-à-vis Belarus (in the form of travel bans and freezing of assets of government officials and judges, and three companies linked to Lukashenko personally). The sanctions are, however, half-hearted at best, as Belarusian companies, which are crucial for the transport and processing of Russian gas for export to the EU, are not affected.[15] The Commission, and especially the Cabinet of the Commissioner for Enlargement and Neighbourhood Policy, Štefan Füle, has opted for a 'critical engagement' with Belarus, including more support for civil society in Belarus but also a continuation of financial assistance to the Lukashenko regime in regional cooperation programmes, and engagement in 'low-politics' areas of mutual interest (such as the Northern Dimension Partnerships for Environment and Transport or the EaP Flagship Project on border management).[16] When asked about the EU's strategy and future engagement with the Belarusian regime, it appears that every EU official involved in the development or implementation of the EU's policy towards Belarus holds a different view, ranging from 'irritating the Belarusian regime with sanctions', to 'keeping communication channels with the regime open for interest-based cooperation', to 'no engagement or deals with that authoritarian regime until Lukashenko is gone'.[17] In other words, there is still no agreement among EU institutions and individual member states on whether to pursue a policy based on values or interests vis-à-vis Belarus. The EU's policy towards Belarus is therefore not driven by values or security interests in relations with the Belarusian regimes as such, but rather by changing coalitions and constellations of policy entrepreneurs who at times shift the EU's policy closer to the values-based approach, and at other times closer to the pragmatic engagement approach based on security interests.[18]

How to deal with the 'the last true remaining dictatorship in the heart of Europe'? A clear response from the EU is still pending after almost two decades of Lukashenko's presidency.

Notes

1 For a more detailed elaboration on the 'nexus' between values and security in ENP and EaP, see: Bosse, G. (2009) 'The Values/Security Nexus: The Limits of EU Governance in Eastern Europe', *Contemporary Politics*, 15 (2), 215–27.
2 Interview by the author with Commission Official, Brussels, 6 March 2008.
3 Ibid.
4 Interview by the author with Commission Officials, Brussels, March 2008.
5 Ibid.
6 Ibid.
7 Ibid.
8 Ibid.
9 The platforms are (1) 'Democracy, good governance and stability', (2) 'Economic integration and convergence with EU policies', (3) 'Energy security' and (4) 'Contacts between people'.

10 Interview by the author with Commission Official, October 2009, Brussels.
11 Private conversation with a Member of the European Parliament, November 2009, Brussels.
12 Ibid.
13 Interview by the author with independent expert, Minsk, June 2010.
14 Ibid.
15 The transport and processing of Russian gas for export to the EU constitutes the largest chunk of Belarusian exports to the EU and therefore the single most crucial revenue for the Lukashenko regime.
16 Interviews by the author with officials from the Commission and the European External Action Service, November 2011, Brussels.
17 Ibid., including interviews by the author with Members of the European Parliament, November 2011, Brussels.
18 For a detailed analysis of the role of policy entrepreneurs in shifting the paradigms of EU policy towards Belarus, see Bosse (2012a). For detailed analysis of EU policy towards Belarus after the 2010 presidential elections, see Bosse (2012b).

PART III

Hard and soft security challenges

ELENA BARACANI

8

The EU and ethno-political conflicts: a secure Europe in a more peaceful neighbourhood?

Introduction

According to key EU documents such as the Treaty on the European Union and the European Security Strategy, the external promotion of peace seems to be, simultaneously, both a value and a security interest for the Union. Let us assume that the promotion of peace is a value instrumental to securing the Union's interests in internal security. For example, the last EU enlargements (2004 and 2007) have brought distant intra-state conflicts of an ethnic nature in the Union's neighbourhood. The presence of these conflicts poses several security challenges to the EU, since these conflicts, even if apparently 'frozen' or not active at present, might escalate at any time (as shown in the case of South Ossetia in August 2008), and have contagion effects on other conflicts in the Union's 'near abroad'. In addition to these traditional security challenges, there are new forms of insecurity for the EU that can emerge from ethno-political conflicts. For example, it is well known that EU member states are highly dependent on oil and gas provided by Russia, the Middle East, and Northern African countries, while Turkey and the Southern Caucasus countries too (especially Azerbaijan and Georgia) are becoming of increasing strategic importance as energy transiting and producing countries. As such, the escalation of conflicts in these areas could reduce the stability of energy supply for EU member states. Another example of a non-conventional security risk for the EU is the negative impact that conflict escalation can have on EU external relations with neighbouring or other third countries. For example, after the escalation of the South Ossetia conflict in August 2008, which led to the intervention of Russian troops, EU–Russia relations deteriorated. All these factors help explain why the Union's internal security is increasingly dependent on a more peaceful neighbourhood. The EU is aware of the fact that promoting peace in its surrounding circle of states is essential for both its internal security and its broader foreign policy goals. Therefore, the aim of this paper is to describe and assess the EU's activity to build peace in its neighbourhood and thus to improve its internal security. This means that the dilemmas the EU faces with 'frozen conflicts' in its neighbourhood should be best considered as an example of the typology 'security as a value' (see Chapter 1 of this volume).

At present the EU has both short-term instruments to manage conflict escalation and post-conflict rehabilitation (mainly Common Security and Defence Policy military and civilian missions), as well as long-term instruments for the prevention of conflict escalation and for building peace. While the EU's crisis management capabilities have developed recently, since the late 1990s following the Union's failures in the western Balkans, instruments for conflict prevention and peace-building are part of the first pillar. These are 'structural conflict prevention' tools (see Keukeleire 2004; Keukeleire and MacNaughtan 2008: 28) – as for example strengthening regional cooperation or building trade links – used by the EU to tackle the root causes of the conflict, and which favour long-term changes in the political, legal, socio-economic, security and mental structures of third countries at the levels of the individual, society and state. The concept of 'structural conflict prevention' is very close to the notion of 'conditioned anchoring' on the conflicting parties used in this chapter, and which can be defined as 'a process in which an external actor keeps close to itself a conflicting party, offering some incentives (metaphorically the anchors) in exchange for the respect of certain conditions for the settlement of the conflict'. According to this definition, the main dimensions of EU-conditioned anchoring that can be empirically detected are institutional links (the current status and final objectives of bilateral relations), economic assistance (and trade with its member states), and demands to comply with certain conditions for the settlement of the conflict. This concept is preferred to 'structural conflict prevention' for two main reasons. First, it allows one to analyse not only what the EU is offering to the conflicting parties but also what the EU is asking the conflicting parties to do in order to contribute to conflict settlement. Second, it focuses only on the potential changes produced at the level of the conflicting parties on their security, political behaviour and attitudes. Therefore, this paper describes the EU-conditioned anchoring on the conflicting parties, trying to assess its potential limits to favouring a positive transformation of the conflicting parties' behaviour, i.e. to contributing to peace-building in its neighbourhood and to strengthening the Union's internal security. In order to do so, after a comparative analysis of two ethno-political conflicts in the EU's neighbourhood, the main dimensions of the EU's 'conditioned anchoring' on to the conflicting parties are assessed.

Two ethno-political conflicts in the Union's neighbourhood

Table 8.1 lists the most important ethno-political conflicts in the EU's neighbourhood and their main characteristics. The Israeli–Palestinian conflict and the South Ossetia conflict have been selected as case studies to investigate what the EU has been and is currently doing to promote peace in its southern and eastern neighbourhood because of their relevance in the areas in which they are located. This is an important selection criteria since a comprehensive EU approach to peace-building requires an enormous amount of financial resources, as well as political, diplomatic and bureaucratic time and energy that can be expected and afforded by the EU for a limited number of cases that are at the heart of its strategic interests (Keukeleire and MacNaughtan 2008: 218). A comparative analysis of these two conflicts shows up certain key similarities and differences, with differing consequences for the settlement of conflicts. The first similarity is that they are both intra-state conflicts of an ethnic nature in which the primary parties are the state's government (the Israeli and Georgian governments) and an ethno-political group (and Palestinians and South Ossetians). Second, for both conflicts the incompatibility between the parties is over the territory, which means that opposition groups struggle to control a part of the state's territory for their own ethnic group. Third, both conflicts can be defined as internationalised intra-state conflicts, as at least one primary party is supported, officially or unofficially, by a secondary party (another state). This means that it is more difficult for a third party such as the EU to promote conflict settlement, given that the positions of all relevant players (not only the primary parties, but also the secondary parties) have to be taken into consideration. Another similarity is that they are the only ethnic conflicts in the Union's neighbourhood to have been active for at least one year, in the recent decade. This means that the EU's activities should aim not only to promote peace in the long term, but also to manage short-term crises when the conflicts escalate.

A first difference between the two parties is that while the South Ossetia conflict is a 'simple' conflict, for it is composed of only one dyad, the Israeli–Palestinian conflict is a 'complex' one made up of more than four dyads simultaneously (such as the government of Israel versus Hamas, the government of Israel versus Al Fatah, etc). This means it is more difficult to solve as there are more veto-players, and even when a peace agreement is reached it is more likely to be followed by a post-settlement armed conflict. A second difference is that while the Israeli–Palestinian conflict is a 'highly protracted conflict', which means that it has been active for more than ten consecutive years, the South Ossetian is not; as such, the Israeli–Palestinian conflict is more difficult to solve because it has been entrenched in society for a long time and because the parties have learned how to block any peace efforts.

Table 8.1 Main ethno-political conflicts in the EU's neighbourhood

Ethno-political conflict	Dyad: 2 primary parties		Key aspects				
	State's government	Ethno-political group (opposition organisation/s in 2008)	Incompatibility (when the conflict reached 25 battle-related deaths for the first time)	Status in 2008 (latest range of years in which the conflict was active)	Intensity	Risk of escalation	Additional aspects
Transnistria	Moldova	Slavs [Russians and Ukrainians] (Pridnestrovian Moldavian Republic)	Territory (1992)	Not active (1992) but incompatibility not solved	Minor	Medium	Inter-nationalised internal conflict
South Ossetia	Georgia	South Ossetians (Republic of South Ossetia)	Territory (1992)	Active (not applicable)	Minor	High	Inter-nationalised internal conflict
Abkhazia	Georgia	Abkhazians (Republic of Abkhazia)	Territory (1992)	Not active (1992–93) but incompatibility not solved	Minor/ War	High	Intern-ationalised internal conflict
Nagorno-Karabakh	Azerbaijan	Armenians (Nagorno-Karabakh Republic)	Territory (1991)	Not active (1991–94; 2005) but incompatibility not solved	Minor/ War	High	Inter-nationalised internal conflict
Israel–Palestine	Israel	Palestinians (Fatah, Hamas, Palestinian Islamic Jihad, etc)	Territory (1965)	Active (2000–08)	Minor	High	Inter-nationalised internal conflict; highly protracted conflict; complex conflict
Western Sahara	Morocco	Saharawis (Polisario Front)	Territory (1974)	Not active (1975–89) but incompatibility not solved	Minor/ War	Medium	

Sources: Uppsala Conflict Data Program (UCDP), Minorities at Risk Program (MAR) and Ethnic Power Relations Dataset (EPR) (author's elaboration)

The following paragraphs reconstruct, for each conflict, the four main common phases of development: the origin of the conflict (that means, for this type of conflict, the politicisation of the ethnic question); the escalation and de-escalation of the conflict; the internationalisation of the conflict; and the Europeanisation of the conflict.

The Israeli-Palestinian conflict and its Europeanisation

The politicisation of the ethnic question started when the Palestinians began to organise their resistance. On 10 October 1959 Yasser Arafat, together with other Palestinian refugees, founded Fatah, whose goal was the liberation of Palestine through armed struggle. Even if the first use of armed force dates back to January 1965, when the first Fatah raid on Israeli soil took place (Uppsala University 2010), the conflict escalated mainly in December 1987, when in the West Bank and Gaza (so-called occupied territories) local Palestinian leaders initiated violent demonstrations against the Israeli occupation, the so-called Intifada (uprising), which only diminished in the early 1990s when Palestinians and Israelis initiated negotiations about the future status of these territories. These negotiations led to the Oslo Peace Accords of 1993 and 1995, and the transfer of territory (a third of the West Bank and almost the entire Gaza Strip) to the Palestinian Authority (PA). Thanks to these negotiations, the conflict became inactive between 1997 and 1999, but in September 2000, following the breakdown of the Camp David talks, the conflict escalated once more, becoming yet more intense. At this time the conflict was characterised by the outbreak of the Second Intifada, which never officially ended, but can be seen as having come to an end with the Israeli–Palestinian ceasefire of February 2005. The electoral victory of Hamas in January 2006, which meant a refusal to recognise Israel and failure to respect previously signed agreements, led to another escalation in the conflict, with a ceasefire reached only in late November. The year 2007 was characterised by the continuation of Israeli–Palestinian fighting. During 2008, while Israel's ongoing negotiations with the Fatah-dominated section of the PA brought a reduction in fighting in this dyad (which became inactive), rocket fire from Gaza towards southern Israel, as well as Israeli targeting of Hamas and the Palestinian Islamic Jihad continued, and culminated on 27 December, when Israel launched a massive air assault on Hamas throughout the Gaza Strip. The Israeli military intervention in the Gaza Strip lasted until January 2009.

The Israeli–Palestinian conflict has been coded by Uppsala University (2010) as an intra-state conflict, thus without any official secondary party involvement. However, states known to have aided the Palestinian warring parties have been Iran, Lebanon and Syria. Israel, in turn, has received aid primarily from the US in the form of political support and military and economic grants. Several third actors have been involved in mediation efforts between the conflicting parties (mainly the US, but also Egypt, Norway, Sweden, Denmark, Italy, Switzerland, Turkey, Jordan, the EU, the UN, Russia and Qatar) and several partial peace agreements have been reached.

The EU's concern for the situation in the Middle East dates back to the first European Political Cooperation meeting of November 1970. A few years later, the European Community started supporting the Palestinians' right to self-determination (see European Council 1973; European Council 1977;

European Council 1980). This is the reason why several Israeli governments during the 1980s rejected any formal involvement of the European Community in the conflict. The European Community began to get directly involved in the Israeli–Palestinian conflict, even if only with an economic dimension, in the framework of the Madrid Peace Conference of 1991, which it sponsored. In particular, in the multilateral track of the peace process, the Community was handed responsibility for the Regional Economic Development Working Group, which brought together Palestinians, Israelis, Jordanians and Egyptians, in order to develop economic cooperation projects in the region (see Peters 1996a; Peters 1996b; Yacoby and Newmann 2008). This initial emphasis on the economic dimension of the EU's involvement in the Israeli–Palestinian conflict continued during the 1990s, as demonstrated by the increase in trade relations between Israel and the EU, the fact that the Union became the main donor for the PA, and the signing of Euro-Mediterranean Association Agreements (EMAAs) with Israel and the Palestinian Liberation Organisation (see also and Olson 1997: 79 and Perthes 2004). However, at the same time, the EU also began to develop its own political stance on the conflict. First of all, in 1996, at the insistence of France and other member states that felt the need to enhance the profile of the Union in the peace process, the EU appointed the former Spanish Ambassador, Miguel Ángel Moratinos, to Israel, as the first EU Special Envoy for the Middle East Peace Process, with two main tasks: to represent the Union, and to provide input into the EU foreign policy-making process. Second, the 1999 Berlin Declaration directly called for the establishment of an independent Palestinian state (see Alpher 2000). After the outbreak of the Second Intifada, the political role of the EU in the conflict partially increased, as demonstrated by the EU's formal role as a member of the Quartet, the diplomatic forum established in 2002 to mediate the peace process (the other members being the UN, the US and Russia). Other developments included the replacement in July 2003 of Moratinos by Marc Otte, who was given a larger mandate: to ensure regular contact with the parties and other relevant international actors; to monitor the situation on the ground; to promote confidence-building measures; to report on the options for the EU intervention in the peace process; and to support the proceedings of the Middle East Quartet. Then, at the end of 2005, the EU deployed two European Security and Defence Policy (ESDP) civilian missions in the Palestinian territories, the EU Police Mission in the Palestinian territories (EUPOL COPPS) and the EU Border Assistance Mission at Rafah (EUBAM Rafah). EUPOL COPPS expanded the work of the previously established Coordinating Office for Palestinian Police Support (COPPS), its assistance coming in the form of 33 unarmed personnel from EU member states, with another mandate: to advise and closely monitor the Palestinian Civil Police; to coordinate and facilitate EU and member state assistance; and to advise on police-related criminal justice elements. EUPOL COPPS has been praised as being focused on creating a single police force, but most funding has gone to providing anti-riot equipment and other material, and most Palestinians have seen COPPS as a programme helping to quash Hamas rather than supporting a security sector reform (Youngs 2007). EUBAM, which was active between November 2005 and May 2008 aimed to 'monitor, verify and evaluate PA performance with regard to implementation of Agreed Principles for Rafah Crossing and act with authority to ensure that PA complies with relevant rules and regulations; contribute to PA capacity building in all aspects of border control and customs operation; and contribute to liaison between Palestinian, Israeli and Egyptian authorities regarding management of Rafah crossing'. Assistance was in the form of 70 personnel drawn primarily from EU member states, who had to oversee the work of the Palestinian border guards in Rafah.

The South Ossetia conflict and its Europeanisation
The politicisation of the ethnic question dates back to 1989, when the Popular Front within the South Ossetian regional council demanded an upgrade of South Ossetia's status from an *Oblast* into an autonomous republic. The conflict escalated when, in October 1990, literature professor Zviad Gamsakhurdia, who championed the interests of ethnic Georgians and demanded Georgia's independence from the Soviet Union, won over the Communist alternatives in Georgia's first multi-party elections. First of all, in December 1990, Gamsakhurdia abolished South Ossetia's *oblast* status, and in January 1991, mobilised Georgian military units to 'liberate' ethnic Georgians living in the region of South Ossetia from the control of the Ossetian elite (Wheatley 2010). This led to an equally fierce counter-mobilisation by Ossetians. On 21 December 1991 South Ossetia voted for independence from Georgia, and hostilities intensified. The ceasefire agreement, reached in June 1992 and signed between Georgian and Russian Presidents, included the withdrawal of all armed forces from South Ossetia and the set-up of a 1500–strong tri-ethnic peace-keeping force drawn equally from Georgian, Russian and Ossetian soldiers. This agreement also established the Joint Control Commission (JCC), a body of Georgians, Russians and North and South Ossetians, established to direct and control the Joint Peace-keeping Forces.

The South Ossetian conflict escalated again in 2004 and 2008. In January 2004, Mikhail Saakashvili came to power, stating that one of his main priorities was to restore the country's territorial integrity. In particular, his government launched a large anti-smuggling campaign, aiming to deny the South Ossetian regime its incomes from the lucrative black market, and leaving the local authorities unable to deliver basic services to the population (Uppsala University 2009). The final objective of this strategy was to weaken the popular support for the *de facto* South Ossetia President, but it had the opposite result. The situation grew increasingly tense, with the number of Georgian troops and road blocks swelling in connection to the anti-smuggling campaign. The South Ossetians perceived this military build-up as preparation for military action, and in August tensions exploded and took the region to the brink of war. The Joint Peace-keeping Force ceased to function, and peace-keepers from Georgia and South Ossetia started to fight each other. A ceasefire was signed and a precarious peace remained in place until the first half of 2008 when the security situation deteriorated again as the quantity and intensity of gunfire exchanges increased (Uppsala University 2010). These tensions culminated on 7 August 2008, when only hours after having declared a unilateral ceasefire, President Saakashvili launched a large-scale military offensive on Tskhinvali, the capital of South Ossetia, to take control of the city.

Neighbouring Russia openly sided with South Ossetia and immediately sent its military support to repel the Georgian army. After five days of heavy shelling and ground fighting, the Georgian troops withdrew from the South Ossetian territory and Russian forces took control of areas far beyond the administrative border of South Ossetia. Mediation by the French President on behalf of the EU resulted in a six-point peace plan signed by Russia, Georgia, South Ossetia and Abkhazia. It established a ceasefire and called for the withdrawal of all parties to the positions held before August, but it did not address the political status of South Ossetia.

The South Ossetia conflict has always been coded by Uppsala University (2010) as an intra-state conflict, with foreign involvement of a secondary party (Russia) only in 2008. According to this source, indeed, before 2008 Russia had formally acted as a third party. However, it can be argued that 'informally' it behaved as a secondary party granting its political, economic and military support to South Ossetia. The involvement of third parties in the conflict started in 1992: Russian soldiers were part of the peace-keeping force, Russians and North Ossetians were members of the JCC, and the Conference for Security and Co-operation in Europe/Organization for Security and Co-operation in Europe (CSCE/OSCE) deployed its mission to Georgia in order to promote negotiations between the conflicting parties.

The EU involvement in the conflict started only in 2001 with a very low political profile, when it started to participate in the meetings of the JCC. Then, in July 2003, in order to reinforce the EU's role in the Southern Caucasus, the EU Council appointed the Finnish diplomat, Heikki Talvitie, as EU Special Representative (EUSR) for the area with the mandate: to develop contacts with governments; to encourage the three countries to cooperate; and to assist in conflict resolution. It was a rather cautious mandate reflecting a new willingness to help settle conflicts in the area, but at the same time taking into account the power balance in the region (Grevi 2007: 56–7). In addition, Talvitie's role was largely affected by the fact that he was based in Helsinki, had limited human and financial resources, and no political adviser based in the region. However, he travelled widely throughout the region and focused on Georgia. He held talks with *de facto* authorities in South Ossetia, but did not regularly participate in OSCE-facilitated negotiations on the conflict (International Crisis Group 2006: 23). In early 2006, the mandate of the EUSR was renewed, and Heikki Talvitie was replaced by Peter Semneby, with a broader mandate: to 'contribute to the settlement of conflict' instead of 'assist in conflict resolution' (Council of the EU 2006b: art. 3). Building on the stronger wording of his mandate, Semneby could participate directly in conflict resolution negotiations. Georgia invited the EUSR to participate in negotiations for the resolution of the South Ossetian conflict, but Russia and South Ossetia opposed it (Grevi 2007: 59–61). In addition to the appointment of a EUSR for the south Caucasus, in June 2004, at the request of Georgian authorities, the Council adopted a Joint Action on the first civilian ESDP mission, in the form of rule of law mission, EUJUST Themis (Council of the EU 2004: art. 2). Notwithstanding the appointment of a EUSR for the area, and the deployment of a civilian ESDP mission in Georgia, the EU's mediating role in the conflict became more active only after the escalation of the conflict in 2008. First of all, French President, Nicolas Sarkozy – on behalf of the EU – mediated the peace plan (six-point agreement), signed on 12 August by Russia, Georgia, South Ossetia and Abkhazia, and then a second agreement, signed on September 8, designed to implement the first one. Then, the extraordinary European Council of 1 September 2008 expressed its firm support for Georgia's territorial integrity and decided: firstly, to dispatch an ESDP civilian monitoring mission (EUMM); secondly, to organise an international donors' conference; thirdly, to appoint an EUSR for the crisis in Georgia; fourthly, to launch the Geneva international discussions; and finally, to establish an international mission of inquiry into the causes of the conflict and the overall strengthening of EU–Georgia bilateral relations. However, notwithstanding all these positive initiatives, it has to be stressed that the EU seems to have ignored the fact that Russia has not been respecting the agreements signed. First of all, Russian military forces have not withdrawn to the lines held before the outbreak of hostilities, as requested by the six-point agreement. Second, in April 2009, Russia sent additional troops to South Ossetia. Third, Russia prevented the OSCE from continuing pre-war activities in South Ossetia, saying that 'new realities' prevail; in turn it recognised the August independence declaration of South Ossetia and concluded bilateral security agreements (see, for example, International Crisis Group 2009).

EU's conditioned anchoring on conflicting parties

The EU has different foreign policy instruments at its disposal in order to contribute to the transformation of conflicts in its neighbourhood (Howorth 2007: 178). Some of these instruments are directly related to the EU's involvement in the conflict, as the appointment of EU Special Representatives or the deployment of CSDP missions (these instruments have been mentioned in the previous paragraphs on the Europeanisation of the conflicts), while others are not, but rather, concern the general relationship between the conflicting parties and the Union. These latter instruments allow the Union to establish a set of linkages (for the notion of political, economic, social and cultural linkages see Levitsky and Way 2005, 2006, 2007) with the conflicting parties (for example, in terms of a membership perspective, higher levels of economic assistance or more preferential trade arrangements) while at the same time exerting some degree of leverage on them. These linkages may be viewed metaphorically as anchors between the conflicting parties and the Union, or 'carrots'. The EU's anchoring may be labelled 'conditioned' since it is used, at least rhetorically, to grant stronger linkages/anchors/'carrots' only in exchange for respect of the values on which it is based, as evidenced in the peaceful settlement of conflicts.

The establishment of strong linkages between the EU and the conflicting parties has two main consequences. First, it indirectly contributes to the socialisation of the conflicting parties with the values and practices of the external actor. Second, when the granting of these linkages is conditioned to the respect of the Union's conditions on the conflict, and when the conflicting parties perceive the granting of these linkages to be relevant benefits or incentives, they can contribute to a transformation of the conflicting parties' behaviour in order to obtain the promised 'carrots'.

Some economic and political science academic literature has used the concept of 'external anchoring' to evaluate if and how an external actor – be it the International Monetary Fund, World Bank or regional organisations such as the EU or the North American Free Trade Agreement – exerts a positive impact on the macroeconomic reforms or democratic reforms of developing or transition countries (Francois 1997; Berglof and Roland 1998; Gros 2001; Tovias and Ugur 2004; Featherstone 2004; Dodini and Fantini 2006; Berger *et al.* 2007; Di Tommaso *et al.* 2007; Önis and Bakir 2007; Ugur 1999; Coricelli 2007; Magen and Morlino 2008). For example, in the only systematic analysis of the impact of the EU's anchoring on the democratic reforms of different countries at the Union's borders, external anchoring has been defined as a process in which national political regimes are subject to variably dense external linkages, pressures and stimuli influencing the conditions for democracy (Magen and Morlino 2008: 28). In a recent comparative description of the EU's 'democratic anchoring' to European post-Soviet countries, I proposed defining 'external anchoring' as a process in which an external actor keeps a target country close to itself by offering some incentives (Baracani 2010: 111). According to such a definition, the anchoring exercised by the EU can be deemed 'democratic' since these incentives – mainly institutional links, economic assistance, and trade with its member states – are conditioned to the respect for democracy. In this paper I propose to extend the use of external anchoring to the field of conflict transformation and use the following working definition of 'conditioned anchoring': a process in which an external actor keeps close to itself a conflicting party, offering some incentives in exchange for the respect of some conditions on the conflict. According to this definition, the main dimensions of EU conditioned anchoring, which can be empirically detected, are institutional links, economic assistance, trade with its member states, and the demand to comply with some conditions on the conflict.

Institutional links

By the expression 'institutional links' I refer primarily to the current status and the final objectives of bilateral relations between the conflicting party (only the government of the state) and the EU. In terms of institutional links, the strongest incentive that the conflicting party (only the state's government) can be offered by the Union is membership. There are also other weaker 'institutional' incentives that the Union can offer to conflicting parties (only the state's government) in the framework of different contractual relations, such as preferential trading arrangements, the liberalisation of the movement of persons, and partial inclusion in EU policies (such as the Free Trade Area, customs union, single market and Schengen regime), as well as participation in EU programmes, association with EU agencies and some political dialogue. The latter represents the minimal form of institutional links, since political dialogue can be developed even without contractual relations. Therefore, it can be offered to both conflicting parties (not only the government of the state, but also the ethno-political group). It refers to all bilateral political contacts between the EU and a conflicting party, and varies in quantity and quality according to the frequency of these contacts and the topics discussed.

In terms of institutional links, of course not all conflicting parties are offered the incentive of EU membership, reducing not only the EU's leverage in terms of 'conditioning' the conflict, but also minimising its potential impact on certain conflicting parties (such as in Georgia and Israel). However, all conflicting parties, with only the exception of South Ossetians, have contractual relations with the EU. Within the framework of the Barcelona Process, in February 1997, a Euro-Mediterranean Interim Association Agreement on trade and cooperation was signed between the EU and the Palestinian Liberation Organisation for the benefit of the Palestinian Authority of the West Bank and Gaza Strip, aiming at establishing the conditions for the increased liberalisation of trade, and to provide an appropriate framework for a comprehensive dialogue between the EU and PA. The Euro-Mediterranean Association Agreement with Israel entered into force in 2000 and included free trade arrangements for industrial goods, and concessions on trade in agricultural products. In this same period of the Euro-Mediterranean Partnership, the EU also started to develop its contractual relations with the former Soviet republics, such as Georgia. Indeed, a PCA between Georgia and the EU was signed in 1996 with the following aims: to provide a framework for political dialogue; to support the country's efforts to consolidate democracy; to complete the transition into a market economy; to promote trade; and to provide a basis for legislative, economic, social, financial, civil, scientific, technological and cultural cooperation. Vahl (2007: 126) underlines that the PCA with Georgia (and the PCAs with the other Southern Caucasus and central Asian countries) were less extensive than the PCAs with Russia, Ukraine and Moldova; only the latter included the prospect of a free trade agreement. Since 2004, EU bilateral relations with the countries at both the southern and eastern flank of the Union have developed in the framework of ENP. Israel and the Palestinian Authority were included in ENP from the beginning, while Georgia was only offered inclusion later. In the framework of this new policy context, in addition to more classical assistance and trade benefits, partner countries are offered the Union's support to meet its norms and standards, develop its internal (domestic) policies and programmes and, ultimately, join the EU single market.

Recently the EU has launched a new policy framework for relations with its six eastern ENP partners, the Eastern Partnership (EaP), as well as a new policy framework for relations with its southern neighbours, the Union for the Mediterranean (UfM). The EaP represents the evolution of ENP for the Eastern partners; it does not preclude their future membership of the EU, and aims at strengthening bilateral relations between Eastern partners and the EU. In particular, the bilateral dimension of the EaP offers partner countries the possibility to sign new 'Association Agreements' (AAs), superseding the PCAs, that 'will provide for the establishment or the objective of establishing deep and comprehensive free trade areas [DCFTA], where the positive effects of trade and investment liberalization will be strengthened by regulatory approximation leading to convergence with EU laws and standards' (Council of the EU 2009b: 7). Georgia is, for example, currently negotiating an AA with the EU. In addition, according to the Joint Declaration (Council of the EU 2009b: 7) the EaP 'will promote mobility of citizens of the partner countries through visa facilitation and readmission agreements' (having full visa liberalisation as a long-term goal for individual partner countries on a case-by-case basis provided that conditions for well-managed and secure mobility are in place).

In contrast to the EaP, the UfM does not aim at intensifying bilateral relations between southern partners and the EU, which will continue to be developed in the framework of ENP. The UfM can be considered as a new phase of the Euro-Mediterranean Partnership, as it recognises the validity of the objectives expressed in the Barcelona Declaration – the promotion of peace, stability and prosperity (the establishment of a Free Trade Area is also endorsed) throughout the region – and it adds six concrete projects for multilateral cooperation: tackling pollution, maritime and land highways, civil protection, alternative energies, higher education and research, and the Mediterranean business development initiative.

Economic assistance

Economic assistance is another main benefit that conflicting parties can be offered by the EU. In order to evaluate the conflicting party's vulnerability when it comes to the EU's conflict conditions, it is necessary to assess whether the EU (which means in this case European Commission plus EU member states) is its principal donor of economic assistance. In order to do this, I compare the total Official Development Assistance (ODA) with the same aid provided only by the European Union. This allows one to assess whether the European Union is the principal donor of economic assistance to the conflicting parties (comparable data are available only for the PA, Israel and Georgia). Data on total aid by all donors in Figure 8.1 show that in the period 1994–2004, Palestinian Administered Areas (PAA) and Israel received much more total ODA than Georgia. The PAA and Israel received almost the same average amount of total ODA each year, about US$1000 million in 2007 while Georgia received only about US$300 million in 2007. But data per capita indicates that Palestinians received the largest amount of disbursements each year (in 2007 about US$268 per capita), while Israelis received US$150 and Georgians US$70.

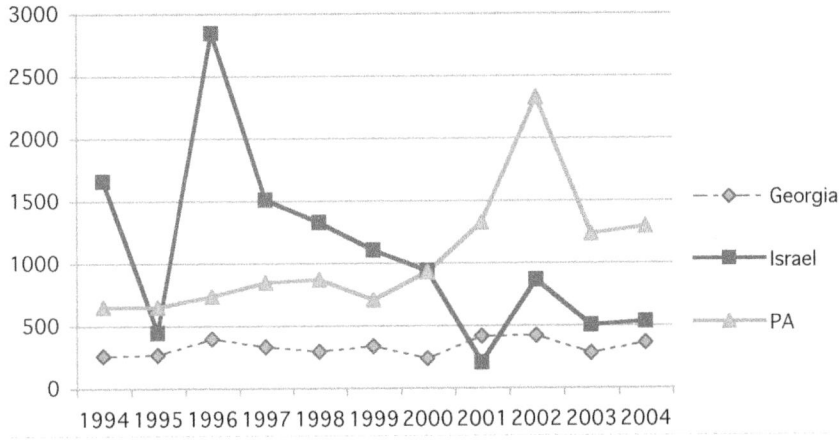

Figure 8.1 Total aid to Georgia by all donors, net disbursements* (2007 US$ millions), 1994–2004

Source: IDS Online-DAC Database – Destination of Official Development Assistance and Official Aid – http://stats.oecd.org/
*Actual expenditure

So is the EU the principal donor to these conflicting parties? Figure 8.2 shows that, in the period 1994–2004, the EU (EC plus EU member states) was the largest donor of economic assistance to Georgia, with an average each year of about US$100 million (in 2007). This means that it gave one third of the total average assistance disbursed each year to Georgia. The US was the second donor with an average each year of US$77 million (in 2007).

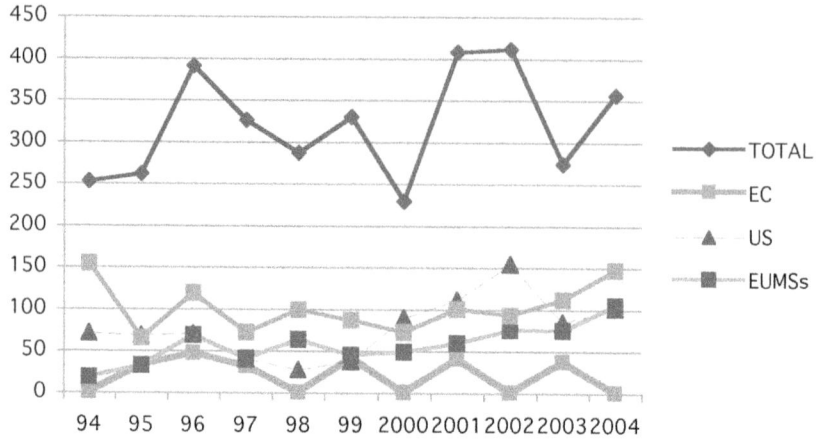

Figure 8.2 Total, EC, US, EU member states and EC plus EU member states ODA to Georgia, net disbursements* (2007 US$ millions), 1994–2004

Source: Data extracted in July 2009 from IDS Online-DAC Database – Destination of Official Development Assistance and Official Aid – http://stats.oecd.org (my compilation).
*Actual expenditure

The case of Israel (see Figure 8.3 below) is completely different, since almost the whole total amount of economic assistance comes from the US.

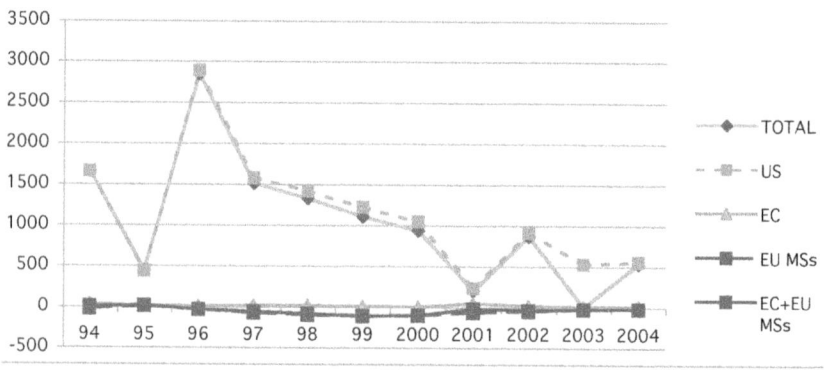

Figure 8.3 Total, EC, US, EU member states and EC plus EU member states ODA to Israel, net disbursements* (2007 US$ millions), 1994–2004

Source: Data extracted in July 2009 from IDS Online–DAC Database – Destination of Official Development Assistance and Official Aid – http://stats.oecd.org (my compilation).
*Actual expenditure

The data in Figure 8.4 shows that in the case of the PAA, as for Georgia, the EU (EC plus EU member states) was the largest donor of economic assistance in the period 1994–2004, with an average each year of about US$390 million (in 2007), that is more than one third of total ODA, followed by the United Nations Relief and Works Agency for Palestine Refugees in the Near East (UNRWA), with an average each year of about US$240 million (in 2007). In this period, the US distributed an average each year of about US$110 million (in 2007).

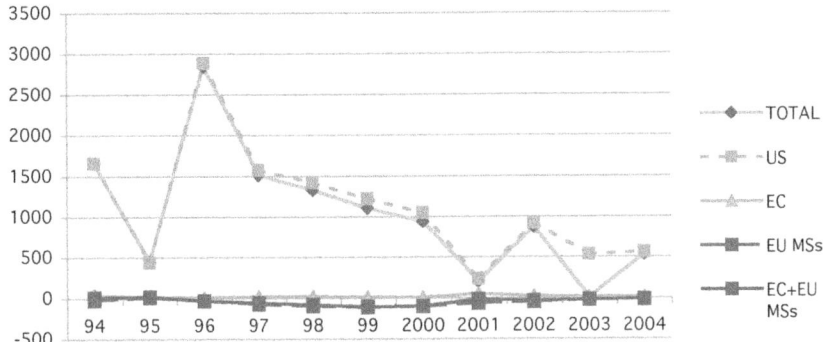

Figure 8.4 Total, EC, US, EU member states, UNRWA and EC plus EU member states ODA to PAA, net disbursements* (2007 US$ millions), 1994–2004

Source: Data extracted in July 2009 from IDS Online-DAC Database – Destination of Official Development Assistance and Official Aid – http://stats.oecd.org (my compilation).

On the basis of this analysis, it can be concluded that, in terms of economic assistance, only Palestinians and Georgians are strongly anchored to the EU, with an average each year per capita, in the period examined, of US$99 and US$22, respectively (2007 constant price).

Conditions on the conflict
This part evaluates the content of eventual EU demands to the conflicting parties in the conflict. This type of information is not available in the case of South Ossetia, as there are no official documents between this conflicting party and the EU. In the case of Georgia, the analysis of official PCA and ENP documents shows that this conflicting party has never been asked to do anything specific to contribute to conflict prevention and resolution. For example, in the ENP Action Plan, adopted in November 2006, Georgia is 'invited to enter into ... shared responsibility in conflict prevention and conflict resolution', but then, according to the paragraph on 'specific actions' it is not clear what the concrete meaning of Georgia's responsibility in this field is, as all the listed actions for the promotion of peaceful resolution of internal conflicts are for the EU rather than for Georgia. In addition, in two

cases, it is written that '[t]he EU points to the need to increase the effectiveness of the negotiating mechanisms', and that '[t]he EU stresses the need for a constructive cooperation between interested international actors in the region ... on additional efforts contributing to peaceful settlement mechanisms', showing that these are actions desired by the EU, but not necessarily by Georgia. Arguably, for Georgia it was very important to establish – as it did in this document – that conflict settlement should be based on the 'respect of the sovereignty and territorial integrity of Georgia within its internationally recognised borders', and that 'the issue of the territorial integrity of Georgia and settlement of Georgia's internal conflicts' should be included in EU–Russia political dialogue meetings.

In contrast to Georgia, in the case of Israel and the PA it is possible to find in the ENP Action Plans some 'actions'; for Israel, these are in line with the requests made by the Quartet (of which the EU is part) to these conflicting parties. In addition, at the beginning of the Action Plans, it is possible to find a formula similar to the one used for Georgia, but which denotes a stronger will of these conflicting parties to engage with the EU in conflict settlement. These formulas read as follows: 'Israel and the EU will strive to intensify ... shared responsibility in conflict prevention and conflict resolution', and '[t]he Palestinian Authority welcomes the EU initiative to enter into ... shared responsibility in conflict prevention and conflict resolution'. This stronger will is also confirmed in the part of the Action Plans on 'priorities for action', in which it is declared that 'the EU and the Palestinian Authority attach particular importance to facilitating efforts to resolve the Middle East conflict, and to alleviate the humanitarian situation', and in the case of Israel that 'particular attention should be given to enhance political dialogue and co-operation, based on shared values, including issues such as facilitating efforts to resolve the Middle East conflict' (EU PA ENP Action Plan 2005: 4).

In the part on 'Actions' in the ENP Action Plan for the PA, it is stated that '[p]olitical dialogue and cooperation should be strengthened and extended to include ... [d]evelopments in the region and prospects for cooperation to resolve the Middle East conflict, including intensified efforts to facilitate the peace process and bring about the implementation of the Quartet Roadmap to a permanent two-state solution to the Israeli–Palestinian conflict'. A longer and more detailed list of actions can be found in the Israel Action Plan. On the whole, however, the EU position on the conflict, including its demands to the two conflicting parties, has been reaffirmed in the Quartet's statement of June 2009. First of all, the Quartet reiterated that lasting peace can only be based on an enduring commitment to mutual recognition, freedom from violence, incitement and terror, and the 'two-state solution'. Therefore, both Israel and the PA have been asked to implement their obligations under a 'roadmap', and to stop incitement and violence against civilians. Moreover, Israel has been urged to: freeze all settlement activity; dismantle outposts erected since March 2001; and refrain from provocative actions in East

Jerusalem – including home demolition and evictions. For its part, the PA has been asked to: continue to make every effort to improve law and order; fight violent extremism; enhance its efforts to build the institutions of the future Palestinian state; commit itself to non-violence; recognise Israel; and accept previous agreements and obligations.

Conclusion

This chaper has proposed using the concept of Europeanisation to describe the EU's position and its involvement in the ethno-political conflicts in its neighbourhood. It has been observed, first of all, that not all the ethno-political conflicts in the Union's neighbourhood have been Europeanised (as in the case, for example, of the Western Sahara conflict) or not with the same intensity, since not all lie at the heart of the EU's foreign policy strategy. Thereafter, for ethno-political conflicts that should be at the heart of policy, the analysis has shown that the EU has started to elaborate its position and adopt several external policy tools of a different nature, and to play a role in these conflicts. For example, it has adopted formal political declarations, participated in peace negotiations, appointed EU Special Representatives and, in the last years, also deployed civilian CSDP missions. This means that the evolution of EU foreign policy has given the EU additional and more effective foreign policy tools – diplomatic, civilian and also military tools – to intervene directly in some selected conflicts, even if the decision to adopt these instruments has always been an intergovernmental one. This last aspect explains why for the EU it is much easier to react to events, such as the conflict escalation of August 2008 in South Ossetia, rather than prevent such developments. The Lisbon Treaty, which entered into force on 1 December 2009, has the potential to further extend the EU's activities directly related to the conflicts, and also ease their adoption. For example, Common Security and Defence Policy (CSDP) missions could have a larger mandate including joint disarmament, military advice and assistance, and conflict prevention and post-conflict stabilisation. In addition, the extension of enhanced cooperation to CFSP (CSDP included), could open new opportunities for a group of willing EU member states (when unanimity cannot be reached) to intervene in countries affected by conflicts. However, one of the main assumptions of this contribution has been that in order to evaluate the potential and main limits of the EU's activity to promote peace in its neighbourhood, it is necessary to analyse not only the Union's activity directly related to the conflict (or the Europeanisation of the conflict), but also the EU's relationship with the conflicting parties, or what has been called the EU's 'conditioned anchoring' to the conflicting parties. This concept – defined as a process in which the EU keeps close to itself a conflicting party, offering some incentives in exchange for the respect of its conditions on the conflict – is preferred to the expression 'structural conflict prevention', even if they both deal with the instruments for conflict prevention and peace-building of what used to be the first pillar.

What has been the potential and what are the main limits of the EU's conditioned anchoring to the conflicting parties? Could the EU, potentially, favour a positive change in the conflicting parties' behaviour and thus contribute to peace-building in its neighbourhood? The analysis of the main dimensions of 'anchoring' has shown that even if the EU does not exploit its entire potential role in terms of institutional links with the conflicting parties, as they are not offered a membership perspective, it could rely on its strong economic anchoring (it is the first donor of economic assistance to Georgia and the PAA, and it is the first trade partner for Georgia and Israel) to ask the conflicting parties to engage much more in conflict settlement. Indeed, the analysis has shown that, in contrast to Israel and Palestine, there are no conditions for Georgia on the conflict. This is due to the fact that in the ENP framework, as opposed to the accession policy framework, the EU's conditions or priorities of action have to be jointly agreed with the partner country. Therefore, even if the EU has a growing number of conventional and structural foreign policy tools at present that would allow it to pursue its security objectives at the same time as it promotes its values (security as a value), it continues to prefer the status quo and react to security challenges rather than preventing them.

MICHAL NATORSKI

9

Deeds not declarations: Ukraine's convergence with the EU's foreign and security policies until 2010

Introduction[1]

This chapter explores European Union–Ukrainian interactions in the field of Common Foreign and Security Policy (CFSP) until the beginning of 2010 when the Treaty of Lisbon entered into force and Viktor Yanukovych was elected as the new President of Ukraine.[2] It argues that the significance of the diplomatic exercise of cooperation goes well beyond the procedural aspects of alignment to CFSP acts and the scope of Ukraine's convergence with EU foreign policy. Concretely, it illustrates how cooperation and association between the EU and Ukraine was motivated by different meanings attached to 'security'. Therefore, the chapter addresses the relationship between different notions of 'security as a value' and the resulting dynamics of 'security versus security' outlined in Chapter 1 of this volume.

In the case of relations between the EU and Ukraine, the divergence between two notions of security has been relatively straightforward. For both actors, the provision of security seems to have acquired the characteristics of 'values', defined as 'notions laden with an absolute (i.e. non-instrumental) positive significance for the overall order and meaning we try to give to our world' (Lucarelli 2006: 10). In this sense, since the mid-1990s, both Ukraine and the EU have come to agree that security encompasses the value of protecting a referent object (Europe). However, until recently, there was a marked disagreement over 'who' was allowed to participate in the community sharing this understanding of an all-European security, namely on whether Ukraine was a member of the European community providing security or, rather, a source of concern for this community. As a result, in order to achieve its aim of being recognised as a wholly European country and security provider, Ukraine wanted to overcome its conventional representation by the

EU as a source of security concerns, which currently excludes it from the community of European states. In short, the value of 'provision of security', as a prerequisite for being considered 'European', explains the Ukrainian predisposition to be engaged in close cooperation in the area of foreign and security policy, and to converge with EU positions. This Ukrainian motivation was additionally enhanced by the EU with its approach of security as a value in itself, trying to ring-fence the insecure external environment beyond its borders (Zaiotti 2007). This interpretation of security based on a rigid distinction between EU insiders (who should be protected) and outsiders (who pose a threat to European security) was brought into being as a result of the idea that conflicts, instability and insecurity in neighbouring states must be managed by the EU in order to avoid them spilling over into its territory (Dannreuther 2006: 195).

This chapter is structured as follows: the second section outlines the theoretical arguments that govern the long-term and short-term motives for convergence between the EU and Ukraine regarding CFSP. The third and fourth sections examine, respectively, the EU's view of the role of Ukraine within the European security system and Ukraine's own consideration of its role. The fifth section describes the evolution of the institutional arrangements that underpin the relationship between the EU and Ukraine regarding CFSP, while the sixth section examines the current degree of convergence between Ukraine and the EU in relation to CFSP acts. The final seventh section concludes by summarising the main findings.

Security as a value in EU–Ukraine interactions

The theoretical argument presented in this chapter is that cooperation between the EU and Ukraine regarding CFSP is driven by Ukrainian attempts to demonstrate that it belongs to the community of European states that constitute the Ukrainian 'Significant We', a we-group to which it attaches positive values (Flockhart 2006: 600). This drive is sustained by an understanding of the European security community as a 'community of meaning' and the constitutive value it gives to being recognised as a member of it.

The idea of 'security as a value' assumes that the notion of security has a meaning, which, if shared by some actors, confirmed through direct and face-to-face interactions, and based on a sense of reciprocity expressing long-term interests and altruism, creates a community (Adler and Barnett 1998: 31). Therefore, we can assume that the existence of different meanings (positive or negative) attached to security may obstruct the emergence of a sense of community and establish borders of inclusion into, and exclusion from, the community. In consequence, intersubjective meanings attached to security integrate some states, but exclude states that do not share similar notions of security. However, the differentiation established by disagreement on the meanings attached to security may lead actors to argue about the meaning of security and eventually to struggle for recognition and inclusion into the community of meaning attached to this particular concept.

The aspiration to be recognised is an existential and constitutive desire for confirmation of one's self-conception and identity. As argued by Markell (2006: 450) 'to be recognized means to be seen or regarded ... under some practically significant description; that is, under a description that makes a difference in the way its bearer is treated, perhaps even shaping the terms in which she understands herself, and which thereby helps to configure her powers and possibilities'. Recognition means confirmation of one's existence, but is also a precondition for association with other actors. According to Rumelili (2004: 38), states associate when they engage in acts that symbolise their membership within the same community and with whom they feel a sense of identity. When the EU associates with other states, in the previously defined sense of 'association', it thereby communicates a recognition that the other states are willing to, and hence might, become more like EU member states. Therefore, such association provides the EU with the institutional means to influence how other states' identities will develop.

Ukraine's official discourses since the mid-1990s reflect ever more clearly that the community of European states that is the EU constitutes for Ukraine an ideationally positive 'in-group' to which Ukraine wants to belong, in addition to its being recognised as a member. Ukraine understands that in order to achieve recognition as a member of the EU security community, it needs to demonstrate a capability and readiness to provide security for Europe, which is a constitutive value for 'European community of security'. For this reason, the Ukrainian concept of belonging to 'Europe' carries both an ethical responsibility to act (Hansen 2006: 50) and a spatial meaning (Hansen 2006: 47) tied to its identity. In practice, in order to demonstrate its attachment to the 'European' value of providing security, Ukraine is attempting to give credence to its sense of responsibility with respect to contributing to the security of the EU's polity, and participating in European and/or Euro-Atlantic institutional forums seeking to provide security, as opposed to Eurasian security institutions dominated by Russia.

In order to achieve its aim of recognition as a fully European country and security provider, Ukraine needs to overcome its conventional representation by the EU as a source of security concerns, which excludes it from the community of European states providing security to the EU. That said, via cooperation with respect to CFSP, Ukraine is attempting to change its image within the EU and acquire the characteristics of association with, and similarity to, the EU states, as an alternative to the previous characteristics of distance and difference. The tension that exists between Ukraine's self-conception as a fully European security provider and the EU's representation of Ukraine as lacking a defined 'Europeanness' and being a source of security concern for Europe, constitutes the background against which Ukraine shapes its attitudes with respect to the CFSP. However, this generally positive Ukrainian attitude towards engagement in the CFSP fails to explain the outcomes of its particular decisions and actions taken within the framework of this cooperation. While the structural, long-term characteristics of Ukraine's leaning towards the EU facilitates the country's convergence with CFSP acts, specific short-term factors may in some cases hinder full alignment. Ukrainian decision-makers regularly have to address the issue of whether to align with a given CFSP act in view of their own short-term considerations.

In the light of studies that address the candidate countries' adoption of EU membership requirements regarding norms and rules (Schimmelfennig and Sedelmeier 2005; Sedelmeier 2006), we can identify two sets of short-term factors that may influence particular decisions adopted by Ukraine: the costs and benefits of adopting particular CFSP positions, and the legitimacy of these positions. The first of these factors relates to the decisions about convergence in specific cases, which must take into account the calculations made by Ukraine regarding the rational utility of the negative and positive incentives offered by the EU.

Ukraine may decide whether to accommodate externally defined CFSP positions, or not, by comparing the costs and benefits of the different courses of action open to it. Ukraine may converge with the EU regarding CFSP when the rewards from the EU for so doing are greater than the costs of the changes needed to be introduced in Ukrainian foreign policy as a result of the convergence.

The second factor relates to the ways in which specific decisions about convergence with CFSP positions may be influenced by normative considerations of their appropriateness. Ukrainian decision-makers will adopt EU positions only if they see them as good, right and legitimate. In cases when there is a disagreement between a CFSP benchmark and a previous Ukrainian position, the EU may use socialisation and persuasion to convince Ukrainian decision-makers of the appropriateness of the CFSP position. In this case, EU strategies 'do not link any concrete incentives to behaviour but rely solely on the use of norms to either persuade, shame, or praise actors into changing their policies' (Kelley 2004: 428). This approach might be successful, given the positive identification of Ukraine with the EU and/or the degree of legitimacy attributed to the CFSP decision-making process wherein the standards for convergence are set out. The degree of acceptance of a certain policy among EU actors and its legal status may also influence the perception of legitimacy of a particular CFSP position in Ukraine itself. When CFSP positions have an adequate legal foundation, and are accepted and implemented across member states and EU institutions, Ukraine may be well-advised to consider them as legitimate.

The uncertainty of Ukraine's role within the European security architecture

Since the beginning of the 1990s, the underlying view of Ukraine within the EU has been in terms of its post-Soviet genesis and of Russia being a principal point of reference for the country. The dominant view of the association of Ukraine with Russia was modified by the EU in the second half of the 1990s, when Ukraine's importance was highlighted in terms of its 'pivotal position in Europe' (Commission 1996: 13). In EU narratives there could also be found a less dominant, vague view of Ukraine being somehow, but not quite, European. The EU Common Strategy on Ukraine summarises this evolving EU narrative on Ukraine, stating that 'geography as well as size, the resources of its population as well as its location along the North–South and East–West axes give Ukraine a unique position in Europe and makes it a determinant regional actor' (European Council 1999: 1). Later on, the EU began to characterise Ukraine as a 'new neighbour' situated in 'an arc stretching through Russia and Ukraine to the Mediterranean' (Prodi 2001: 9). In the EU narrative there were also claims that 'Ukraine is an important member of the European family of nations' (Prodi 2000: 2) and that 'Ukrainians have been consistently and closely linked with wider European cultural and political developments' (Solana 2000). Consequently, the EU discourse on Ukraine reflected the dilemma of inclusion or exclusion, a dilemma that was particularly clear during the drafting of the Common Strategy, when the EU faced 'the most difficult and politically demanding task ... which should provide the answer to the question of defining "Ukraine's place in Europe"' (Council of the EU 1999a: 2). The result was a declaration that 'the EU acknowledges Ukraine's aspirations and welcomes Ukraine's pro-European choice' (European Council 1999: 2), though the precise implications of this statement remain unclear.

The second element which highlighted ideational differences between the EU and Ukraine were security-related concerns about Ukraine being potentially one of the most disruptive states in Central and Eastern Europe, in particular, and in Europe generally. The source of these concerns was a fear of political, economic, and social (inter-ethnic) instability, which could result in domestic and inter-state armed conflicts, with the potential for disruptive effects across the entire continent (Moreno 2006). Ukraine was associated with 'hard' challenges to security, such as its nuclear status, the stationing of nuclear weapons on its soil and its nuclear power plant at Chernobyl. Related to these problems, the EU also represented Ukraine as a source of 'soft', yet still significant, challenges to security. These anxieties came to play a dominant role in EU narratives on Ukraine, especially within the context of the EU's eastern enlargement, which '[would] increase EU awareness of "soft" security threats from Ukraine, in the fields of environment, nuclear safety, justice and home affairs (illegal immigration, organised crime, money laundering, etc.) and public health' (Commission 2001: 1).

The EU narrative also recognised the potential positive contribution of Ukraine to security in Europe. Therefore, the EU underlined Ukraine's involvement 'in the stabilisation of its region and encouraged the strengthening of Ukraine's role in regional cooperation institutions' and its 'commitment to nuclear disarmament as well as its cooperation in the maintenance of European and international peace and security' (European Council 1999: 1). However, such recognition was challenged by the rationale behind the development of ENP, which instead stressed the security concerns of EU member states. The clearest statement of such regional concerns is found in the European Security Strategy of 2003, which stated that neighbours 'engaged in violent conflict, weak states where organized crime flourishes, dysfunctional societies or exploding population growth on its borders all pose problems for Europe' (European Council 2003: 7). Within this general context, ENP was meant to tackle 'soft' security threats such as 'migration, asylum, visa policy, measures to combat terrorism, organized crime, trafficking in drugs and arms, money laundering and financial and economic crime' (Commission 2004b: 17).

In sum, the EU narrative highlighted both the uncertainty of the 'European' character of Ukraine, as well as its status as a country that was itself a source of instability and security problems.

The Ukrainian pursuit of recognition of its European character

In contrast with the EU narratives described above, Ukraine has distanced itself from the Soviet Union and Russia in its international discourse. This pursuit of the recognition of its distinctiveness from Russia formed part of the process of establishing a Ukrainian international identity pursued by Ukrainian elites during the 1990s (Burant 1995: 1137–8; D'Anieri 1997, 1999; Prizel 1998: 365–8, 376–9; Solchanyk 2001: 92–3). In order to carve out its identity, Ukraine sought recognition by other European countries as an independent, viable and predictable actor situated in the centre of the European continent. In this context, Europe constituted a continuously dominant positive point of reference that Ukraine used to express its aspirations to be part of a broader European 'political grouping'.

Ukraine presented itself as a consolidated member of the community of European nations that had 'traversed the road from a quasi-State within the former USSR to a universally recognized European State' (United Nations 1992: 17). This discourse, which emphasised the European character of Ukraine and its aim of integration into European and Euro-Atlantic institutions, was based mainly on 'natural' geographical, historical and geopolitical arguments (Tarasyuk 2000; Wolczuk 2000) and the country's geopolitical importance to the whole continent (Udovenko 1995, 1997; Tarasyuk 1998).

This pursuit of recognition of Ukraine's 'European' nature was closely linked with security considerations. During the first years of independence, Ukraine feared being marginalised or of merely ending up acting as a 'buffer' between Europe and Russia (Udovenko 1996). Ukraine stressed that 'recognition by the European Union of the considerable importance of Ukraine in the creation of a new European security architecture may and shall be utilized as an important tool of realization of Ukrainian interests in the relations with the EU' (Decree of the President 1998). The most recurrent elements of Ukrainian security discourse represented Ukraine as a country that voluntarily renounced nuclear weapons. However, one of the arguments employed to convince European actors of the sincerity of Kiev's 'European' aspirations was the promotion of Ukrainian responsibilities for providing security to the European continent. Ukraine represented itself as a country that supported and actively participated in all undertakings aimed at enhancing security in Europe, and it duly sought recognition by other partners of its role as 'security provider' in Europe (Udovenko 1997; Tarasyuk 1998). Ukraine's contribution to European security was also considered by Ukrainian representatives as proof of its adherence to European values and principles. As argued by the Ukrainian Minister of Foreign Affairs:

> Wherever there is a danger to Europe and its democratic values, and wherever conflicts jeopardize peace and stability, Ukraine will be there to help, because we realize that any local instability poses a threat to the whole of Europe and to unity. Ukraine believes that European affairs are our affairs and our responsibility, now and in the future. (Tarasyuk 2000)

In summary, we may observe that the discourses of the EU and Ukraine, in terms of both its 'European' status and its contribution to the European security system, diverged considerably. Different perceptions of the sources of security challenges, and the question of responsibility for tackling these challenges, reflected Ukraine's desire for recognition as a wholly 'European' actor, thus demonstrating its sense of responsibility for providing security to Europe. This fundamental divergence of views between the EU and Ukraine led Ukraine to propose various measures to institutionalise the relationship between the EU and Ukraine, in order to demonstrate its credentials as security provider.

Institutionalising cooperation on CFSP: Ukrainian expectations and EU reluctance

The issues that fall under the remit of CFSP have constituted one of the significant elements of EU–Ukraine relations since 1998. Since this time, Ukraine and the EU have consulted one another regularly on international issues of interest to both parties. These consultations on issues such as the situation in Belarus, Russia and Moldova, and sometimes on the developments in GUAM, the Balkans and the Middle East, have been commonly held during bilateral and international summits and other bilateral working meetings. During these consultations, Ukraine has demonstrated its predisposition to become further involved in cooperation in the CFSP field, beyond the limited scope of the political consultations foreseen in the Partnership and Cooperation Agreement.

Specifically, Ukraine has shown its willingness to be invited to align itself with the most visible result of the day-to-day operation of the CFSP: the Presidency declarations. In 2000, for example, Ukraine presented far-reaching proposals concerning the nature of EU–Ukraine cooperation on CFSP matters. Furthermore, in 2000, the EU Presidency work plans on the implementation of the 'Common Strategy on Ukraine' raised the possibility of Ukraine's unilateral alignment with EU declarations and Common Positions (Council of the EU 2000b: 4), and even the possibility of an official invitation to endorse the Presidency statements adopted under CFSP (Council of the EU 2000c: 5). Nevertheless, between 2001 and the adoption of the ENP Action Plan in 2005, the EU blocked further cooperation with Ukraine on CFSP matters owing to a rapid deterioration both of the international standing of Ukraine and of bilateral EU–Ukraine relations, especially in the light of the continued violation of human rights and fundamental freedoms by the Kuchma administration (1994–2005). Furthermore, domestic political turbulence in Ukraine, and the struggle between the opposition and the President's administration, confirmed EU concerns that Ukraine constituted a problem for its neighbours regarding security and stability.

Despite the fact that Ukrainian proposals made in 2000 for cooperation in the CFSP field were not officially accepted by the EU, Ukraine began to align itself with EU statements and declarations on a unilateral basis. Although no official record was made public, according to Ukrainian diplomats, during the period 2000–4 Ukraine aligned itself with about 92 per cent of the CFSP acts.[3] Up until 2004, Ukraine and the EU had established various working schemes of cooperation, including consultation on cooperation in the OSCE framework, non-proliferation and disarmament. As a result, before ENP was put into place, the European Commission stated that 'the EU–Ukraine political dialogue has intensified considerably over the past years. It has yielded practical results and paved the way for further discussions, including on regional issues, conflict prevention and settlement' (Commission 2004a: 10). Notwithstanding this positive assessment, CFSP matters included in the EU–Ukraine Action Plan within the framework of ENP were rather narrow, in terms of their scope and degree of cooperation. In fact, all the elements of the Action Plan in the CFSP field improved already existing mechanisms of relations (The Cooperation Council 2005: 10–13).

It was only as a consequence of the Orange Revolution in Ukraine that the EU included one further element of CFSP cooperation in the ENP Action

Plan: that of alignment with CFSP acts. The political decision that 'Ukraine should be invited, on a case by case basis, to align itself with EU positions on regional and international issues' (Council of the EU 2005c: 14) was made public in February 2005. As a consequence, the EU put into practice guidelines on the modalities for Ukraine's alignment with EU declarations, *démarches*, and common positions in the area of CFSP. In May 2005, Ukraine established an internal procedure for decision-making when invited to align itself with CFSP acts. The EU Presidency invitation issued 'on a case by case basis' permits Ukraine, on a voluntary basis, to align itself publicly with CFSP positions previously agreed by the EU member states (Council of the EU 2005b). Therefore, in comparison with the previous practice of unilateral alignments, the EU granted Ukraine the 'publicity' elements that ensured, to some extent, the recognition of membership in a wider community of European countries that cooperate with the EU on CFSP matters.[4] Thereafter, at the end of CFSP declarations or at the beginning of EU Presidency statements delivered within international organisations, there is the clause that Ukraine (and other invited countries) 'align themselves with this declaration/statement'.

As a result, according to Ukrainian experts, since 2005, consultations on CFSP matters have evolved towards a more structured, organised and intensified cooperation (Ukrainian Centre for Economic and Political Studies 2007: 6). Similarly, cooperation on CFSP matters has acquired greater visibility and, since the implementation of ENP, the European Commission has evaluated the cooperation between the EU and Ukraine in the CFSP area positively, observing progress and more regular and intense interactions in this area (Commission 2006b: 2, 2008e: 2, 2009e: 5).

Ukraine's alignment with CFSP acts: instrumental convergence

In this section, we assess of the degree of convergence of Ukraine with the EU in terms of concrete cases of cooperation within the CFSP field, specifically, of alignment with CFSP declarations, EU common positions, EU statements made at the OSCE Permanent Council and voting behaviour at the General Assembly of the United Nations (UNGA).[5] A survey of Ukraine's alignment with the CFSP acts made between June 2005 and June 2009 shows that Ukraine aligned itself with 2056 out of 2285 CFSP acts, i.e. about 90 per cent of all CFSP acts issued by the EU to which Ukraine was invited to align itself. According to the Ukrainian register, the total number of non-alignments was 229 for this 49–month period, which represents an average of 42 acts of alignment and five acts of non-alignment per month. However, the alignment pattern varies considerably in the cases of different CFSP acts issued by the EU.

Table 9.1 Ukraine's alignment with CFSP declarations

	2005 (since June)	2006	2007	2008	2009 (until May)	Total
Total CFSP declarations	99	138	103	152	59	551
Alignment	91	124	91	119	51	476
Non-alignment	5	4	5	21	3	38
Alignment not requested	3	10	7	12	5	37

Source: Author's elaboration using data from Ukraine's register, the *Bulletin of the European Union* and the Council of the European Union website.

Alignment with CFSP declarations

Since June 2005, Ukraine has been invited to align itself with CFSP declarations issued by the Presidency on behalf of the EU. As we can see in Table 9.1, during the four-year period of analysis (June 2005–May 2009) Ukraine aligned itself with 476 CFSP declarations issued by the EU Presidency on behalf of the EU out of the 514 invitations issued, which indicates substantial convergence between the EU and Ukraine on international affairs.[6]

The level of non-alignment with CFSP declarations indicates, in broad terms, the scope of convergence between the EU and the aligning country. During the period of analysis, Ukraine failed to align with only 38 of the CFSP declarations, which covered the broad spectrum of issues, areas and countries concerned. There is only one long-term, clear-cut pattern of non-alignment with CFSP declarations, namely those relating to the political situation and human rights problems in Uzbekistan. In some cases, we may also observe a degree of prudence when it comes to decisions on whether or not to align. For example, Ukraine usually aligns itself with declarations concerning Azerbaijan, Russia, Iran or Taiwan/China, but in these cases Ukrainian decision-makers evaluate cautiously the scope of each declaration and in some cases opt for non-alignment. As explained by one Ukrainian diplomat, such caution is necessary because Ukrainian alignment with an EU act might be perceived as 'hostile', thus impinging on its relationship with countries of 'special interest' to Ukraine.[7]

This high level of alignment by Ukraine with the EU may be explained in terms of the nature of both the incentives in, and the legitimacy of, this mechanism of cooperation. First of all, the low costs of alignment also have to do with their ease of implementation. The changes required within the Ukrainian administration consist only of setting up the technical means of coordination and communication between Ukraine's representation in Brussels and the Ministry of Foreign Affairs in Kiev. At the same time, the ministerial bureaucracy involved in aligning with CFSP declarations acquired additional domestic leverage; the alignment process has had the effect of enhancing the position of the Ukrainian Ministry of Foreign Affairs relative to other branches of the executive involved in foreign policy decision-making.[8]

Secondly, alignment with CFSP declarations essentially signals political support for EU positions on international affairs. It can be considered a significant symbolic reward since it means in some sense participation in EU foreign policy. At the same time, it is not politically costly to align with CFSP declarations. The CFSP declarations address a broad range of issues in thematic and geographical terms, and their content is mainly of a symbolic nature. In most cases, CFSP declarations simply fill in the gaps in Ukrainian foreign policy agenda in those areas where Ukraine has not established its own political position due to a lack of interest or resources, or where such a position does not cause problems of compatibility with previous policies. At the same time, countries that fail to align are not subject to punishment by the EU. Indeed, there exist a variety of different reasons why an invited country might refuse to support a specific CFSP declaration, which may have nothing to do with its political content.[9] As a consequence, refusal to support a CFSP declaration is of relatively low cost because the true reasons for non-alignment are not made public in every case. It is only in exceptional circumstances that non-alignment may incur a cost for nations such as Ukraine, in terms of public criticism. As a result, the country generally avoids public criticism, but gains appreciation and gratitude.

In concrete terms, the statistics on alignment with CFSP declarations were used to illustrate the increase in cooperation and dialogue on CFSP matters. In 2008, the European Commission noted that Ukraine 'aligned itself with nearly all of the EU's CFSP declarations open to alignment' (Commission 2008e: 6). Additionally, in summit declarations both parties have continuously stressed how Ukraine's alignment with EU positions on regional and international issues is a particularly positive example of bilateral cooperation (Council of the EU 2005a: 1–2, 2006a: 2, 2007b: 2) leading to ever-closer political convergence (Council of the EU 2008a: 5). Thus, for Ukraine, as well as for the EU, alignment with CFSP acts has illustrated specific achievements in this policy area.

In terms of the rewards for cooperation described above, Ukrainian elites generally think that a good track record of alignment with CFSP declarations could provide positive arguments, to be used when bargaining with the EU on the further deepening of bilateral relations and on recognising Ukraine's 'European aspiration'. For example, a leading Ukrainian expert has stated that, due to Ukraine's good track record in aligning with CFSP acts, 'it may be assumed that political association in the relations between Ukraine and the EU is *de facto* in place' and that if this tendency continues, 'not only a chance but a need will arise to incorporate the new *status quo* in the new agreement' (Sushko 2007: 166).

Ukraine's high degree of alignment with CFSP declarations also has at its core the desire for greater integration with the EU, because alignment is very much related to the aim of acquiring the image of 'good Europeans' who demonstrate their credentials through 'deeds not declarations'.[10] In fact, the Ukrainian insistence on being involved in CFSP cooperation indicates the high level of legitimacy the country attributes to it. The self-identification of an important group of Ukrainian policy-makers with the European and Euro-Atlantic communities constitutes the background for Ukraine's cooperation on CFSP matters. As stated by Ukraine's Minister of Foreign Affairs, 'sharing EU goals and values, we launched a process of alignment of our foreign policy to the EU Common Foreign and Security Policy. As a sign of our practical commitment to declared policy of European integration we have been aligning with the EU CFSP statements' (Tarasyuk 2006). These sorts of normative utterances have become stronger and more frequent, particularly following the 'European choice' that was made regarding the orientation of Ukrainian foreign policy following the Orange Revolution. Additionally, the dynamics of socialisation have been in place since the beginning of the 2000s, when, in addition to high-level political dialogue, possibilities of dialogue on foreign policy and security matters were also introduced at the working level of diplomats and experts. In 2001, it was noted that 'these contacts made it possible to observe a convergence of opinions on regional issues, particularly relations with Russia, the situation in the Balkans and Belarus, and on questions of disarmament and non-proliferation' (Council of the EU, 2001a: 5). These channels of contact served also to explain to the EU why Ukraine could not align itself with CFSP declarations in some cases.

Alignment with CFSP common positions

Compared to CFSP declarations, common positions are a more demanding kind of act, due to the fact that they contain binding commitments that may have more substantive implications for foreign policy, and usually consist of the introduction of sanctions or other restrictive measures against particular countries, individuals or groups of people. The EU very rarely issues an invitation to align with common positions. During the period of analysis, the EU invited Ukraine to align with only 10 EU common positions. As a result, Ukraine declared that it 'shared the objectives' of six of the common positions and did not align itself with four of them. This lower degree of convergence is relatively invariable over time; in only one case was there a change in a previously held Ukrainian position. Specifically, in March 2007, Ukraine declared that it 'shared the objectives' of the common position on further measures supporting the effective implementation of the mandate of the International Criminal Tribunal for the Former Yugoslavia (ICTY), with which Ukraine had failed to align itself in October 2005.

In contrast, Ukraine has continually refused to align with the common positions on the introduction of diplomatic and/or trade sanctions with Uzbekistan, Belarus, the Transnistrian region of the Republic of Moldova and Burma/Myanmar. Ukraine has provided no official reasons for this. However, Ukrainian diplomats recognise that the cases of Uzbekistan, Belarus and Transnistria are very sensitive and that it is necessary to maintain normal channels of diplomatic relations with these actors. Uzbekistan is cited as being important for Ukraine's energy security, and cooperation with Belarus is deemed as essential for managing issues such as the consequences of the Chernobyl disaster, border management, and immigration policies.[11] In the case of the common position on the Transnistrian leadership, Ukraine participated in the diplomatic negotiations on conflict settlement within the OSCE and, therefore, views it as counterproductive to adopt measures that would limit its room for manoeuvre in this area. In such cases, the potential long-term rewards do not compensate for the short- and mid-term costs of supporting the EU positions. In this context, it is not absolutely clear why Ukraine did not align with common positions on Burma/Myanmar, but it seems that Ukraine was attempting to maintain profitable arms trade contracts with this country.[12] This points to the considerable importance of Ukraine's cost–benefit calculations in determining whether or not to align itself with common positions, as for example made clear in its aligning with those aimed at combating terrorism, Zimbabwe, the Former Yugoslav Republic of Macedonia, Congo and the International Criminal Tribunal for the Former Yugoslavia, all of which are related to issues not considered to be high priorities on Ukraine's foreign policy agenda.

Ukraine's alignment with EU common positions also varies in terms of the legitimacy with which it views them, ascribing a lower level of authority to one particular group of common positions than others. The low degree of EU coherence in the common positions on the introduction of restrictive measures against Uzbekistan and Belarus has traditionally served to justify Ukraine's refusal to align with them. The common positions on these countries have hitherto prompted disagreement among member states, thus limiting the legitimacy attributed to them by Ukraine. In addition, these specific cases are perceived by Ukraine from the broader perspective of other conflicts existing within Europe and the post-Soviet space, in which the EU appears to be a rather inconsistent actor. The lack of a consistent EU approach to 'frozen conflicts' has been raised by Ukraine on many occasions, thus justifying its reluctance to accept EU political positions on the security problems that exist in the post-Soviet area. Ukrainian diplomats have highlighted their view that the EU lacks comprehensive policy on these issues, which are of primary concern for Ukrainian security policy. For example, Ukraine has concerns that the status of Kosovo may set a precedent for frozen conflicts in other post-Soviet countries, such as Transnistria in Moldova, Abkhazia and Southern Ossetia in Georgia, and Nagorno-Karabakh in Azerbaijan. Ukraine has also expressed the view that the EU has no well-established political stance on the problems affecting this area, due to a lack of specific 'knowledge and experience' in dealing with the post-Soviet countries. It would thus appear that Kiev does not really perceive the EU as an authoritative actor in any position to contribute to the settlement of conflicts and crises in the region.

Alignment with Presidency Declarations at the OSCE Permanent Council

The OSCE Permanent Council is a body that consists of permanent representatives of participating countries, which meets weekly and whose aim is to discuss and make decisions on all issues related to areas of OSCE competences and interest. It is common practice for the EU Presidency to adopt positions and issue declarations on behalf of all member states. Since 2005, it has been common practice for Ukraine to align itself with these declarations as well. During the Permanent Council sessions between June 2005 and May 2009, Ukraine aligned itself with 343 declarations (69 per cent) while failing to align in 154 cases (31 per cent). This is a much lower degree of alignment than with CFSP declarations, which might be attributed mainly to cost–benefit calculations.

As in the case of the common positions, alignment with EU Presidency statements at the OSCE is considered by Ukraine to be a relatively high-cost decision. The issues most frequently debated by the OSCE relate to the post-Soviet countries, a region for which Ukraine has a well-established foreign policy agenda. This is especially true for Uzbekistan, Tajikistan, Kazakhstan, Turkmenistan and Belarus, with whom Ukraine has tried to develop its own independent set of policies aimed at ensuring a continued energy supply and markets for Ukrainian products. In addition, alignment with EU statements in relation to these countries is particularly costly, due to the fact that the statements are made during sessions of the OSCE Council and normally trigger harsh criticism from the representatives of the states concerned. It is thus hardly surprising that Ukraine fails to align itself with many of the declarations concerning these countries, especially those condemning the violation of human rights and fundamental freedoms. Similar political factors come into play in a second set of cases of non-alignment, which includes statements related to Georgia, Azerbaijan and Moldova. Nevertheless, Ukraine has firmly supported many EU statements and declarations concerning the situations in South Ossetia and Abkhazia.

At the same time, more than half the Ukrainian non-alignments are related to EU statements of a more ceremonial or procedural nature. These include, for example, statements made following addresses delivered by high-ranking officials during Council sessions (in most cases Ministers of Foreign Affairs of OSCE member states) and statements about reports from different OSCE missions or from other OSCE bodies pertaining to their activities.

Alignment with EU voting at the General Assembly of the United Nations

The strengthening of cooperation in 2005 between the EU and Ukraine regarding CFSP was also reflected at the United Nations. The new mechanisms of cooperation allowed Ukraine to position itself closer to the EU (or at least a majority of its member states) during voting on resolutions in the UNGA. In a similar way to the case of CFSP declarations, this also indicates that Ukraine attributes a high degree of legitimacy to EU positions on international affairs. In addition, voting on these resolutions is relatively low cost due to the fact that resolutions generally constitute a political compromise adopted by an overwhelming majority of states. Only in a small number of instances do resolutions cause serious divergences among states, in which case voting behaviour acquires political significance.

During the three sessions of the General Assembly (GA) analysed (2002–4) prior to the strengthening of the cooperation between Ukraine and the EU on CFSP matters, Ukraine diverged from the common position of the EU in 17 to 20 per cent of the recorded votes on resolutions. Conversely, in 2005 this divergence dropped to 6.8 per cent of votes, and during the following two GA sessions, Ukraine's voting was aligned almost fully with that of the EU. The only exceptions were voting on the very sensitive and problematic Declaration on the Rights of Indigenous People in September 2007 (adopted after 20 years of negotiations) and on the resolution on the situation in the occupied territories of Azerbaijan. In the first case, Ukraine abstained, along with 11 other countries (e.g. Georgia, Azerbaijan, Russian Federation), while the EU voted in favour of this declaration (with the exception of Romania, who was absent), despite concerns raised among member states regarding references to self-determination and collective and individual rights. In the second case, support of continued negotiations on the Nagorny Karabakh conflict within the framework of the OSCE's Minsk Group, Ukraine voted in favour, while France voted against, and the remaining EU member states abstained. In those cases where there was no EU common position during the voting on resolutions, detailed scrutiny of the votes recorded places Ukraine in the mainstream of the positions adopted by member states. During the period 2002–8, EU votes were divided in 108 cases, and Ukraine voted in line with the majority of EU member states in 79 cases.

Analysis of the voting on concrete resolutions is especially illustrative of this tendency to follow EU voting patterns. During the six sessions of the GA of the United Nations during the period 2002–8, Ukraine's votes diverged from those of the EU in 21 resolutions on a variety of different topics. However, in 2006, a major policy shift was observed when Ukraine changed its pattern of previous votes in seven of the resolutions subject to annual voting, thus indicating an intent to align with the EU position in these areas.[13] In order to achieve this alignment, Ukraine changed its voting behaviour on resolutions related to questions of international security and, in particular, paradoxically on resolutions on nuclear weapons issues, thus diverging from the traditionally strong Ukrainian support for denuclearisation initiatives. These observations, as well as the continued alignment with EU statements during the debates of the GA, leads one to conclude that Ukraine has incorporated alignment with EU positions into its general behaviour at the UNGA. However, in 2005, Ukraine faced serious dilemmas concerning two resolutions on human rights in Uzbekistan and Turkmenistan. In both cases, Ukraine abstained from adopting any position on those issues in order to avoid criticism by the EU and/or the Central Asian countries. Finally, the tendency for Ukraine to align with the EU is confirmed when its voting pattern is compared with that of the United States or Russia. For example, during voting on 85 resolutions of the 61st session of the UNGA, Ukraine and the United States voted differently in 63 cases, and Ukraine voted differently from Russia in 31 cases.

Conclusion

In Ukraine's alignment with CFSP acts, it can be seen that EU policies in the security field have had a considerable impact on Ukraine. Out of the four cases addressed, two show a strong effect on alignment (CFSP declarations and voting behaviour at the UNGA), and the remaining two, a medium effect on alignment (common positions and EU statements made at the OSCE Permanent Council). The cases of medium effect reveal the importance of short-term costs within the structure of incentives. More precisely, it is this variable that offers the most convincing explanation for Ukrainian alignment with the EU. In the two cases where convergence is considered 'medium', the short-term costs were considered to be too high to be compensated for by future rewards. In addition, it has been shown that the cases of medium effect were also brought about by Ukraine's perception that the EU is not really a consistent and authoritative actor. Notwithstanding these exceptions, the overall high convergence with EU policies regarding CFSP shows that Ukraine has demonstrated a high level of receptiveness to EU policies. However, this influence of the EU on Ukrainian foreign policy reveals a broader phenomena of Ukrainian association with the European security community.

As we have seen in this chapter, the EU and Ukraine have approached security as a value, but meanings attached to it were initially at odds. Both actors have shared the idea that the provision of security is closely associated with the notion of being 'Europeans', but uncertainty has been felt as to whether Ukraine might be considered a member of the European security community or rather a source of concerns for it. This notwithstanding, Ukraine overcame EU reservations and engaged in a process of associating with EU positions on international affairs. The explanation for Ukraine's persistence in engaging in closer cooperation with the EU on foreign policy matters is related to Ukrainian considerations that it has to prove its role as security provider in Europe and, as a consequence, improve Ukrainian chances of being recognised as a member of the European security community. Ukraine's self-identification with Europe allowed the EU to enjoy considerable leverage in the process of drawing Ukraine closer to its positions and world views on international affairs. As a result, this diplomatic cooperation between Ukraine and the EU has two implications: firstly the EU opened the gate (at least partially) to the community of meaning attached to security to include a former 'outsider', and secondly the mechanisms of geographical differentiation and bilateralism included in ENP provided flexible forms of cooperation in this particular field.

Notes

1. This chapter falls within EUPROX 'Coordinación, Integración y Europeización en la Proximidad de la Unión Europea (Mediterráneo y Europa Oriental)', a research project of the Observatory of European Foreign Policy funded by the National Plan R+D of the Spanish Ministry of Education and Science (SEJ2006–03134/CPOL). I am grateful to Ulrich Sedelmeier, Anna Herranz Surrallés, Ignasi Guardans and the editors and authors of this volume for their comments on earlier drafts.
2. First, the Treaty of Lisbon changed the EU's mechanisms of institutional cooperation with third countries in the CFSP field. Second, the new President introduced some changes to Ukraine's overall approach to cooperation with the EU. Both facts influenced Ukraine's convergence with the EU in foreign and security policies, but it seems that their exact consequences remain circumscribed rather more to some institutional problems of everyday interactions than to a general shift in the dynamics of convergence analysed in this chapter. However, at the moment of drafting this chapter it was still premature to draw any comprehensive conclusions on the Ukraine–EU cooperation in the CFSP field after 2010.
3. Interview with Ukrainian diplomat, Brussels, 29 March 2007. Similarly, in 2004 the European Commission recognised that Ukraine aligns itself unilaterally with a 'large number of EU declarations in the framework of CFSP' (Commission 2004a: 10).
4. The procedure of alignment with CFSP declarations was introduced in the 1990s for candidate countries or members of the European Free Trade Area. Since 2003, it has been possible for members of the Stabilisation and Association Process to align themselves with CFSP declarations as well.
5. All data presented to illustrate these cases are based on the author's calculations and drawn from primary source documents available to the wider public, namely the *Bulletin of the European Union*, minutes of OSCE Permanent Council sessions, and minutes of General Assembly of the United Nations sessions.
6. In 37 cases, the EU did not issue an invitation to align, mainly in cases that were particularly urgent or politically very sensitive.
7. Interview with a Ukrainian diplomat, Barcelona, 29 January 2009.
8. Ibid.
9. According to the author's correspondence with the Secretariat General of the Council of the European Union (DGF – information to the public, 18 February 2008), the EU itself may not invite a specific country to align; secondly, the decision on alignment

may be received after the deadline; thirdly, the invited country may not reply to the invitation at all. Only in a fourth case may an invited country refuse to align with a CFSP declaration. As confirmed by the Ukrainian Ministry of Foreign Affairs there have been several cases of non-alignment due to administrative and temporal constraints that have led to late replies.
10 Interview with a Ukrainian diplomat, Brussels, 29 March 2007.
11 Ibid.
12 A Ukrainian company signed an arms contract in 2003 for a 10-year period for delivery of 1000 armoured personnel carriers worth $500 million. However, further to this, it was reported that Myanmar failed to meet its payment obligations on time and the prospects for this contract are unclear (Parker 2006).
13 Among the 21 cases of diverging resolutions, only 10 resolutions were voted on during all the sessions of the GA analysed in the period 2002–7. In the same period, the EU changed its position only once in a way that resulted in alignment with the Ukrainian position. Five resolutions were voted on only once in the period analysed. It is thus not possible to observe any changes in these positions.

Anke Schmidt-Felzmann

10

Conducting relations with a difficult neighbour: the EU's struggle to influence Russian domestic politics

Introduction

The Russian Federation has a special place in the EU's relations with its neighbours. Russia remains, by its own choice, outside the political umbrella of the European Neighbourhood Policy (launched in 2005) and the EU's 'eastern dimension', the Eastern Partnership (EaP, launched in 2009). Since Russian political elites rejected the EU's plan to group Russia together with the countries of the Community of Independent States (CIS) and the Southern Mediterranean states, the EU pursues its official relations with Russia separately from the EaP (Commission 2008c) despite the fact that developments in the EU's Russia policy are in practice influenced by, and intertwined with, the EU's policies towards the EaP states and the Central Asian states that remain outside the EaP framework.

Despite the close links between the EU's relations with Russia and relations with the other Eastern and Central Asian states in the EU's proximity, the EU's engagement with Russia is qualitatively different from that with the other 'neighbours' in the East and South. The Russian Federation is regarded as a 'strategic partner' of major importance to the EU (European Security Strategy 2003): Russia is the single most powerful state among the EU's neighbours by virtue of its elevated international status that stems from its historical position of power, its nuclear capabilities and its vast natural resources. The country is also of considerable importance as a market for EU goods and as a supplier of primary energy resources. As the largest neighbour of the EU, it shares land or sea borders with more than a third of all EU member states.[1] The close proximity, its status as major nuclear power and its importance as a major energy producer, mean that political and economic developments in Russia are of considerable importance to the EU as they are likely to directly affect EU member states. Geographically, politically and economically, these are key reasons why EU member states and the supranational institutions have invested considerable resources and efforts in developing the EU's relations with Russia in a fruitful, constructive manner, and why guaranteeing Russia's domestic political and economic stability is regarded as an overriding priority.

The promotion of the EU's fundamental, constitutive values has been a key objective pursued by the EU in its relations with Russia. The Maastricht Treaty (Treaty on European Union, TEU) of 1992, which created the modern EU, declared that the principles of liberty, democracy, respect for human rights and fundamental freedoms were the central values of the EU (TEU 1992, art. 6) stipulating the promotion of these values as a core component of the EU's external relations. The Treaty demanded that the EU member states 'safeguard the common values' and 'develop and consolidate democracy and the rule of law, and respect for human rights and fundamental freedoms' in their relations with third countries (TEU 1992, art. 11 (1)). The Lisbon Treaty (Treaty on the Functioning of European Union, TFEU[2]) of 2007 reiterated these fundamental principles (TFEU 2007, art. 2; see also Preamble and art. 6) and the need for the member states to promote and uphold them in their external relations (TFEU 2007, art. 3 (5); see also art. 8).

The new Russian constitution of December 1993 also enshrined democratic principles and, with Russia's accession to the Council of Europe in January 1996, Russia became formally committed to implementing the human rights standards and democratic principles which are enshrined in the Council's legally binding agreements. The EU–Russian Partnership and Cooperation Agreement (PCA) of 1994 which entered into force in 1997 also declared the importance of democratic principles, respect for human rights and the rule of law and the joint ambition to ensure Russia's consolidation as a democratic country (PCA 1994, Preamble, art. 1 and Title I, art. 2). Operating on the assumption that the values of democracy, a multi-party system, respect for human rights and civil liberties, and the rule of law are 'essential prerequisites for political stability' (Commission 2003b: 7) and that their effective promotion thus forms a precondition for achieving prosperity, stability and consequent long-term security in the EU's neighbourhood ('values as part of security'), EU officials and national governments undertook considerable efforts over the course of the 1990s and 2000s, in terms of financial and technical assistance, to aid in Russia's political and economic transition.

Despite strengthening cooperation in a broad range of policy fields, a European Parliament report of 2004 noted that: 'Russia has not gone through a transition of the kind foreseen when ... the EU, formulated its basic response to developments there a decade ago ... instead, and against the common values on which the EU–Russia bilateral relationship is to be built, a "managed democracy" is being consolidated, contrary to key EU principles'

(European Parliament 2004: para AB). Furthermore, towards the end of the decade, observers noted that Russia's domestic political reforms had stalled, some arguing that the democratisation process had been effectively reversed with Russia becoming a semi-authoritarian political system during Putin's second presidential term – despite Russia's formal status as an electoral, multi-party democracy (see Light 2009; Pridham 2009; Sakwa 2008). By 2008, Russia experts including Richard Sakwa (2008: 897) deemed the democratisation process to have been effectively 'derailed'; Margot Light (2009: 88–9) put forth that the Russian Duma had turned into a 'pocket parliament', seriously undermining Russia's status as democracy.[3] Russia's political trajectory is in marked contrast to the leverage the EU has exerted over political and economic developments in the countries of Central and Eastern Europe, including its success in getting the 12 new member states that joined the EU in 2004 and 2007 to radically transform their political and economic systems in preparation for EU accession. Russia remains – besides Belarus (see Bosse 2013, this volume) – the Eastern neighbour that the EU has most struggled to influence since the collapse of the Soviet Union in 1991.

This chapter aims to shed light on why the EU has held so little sway over developments in Russia since the end of the Cold War. Despite the importance EU member states have attributed to Russian reforms and their individual and collective investment of human resources and financial and technical aid to help along Russia's transition, the EU has struggled to influence Russia since the collapse of the Soviet Union. The EU's difficulties in bringing about the desired changes in Russia have primarily been attributed to two reasons: a lack of leverage and internal divisions among the member states (see, e.g., Gower 2007; Timmins 2007; Blockmans 2008). This chapter examines both assumptions: it explores the reasons for the EU's weak performance as a 'values promoter' by identifying, firstly, the obstacles the EU faces in its engagement with Russia externally, and secondly by identifying the internal difficulties that the EU faces in forging and pursuing a common policy towards Russia. The analysis shows that the EU's limited internal and external effectiveness (see Laatikainen and Smith 2006) account for the EU's consistent failure as a promoter of democracy, human rights and the rule of law in Russia. The EU's external effectiveness is measured and analysed by examining the EU's capabilities and bargaining power in relation to Russia and its position and attractiveness for Russia. The internal effectiveness of the EU is measured and analysed by the extent to which the EU member states' preferences are congruent: a congruence of views can be regarded as a precondition for successfully pursuing Russia's democratisation and for promoting the respect for human rights in Russia. By exploring a prevailing claim in the literature that certain trade and energy supply interests prevent national governments from promoting Russia's democratic development, this chapter argues that the EU's considerable difficulties in achieving the desired transformations in Russia are a result of a divergence of objectives: between the EU and Russia regarding Russia's future, and a consequence of the incongruence of member states' objectives and consequent lack of leverage of the EU vis-à-vis Russia. This highlights specifically the problems in reconciling democracy and human rights promotion with the protection of trade opportunities and energy supply security and provides insights into the extent to which the five typologies (see Chapter 1, this volume) help us understand the 'values/security' dilemma(s) faced by the EU in its efforts to promote democracy, human rights and the rule of law in Russia.

The first part of this chapter discusses the mechanisms of democracy and human rights promotion in Russia. The second part examines the EU's capabilities and its ability to influence Russia by scrutinising its bargaining power and also the congruence of the EU's objectives with those of Russia. The third part scrutinises member states' individual policies towards Russia, examining their approaches to the promotion of democracy and the protection of human rights in Russia. The fourth and final part summarises the findings and considers their implications in light of new developments during 2011 and 2012 in the economic and political sphere.

The processes and instruments of democracy and human rights promotion

In order to find out which factors have contributed to the lack of success in the EU's efforts to directly influence Russia's transformation, we need to know what the mechanisms and the conditions are that have to be present for the successful promotion of democratic principles, the respect for human rights and the rule of law in a third country such as Russia. Rational choice and social constructivist theories focus on different aspects in this regard and rather than being mutually exclusive, both perspectives provide complementary explanations of the EU's potential to influence Russian policy-makers and achieve the desired changes in Russia.

From a rational choice perspective, Russian policy-makers will only undertake the democratic reforms that the EU advocates if they – or Russia as a whole – have something to gain from doing so or something to lose from failing to implement the reforms that the EU and its member states expect it to undertake. For the EU this means that rewards have to be promised to Russia for implementing the desired changes and a failure to undertake the desired reforms would have to be met with sanctions. The Russian government can be expected to respond in the desired way only if the EU is sufficiently powerful and Russia is vulnerable to such pressures or if the EU has enticing incentives to offer that the Russian government is keen to obtain (see Jurado 2006). However, even governments of states that respond well to material incentives have been found to implement changes that are rather cosmetic and subject to reversal when incentive structures change (Jurado 2006). So although the Russian government may formally subscribe to the

EU's values regarding democracy, human rights and the rule of law, Russian officials may not regard it as necessary or desirable to act in accordance with them, and may instead interpret these values in a fashion that is more compatible with their own interests (see Schimmelfennig 2000; Sedelmeier 2005). This would mean that the adoption of these principles remains at a superficial level. For example, Kristi Raik (2005) found that the East European states that joined the EU in 2004 complied with the accession criteria imposed by the EU as 'recipients of instructions', but did not fully incorporate the norms and standards of the EU (see also Pridham 2006, 2009).

In contrast, social constructivists place greater emphasis on the effects of political elites' interaction and the power of the better argument (see Risse 2000). They expect that the Russian government's policies will be altered as a result of socialisation of Russian policy-makers, through regular interaction with representatives of EU member states and the EU institutions. Russian policy-makers would thus become gradually acquainted with the normative principles that EU officials and national representatives 'diffuse', and/or convinced by EU and national officials that the reforms regarded as important to ensure Russia's long-term stability and prosperity are desirable and necessary. The process of adopting and implementing the EU's fundamental values thus differs substantially from that which rational choice theory depicts.

Elena Jurado (2006) combines the constructivist and the rational choice perspectives, arguing that norms promotion in third countries should be viewed from a 'sequencing perspective'. In essence, the target state's actions are initially driven by instrumental reasons, but the state will develop a new identity and adopt rule-consistent behaviour in the course of its engagement with the 'values promoter'. Effective values promotion relies during the first, instrumental stage, on superior bargaining power by the values promoter over the target state; following on, practices of states change only in a lasting manner when the principles guiding their behaviour become genuinely embedded in the belief system of national decision-makers (see Sedelmeier 2005; see also Pridham 2006, 2009). Alternatively, if one departs from the view that democracy cannot be effectively established from the top down, but rather from the bottom up through civil society movements, practices of national governments will only change in a lasting manner if normative principles become embedded in the minds of the general population who will then push the governing elites to shift their priorities, or replace those that do not share their principles and belief system with candidates that do.

The EU relies on inducements, constructive engagement, critical dialogue and persuasion to influence third countries' actions, notably on normative issues (McCormick 2007; Toje 2008; Forsberg and Seppo 2009). A credible conditional EU membership prospective is considered to be the most powerful incentive for third states to undertake substantial domestic change in line with the EU's demands (see e.g., Schimmelfennig 2008): candidate countries' eagerness to join the EU has made them willing to accept and meet the conditions imposed on them by the EU (see Schimmelfennig and Sedelmeier 2004; Lavenex and Schimmelfennig 2009). In contrast, the EU's ability to influence third states not wishing to join the EU is severely constrained, especially when the target state is both uninterested in implementing reforms and powerful enough to resist the EU's pressure (Schimmelfennig and Seldelmeier 2004).

Frank Schimmelfennig and Ulrich Sedelmeier (2004) have set out the conditions that have to be met for the EU's use of conditionality to be effective. They have found that the main requirement for effective EU conditionality is that both the offer of rewards and the withholding of such rewards when the conditions are not being met are credible (Schimmelfennig and Sedelmeier 2004; Schimmelfennig 2008). Credible conditionality arises when the EU has superior bargaining power, since threats would otherwise not be convincing. Second, conditionality is credible when the EU is less interested in giving the reward than the target government is in getting it. Thirdly, conditionality is credible when the EU is consistent in its allocation of rewards (Schimmelfennig and Sedelmeier 2004). However, if the EU subordinates conditionality to other political, strategic or economic considerations, the target state (Russia) might hope to receive the benefits without fulfilling the conditions (see Schimmelfennig and Sedelmeier 2004), thus limiting the effectiveness of conditionality. In addition, if there are conflicts among EU member states about the use of conditionality, the target state (Russia) will receive inconsistent signals, and will likely be tempted to manipulate these divisions to its advantage (see Schimmelfennig and Sedelmeier 2004).

Because Russian political elites are very concerned about Russia's image in the West (see Feklyunina 2008), the EU can also try and 'shame' the Russian government into compliance through the 'public exposure of undesirable actions' (Schimmelfennig 2005a). Regardless of whether Russian political elites declared their support for the EU's fundamental values out of a sincere belief in their rightfulness and desirability of adhering to them or for instrumental reasons, the fact that they have formally committed to upholding these principles enables the EU to shame the Russian government when it deviates from these values by exposing inconsistencies between the political elite's declarations and their current behaviour (see Schimmelfennig 2005). But, as Schimmelfennig (2000: 117) argues, 'states do not have to internalize values and norms but they have to live up to them in a credible way'. It is conceivable that the Russian political elites made a formal commitment to the democratic and human rights principles for mainly instrumental reasons, such as gaining access to Western institutions and receiving financial and technical aid to help along Russia's economic transition. However, Russian political elites are concerned with what the public exposure of 'illegitimate' behaviour will do to their international standing and reputation (see

Schimmelfennig 2005a). Even if the normative commitment it made does not affect Russia's underlying interests, the Russian government will include reputation in its cost–benefit calculation regarding the implementation of the democratic and human rights principles (see Sedelmeier 2005).

I will next examine whether the preconditions that can be expected to increase the effectiveness of the EU's 'values' promotion efforts in Russia have been met: first, whether the Russian government is ready and able to undertake the reforms necessary to achieve the country's full democratisation and respect for human rights and the rule of law; second, whether the EU possesses superior bargaining power and whether it has enticing incentives that it can offer to reward the Russian government for implementing the desired reforms; third, whether the EU is internally 'effective', as a precondition for its external effectiveness: whether the member states are in agreement about the need to promote democratic principles and respect for human rights and the rule of law in Russia and, secondly, whether member states' views on the strategy to be pursued towards Russia converge – as any disagreements would allow Russian officials to exploit inconsistencies and use them to justify a policy that conflicts with the EU's fundamental principles.

The external obstacles to the EU's influence over Russia

I will now go into greater detail about how far the EU's lack of success in influencing Russian domestic developments can be attributed to a divergence of views between the two parties on how Russia's political and economic systems should evolve in order to ensure long-term stability and prosperity in Russia. This section will also explore the leverage and the incentives that the EU can apply in order to get Russian decision-makers to implement the desired reforms.

The EU's and Russia's contrasting ambitions
The EU has long faced serious difficulties in the promotion of Russia's democratisation and respect for human rights. This is despite the fact that, at the most basic level, the EU's and Russia's objectives appear to converge or at least overlap: both want to ensure that Russia transforms into a stable and prosperous country. Nevertheless, when examined more closely, it becomes evident that the Russian government's vision diverges in fact substantially from the EU's vision of the way in which the apparently shared goals should be achieved. Whereas the EU's belief is that democracy, pluralism, respect for human rights, civil liberties and the rule of law constitute 'essential prerequisites for political stability' (Commission 2003b: 7), the Russian political elites' belief is that the democratisation of Russia must be controlled by the state and that it is impossible to address the economic and social problems in the country in the absence of a strong state, or an autocratic government

(Kobrinskaya 2005). Russian political elites insist that democracy has to be 'phased in' (Putin 2005)[4] as this is the only way of protecting and strengthening the state and protecting its sovereignty in the long term, emphasising that the 'initial haste' with which democracy developed in Russia has exacerbated domestic threats to the Russian state (*Der Spiegel* 2005; Ryzhkov 2005a, 2005b; Tretyakov 2003). Both Vladimir Putin and Dmitri Medvedev have insisted, in their capacity as President of Russia, that a 'dictatorship of the law' is necessary to support civil society, to protect and strengthen democratic institutions and to safeguard democracy in Russia by maintaining order (Putin 2000, 2004a, 2005; Medvedev 2008a, 2008b, 2009). At the beginning of his presidency, Dmitri Medvedev also underlined that '[c]ivil society needs a strong state as a tool for development and maintaining order, and for protecting and strengthening democratic institutions', although he acknowledged that 'an all-powerful bureaucracy' could pose a 'mortal danger for civil society' (Medvedev 2008a). However, the adoption of new restrictive legislation in January 2006, limiting the ability of foreign non-governmental organisations (NGOs) to operate in Russia (for details see Commission 2008f, Annex 86; Light 2008; Saari 2009) and increased scrutiny of Western-funded organisations, including the forced closure of a number of British Council offices in Russia in January 2008, increased the impression that the development of civil society in Russia was being systematically restricted following the 'coloured revolutions' in Georgia and Ukraine (which, from a Russian point of view, seemed to indicate that NGOs that are funded by 'the West' could bring about undesirable political change).

The importance of the domestic dimension for the Russian leadership cannot be disregarded in this context. While Western scholars have criticised Russia's 'tutelary democracy' (Sakwa 2008: 882) or 'regulated democracy' (Light 2009: 88) as a sign of 'democratic backsliding' (Frellesen and Rontoyanni 2007: 240), with some going as far as to describe developments in Russia towards the end of the 2000s as a 'reversal of systemic change' (see, e.g., Pridham 2009: 53) – being *seen* to be strong and assertive has been of considerable importance for the Russian President(s) during the 2000s as a means of ensuring political stability after the rather chaotic years of President Yeltsin's reign during the 1990s.[5] The need for a consistent display of strength thus led to the implementation of legal changes designed to regain control over the federal regions and the strategic sectors of the economy, resulting in stronger state control in both the political and the economic sphere while the favourable economic climate, especially the speedy economic recovery through rocketing oil prices, ensured that the Russian President could maintain the public's support. This resulted in a situation where the same policies that made the Russian President popular at home moved Russia further away from a 'true' Western democracy (Schuette 2004).

An important reason for the Russian political elites' emphasis on a 'strong state' has arguably also been the ambition that Russia regains its status and influence as a global power on the international stage (see Feklyunina 2008). A strong state is required to propel Russia back into a leading position in the international arena, since a strong, determined leadership is better able to position the country internationally than a divided, weak government would be able to do. The policy aim that 'in a not too far off future, Russia will take its recognised place among the ranks of the truly strong, economically advanced and influential nations' (Putin 2003a; see also Putin 2004a, 2005) plays an important role and helps explain the priority that is attached to the strengthening of the state, and the willingness to compromise certain democratic and human rights standards. The 'need' for a strong state, notably the need for Russian political elites to retain control over the country to enable a gradual transition towards a democratic form of government in Russia, is endorsed by a large part of the Russian population, especially against the backdrop of a certain destabilisation of public life caused by several attempts by separatists (generally labelled as 'terrorists') to disrupt public order and the economic failures of the 1990s. The installation of a more authoritarian, rather than fully democratic, political regime as well as the strengthening of state control over strategic resources has for that reason not been as strongly resisted by the Russian population as Western observers might have hoped. The Russian people '[look] back at the Yeltsin years as a time of a failed western democracy export that only ended in "chaos" and of the triumph of robber capitalism that benefited only a few' (Kobrinskaya 2005). Schmidt (2005) argued in that context that democracy is defined in Russia primarily in terms of wealth and a balance of powers, namely the restriction of the oligarchs' power and influence over the political sphere. The Russian government's primary task, seen from that perspective, has therefore been to maintain Russia's 'integrity and sovereignty, protect the country against threats emanating from disruptions caused by demonstrations [and] elections etc.': in short, to limit the unwanted side effects of (EU-style) democratic procedures (Ryzhkov 2005a).

The more authoritarian turn in Russian politics that began during Putin's presidency is, from this vantage point, a safeguard for Russia's democratic development rather than the sign of a decline of democracy (Schmidt 2005). There are also voices in the EU who have argued that the objectives of promoting the democratisation of Russia and maintaining stability (both economic and political) may actually be in conflict with one another. Russia is such a vast country that strong state institutions are necessary to ensure order and stability. As a report to the European Parliament pointed out at the end of Vladimir Putin's first term as President, the threat that a 'resurgent and increasingly strong Russia' may pose to its neighbours may well be preferable to the 'perils of a weak, poor and possibly drifting and disintegrating Russia' (European Parliament 2004: 17). In addition, Russian officials have repeatedly insisted that the shape of Russia's democracy has to be adjusted and customised to the special conditions in the country (see Feklyunina 2008).

This is because, as Putin himself has argued, only reforms 'dictated by the impulses of the political life of that state itself' will create a stable and effective form of government that corresponds to 'historical realities and to the particular experience of the country in question' (Putin 2003b). A 'blind' transfer of Western models of democracy would simply not be successful in Russia (see Ivanov 2008). Therefore, Russia 'as a sovereign nation' must decide for itself the timeframe and conditions for its progress along the 'road' towards democracy, taking into account Russia's particularities (Putin 2005). Since Russian officials defend the legitimacy of the measures that the Russian government has implemented as necessary to safeguard Russia's democratic development, it is difficult for EU member states to achieve any progress by means of 'shaming' Russia. This is even more the case since some of the political elites in EU member states, foremost German Chancellor Schroeder and Italian Prime Minster Berlusconi, gave credence to Russian officials' claims that democracy in Russia has to be phased in to be sustainable (Hamburger Abendblatt 2004; Focus Online 2006; Frellesen and Rontoyanni 2007).

The differences between the EU's understanding of what the democratic values, human rights norms and rule of law mean in practice and what some leading Russian officials claim to understand by them is perhaps not as far apart as the EU's own values conception and that of the Arab states for religious, political and historical reasons (see Bezen Balamir Coskun 2013, this volume). Nevertheless, the EU's interpretation of what these values entail and how the democratisation should be pursued clash, as we have seen, with that of the Russian proponents of democracy 'à la Russe' (Bogutcaia et al. 2006), presenting EU officials and national policy-makers with a dilemma ('values versus values') of whether or not they can accept the 'translation' of the EU's fundamental values into the Russian political, historical and cultural context or whether such a translation conflicts with the essence of their values understanding.

The EU has faced two significant obstacles in its attempts to influence Russian domestic developments from the outside: first, the contrasting views that Russian officials hold about how Russia's political system should develop and the apparent support for this form of government by the Russian people; second, the Russian government's refusal to allow external state and non-governmental actors to 'interfere' in Russia's internal affairs. In order to exert its influence under these circumstances, the EU requires enticing incentives or powerful coercive instruments to effectively foster changes in Russian domestic political and economic practices.

The EU's capabilities and bargaining power
The EU's main bargaining chip to influence third or external states in its neighbourhood has been the prospect of EU membership. Scholars have emphasised that the EU's 'norm dispersion' is most effective when in the

target state there is a clear desire for, and credible prospect of, accession to the EU (e.g., Balfour 2006; Le Gloannec and Rupnik 2008; Nygren 2008). Throughout the 1990s, while Russia was economically weak and struggling with domestic political instability after the collapse of the Soviet Union, Russian political elites regarded close cooperation and integration with the major economic trading block on the European continent as important for assisting in Russia's speedy economic recovery (Newton 2003). In the transition period following the end of the Cold War, Russian political elites even seriously considered the possibility of Russia's accession to the EU as a long-term goal as it was felt that closer integration with the EU could help Russia recover its international influence (Leshukov 1998).

Russia's rapid economic recovery (see Figures 10.1 and 10.2) and its domestic political stabilisation in the early 2000s seemed to be a sign of President Putin's successful policies. With the steep increase in revenues from the export of its oil and gas, helped along by the rising oil prices on the world market, Russian elites' confidence in their country's own potential as an independent pole in the international arena grew significantly. In addition, the Russian government managed to repay most external debt and started building up substantial financial reserves in the form of a sovereign wealth fund that could be used to buffer the effects of the financial crisis in 2008 (see Pravda.ru 2006; Ivanov 2008). As a result of the economic recovery, the aspiration to EU membership was quickly abandoned and a unilateral approximation of Russia's political, legal and economic rules and standards to the EU's *acquis communautaire* was rejected as it conflicted with Russian aspirations of regaining the status of independent great power (see e.g. Tsygankov 2010). Another result of Russia's economic recovery was that the financial and technical aid that the EU and its member states had provided during the 1990s and early 2000s to support Russia's transition from a planned economic Communist state towards a democratically governed state with an open market economy, could no longer act as an incentive to undertake further reforms and conditional aid provision could no longer serve to influence Russia's reform process (see Youngs 2009).

Since membership in the EU has long ceased to act as an incentive for Russian policy-makers to implement the political and economic reforms that the EU would like Russia to introduce, and as the EU has been unable to win over Russian policy-makers with the power of the better argument (see Risse 2000), the EU's ability to influence Russian domestic politics effectively hinges on its capacity to coerce or coax Russia into implementing the desired reforms. The EU's strength as a major global trade actor and the size of its single market are generally regarded as key sources of power in relations with third states (Bretherton and Vogler 2006; Keukeleire and MacNaughtan 2008; Meunier and Nicolaidis 2011). The EU maintains a dominant and completely unrivalled position in Russia's external trade, with a 45 per cent share in Russian imports, around 60 per cent share in Russian exports and around 50

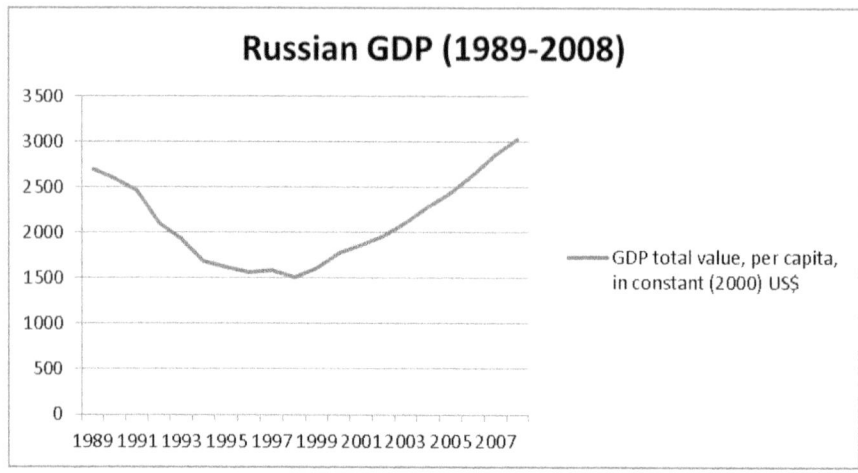

Figure 10.1   The development of Russian GDP volumes

Source: World Bank (2010). NB: figures have been rounded by the author.

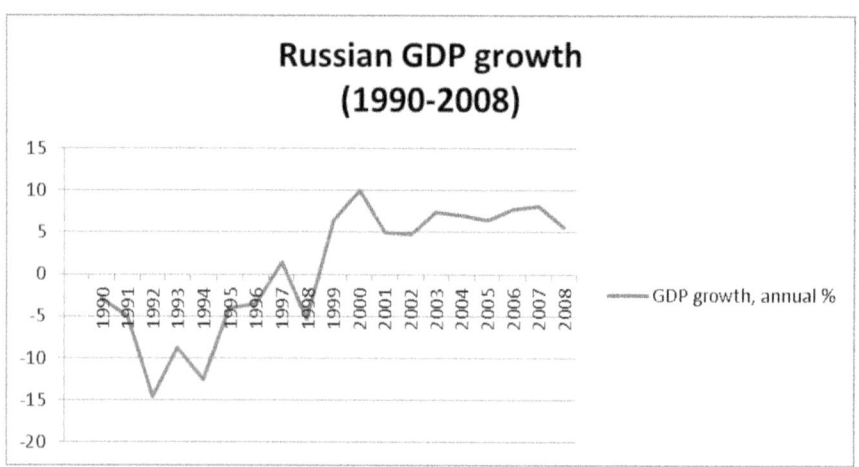

Figure 10.2 The growth of Russian GDP in the post-Cold War period

Source: World Bank (2010). NB: figures have been rounded by the author.

per cent in Russian trade overall (Commission 1995; Eurostat 2001, 2006, 2009, 2010; DG Trade 2005, 2007, 2010). Russia in contrast occupies only a comparatively small share of EU total external trade, between 5 per cent to 10 per cent, although it has grown substantially during the 2000s (see Eurostat 2001, 2006, 2009, 2010; DG Trade 2007, 2010). Economically, the EU is placed in a powerful position vis-à-vis Russia, with the EU's superior bargaining power derived from its position in global and bilateral trade, which could be expected to enable the EU to achieve its policy goals (Bastian 2006).

Despite the EU's superior resources as a global trade power and the strong asymmetry in overall trade and investment between the EU and Russia that could be expected to give the EU significant leverage, the EU does not actually possess all that many trade 'carrots' that it could employ to influence Russian domestic politics. Most of the credible trade-related incentives were already handed over to the Russian government in the 1990s and early 2000s when Russia was granted privileged access to the EU's single market. This occurred in the wake of Russia's severe economic crisis of the late 1990s, as a result of which effective support for Russia's economic recovery was ranked higher than the insistence on Russian political reforms. The priorities shifted again after Russia's swift stabilisation following the rise in global oil prices, but by then the EU's leverage was regarded as rather weak. In 2004 a European Commission Communication cautioned that the EU's leverage should not be overestimated in view of 'Russia's economic self-sufficiency and geopolitical history' (Commission 2004c, Annex II). A diplomat from one of the eastern member states cautioned in late 2007 that EU member states 'need more from Russia than Russia needs from [them]' and that the EU's leverage is very limited.[6] Even though the EU may lack enticing trade incentives, it could be expected that it possesses some leverage due to the size of the single market and the possibility of thus applying pressure by means of sanctions.

In order to assess each party's bargaining power, it is necessary to consider in addition to the total share of both parties' goods in imports and exports of the other party, the cost of adjusting to changes if one party was to suspend its trade with the other (see Keohane and Nye 2001). If one party has difficulties substituting goods from the other, the one that supplies these goods has much greater leverage than is the case vice versa. It is in this regard significant that Russia imports mainly manufactured goods from the EU whereas the EU imports mainly primary sources and Russia supplies large quantities of the EU's natural gas, crude oil and coal which account for a considerable share of total energy imports and play an important role for member states' domestic energy consumption and electricity generation (see Figures 10.3 and 10.4). A real dependence on Russian supplies exists with regard to natural gas supplies. Russia provides altogether 42 per cent of the EU's total natural gas imports and supplies two-thirds of the member states with gas (Commission 2008g; see also Commission 2007a, Annex 2: 25). The dependence is exacerbated by the fact that natural gas differs as a commodity from oil and coal in that its transport is predominantly dependent on pipelines and that relative geographic proximity to the source is therefore necessary, so importing states have little flexibility in their choice of suppliers and in implementing any changes in their supply sources and the volumes they receive from each supplier; this is also due to the disproportionate cost of alternative supplies (see, e.g., Bouzarovski and

Konieczny 2010). Although natural gas can be transported by ship, this requires special liquefied natural gas (LNG) infrastructure which only a few member states importing gas from Russia have in place (Belgium, France, Greece and Italy) whereas quite a few – especially the Eastern member states – have only very limited access to alternative sources of supply due to their geographic location and small market size.

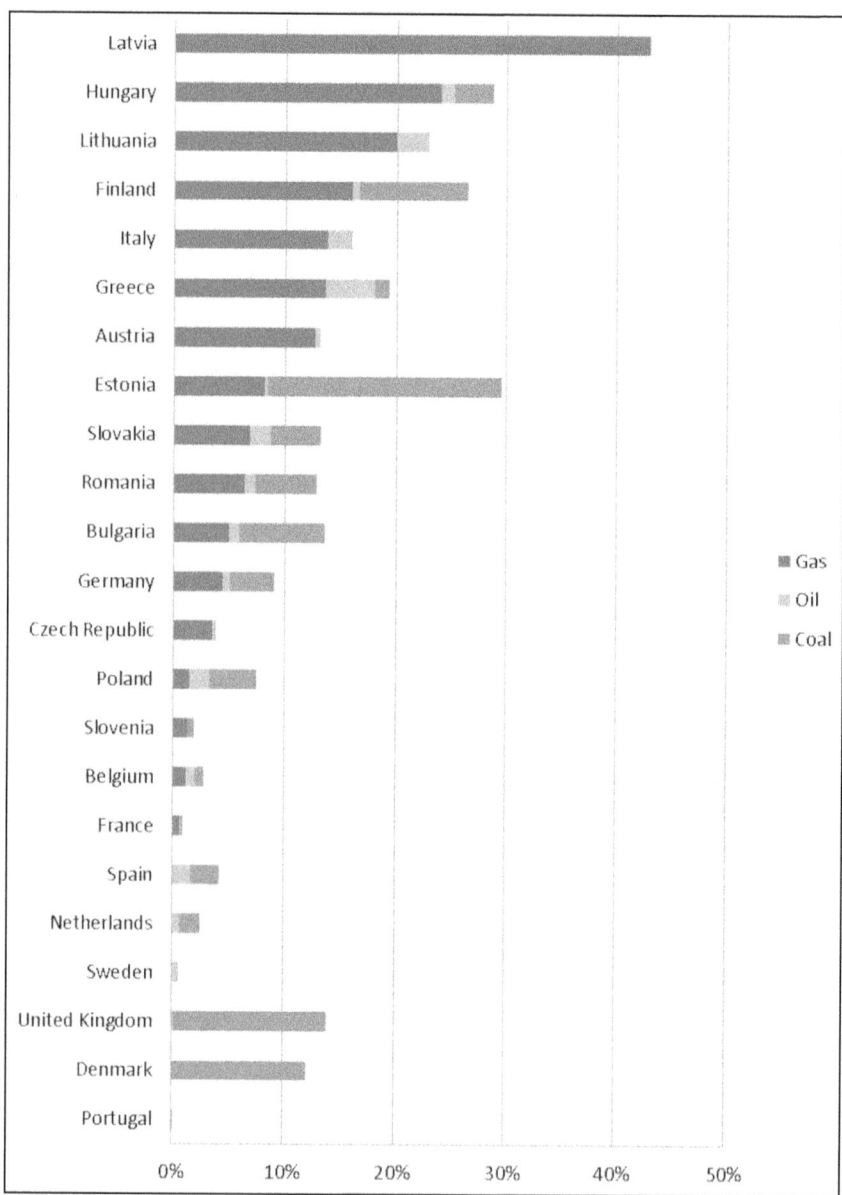

Figure 10.3 Russian energy in member states' electricity generation (2006)

Source: Authors' own calculations from Commission data (Commission 2008b, Annex)

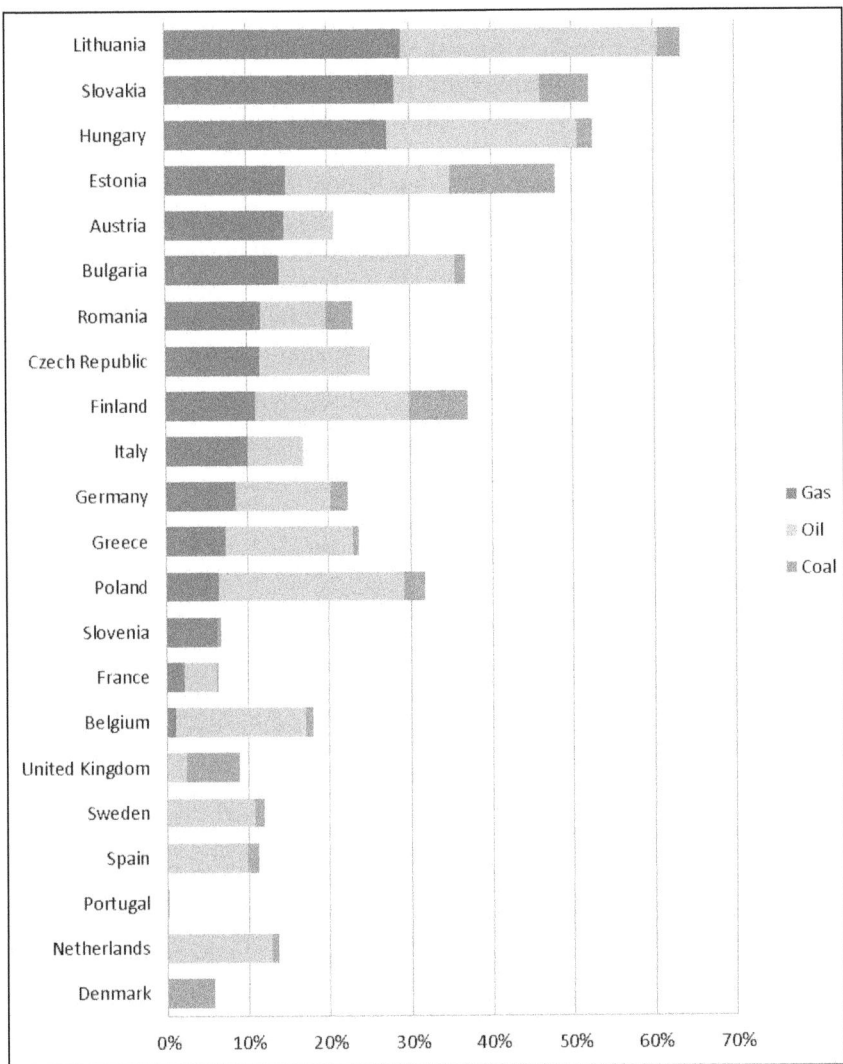

Figure 10.4 Russian energy in member states' total consumption (2006)

Source: Authors' own calculations from Commission data (Commission 2008g, Annex)

This asymmetry in trade between the EU and Russia is significant because while Russia can substitute many of the manufactured goods that it receives from the EU from various competing suppliers on the global market, the EU has difficulties substituting its energy imports from Russia. Whereas for example an oil import embargo can be imposed on Iran at no particular cost to the EU's member states because national energy companies are able to purchase and use alternative supplies from various other producers on the world market, comparable sanctions on Russia might trigger a gas supply cut which would most likely affect the EU's energy supply security. Of course, energy sales to the EU make a substantial contribution to the Russian state budget, and the existing pipeline infrastructure that is directed towards EU member states constrains Russian producers in their ability to redirect energy supplies to alternative customer bases in the short and medium term, but as the gas supply crisis of January 2009 has shown (see Roth 2011; Schmidt-Felzmann 2011) many member states would have considerable problems substituting the gas they receive from Russia from other sources and would incur considerable economic losses should Russian gas supplies be cut off for a prolonged period of time, even if some of the technical obstacles to replacing shortfalls from other sources have been addressed in the wake of the 2009 supply crisis (see Figure 10.5).

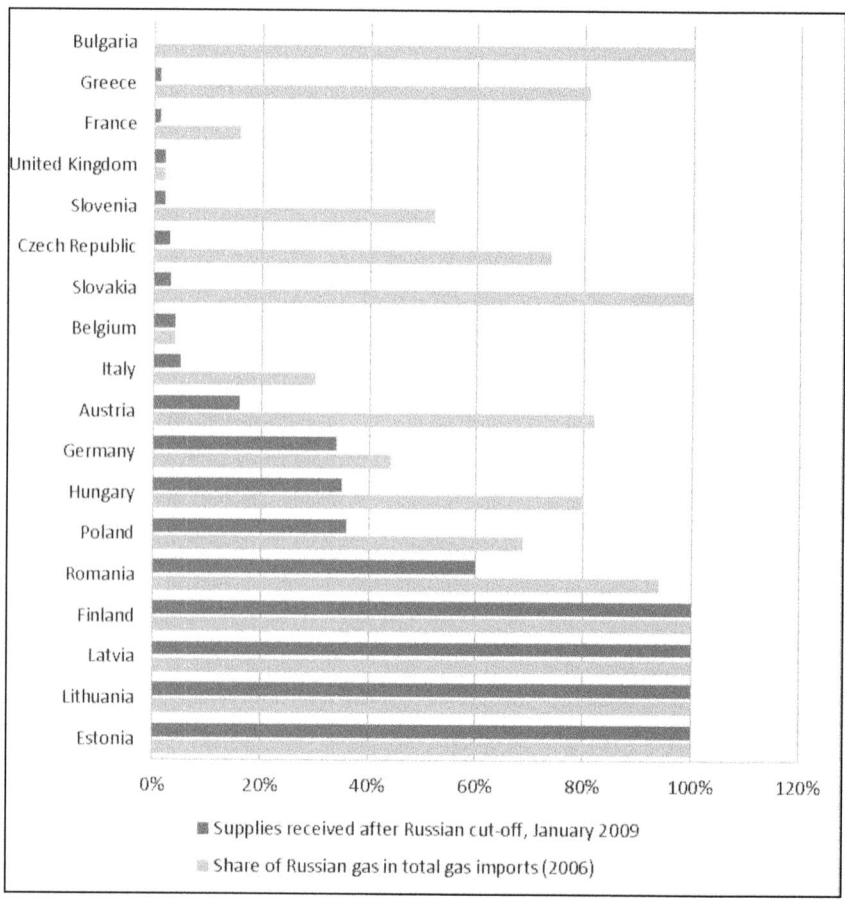

Figure 10.5 Russian gas supplies and the effects of the January 2009 disruptions
Source: Author's compilation (Stern 2005; Commission 2008g; Commission 2009c; House of Commons Deb, 4 March 2009, c1668W).

Any other trade measures that the EU could impose – especially withdrawing Russia's privileged access to the internal market – to apply pressure on the Russian government to undertake domestic political and economic reforms, would have harmed the member states themselves as the 'new' re-empowered Russia during the 2000s was likely to reciprocate and impose barriers restricting member states' access to the Russian market. The range of Russian import embargoes and export tariffs that were imposed by the Russian authorities on certain products in order to protect the Russian market and/or foster Russia's domestic industry have made this clear.[7] Since Russia is regarded as an important market with a considerable potential for growth, especially for the trade of EU goods and services (Commission 2004c, 2008f), the imposition of restrictions would have inflicted costs on the member states. After the endorsement of Russia's World Trade Organization (WTO) membership by the WTO Ministerial Conference in Geneva in December 2011 and Russia's subsequent WTO accession in the second half of 2012, the imposition of trade distorting measures (including special preferential treatment) is no longer possible for either party as both are now bound by WTO rules on non-discrimination.

It is important to note that asymmetric economic interdependence does not necessarily mean that the economically more dominant party will be able to exercise political influence over the economically weaker party (Wagner 1988) and it is important to consider whether the actor possessing the necessary resources to achieve certain policy goals actually also has the resolve and determination to deploy them (see Moravscik 1997). The weaker state may well be more committed than the stronger state and may therefore, as a matter of principle, be more willing to suffer costs when faced with coercive measures or successfully pretend that it is willing to do so (Keohane and Nye 2001). What we can take from this is that if Russia is more determined to mobilise its resources, regardless of the cost, than the EU's member states are (who ultimately have to (agree to) deploy their capabilities and resources), the Russian government is likely to withstand the EU's attempts to influence Russian actions. In the context of the various import bans and export tariffs that have been imposed by the Russian government on a range of products and services during the 2000s, there can be little doubt about the Russian authorities' resolve and willingness to use punitive action as a matter of principle, even when such measures create costs for the Russian state. In contrast, we have seen that the EU faces considerable difficulties in its attempts to influence Russia's domestic political and economic developments which has to do both with the contrasting approaches of the EU and Russia to achieving Russia's democratic consolidation and the EU's lack of strong incentives or coercive tools that could enable it to get Russia to implement the desired changes.

Some commentators (e.g., Secrieru 2009) argued that in the aftermath of the financial crisis of 2008/2009 the Russian government would become more willing to allow external actors more influence in Russia. and indeed many EU and national officials argued that Russia's WTO accession would improve the climate for business and have a positive impact on the state of the rule of law and transparency in Russia.[8] Nevertheless, they acknowledge that any shift in Russian policies towards the EU and 'the West' in general will primarily be motivated by long-term calculations that are driven by Russia's economic vulnerabilities and security imperatives (Secrieru 2009) and cannot therefore be interpreted as a sign of success of the EU's efforts. The renewed keen interest in close engagement and even (economic) integration with the EU that was highlighted by Vladimir Putin in his capacity as Prime Minister (for details of his proposals, see Putin 2010) and followed by the adoption of the concept of 'modernisation partnerships' at the EU level and the conclusion of bilateral 'modernisation partnerships' with Russia by most EU member states, is clearly based on the desire of Russian political elites to modernise the Russian economy by taking advantage of the know-how and capacity of the EU's internal market, without however allowing policy-makers in the EU any influence over Russian political developments.

In order to wield any influence over Russian domestic political developments under these circumstances the EU has to pursue its objectives with determination. In order for that to happen, member states' preferences and approaches to Russia must be congruent since disagreements and conflicts among them would, as Jurado (2006) pointed out, allow Russian officials to exploit inconsistencies to justify the need for a 'customised' adaptation and implementation of the fundamental democratic principles and the respect for human rights and the rule of law according to Russia's 'needs' as such disagreements are indicative of a lack of consensus of what is required for Russia's consolidation as a democratic country.

The implications of the EU's internal problems for its external influence

After having investigated the external obstacles to the EU's success as a values promoter regarding Russia, this part examines the extent to which internal difficulties are weakening the EU's ability to influence Russian domestic politics.

The 'values versus (energy supply) security' dilemma
Divisions among the EU's member states on a range of foreign policy matters are frequently blamed for the EU's failure to achieve its foreign policy goals. Many scholars have emphasised that the 27 member states and the different EU institutions and agencies each pursue their own agendas and thereby weaken the EU's ability to take decisions and implement them (Hill 1993, 1998; Bretherton and Vogler 2006; Gower 2007; Keukeleire and MacNaughtan 2008; Whitman 2010). If the member states are in

disagreement about the policy and strategy that should be pursued towards Russia and are not able to reach agreement on a common policy or if they pursue their bilateral relations with Russia in a fashion that conflicts with and undermines the common policy, this would considerably weaken the EU's collective capacity to influence Russia.

Russia is often described as the country that reveals internal differences and the incoherence of EU policy most sharply, with the then EU Trade Commissioner Peter Mandelson (2007) declaring that '[n]o other country reveals our [i.e. EU member states' and the EU institutions'] differences as does Russia'. That EU member states have a diverse range of views and interests regarding Russia is understandable given their divergent historical experiences. National political elites' views diverge significantly on the kind of country that contemporary Russia is and on the assessment of the intentions of Russian policy-makers which vary from regarding them as close friends and allies (at one extreme) to individuals that cannot be trusted and whose policies pose a potential threat to their countries (at the other extreme). A particular obstacle to forging and pursuing common policies is their contrasting view on whether or not the Russian government can be regarded as a reliable and trustworthy partner that can be 'socialised' or if Russian political elites will have to be coerced into implementing the desired (and from the EU's point of view necessary) domestic changes in Russia. The differences in member states' assessments of Russia have implications for how the values promotion is being pursued at the European level as they essentially advocate two contrasting approaches of how Russia's transformation can be achieved.

Many of the 'old' member states consider Russia to be a reliable partner that is both needed to address international challenges and offers important trade opportunities. These member states are convinced (or at least hopeful) that Russia is developing towards fully fledged democracy even if the transformation is currently being halted – as exemplified by Gerhard Schröder's statement that President Putin is an impeccable democrat ('ein lupenreiner Demokrat') (Hamburger Abendblatt 2004) and that critics of developments in Russia should remember that the process of democratisation inevitably bears difficulties, but that this does not mean Russia is returning to an authoritarian form of government (see Focus Online 2006). National governments that endorse this view of Russia tend not to perceive the country as a 'problem' or 'threat', but as a trustworthy partner and, given the potential of the Russian market, they contend it would be foolish not to engage with Russia in a 'pragmatic' fashion. The member states that regard Russia as an opportunity and important partner insist that a deepening of the EU–Russian cooperation will gradually bring about the desired transformations in Russia through a process of 'socialisation'. This approach, which could be termed *interlacing*, assumes that Russia will gradually become interlocked with the EU and in this process implement and adhere to the EU's fundamental values. The most prominent proponent of interlacing is Germany's Foreign Minister

Steinmeier who attempted in 2007 to launch a new 'Ostpolitik' with the slogan *'Annäherung durch Verflechtung'* (moving closer by means of interlacing).[9] The belief is that this will bring Russia into the EU's orbit where it will gradually be transformed into a 'Western-style' liberal democracy (see Leonard and Popescu 2008), thus drawing on the very ideas that were at the heart of the creation of the European Communities: namely that intensifying economic cooperation can create a level of interdependence that will also condition the political sphere. Proponents of interlacing have argued that disengagement would risk alienating Russia rather than result in its transformation (Steinmeier 2007; see also European Parliament 2005) and that Russia is in fact a strategic partner that the EU 'cannot do without' – too important in any case to 'drive it away' through 'excessive criticism' (see Gathmann and Fischer 2007).

Among the other group of states, consisting mostly, but not exclusively, of 'new' member states, there is a broad consensus, originating particularly from these states' experiences with the Soviet Union, that Russia constitutes a (latent) threat. Their assessment of the current political situation in Russia is characterised by scepticism as to the likelihood of democratic consolidation in Russia, exemplified by the Lithuanian President Adamkus who argued in a 2008 public speech that Russian democracy is on a downward spiral towards authoritarian rule (Adamkus 2008). This view has primarily been shared by the Central and Eastern European countries, but the 'tougher line' regarding Russia has also found support among many 'old' member states such as the Nordic countries, Austria and to some extent Britain (see Vahl 2007).[10] Lithuania's former president, Vytautas Landsbergis (2008), declared that Russia is a threat to Western democracies. Those states that regard Russia as a potential threat argue that Russia's respect for the shared democratic and human rights principles that are enshrined in the PCA should be a precondition of the EU's closer engagement with Russia and not the endgoal.[11] This approach could be termed *conditional* or *coercive engagement*. Advocates of this approach have argued for a distancing of the EU to penalise Russia for its failure to comply with its values-based commitments and thereby coerce it into playing by the EU's rules. As Hughes (2007) argues, many of the political leaders of the new member states harbour suspicions of Russia for historical reasons and oppose a strengthening of the EU's engagement with Russia. They argue that enforcement of Russia's adherence to the 'shared norms and values' which are supposed to be underpinning the EU–Russian relationship is the only way forward, since interlacing has not rendered the desired results over the course of the past fifteen years (Adamkus 2008). The proponents of this approach argue that even if short-term political and economic costs may be incurred, in the long term significant achievements would be made.

Besides the contrasting assessment of Russia and consequently the contrasting approaches to promoting Russia's adoption and adherence to the EU's fundamental values that national officials favour, a key area of contention among national governments has been the question of whether, and if so how, their material interests regarding Russia are linked with the promotion of the EU's fundamental values. On the one hand, national officials emphasise the close linkage between the promotion of democratic institutions and a strengthening of the rule of law in Russia. They stress the fact that both are necessary to ensure greater transparency for investors and thus constitute a prerequisite for the efficient exploitation of Russia's natural resources and thus for ensuring EU member states' supply security.[12] Indeed, analysts have long pointed out the serious negative side-effects of corruption in Russia's energy sector and in particular the lack of transparency and the persisting questions about the rule of law in Russia for investors. This situation has already, as scholars and analysts have demonstrated in various analyses over the course of the 2000s, resulted in insufficient investment levels in the energy sector and consequently also falling oil and gas production levels which are likely to affect consumers in EU member states in the not too distant future (Spruds 2002; Heinrich 2004; Wasilewski 2004; Berg 2008; Goldthau 2008; Mandil 2008; Noël 2008; Tkachenko 2008; Westphal 2008; Whist 2009). The promotion of the EU's fundamental values, in particular the adherence to democratic principles and respect for the rule of law, will from this perspective also ensure member states' energy supply security ('values as part of security').

But whereas many observers and policy-makers regard energy supply security and the promotion of the EU's democratic values, human rights principles and the rule of law as intrinsically linked,[13] the two objectives seem to be nevertheless difficult to reconcile in practice. In the scholarly debate about the promotion of the EU's fundamental values abroad, attention has been paid in particular to the question of where the 'values promotion' fits and how high it ranks on member states' list of priorities in their foreign relations with third states. Hyde-Price (2006, 2008a, 2008b) has questioned outright the compatibility of normative objectives (reflecting the 'principles and values' each country adheres to which are *not* vital to their security or prosperity) and the pursuit of core national interests that play an important role for the security and prosperity of the state. Keukeleire and MacNaughtan (2008) have also found that the 'values promotion' stands generally in conflict with important economic interests. Policy-makers are therefore confronted with a dilemma regarding which objectives they should attribute greater importance to ('values versus security').

Indeed, the prioritisation of bilateral commercial deals of some member states with Russia, especially in the energy sector, has been regarded by critics as the biggest obstacle to the EU's successful pursuit of democracy and human rights promotion in Russia. Member governments' reservations about values promotion at the bilateral level stems from the correlation of criticism of Russia's state of democracy and human rights protection being followed by trade sanctions. There is no incontrovertible evidence that could *prove* that the Russian authorities retaliate against criticism by imposing sanctions on the respective state, but past events have created the impression that the two are closely linked. A report by Larsson (2007) concluded that there is a high correlation of public criticism of Russia's democratic failings being followed by economic reprisals, including the cut-off of energy supplies from Russia. The possibility that an active promotion of the EU's 'fundamental values' can cause material losses is bound to influence national policy-makers in their assessment of costs and benefits of pushing Russian decision-makers on normative issues. If the pursuit of normative objectives and material interests in equal measure is impossible because of Russia's negative response to attempts at pushing the values agenda, a trade-off necessarily has to take place.

Research has revealed, and national diplomats and EU officials working on relations with Russia are also of the view, that national governments indeed tend to prioritise in their bilateral relations with Russia the conclusion of trade and energy supply agreements over the promotion of the EU's fundamental values. Specifically, those member states that are highly dependent on Russian energy supplies tend to downplay Russian human rights infringements and failures in the democratic reform process, while the least dependent states have been found to be more willing to push Russia to respect the 'shared' fundamental values (Götz 2004; European Parliament 2005; Handke and de Jong 2007; Kausch 2007; Sánchez Andrés 2007; Keukeleire and MacNaughtan 2008).[14] The extent to which individual governments really are driven by a choice between 'values' or 'energy supply security' is debatable, but it is clear that there are significant differences among the member states in terms of the importance they attribute to promoting the EU's 'normative agenda' in relation to other material and in particular energy supply security interests.

As the successful promotion of the EU's values agenda vis-à-vis Russia relies on the full support of 'common' objectives by the member states – not just at the EU level, but also in their unilateral dealings with Russia – the incongruence of their policy objectives in terms of whether to prioritise 'values' or 'material/security interests', and the approaches that they advocate to achieve the desired reforms in Russia, would appear to significantly weaken and limit the EU's ability to promote the fundamental values effectively in Russia. Nevertheless, national diplomats working in Brussels have observed a gradual change in the years following the accession of the new member states (post-2004 and post-2007) regarding the assessment of Russia and of the kind of policy that should be pursued to promote Russia's 'normative approximation' at the European level. They have noted a gradual conversion of member states' perspectives on Russia as a result of certain 'excessive' foreign policy actions on the part of the Russian government and they believe that there are far fewer and less pronounced differences among the national positions at the EU level.[15] So, while the challenges to the EU's external effectiveness posed by

Russia's economic recovery and Russian political elites' determination to prevent outside interference in Russian domestic affairs remain, and have somewhat increased as a result of the Eurocrisis, the internal obstacles to a successful pursuit of the EU's values agenda vis-à-vis Russia seem to have decreased substantially.

Conclusions

Three main conclusions can be derived from this analysis of the EU's relations with Russia: first, that it is not possible to capture the reality of the EU's relations with Russia with just one 'typology' (see Chapter 1, this volume). Second, the formal adoption of democratic principles along with legislation designed to ensure the respect for human rights and the rule of law offers no guarantees that reforms will be followed through and translated into practice. Thirdly, the EU is unable to pull its weight in the countries that do not have an accession perspective and/or do not seek EU membership. I will elaborate below on each of these observations and their implications for the EU as a values promoter, and for the state of play in Russia.

The analysis of the EU's relations with Russia has underlined the fact that policy-makers in the EU and at the national level are confronted with a range of obstacles and difficulties in the development and implementation of a common 'values promotion policy' towards Russia. The relationship between 'values' on the one hand and 'security' on the other hand is more complex that might appear at first sight. The analysis has shown that the EU's and Russia's interpretations of what the 'shared values' (as enshrined in the PCA) entail differ substantially ('values versus values'), but that there is also, to a certain degree, a conflict between the promotion of democratic and human rights principles and the rule of law on the one hand and security, stability and prosperity (both in Russia and in EU member states) on the other. At the same time, this apparent conflict between 'values' and 'security' goals ('values versus security') is not actually perceived as such by many policy-makers who believe instead that the achievement of material/security interests is intrinsically linked with the effective promotion of the EU's fundamental values ('values as part of security').

The analysis has revealed that the EU has failed to exert its influence over Russian domestic developments, despite investing considerable efforts. The Russian case appears in fact to confirm Jurado's predictions that states respond well to material incentives while they are vulnerable, but that democratic reforms are subject to reversal when the incentive structure changes between the values promoting agent (the EU and its member states) and the target state (Russia), if the 'values' or democratic principles have not already been fully incorporated at that point. The empirical evidence suggests that Russia's values-adoption did not progress beyond the first stage and that it did not enter the 'socialisation' stage before the incentive structures radically changed with the speedy recovery of the Russian economy and the stabilisation of the Russian political system under Vladimir Putin's strong leadership. Quite to the contrary, the reforms of the political and legal system that were implemented in Russia during the 1990s seem to have been reversed rather than consolidated during the 2000s. It is doubtful that a changed incentive structure, notably the negative effects of the international financial crisis on the Russian economy, will make Russian policy-makers more inclined to accept external influence over Russian domestic political processes. Policy-makers have in fact highlighted the negative consequences of the financial crisis, and particularly the EU's struggle to cope with the Eurocrisis, on the EU's image and on the 'power of attraction' of the EU's political and economic system which could, as a result, act rather as a disincentive for governments in third states to emulate the EU's example.[16] It also remains uncertain if Russia's WTO accession and thus its integration into the global multilateral trading system (which will enable third parties to take legal action through the WTO's dispute settlement procedure against trade distorting measures) will really strengthen the rule of law in Russia and ensure greater respect for human rights and the adherence to democratic principles by the governing elites, as many EU officials and national policy-makers are hoping.

The track record to date indicates that contrasting interpretations on the EU's and the Russian side of how Russia's democratic 'consolidation' should be promoted continue to make it difficult for the EU to influence the course of developments in Russia. This is also due to the fact that the EU lacks the necessary compelling instruments to coax or coerce the Russian government into implementing the desired political reforms, and due to the fact that the member states are also divided over the question of how to promote the shared normative objectives in Russia, although differences between them have become less pronounced since the late 2000s. However, the divisions between the EU and Russia remain and the EU is unlikely to gain substantial leverage over Russia as long as the Russian state continues to reap substantial profits from the sale of oil and gas on the world market. What is more, if the EU's struggle to cope with the Eurocrisis continues, it may well forfeit the bargaining power that the size and potential of its internal market has granted it since the creation of the single European market. It is, as a result, therefore unlikely that the EU will be able to record much progress in the promotion of its 'fundamental values' in Russia in the foreseeable future. Meanwhile, Russian civil society is bound to play a considerably more prominent role, although not because of the EU's efforts, but rather because of the spread of the new media and the more successful mobilisation of the masses by Russian bloggers through Twitter, Facebook and the like (see BBC News Europe 2011). In view of the continuing popularity of Vladimir Putin as political leader and the effective splinter tactics employed by the ruling elites against the opposition it is nevertheless unlikely that a 'Russian Winter' or 'Russian

Spring' movement will overthrow the existing political system in the near future (*Dagens Nyheter* 2011a, 2011b, 2011c; Gustafsson and Kott 2011). However, in light of the growing dissatisfaction among the Russian people with the existing regime, illustrated by the repeated mass demonstrations of December 2011 in Moscow and other parts of the country against the victory of the ruling United Russia party in the Duma elections (see *Dagens Nyheter* 2011a), it is much more likely that any political reforms in Russia will be triggered and pushed forward by domestic actors rather than that they will be brought about by the efforts of the EU and its member states.[17]

Notes

1. Finland, Poland, Lithuania, Latvia and Estonia share a land border with Russia; Sweden, Finland, Denmark, Germany, Poland, Lithuania, Latvia and Estonia share a sea border with Russia in the Baltic Sea region and Bulgaria and Romania share a sea border with Russia in the Black Sea region.
2. I refer here to the consolidated version of the TFEU.
3. For a detailed discussion of the 'derailed' Russian democracy, see Fish (2005). For an account of the early stages of the Russian democracy in the early 1990s after Yeltsin took power, see Kagarlitsky (1994).
4. The English language quotations of President Putin's and President Medvedev's respective Addresses to the Federal Assembly are taken from the official translations provided on the website of the Presidential Administration at http://archive.kremlin.ru/eng/sdocs/speeches.shtml?stype=70029 (accessed 10 October 2010).
5. The swift succession of five different prime ministers between March 1998 and August 1999 is just one indicator of the domestic political problems experienced in Russia during the 1990s.
6. Author's interview with a diplomat of an EU member state, July 2007, Brussels.
7. These have included, *inter alia*, embargoes on meat and plant products and tariffs on the export of Russian timber which have affected a considerable number of EU member states and inflicted damage on the respective industry sectors in the affected member states (see, e.g., Roth 2009).
8. Author's interviews with diplomats of several EU member states, November–December 2011, Brussels.
9. It should be noted that the German Chancellery under Angela Merkel's leadership did not support the launch of this 'new' Eastern policy and a few German diplomats were also critical of this strategy (author's interviews with German diplomats, June 2007, Ministry of Foreign Affairs, Berlin).
10. Author's interviews with diplomats of several EU member states, June, November–December 2007 and November 2011, Brussels.
11. Author's interview with a European Commission official, DG RELEX, December 2007, Brussels.
12. Author's interviews with diplomats of several EU member states, November–December 2011, Brussels.
13. Ibid.
14. Author's interviews with European Commission and European External Action Service officials and diplomats of several EU member states, November–December 2011, Brussels.
15. Ibid.

16 Ibid.
17 It is noteworthy that most observers were in agreement that the mass demonstrations in and of themselves would not threaten the political establishment in Russia, but that since in particular the young and well-educated Russians in Moscow took to the streets, a slump in global oil prices and consequent negative impact on the Russian economy could quickly erode the support that 'Putin's' political system has enjoyed (see *Dagens Nyheter* 2011a).

Florian Trauner, Imke Kruse and
Bernhard Zeilinger

11

Values versus security in the external dimension of EU migration policy: a case study on the readmission agreement with Russia

Introduction

Since the entry into force of the Amsterdam Treaty, the creation of a European Area of Freedom, Security and Justice (AFSJ) has become a major treaty objective of the EU.[1] Although primarily thought of as an EU internal security regime, the EU has developed an external dimension to its justice and home affair policies, which has in turn impacted on the EU's interactions with the outside world. The efforts to create a closer internal–external security nexus have been based on the understanding that the EU may increase its problem-solving capacity in relation to transnational challenges such as the fight against irregular migration, organised crime or terrorism, if it manages to engage third countries – in particular those countries neighbouring the EU – in achieving its JHA-related objectives. This development has received a great deal of scholarly attention. For instance, Rijpma and Cremona (2007: 12) have described it as the 'extra-territorialisation of EU migration policies and the rule of law' (see also Bigo and Guild 2005; Balzacq 2009; Wolff *et al.* 2009; Carrapico and Trauner 2012).

Against the background of the EU's efforts to minimise irregular migration into the Union, migration control policy has become a particularly important issue area in the EU's cooperation with third countries (see e.g., Lavenex 2006). In fact, when the Schengen agreements shifted the focus from nation state borders to external borders, an effective 'common return policy' to enforce border control moved to the centre of the EU's attention (Council of the EU 2001b: 2). Consequently, readmission agreements – a long-standing instrument of nation states to facilitate the return of irregular migrants and rejected asylum seekers – have increasingly been discussed as a Community instrument on the supranational level (Council of the EU 1998, art. 133). The EU's efforts to reach a high number of readmission agreements with all states around its territory, and even with more distant transit and origin countries, represents an attempt to create concentric circles of demarcation; this attempt seeks to both extend the redistributive system for the examination of asylum claims to non-EU countries, and to transfer irregular immigration to outside territory (Council of the EU 1998, art. 60).

The EU's readmission policy therefore presents a clear – probably even the clearest – manifestation of a security logic driving the EU's external action in the migration field. It illustrates a 'hard case' concerning place and relevance of values when the EU cooperates in a 'security logic' with neighbouring states. Inspired by this book's conceptual underpinnings (see Chapter 1 of this volume), the main research questions for this chapter are as follows: does the EU include and acknowledge values as part of security, or are there areas characterised by tensions between values and security? Or, in more empirical terms, do EU and non-EU actors effectively consider international humanitarian and refugee protection norms when implementing EU readmission agreements, and if so, what does this look like in practice?

In order to answer these questions, in this chapter we will focus on one single readmission agreement as a case study: the EU readmission agreement with Russia. Negotiations between the European Commission and representatives of Russia were concluded in May 2006 with the agreement entering into force in June 2007. For our analysis, the EU–Russia agreement is a particularly good example for two reasons: first, the signing and implementation of the readmission agreement with Russia – an increasingly important country of origin and transit of irregular migration – has become a strategic priority for the EU. However, we know that the EU is not in a position to just impose its own standards, processes and institutional infrastructure on this particularly powerful neighbouring state. Russia has been relatively resistant to the EU's efforts of projecting its values, norms and practices onto the country (Gänzle, 2008; Debardeleben, 2008: 76–9). The Russian case is therefore likely to show whether the EU compromises on its values standards when pursuing security interests. Second, the EU–Russia readmission agreement has entailed a three-year transition period before the obligations concerning the readmission of third-country nationals and stateless persons have become applicable. During this three-year period, Russia has had the chance to establish all relevant infrastructure and to prepare for implementing the agreement. Thus, by observing the activities of the Russian government and by looking at the role which the EU has been playing during this transition period, we may gain insight into what roles both security and values have played in recent EU–Russia relations.

The chapter proceeds as follows: to set the stage for the empirical examination, we first give a short overview of the development of readmission agreements as a standard policy tool at the EU level, and show how the way in which they have been framed as a legitimate policy instrument has changed in recent years. Next, the research focus shifts to the case study on the EU–Russia readmission agreement. After presenting the background and the legal stipulations, we illustrate the EU's efforts to ensure the implementation of the agreement on the Russian side. This more descriptive analysis allows us to then identify three aspects of the EU–Russia readmission agreement where the two logics 'values versus security' come into conflict with each other.

The development of an EU readmission policy: does it have values?

With signatures on a readmission agreement, both parties agree to readmit their own nationals, or third country nationals who have transited through their country, and who do not, or no longer, fulfil the conditions for entry or stay in the territory of the requested country. Such agreements are signed on the basis of reciprocity, meaning that all contracting states must be prepared to readmit not only their own citizens, but also third country nationals on the same terms. However, with regard to Community readmission agreements with third countries of transit or origin, it is hard to imagine a situation where, for example, Russia would face difficulties in readmitting EU nationals to the EU who have irregularly entered or stayed in the country. Rather, the empirical case only appears valid the other way around.

Between 1999 and 2001, when the European Commission's activities in justice and home affairs was primarily concentrated on legal residence and refugee protection, the issue of readmission had primarily been discussed in the broader context of legal immigration. The underlying idea was that only if calls for voluntary return have no effect, could readmission agreements serve as a valuable instrument to facilitate returns as a last resort (see e.g., Commission 2000). However, since then, the European Commission has turned its attention to irregular immigration as the missing link in a comprehensive immigration and asylum policy, and, in this context, readmission has received increasing attention in its own right. The focus in EU migration policies significantly changed in parallel with a change of tone in public discussions, and in this context the call for Community readmission agreements became 'louder'.

The EU became increasingly aware of the insufficiency of domestic border controls if they are not backed up by cooperation with countries of origin and transit. This way of thinking has boosted the creation of the external dimension of justice and home affairs policies. One can generally distinguish two approaches to dealing with the external dimension of EU migration policy: the first approach seeks to externalise the traditional tools of national and/or EU migration control, for example by strengthening border controls in countries of origin or transit. The second approach is preventive in nature and strives to eliminate the root causes of migration

(Boswell 2003). These two approaches differ fundamentally in their perception of how to deal with substantial numbers of immigrants and affect the EU's relations with third countries in different ways. The first is a restrictive approach based on the security logic in which the EU passes classical migration control instruments on to non-member countries, who have to accept the provisions for facilitating the return of irregular migrants and rejected asylum seekers. The second approach recognises values, seeking to abolish circumstances in the countries of origin that force people to migrate to the EU, and builds on mutually beneficial forms of cooperation between the EU and third countries.

The EU has the power to sign readmission agreements since the Treaty of Amsterdam, although the instrument has had a long prior tradition in EU member states (Cassarino, 2007; Kruse, 2006; Schieffer, 2003). Within the external dimension of EU justice and home affairs, the EU has repeatedly emphasised the need to take both the security logic and values into account (Commission 2000; Council of the EU 1999). However, the security logic – for which readmission agreements are a case in point – has dominated the debate, particularly since the early 2000s.

The signing of EU readmission agreements with third countries is considered as *the* key instrument to restrict irregular migration to the EU. How readmission policy is framed is of particular significance for the EU's position towards countries of origin and transit. The high priority increasingly given to negotiations on EU readmission agreements with third countries illustrates the contemporary focus on restrictive policies of demarcation; they are the most visible manifestation of how the EU's security logic is driving its migration and asylum policy.

During negotiations on the first Community readmission agreements with third countries, human rights issues did not play a prominent role (for more details on the negotiations, see Kruse 2005). On the contrary, EU member states were mainly concerned with the slow progress made in negotiations and the difficulty of exerting leverage on non-EU countries in order to reach an agreement. It is widely known that the infrastructural conditions for receiving, hosting and returning third country nationals fall short of EU required standards in third countries like Russia. Although the 2002 EU return action programme[2] had underlined the importance of respecting human rights in readmission and upholding international standards, it was the European Parliament that had to remind EU member states of their international human rights obligations in the context of readmission.

In case of the Hong Kong and Macao readmission agreements – the first to be signed at Community level – the 'non-affection' clause merely stated that 'this Agreement shall be without prejudice to rights, obligations and responsibilities arising from International Law applicable to the Community, the Member States and the [partner country]' (Council of the EU 2002: 23). Criticism by the European Parliament and non-governmental organisations was harsh. In consequence, the wording of the Albanian agreement became more precise:

> This Agreement shall be without prejudice to the rights, obligations and responsibilities of the Community, the Member States and Albania arising from International Law and, in particular, from the European Convention of 4 November 1950 for the Protection of Human Rights, the Convention of 28 July 1951 and the Protocol of 31 January 1967 on the Status of Refugees, and international instruments on extradition. (Council of the EU 2005f: 22)

Again, several non-governmental organisations and the European Parliament criticised the human rights clauses for being too weak. The readmission agreement with Russia was signed next. Even though it did not refer to a non-affection clause but 'relation to other international obligations', the list of legal documents to be considered, according to article 18, grew even longer:

> This Agreement shall be without prejudice to the rights, obligations and responsibilities of the Community, the Member States and the Russian Federation arising from International Law and, in particular, from: (a) the Convention of 28 July 1951 and the Protocol of 31 January 1967 on the Status of Refugees; (b) the European Convention of 4 November 1950 for the Protection of Human Rights, (c) the Convention of 10 December 1984 against Torture and other Cruel, Inhuman or Degrading Treatment or Punishment; (d) international treaties on extradition and transit; (e) multilateral international treaties containing rules on the readmission of foreign nationals, such as the Convention on International Civil Aviation of 7 December 1944. (Council of the EU 2007d: 27)

With regard to human rights considerations, the wording of the EU–Russia readmission agreement became the standard model for the readmission agreements later signed by the EU (Trauner and Kruse 2008; Hernández i Sagrera 2010). In its Council conclusions defining the EU strategy on readmission, the Justice and Home Affairs Council mentioned the respect for human rights as a guiding principle of the EU's overall external relations policy, reiterating that human rights standards would continue to be fully respected in the framework of the EU's return policy (Council of the EU 2011: 2). However, no conclusions were adopted concerning human rights, illustrating that the Council does not see any need for improvement.

Whether or not these human rights-related paragraphs of the EU–Russia readmission agreement are being properly considered in practice, is discussed in the following section.

'Values versus security': putting the EU–Russia readmission agreement into practice

The readmission agreement constitutes an important element of the EU–Russian 'Common Space on Freedom, Security and Justice' (CSFSJ), which provides the overall framework for dealing with JHA issues.[3]

Cooperation within the Common Space framework is guided by a roadmap jointly adopted in 2005 that placed an emphasis on the fight against illegal cross-border activities, including organised crime, money-laundering, illegal trafficking in human beings, drug trafficking and irregular immigration (Council of the EU 2005e). To implement the roadmap and to organise cooperation within the Common Space, the EU and Russia set out an institutional structure, the highest level of which constitutes the EU–Russian Permanent Partnership Council on Justice and Home Affairs.

The EU has been motivated to intensify cooperation in these soft security-related issues due to insecurity spill-over from Russia, including in the area of irregular migration. Russia has not only been a country of origin, but also a country of transit of irregular migration. A considerable number of the irregular migrants coming from Central Asian and Asian countries cross Russia and the Ukraine before they enter the EU's territory. The Federal Police of Germany, for instance, reported in 2007 that the second highest number of irregular migrants apprehended at German borders originated from Russia (Bundesamt für Migration und Flüchtlinge 2008). In 2009, 6.1 per cent of irregular migrants apprehended at German borders were Russian citizens (Bundesamt für Migration und Flüchtlinge 2011: 186). Also, the European Commission draws attention to the porousness of the Eastern borders by stating that 'more than 80 per cent of all illegal migrants come from CIS countries, others from China, south-east Asia and Africa ... Over recent years, Russia has become a country of origin, transit and destination for migrants' (Commission 2007d: 9).

Despite its focus on security, the EU–Russian cooperation within the Common Space of Freedom, Security and Justice ascribes importance to 'common values' such as democracy, rule of law and the respect of human rights. The relevance of these values is also underlined in the preamble establishing the CSFSJ (Council of the EU 2005e: 20). They should be monitored in the context of ministerial meetings of the bi-annual EU–Russia Permanent Partnership Council of Justice and Home Affairs, and other meetings related to the CSFSJ. In addition, human rights abuses can be addressed during human rights consultations with Russia.

The negotiations on the EU–Russia readmission agreement were initially very difficult and made little substantive progress (Potemkina 2004; Kruse 2005). Only once the EU had accepted the notion of facilitated EU visa requirements for certain categories of people (e.g. businessmen, students), in exchange for the signing of the readmission agreement, could the negotiations be finalised at the 15th EU–Russia summit in Moscow in 2005. The deal was generally seen to be beneficial for both parties. Russia was provided with facilitated travel opportunities for bona fide travellers, while the EU acquired a lever to encourage Russia to sign a readmission agreement and increase its reform efforts in the sectors of justice and home affairs (Trauner and Kruse 2008). At the same summit, both parties agreed to intensify cooperation in a range of related JHA issues, in particular border control, irregular migration, document security and data and information sharing (Council of the EU 2005d).

In May 2006, Russia and the European Union finally approved the visa facilitation and readmission agreement, which has opened the way for easier travel and contacts between the EU and Russia, while providing a legal framework for the readmission of irregular migrants. The objective of visa-free travel has been subject to further conditions set by the EU, among which are the smooth implementation of the readmission agreement and the improvement of border management and document security.

In an examination of the implementation process itself and the role of values therein, the following section investigates the nature of the agreement and separates elements of the security logic from values referring to international obligations on fundamental rights.

The stipulations of the EU–Russia readmission agreement
The EU–Russia readmission agreement entered into force in June 2007, with the exception of stipulations on third country nationals and stateless people (which later entered into force in June 2010). Although the European Commission was responsible for the negotiations with Russia, the actual readmission of persons remains the sole responsibility of the individual EU member state.

Obligations relating to the security logic: who has to be readmitted and under what conditions?
The EU–Russia readmission agreement sets out clear obligations and procedures for the contracting parties as to who can be readmitted and under what conditions. It includes technical rules on the readmission procedure and transit operations, including on the contents and format of readmission applications, the means of evidence for establishing nationality, data protection and the respect of international obligations and standards. Overall the agreement is organised in eight sections, with some additional annexes and special protocols clarifying the relevance of the agreement for Denmark, Iceland and Norway:

- Readmission obligations by the Russian Federation
- Readmission obligations by the Community
- Readmission procedure (information exchange, mutual recognition of verdict)
- Transit operations
- Costs
- Data protection
- Implementation and application
- Final provisions

The readmission obligation rules concern the category of people that can be readmitted among the contracting parties: country nationals, third country nationals and stateless persons. A fourth category can be added, namely those persons readmitted under the agreement who, in the course of new investigations, were discovered to have no link whatsoever with the requested country; the literature refers to these cases as 'readmission in error' (Balzacq 2008: 22).

The stipulations on the readmission procedure provide technical and detailed specification with regard to the process of readmission, including verifying the purpose of readmission to the requested country and formally submitting a readmission application as well as transferring a person.[4] A special accelerated procedure applies to persons who are apprehended in border regions. They may be returned within a few days (art. 6 (2)).

The costs of readmitting a person, including transit costs, shall be borne by the requesting party (art. 16). However, there is no institutionalised mechanism to prevent the respective state from requesting these costs from the readmitted migrant – something which has met with criticism on the grounds that it might lead to abuse: 'For instance, how could the EU check that the individuals concerned are not sent to jail, for failure to pay back the costs incurred by the state in readmitting them?' (Balzacq 2008: 24)

With regard to the guidelines on data protection (art. 17), both parties agreed that personal data should only be exchanged, if necessary, for implementing the readmission agreement, and should be processed fairly and lawfully. Personal data must be 'adequate, relevant and not excessive in relation to the purpose' (art. 17) for which it is collected. However, while EC member states are requested to abide by the data protection directive 95/46/EC, the readmission agreement lacks similar obligations on the Russian side; it only refers to the legislation in the respective contracting country.

Even though the issue of data protection has been discussed within the remit of security-based obligations, the lack of any concrete and effective data protection rules applying to the Russian government has important value-related implications. The lack of sufficient protection of personal data in the context of readmission places the individual migrant in severe danger and violates international human rights standards. The following subsection discusses further values-based obligations in the EU–Russia readmission agreement.

Obligations relating to values

As outlined in the previous section, article 18 of the readmission agreement clarifies all relevant obligations with regard to international humanitarian and refugee protection, including, in particular, the principle of *non-refoulement*.[5] Moreover, some reference to the obligations and rights of returned persons can be found in other parts of the agreement. In the stipulations on the transit of third country nationals and stateless persons, it is outlined that the transit may be refused on the grounds that:

(a) If the third-country nationals or stateless persons run the risk of being subjected to torture or to inhuman or degrading treatment or punishment or the death penalty or of persecution because of race, religion, nationality, membership of a particular social group or political conviction in the State of destination or another state of transit; or
(b) If the third-country national or the stateless person will be subject to criminal prosecution or sanctions in the requested state or in another State of transit; or
(c) on grounds of public health, domestic security, public order or other national interests of the requested state. (Council of the EU 2007d: 21)

Taking into account the ill-developed Russian tradition for dealing with asylum seekers and refugees and the weak legislation in this area in Russia, both parties agreed on a transition period of three years on readmitting third country nationals and stateless people. During this period, Russia agreed to improve the legislative framework and enhance the administrative capacity.

Referring to remarks made by the Russian Foreign Minister, Sergey Lavrov, Roig and Huddelston (2007: 373) argue, however, that the transition period was used by Russia first and foremost as a strategy for circumventing the obligation of returning non-nationals. In addition, the transition period gave Russia the possibility to sign as many bilateral readmission agreements as possible with its neighbouring countries, and other countries of origin, in order to make it possible to readmit third country nationals that were being readmitted from the EU further to other countries of transit or origin.

EU efforts to help implement the agreement

The EU and Russia have deepened their cooperation in several areas in order to help implement the readmission agreement. Three principal areas can be identified:

1. Establishing a comprehensive institutional framework to evaluate the current situation on readmission, to monitor the agreed obligations and to regulate the execution of the respective policy;
2. Enhancing co-operation between EU agencies, such as EUROPOL and FRONTEX, with state authorities of Russia, such as police and intelligence forces and State Border Guards (SBG), in order to exchange information and expertise on the use of biometrics, data protection, document security etc;
3. Providing technical and financial assistance to support the implementation of the readmission agreement.

With regard to the first aspect, both parties put in place a joint readmission committee for the practical implementation of the agreement. It meets twice a year and has the task of monitoring the application of the agreement, arranging the execution of the agreement, exchanging information, and proposing amendments to the agreement, if deemed necessary. It consists of representatives of Russia and the European Commission acting on behalf of the European Community. The EU is also represented by experts from the member states. The joint committee decisions are binding in nature for the contracting parties (art. 19 of the EU–Russia readmission agreement).

Concerning the second point, cooperation on readmission between Russia and the European Commission's Directorate General for Home Affairs is supported by two EU agencies: the European Agency for the Management of Operational Cooperation at the External Borders of the Member States of the European Union (FRONTEX) and the European Law Enforcement Organisation EUROPOL. Both agencies coordinate the operational aspects of readmitting irregular third country nationals and, thus, play a decisive role in implementing readmission agreements (for more details, see Carrera 2007; Jorry 2007). For instance, FRONTEX has developed a practical guide for the implementation of return operations, which includes recommendations on ways to adhere to human rights standards at each stage of the returns procedure, and organised joint training sessions for national border guards. EUROPOL also makes efforts to foster close cooperation with Russian police and intelligence forces with a view to exchanging information on migratory flows.

Thirdly, the EU provides financial and technical assistance to help Russia assume its responsibilities deriving from the readmission agreement, and to enhance efficiency in return procedures. Several Russian projects have benefitted from financial and technical assistance of the European Neighbourhood and Partnership Instrument (ENPI, formerly TACIS) and the Technical Assistance and Information Exchange (TAIEX).[6] In addition, in the period from 2007 to 2010, the new 'thematic programme on cooperation with third countries in the areas of migration and asylum' provided €50 million for the assistance of countries along the eastern migratory route (Commission 2006j: 3). With regard to readmission agreements, the thematic programme provided financial and technical assistance for the social and professional reintegration of returnees – money meant for establishing adequate humanitarian conditions in detention centres, and for strengthening third countries' institutional capacities to both provide asylum and international protection and develop national legal frameworks in line with the agreement (Commission 2006j: 3). In the period 2011–13, the indicative budget of the thematic programme is €179 million, of which €29 million is allocated for Eastern Europe and Central Asia.

When trying to help implement the EU readmission agreement in Russia, the EU endeavours to cooperate with international organizations, in particular, the International Organisation for Migration (IOM). For instance, the IOM implemented a project called 'Assistance to the Government of the Russian Federation in Establishing Legal and Administrative Framework for the Implementation and Development of Readmission Agreements (DIRA)'.[7] It aimed at improving the Russian government's organisational, practical and legislative capacity to implement the readmission agreement. The project was described as 'a platform for the expertise and knowledge interchange between the EU and Russia in the field of migrants' readmission and return' (IOM 2008). More broadly, the IOM has helped implement several EU projects on JHA topics together with the Russian authorities e.g. on using biometrics, facilitating reception centres for readmitted people and training authorities on new procedures in readmitting people.[8]

In short, the EU has sought to help Russia implement the readmission agreement in various ways. A strong focus has been placed on capacity-building in the areas of border management, risk analysis and information-gathering. Although the EU officially stresses the respect of fundamental rights for readmitted individuals in all its documents and agreements, there appears to have been little practical action in this area, except for organising training sessions for executing authorities and the equipping of reception centres. The following section analyses the security logic driving the EU's external activities in the field of readmission and, more broadly, migration conflict with values derived from international human rights and refugee protection standards.

Tensions between security and values-based logics
The European Parliament (2007b: 6) has noted that 'a policy to regulate illegal immigration has to be linked indissolubly to a human rights policy' in order to be legitimate and in line with the EU's self-understanding as a civilian power on the international stage. By elaborating on this link, we identify three areas particularly characterised by tensions between security-based and values-based external action.

Missing effective control and monitoring instruments
As previously shown, some NGOs, as well as the European Parliament, have strongly pushed for a greater emphasis on international humanitarian and refugee protection obligations in the context of the EU's readmission policy. However, with regard to the EU–Russia readmission agreement the EU has *de facto* few possibilities to ensure these standards are implemented, even if they are contractually regulated. There is basically no human rights or refugee protection clause in the readmission agreement, the violation of which could result in the temporary suspension or denouncement of the agreement.[9] The only conditionality principle in the agreement can be found in the link between visa facilitation and readmission: since the facilitation of short-stay visas is understood as being a first step towards a visa-free regime, further concessions can be made, conditional to human rights standards in Russia being upheld. During negotiations between the European Commission and the Russian government on visa facilitation, the European Parliament called for a formal human rights and democracy clause to be included in the agreement, though to no avail:

The European Union's relations with Russia should be made subject to a conditionality principle, as is the case for the European Neighbourhood Policy. According to this principle, there can be no visa facilitation of visa-free travel without compliance with the rules of democracy and the rule of law. (European Parliament 2006b: 9)

Moreover, the EU lacks effective monitoring tools with regard to the practice of readmission. The joint readmission committee does not have any power to monitor the upholding of human rights standards at the different stages of the readmission procedure. Rather, it approaches it in a relatively non-politicised and technical way, prompting the European Parliament (2007: 10) to ask whether an agreement that relates to persons can indeed 'be treated as a purely technical agreement'. To assess human rights practices, the EU has to rely on the information provided by its Russian partners and by non-governmental organisations (such as UNHCR, Amnesty International and IOM) who are, however, not part of the joint readmission committee. It is worth mentioning that the EU's readmission policy does not stand alone in this regard. In Russia, the EU's external influence on human rights violations and the development of human rights law according to international standards is generally low (Gänzle 2008; Debardeleben 2008: 76–9).

Low human rights and refugee protection standards
Although the readmission agreement includes safeguards for protecting the human rights of returned persons, it is not comprehensive in this respect. According to the European Parliament (2007b), the agreement lacks clear legal stipulations in two areas in particular. Firstly, the safeguards on the basis of which the transit of a third country national or stateless person may be refused do not include measures to protect children and the family unit or recognise the physical and psychological inviolability of irregular immigrants – elements which are essential since they 'constitute the indispensable core of a principle of humanity that has to be observed if the agreement is to be valid in the light not only of Union values, but also of the unwritten principles of international law' (European Parliament 2007b). Second, the provision dealing with accelerated procedures for persons apprehended in border regions does not outline how to safeguard the rights of the apprehended person. If such a person is readmitted within a very short time period, 'how can the procedure be reconciled in practice with the specific status of asylum-seekers in international law?' (European Parliament 2007b: 10).

Similar practices by EU member states in other geographical settings were criticised for directly contravening international law. For instance, in May 2009 when Italy discovered 227 migrants some 35 miles off the island of Lampedusa and acted to remove them within 24 hours to Libya, NGOs forcefully protested that these migrants were being prevented from lodging an asylum claim and, in the worst case, were being directly pushed back into the arms of their persecutors (Jesuit Refugee Service 2009).

Even more critically, we can assume that there is a substantial gap between the formal adoption of international refugee protection standards and the actual degree of compliance with them. With the help of EU financial assistance, Russia has made progress in reforming its national migration and asylum legislation according to international standards, on paper at least, since the degree of actual implementation remains questionable. Although they did not include Russia as a case study, Freyburg *et al.* (2009) demonstrated that in several ENP participating states the EU might be able to succeed in bringing these countries' domestic asylum legislation in line with internationally recognised standards, but that 'successful rule adoption does not necessarily lead to rule application' (Freyburg *et al.* 2009: 916). By looking at rule adoption and rule implementation in Moldova, Ukraine and Morocco, they showed that practical deficiencies remained, despite the adjusted legislative framework – these deficiencies include the non-application of a human rights approach, weak administrative capacities for dealing with asylum seekers, and shortcomings in the justice system concerning fair asylum procedures.

The same kinds of concern are of relevance for Russia. The question is to what extent Russia is actually capable of providing, and willing to provide, fair asylum procedures, against a background of reports of widespread torture and the ill-treatment of detainees throughout Russia (see, e.g., Amnesty International 2009). Moreover, with an over-politicised justice system, whose independence is questioned, the work of lawyers and human rights defenders is increasingly restricted and subject to harassment (International Commission of Jurists 2009). The 'safe third country' principle in general overemphasises formal criteria while neglecting the actual procedures and practices.

Shifting responsibility and chain deportation
The danger of human rights violation is of particular relevance with regard to the return of third country nationals from the EU; subject to further readmission beyond transit countries. The EU–Russia readmission agreement lacks any possibility to prevent Russia from sending third country nationals and stateless persons to countries that are widely recognised as committing human rights violations. The agreement does not interfere with other bilateral readmission agreements that Russia has signed or intends to sign with other third countries. The EU simply has no option for effective action if Russia signs bilateral readmission agreements that may fall short of internationally recognised safeguards or protection standards. This may lead to a situation whereby third country nationals returned from the EU's territory on the basis of bilateral agreements, end up being transferred on to third countries known for human rights abuses and which do not fulfil the standards of 'safe third countries'. The only way to make sure that no human rights abuses later occurred would be to determine beforehand the readmission of the third country national to Russia.

An example is the 2007 bilateral readmission agreement between Russia and Uzbekistan. The content of this agreement has not been made publicly accessible. This means that people readmitted by the EU to Russia might be further transferred to Uzbekistan, regardless of the fact that the EU imposed sanctions on Uzbekistan after the killing of numerous civilians in Andijan in May 2005 (Balzacq 2008: 30). According to the 2009 country report by Amnesty International, Russia attempted to extradite several individuals wanted by Uzbekistan in connection with the 2005 Andijan protests, thereby overlooking the risk of torture and ill-treatment for these people and violating the obligation of *non-refoulement* defined by the Geneva Convention. In at least two cases, extradition was halted due to intervention by the European Court of Human Rights, though Russia has so far refrained from generally suspending extraditions to Uzbekistan (Amnesty International 2009). What is more, in at least one case, Russia went ahead with the extradition irrespective of interim measures laid down by the European Court of Human Rights (International Commission of Jurists 2009: 8).

In interviews, Commission officials and representatives of EU member states advanced the view that in practice the member states always try to readmit people directly to their country of origin. However, if they know that Russia may thereafter send the returned person on to a country where there is high risk of human rights abuse, the member states will refrain from readmitting. There is, however, no legal clause in this respect, and it is up to the individual member states to decide on a case by case basis. Legal guarantees are lacking, as is public control. The agreement provides for establishing a readmission joint committee in which representatives of Russia and the European Commission, together with experts from member states, meet on a regular basis to review the agreement's implementation. In addition, the EU's border management agency, FRONTEX, coordinates the operational aspects of readmission of irregular third country nationals. However, in both instances, these provisions do not constitute independent bodies that can be called upon in the case of insufficient or non-existent implementation. There is no such independent body, be it a regulatory authority or court, to deal with Community readmission agreements. The absence of any independent third party should cause concern, especially given the costs and negative implications of readmission agreements for transit countries – this might entice the governments of such transit countries to further readmit third country nationals to the next country regardless of their human rights situation.

Conclusions

The aim of this chapter has been to discuss the tension between values and security in the external dimension of EU migration policy, by exploring the implementation of the EU readmission agreement with Russia. The EU's foreign policy tool of readmission agreements is probably the strongest expression of a security logic underlying the external dimension of EU migration policy. This raises the question as to the role and importance given to self-proclaimed values relating to international humanitarian and refugee protection standards when implementing Community readmission agreements. Moreover, given the importance attached to values-based policy instruments, does the EU really have the power to assure their implementation?

In the last two decades, the focus of return policies in EU member states changed from voluntary return to an ever more restrictive approach that considered forced return to be a legitimate policy goal. The abolition of border controls within the Schengen area has resulted in a much stronger focus being placed on external borders; as a result, more attention has been given by the EU member states to an effective common returns policy to enforce border control, as expressed most significantly with the Community readmission agreements. By its very nature, this security logic creates a challenge for international humanitarian and refugee protection standards. As the analysis has illustrated, the EU struggles to find an appropriate place and emphasis for human rights aspects when defining a common readmission policy. Only in reaction to strong criticism by the European Parliament and NGOs, was the list of international obligations and legal documents to be considered by the contracting parties substantially lengthened. The wording of the EU–Russia readmission agreement became the standard model for the agreements that followed. Securing a signature for the agreement was a priority for the EU within the framework of EU–Russian cooperation in the JHA domain, yet the EU only succeeded in what were tedious negotiations after it accepted the link between readmission and visa facilitation. In its concrete stipulations, the EU–Russia readmission agreement contains detailed information concerning the obligations of those readmitted, and under what conditions, combined with certain value-based human rights and refugee protection standards. With regard to the most continuous question, that is the readmission of third country nationals and stateless persons, the EU and Russia agreed on a transition period of three years, which expired in July 2010. In the process of implementing the agreement the EU has provided a range of technical and financial assistance to help Russia enhance law enforcement and capacity-building.

This chapter has advanced the argument that tensions between the security logic and values exist, particularly concerning three aspects. The first refers to the lack of effective control and monitoring instruments. Although demanded by the European Parliament, the Commission and Council have refrained from making compliance with human rights and refugee protection standards subject to its external conditionality, as well as from including a formal human rights and democracy clause in the EU–Russia readmission agreement. The monitoring possibilities of the EU are limited in this respect. Second, the readmission agreement excludes references to certain aspects of human rights and refugee protection standards, and particularly on how to assure compliance with them. Instead, the EU only focuses on the formal adoption of human rights standards without taking care of the actual degree of compliance. However, there is a considerable gap between the transposition of human rights and refugee protection standards and their actual degree of implementation in Russia. Finally, the EU did not include legal safeguards for preventing Russia from sending on readmitted third country nationals and stateless persons to countries with human rights violations. EU member states therefore consciously risk contributing to the carrying out of human rights abuses directly by others. EU officials maintain that no member state would readmit a person if doubts existed about the adherence to human rights and refugee protection standards in the country to which an individual was to be sent. However, readmission cases where rights are not being respected and standards not upheld are reported by national NGOs and international organisations such as UNHCR on a regular basis.

Overall, therefore, the case study on the EU–Russia readmission agreement has demonstrated that the EU has been willing to sideline values when proceeding in favour of security interests. This sheds a different light on the EU's self-proclaimed objectives of promoting the rule of law and good governance in the wider European region.

Notes

1. We would like to thank Heidrun Maurer and the editors of this book for their helpful comments on earlier versions of the chapter.
2. 'Respecting international obligations and human rights Article 6 of the Treaty on European Union affirms that the Union is founded on the principles of liberty, democracy, respect for human rights and fundamental freedoms, and the rule of law, principles which are common to the Member States. In consequence, the full respect of human rights and fundamental freedoms is the natural and basic prerequisite for a European return policy' (Commission 2002; see also Directive 2008/2115/EC).
3. The thematic common spaces within the framework of the Partnership and Cooperation Agreement are as follows: 1) Common Economic Space; 2) Common Space of Freedom, Security and Justice; 3) Common Space of External Security; and 4) Common Space of Research and Education.
4. Contrary to most readmission agreements signed between the EU and third countries, the EU–Russia readmission agreement contains a strict timeframe for submitting an application for readmission. Russia insists on a submission 'within a maximum of 6 months of the requesting State authority having received information indicating that a third country national or a stateless person no longer fulfils the conditions in force

for entry, presence or residence' (article 11: 1).
5 The principle of *non-refoulement* is laid out in article 33(1) of the 1951 Convention on the Status of Refugees (known as the Geneva Convention) which states that 'no contracting state shall expel or return (*refouler*) a refugee in any manner whatsoever to the frontiers of territories where his life or freedom would be threatened on accound of his race, religion, nationality, membership of a particular social group or political opinion'.
6 Between 2004 and 2006, targeted assistance was offered within the AENEAS programme, which had an overall budget of €120 million.
7 This project was funded by the EU under the AENEAS 2005 programme and by the governments of Germany and Finland.
8 According to interviews with EU officials in Moscow in May 2009, IOM has been the most important cooperation partner of the EU in Russia with regard to readmission. Other cooperation partners are, e.g., UNDP and UNHCR, the EU member states acting as donors, and national implementing institutions, such as the Danish International Development Agency (DANIDA) and the Swedish International Development Cooperation Agency (SIDA).
9 However, in article 23(5) there is an unconditional possibility to denounce the agreement by either contracting party.

KAROLINA POMORSKA AND GERGANA NOUTCHEVA

12

Conclusion: conceptualising the EU's role in the European neighbourhood

This book has set out to examine the complex interaction between values and security in shaping the EU's policy towards its neighbours. It has looked at the normative and strategic dynamics of EU's foreign policy through the prism of five typologies: (i) 'security as a value', (ii) 'values as part of security', (iii) 'values versus security', (iv) 'values versus values' and (v) 'security versus security'. The contributors to the volume have demonstrated the utility of combining different conceptualisations of values and security in their empirical investigation of concrete EU policies vis-à-vis (groups of) neighbouring states. They have shown the complexity of motives behind the EU's external actions and analysed various tensions that prevent the EU from having greater impact on its neighbourhood.

In this concluding chapter, we examine the implications of the analysis at three levels. First, we discuss the implications of the approach favoured in the book for European foreign policy research, emphasising the advantages of building bridges across research traditions for our understanding of European foreign policy dilemmas. Second, we look at the implications of the empirical findings of the book for the EU's foreign policy 'actorness'. Third, we explore the implications of the analysis for the European Neighbourhood Policy and the EU's future relations with its neighbours.

Theoretical implications

This book has argued in favour of ontological and methodological openness in European foreign policy research taking the example of ENP and the EU's relations with its neighbouring states, broadly defined. Bringing in perspectives from seemingly opposing theoretical schools and combining methods linked to different research traditions have proved useful for unpacking the complexities of phenomena occurring in the world of policy and practice. This is not to negate research embedded in single theories but to complement it and to show the advantages of building bridges across competing paradigms (Checkel 2010; Sil and Katzenstein 2010). In this section, we discuss first the research questions addressed by the contributions. We then summarise the methods employed by the authors in their analysis of concrete empirical puzzles. Finally, we demonstrate the strategies used by the contributors to transcend the boundaries of rationalism and constructivism and to combine insights from both in their research designs.

Research questions
The book has been driven by a substantive policy-oriented problem, while searching for a middle-range theory that would help us understand better the empirical puzzles identified in Chapter 1. To repeat what we have identified as the main questions of this volume:

1. Can the EU pursue norm export in the wider neighbourhood and, at the same time, ensure the cooperation of neighbouring states on hard and soft security matters?
2. Can these two goals be pursued simultaneously and what are the implications for the Union's influence in the neighbourhood and its status in global politics?
3. Is the choice between values and security unavoidable by the EU and its neighbours?

The contributors engaged with the debate on the different conceptualisations of security and values and employed different methods for examining the tensions between them. Their analysis has shown that the EU foreign policy-makers face policy dilemmas which are not sufficiently captured and properly analysed by the narrow focus and methodological foundation of individual IR paradigms. To remain policy-relevant and close to real world problems, European foreign policy research has to transcend the boundaries of different research traditions and remain flexible about the research questions it asks, the ontological premises it starts from, the methods it uses and the statements it makes about causal mechanisms in explanatory accounts. In the words of Sill and Katzenstein (2010: 418), 'the kinds of problems addressed by eclectic scholars are more likely to have concrete implications for the messy substantive problems facing policymakers and ordinary social and political actors'.

In concrete terms, the specific research questions tackled by the chapters fall within two broad categories. One concerns the driving factors behind the EU policies vis-à-vis specific (groups of) neighbours and the second relates to the reasons for the EU's (lack of) impact on the neighbourhood in specific policy areas. In the first vein, we find the chapter by Bechev on the sources, facets and manifestations of EU power in relation to its neighbours enquiring into the material pre-conditions for a hegemonic order centred on the EU's internal market. Similarly, the chapter by Dimitrovova examines the existence of a hegemonic discourse based on the EU values that underpins the power relationship between the EU and its neighbours. Two other chapters, one by Balfour and another by Bosse, look at the continuity and change in the EU's policies towards the Mediterranean and Belarus respectively, and ask about the causes of EU policy continuity or change. Trauner, Kruse and Zeilinger investigate the motivation behind the EU's readmission policy vis-à-vis Russia.

In the second vein, we find authors who refer the value and security dimension of EU policies to explain the (lack of) EU's impact on the neighbourhood. In particular, Coskun enquires into the reasons for the EU's failure of promoting democracy in the Middle East; Simão asks about the EU's lack of impact on security in the Southern Caucasus; Baracani investigates the EU's record of promoting peace in the neighbourhood; whereas Schmidt-Felzmann examines why the EU has failed to influence democratic developments in Russia in the post-Cold War period.

In sum, all chapters engaged in the discussion about motivations or the impact of the EU's policy in the neighbourhood. In different ways, all of them exposed tensions in the policy-making process, either between values prioritised by the EU member states or the European Commission and between security interests and/or values as perceived by the EU member states and the neighbouring countries. A useful conceptualisation was proposed by Balfour, who wrote about the 'logics of diversity', which can be applied to almost every chapter in the volume. The authors have thus moved the discussion away from the *leitmotiv* of the recent literature on ENP, the issue of incentives offered to the countries in the neighbourhood, inspired by the enlargement debate, and have anchored the study of the ENP in the field of foreign policy analysis.

Methodology

The book has not outlined a set of hypotheses for the contributors to test but has provided five possible conceptual frameworks as a point of departure for the analysis. The rationale behind this approach is to attempt to break out of the strict ontological and methodological divisions between different theoretical schools and build bridges between them (Zürn and Checkel 2005). All contributors were encouraged to choose the methods that provide the soundest methodological foundation for their research designs and to be open-mined about the interpretation of the empirical evidence. In effect, the authors have opted for a variety of methodological tools mostly related to the positivist view of knowledge. The volume is thus based on a positivist epistemology which is open to methodological pluralism.

In line with the theoretical plurality, the book brings together different levels of analysis, focusing on the individuals (e.g. officials from the European Commission, Dimitrovova), the EU member states (e.g. Schmidt-Felzmann; Balfour) or the EU itself (Bechev; Trauner, Kruse and Zeilinger). By engaging with analysis at different levels, the book provides the reader with a more complex view on the fundaments of the EU's relations with its neighbours. The analysis of Bechev is structural and related to the international system, in which the EU is portrayed as a hegemon by default. A similar structural view is taken by Dimitrovova, who argues that the EU is acting as an empire. In a similar vein, the analysis of Trauner, Kruse and Zeilinger focuses on the EU as a level of analysis. Balfour focuses on the EU member states, showing the South–North divisions within the EU. Natorski and Schmidt-Felzmann also analyse the positions of governments: Natorski that of an outsider (Ukraine) and Schmidt-Felzmann those of the EU member states. Bosse concentrates on the European Commission.

The most frequently employed method in the book is discourse analysis. Dimitrovova analyses the official documents and compares them with the unofficial discourse of European Commission officials, obtained through interviews. A similar technique is used by Bosse and Natorski, who studied both official documents and interview data, while Trauner, Kruse and Zeilinger conducted an analysis of legal documents.

Collectively, the contributions demonstrate that there is no single methodology that is better suited to study the EU's policy and impact on its neighbourhood. It is therefore justified to be open-minded methodologically and ready to combine methods associated with different research traditions with the aim of unpacking the complex causal relationships between variables that hold to key to explaining empirical developments.

Theoretical approaches: bridge-building in practice

The two main strategies suggested in the literature for connecting different theories in research designs are domain of application and temporal sequencing (Checkel 2010: 11). The former employs a synthesis approach which specifies how different explanatory factors derived from competing theoretical schools combine to explain different aspects (or domains) of an empirical puzzle. The latter suggests a temporal difference in the application of competing theories to a real-world problem. The strategy favoured in this book is that of domain of application, where independent explanatory variables associated with different theories are employed in individual research designs to help us understand better 'the empirical world' (Checkel 2010: 11).

The book thus favours analytical eclecticism and has made an attempt at combining constructivist (idealist) and rationalist (materialist) approaches. As emphasised by Sil and Katzenstein (2010), such a pragmatic approach is recommended when one seeks 'engagement with the world of policy and practice' (2010: 411). The authors adopt different conceptualisations of values and security throughout the book. Dimitrovova clearly operates within the values versus values typology and classifies security as one of the values pursued (with priority) by the EU. Simão and Natorski in their contributions also opt for including security in the values nexus. Balfour places her chapter within the 'values versus security' typology, but recognises also the 'values versus values' clash and competing perceptions of values. She also conceptualises engagement and cooperation as values. While Coskun continues with the emphasis on values, the notion of interest comes across in her chapter, clashing with political values related to democracy promotion. Bosse shifts the analysis to a more straightforward contrast between pursuing *realpolitik* on the one hand and idealist-driven policies on the other. It is now the nexus 'values versus security' that informs the analysis, which also continues in the chapter of Schmidt-Felzmann, who examines the 'values versus energy security' nexus. The clash between the traditional rationalist interpretation of security linked to interests and the idealistic perception of values comes up in the analysis of Trauner, Kruse and Zeilinger as well, even though they consider the possibility of values as part of the security logic too.

The book contributors also took up the challenge of combining different theoretical approaches by including both values and security and the relationship between the two in their explanatory accounts of EU policy. While some positioned themselves clearly in the constructivist or the rational school of thought, all of them addressed the tensions between values and security, albeit in a different manner.

Bechev argues that value projection is part of the security order built around the EU and designed to advance the EU interests. According to his analysis, the rhetoric on values is used to justify certain policies that serve to strengthen the position of the EU at the expense of its peripheries. In the conceptualisation of power, he underlines the EU's ability to shape the 'rules of engagement' (norms). Thus, both security interests and values underpin the EU power resources turning the EU into an 'unintentional hegemon'. The power asymmetry between the EU and its neighbours explains the relations between the EU core and the various circles of countries around the EU with receptivity of EU values in periphery societies marking the outer limits of the EU's hegemony.

Unlike Bechev, Dimitrovova adopts the 'opposite' approach and conceptualises security as a value that can undermine other values in the EU's policies. She argues that the EU's relationship with its neighbourhood is of a neo-imperial character since it reflects the EU's civilising mission of projecting its own values onto the neighbours. She emphasises that this is only possible because of the asymmetrical teacher–pupil relationship between the EU and its neighbours. Dimitrovova also maintains that the values the EU promotes should not be considered as 'neutral', but rather seen as an expression of the EU's strategic interests. Thus, both rational and normative reasons combine to explain the dominant values-based discourse in ENP.

Similar to Dimitrovova, Simão also conceptualises security as a value and argues that the strategic goals of the EU are negatively affected by the Union's negligence of its normative agenda. She has chosen to use the security networks approach in order to explain the (non-)emergence of a security community between the EU and its neighbours. Drawing on evidence from the South Caucasus, Simão observes that the EU's goals and its normative agenda are undermined by its unwillingness to engage in conflict resolution. As a consequence, the Union is perceived as a 'weak political player' in the region, who is unable to change the context into a more favourable one for domestic reforms in neighbouring states. The discrepancy between the EU's normative approach to security and local preferences for hard security guarantees (security versus security) is a key determinant of the EU's limited impact in the area. For Simão, therefore, the values-based logic is better placed to explain the EU's policies whereas the rationality-based logic is more suitable for understanding neighbouring states' reactions to the EU's (in-)actions.

Balfour, similar to Dimitrovova and Simão, conceptualises security as a value, but operates within an even broader understanding of what qualifies as a value. She argues that partnership and engagement, next to multilateralism, should also be considered as a value, bringing a new perspective to the debate. Balfour concludes that the 'logic of diversity' is prevalent in the perceptions of security and values among the EU member states, often resulting in lowest common denominator policies at the EU level. Given the internal inconsistencies and complexities, the normative and the rational become impossible to disentangle as drivers of EU policy but interact to shape the EU's external positions.

Coskun in her chapter brings in a historical perspective on the 'security versus values' dilemma and explains the EU's motives by both its material interests (which tend to prevail in her case study) and its values. Historical background explains the different perception of political values in the EU and in the Middle East (values versus values), which, in turn, undermines any efforts of the Union to promote democracy in the region. In this sense, security trumps democratisation or other values discussed in the volume. But both the security and the value logics inform our understanding of the EU relationship with the Middle Eastern countries.

A somewhat similar strategy is taken up by Michal Natorski, who places his analysis of EU–Ukraine foreign policy cooperation in the 'security as a value' typology, while showing the tensions between different perceptions of security by the EU and its neighbours. This then becomes a security versus security tension, all conceptualised in a normative framework. He highlights the detrimental consequences of such divergent understandings of values for EU–Ukraine relations. Ukraine strives to assert its 'Europeanness' by presenting an image of a security provider entitled to be part of the European security community while the EU treats the country as a security threat that does not belong to the European core.

Like Coskun and Natorski, Schmidt-Felzmann also shows how different perceptions of values between the EU and a neighbour, Russia in this case, inhibit the EU's impact. In particular, the divergent perceptions of democracy between Russia and the EU explain partly the EU's incapacity to influence the country's internal political development. In addition, and perhaps more importantly, she exposes the internal tension between diverging interest perceptions of the EU member states, revealing a clash between the material interests of the EU member states and the value-oriented policies of the EU.

In a similar vein, Bosse illustrates the classical clash between security and values and the oscillation of EU policy between these two poles depending on domestic circumstances in neighbouring states, Belarus in this case, and the perceived effectiveness of policy instruments used by the EU. According to her analysis, a shift in emphasis from values to security explains the change in EU policy from negative conditionality and isolation of the Belarusian regime to engagement and dialogue and from support of civil society to pragmatic privileging of relations with the government.

A similar dichotomy is also prevalent in the chapter by Trauner, Kruse and Zeilinger, who show the disparity between the EU's normative agenda and its 'security logic' in the case of the EU's readmission policy. The authors demonstrate that when faced with the choice of protecting its internal security or the human rights of illegal immigrants trying to enter the Schengen zone, the EU expresses a clear preference for its own security at the expense of upholding human rights principles enshrined in international law. Their analysis is thus more in line with the rationalist tradition in social sciences but the authors do not exclude the normative dimension from the EU's security rationale.

Baracani includes both normative and strategic elements in her explanation of EU's conflict resolution policy instruments. While many 'soft tools' are used in pursuing the 'conditional anchoring' of conflict parties to the EU's institutional framework and policy space, she concludes that it is the strategic interest of the EU that pre-determines the choice of conflicts in which the Union becomes involved. Baracani argues, on the same lines as Simão, that the promotion of peace as a value is instrumental to achieve the EU's strategic interests in its internal security. The Union can achieve it by providing conditional support to conflict parties in exchange for their compliance with the EU's values.

Collectively, the chapters demonstrate the diversity of bridge-building approaches that can be applied to the study of the EU's relations with its neighbours. They highlight the utility of combining explanatory variables from the rationalist and constructivist research traditions in single research designs thus enriching our understanding of real world policy dilemmas. In

Implications for the EU's foreign policy 'actorness'

The research findings of the book contributions reveal a number of important implications for the EU's foreign policy 'actorness' in general and its impact on the European neighbourhood in particular. Three themes merit a special mention as they run throughout the volume and appear to challenge conventional wisdom about European foreign policy. First, the volume has brought to light some severe internal divisions among the EU member states over values and security and their prioritisation in EU's foreign policy. Second, some of the contributions have unearthed important differences between the EU and its neighbours about conceptions of values and security, closely linked to contradictions between the formal EU discourse on ENP and the rhetoric of EU officials involved in the EU policy-making process. Third, as a result of the internal and external tensions over values and security, the EU's impact on the neighbourhood has been shown to be limited, a finding directly challenging much of the existing literature on ENP's transformative power in neighbouring states. We address consecutively these three implications in greater detail below.

The EU's divisiveness over values and security

Several authors in this volume have put forward the argument that the internal divisions in the EU are to blame for the EU's inability to exert influence in the neighbourhood. In this context, Balfour has been writing about the 'logic of diversity' often leading to lowest common denominator policies at the EU level. This is vividly illustrated in the chapter on EU–Russia relations, where Schmidt-Felzmann shows the divisions among the member states when it comes to the weight of trade and energy security interests, on the one hand, and EU political values, on the other hand. These differences inhibit the emergence of a coherent value-consistent position on Russia (security trumps values). Bechev argues, in a slightly different manner, that the divisions between the EU member states regarding the prioritisation of certain values do not necessarily impede the EU from diffusing its norms, but the dynamics of this diffusion is more gradual and technocratic.

A number of different divisions were shown in the book: those between the 'core' member states and the rest (Bechev), the South and the North (Bechev, Balfour, Schmidt-Felzmann), those putting greater emphasis on the

EU's security interests and those insisting on a more value-driven foreign policy. What policy ultimately prevails at the EU level is case-contingent. Coskun, for instance, observes that in the case of the EU's policy towards the Mediterranean, security is the main interest, while democracy promotion is conditioned by the strategic interests and priorities of the member states. Bosse argues that it is *realpolitik* that clearly dominates the EU's policy towards Belarus, even though the normative elements are also present.

These findings go against the bulk of literature that emphasises the transnational character of CFSP and the consensus-orientated culture that dominates EU foreign policy-making. In particular, the Europeanisation research has sought to trace the changing patterns of member states' foreign policies as a result of the institutionalisation of foreign policy exchanges within the CFSP framework (Manners and Whitman 2000; Tonra 2001; Wong 2005; Wong and Hill 2011). The underlying expectation of some Europeanisation literature is foreign policy convergence among the member states, which in concrete terms means the 'emergence of shared norms and notions of European interests' (Wong 2007: 325). The mechanisms through which such convergence may occur remain contested even though elite socialisation through intense institutionalised contacts have largely been anticipated to account for changes in that direction over time (Tonra 2001; Wong 2007). Our findings, in line with other studies, reveal the limits of 'Europeanising' national foreign policy and the persistent relevance of national foreign policy preferences (Gross 2009).

Different perceptions of values and security between the EU and its neighbours

The divergent perception of values and security are not only present among the EU member states (the internal EU dimension) but also between the EU member states and the EU's partners in the neighbourhood. Natorski, Simão and Schmidt-Felzmann demonstrate the negative effects of the differences in perceptions of security between the EU and its neighbouring states. Dimitrovova, Coskun and Schmidt-Felzmann show the negative consequences of the differences in perceptions of values between the EU and its partners. Similar negative effects of the growing gap between the EU's capabilities and external expectations ('capabilities–expectations gap') were already shown in the early CFSP literature e.g. by Christopher Hill (1993). Ole Elgström and Michael Smith suggested that, in addition, we may consider the existence of the 'conception–performance gap', which would capture the discrepancy between what the EU proclaims as its role and the perceptions of the outsiders (Elgström and Smith, 2006: 248). This book's findings reinforce what we have learnt from recent literature exploring the difference between the EU's self-perception and the way it is viewed from the outside, for example in Russia (Morini *et al.* 2010). In this respect, the chapters provide new evidence from the European neighbourhood adding insights to the cases that have so far mostly focused on the perceptions of the EU by major world powers or international organisations (e.g. Lucarelli and Fioramonti 2010).

Some of the differences over perceptions stem from the contradictions in the EU's discourse over the nature of ENP. These contradictions become especially apparent in the chapter by Dimitrovova. While the official discourse favours partnership and joint ownership (classified by Balfour as important values in their own right), informally, the EU officials' discourse is often 'mentoring and paternalistic'. This mismatch between the formal normative discourse on ENP and the security-driven discourse of the readmission agreements is also demonstrated by Trauner, Kruse and Zeilinger. A substantial gap exists between the rhetorical adherence to human rights principles and the implementation of policies leading to the actual protection of the human rights of illegal immigrants and asylum seekers. Such inconsistencies do not go unnoticed by the partners from the neighbourhood and negatively influence the relationship between the two. Rosa Balfour also points at the direct tensions and contradictions in the EU's discourse over ENP, especially between the political values and security aims on one hand and maintaining relationships with certain countries on the other. The resulting mixed signals sent to the partners undermine the EU's credibility, a danger clearly flagged also by Bosse regarding the EU's policy towards Belarus.

The EU's impact on the European neighbourhood

The empirical findings of the volume have important implications for the EU's impact on the European neighbourhood. While there is no lack of literature that asserts the limited influence of ENP on partner countries to date, the majority of it attributes the EU's failure to transform the neighbourhood to the size, speed and credibility of EU incentives offered to the neighbours (Smith 2005a; Weber, Smith and Baun 2007; Whitman and Wolff 2010). This volume claims that the reasons for the EU's ineffectiveness in the neighbourhood are more fundamental and have to do with core disagreements at the heart of the EU. In a way, the EU's hesitation to offer stronger incentives for reform to the neighbours is a consequence of the internal EU divisions over values and security and how to prioritise different objectives in the EU's external relations. In this sense, our understanding of ENP's transformative potential must include an analysis of the strategy behind ENP (to the extent that it exists) and the internal EU support for it, an angle that has largely escaped the focus of ENP research so far. This volume has aimed to fill in this gap in the literature.

The contributors have shown that the internal and external tensions regarding values and security have affected all policy areas of EU external action. In the domain of democracy promotion, the EU has been cautious about putting its resources behind its political values and has achieved limited results as a consequence, both in the South and in the East (Balfour, Coskun, Bosse, Simão, Schmidt-Felzmann). In the area of conflict resolution, the EU has been uncertain about its security priorities and has punched below its weight with the instruments it has been willing to commit (Simão, Baracani). It has managed to entice partners to cooperate on foreign policy dossiers (Natorski) but this has not changed the security dynamics in the neighbourhood. In other fields of soft security such as energy policy and immigration policy, the differences between the EU member states have brought to the fore a more self-regarding EU concerned more with its own security than with its normative impact on neighbouring states (Schmidt-Felzmann, Trauner, Kruse and Zeilinger).

Overall, the book paints a complex picture of the EU as an actor in international relations: it is undecided about its goals, which are often in competition (or even contradiction) with each other; it is internally divided about the values and interests to be promoted in the neighbourhood; it sends mixed messages to its partners, often in a paternalistic tone. The normative agenda is present in the official discourse and in internal debates with several EU member states pressing for attaching more significance to democracy promotion in the EU's external policies but divergent perceptions among the member states stand in the way of a more robust norm-consistent EU policy. Simultaneously, differences over security objectives and means to enhancing security, both internally and in the neighbourhood, have often paralysed the EU and left its neighbours struggling for its attention.

The book itself is not free from tensions apparent in its findings: can the EU be an 'unintentional hegemon' and conduct a strategically oriented, asymmetrical, *realpolitik* towards its neighbours? Can it be a 'weak political player' and yet have the power of attraction to draw its neighbours to its policies and institutions? These contradictions do not invalidate the analysis but emphasise once again the need to open up our conceptual paradigms and methodological tools for the complexities of the real world in order to gain more insight into the multifaceted dynamics at play.

Implications for ENP

The conceptual dilemmas identified in this volume have reflected the policy dilemmas confronting European foreign policy-makers. They continue to be relevant prisms through which to examine policy outcomes of past decisions and policy options for the future. We will demonstrate now how they apply to the strategic review of ENP conducted over the course of 2010 and released in May 2011. In particular, we will discuss the impact of the Arab Spring on the EU's policies vis-à-vis the neighbours and how the values and security aspects of ENP interact to define the EU's future strategy with regard to the southern and eastern neighbourhoods.

Policy failure based on a 'values versus security' logic?
The Arab Spring of 2011 exposed the false premises of decades-long EU policy towards the Mediterranean which for years paid lip service to the EU's normative principles while in practice backed the authoritarian leaders in the region in exchange for their cooperation on security issues. Support for the status quo provided an illusionary feeling of stability which proved unsustainable given the internal dynamics of Arab political regimes. The events on the ground revealed unequivocally the short-sightedness of privileging engagement with autocrats and ignoring the aspirations of Arab societies. The Arab youth decisively denounced the unholy alliance between autocracy and deceptive stability and expressed a clear preference for different normative fundamentals and security arrangements of their polities. In addition, the Arab societal demands for change were made in a peaceful way, rejecting the violent extremism and religious fundamentalism of radical movements from the region that have provoked Western security concerns since the 9/11 attacks.

Towards complementarity of values and security in the EU's policy?
How has the EU responded to the momentous changes in the Mediterranean? While ENP was under review well before the Arab uprisings of 2011, it took a political upheaval of that scale for a radical rethink of the EU's approach to the southern neighbourhood particularly and the whole neighbourhood more generally. While the events on the ground were still unfolding, the European Commission (2011a) announced the launch of a 'Partnership for Democracy and Shared Prosperity with the Southern Mediterranean' in March 2011 followed by a strategic review of ENP in May 2011entitled 'A New Response to a Changing Neighbourhood' (2011b). The two documents are intended to outline the EU's new strategic vision for its relations with the neighbouring countries but do they amount to a 'grand strategy'?

First, there is a clear attempt at the rhetorical level to admit the mistakes of the past. As the European Commissioner for Enlargement and Neighbourhood Policy Štefan Füle put it in a speech to the European Parliament on 28 February 2011 (Füle 2011):

> [W]e must show humility about the past. Europe was not vocal enough in defending human rights and local democratic forces in the region. Too many of us fell prey to the assumption that authoritarian regimes were a guarantee of stability in the region. This was not even Realpolitik. It was, at best, short-termism – and the kind of short-termism that makes the long term ever more difficult to build.

Second, the new approach advocated for the EU's relations with the neighbourhood emphasises the need to rebalance the security and the value dimensions of EU policy by placing the normative component at its heart. Standing by the side of democracy in the Arab uprisings is also riding by the tide of history so there were no surprises when the EU announced a renewed focus on democracy support, with the objective this time of 'building deep and sustainable democracy' in the neighbourhood (Commission 2011b: 3). What is meant by 'deep democracy' is not specified yet but the term used seems to put a clear distinction between what used to be a rhetorical commitment to democratisation with very little practical support for democracy-building and a newly invigorated policy of helping the Arab societies fulfil their aspirations for human dignity, social justice and equal opportunities. There is also a notable shift of emphasis in the EU rhetoric from establishing a partnership based on 'common values' with the EU's political principles setting the normative benchmark to a relationship reflecting a shared commitment to 'universal values' (Commission 2011b: 2). The change in the justification of the EU's policy is probably not incidental given the long-standing criticism of the EU as patronising its partners and imposing its values on other societies. Every attempt is made to present the EU as a humble player, ready to assist but letting endogenous actors take the lead in determining the parameters of democratic transitions in the region.

Third, the EU has also made a pledge to support the democratic transformation of the Mediterranean with more resources. The EU High Representative for Foreign Affairs and Security Policy Catherine Ashton has defined the three pillars of the EU's new approach as the '3 Ms' – money, market access and mobility – committing the EU to a more generous policy vis-à-vis the neighbours with regard to financial assistance, trade openness and visa facilitation to boost people-to-people contacts (Ashton 2011). The EU has also vowed to stick strictly to the principle of conditionality in offering support to the neighbours. The 'more for more' approach (implying also 'less for less') is meant to differentiate more systematically between partners and help those that are willing to advance domestic reforms in line with shared expectations (Commission 2011a: 5). Furthermore, the EU has recognised the necessity to support more decisively the civil societies in partner states as a counterbalance of government policies and in order to strengthen the internal checks and balances of the neighbours' political regimes (Commission 2011a: 6; Commission 2011b: 4). To that end, the European Commission has announced the setting up of a special Civil Society Neighbourhood Facility and a European Endowment for Democracy. The parameters of these instruments are not clear yet and it is too early to say whether they will constitute a radical departure from the EU's privileging of relations with governments that had previously discredited its policies in the eyes of neighbouring societies.

Obviously, the EU will have to shed some long-standing taboos in its policies to be able to deliver on its promises. One refers to its fear of increased flows of irregular migration from the South. Another relates to its fear of losing business opportunities with increased market opening. A third concerns its fear of engaging political organisations that espouse non-violent

Islamic ideologies. If the EU is able to overcome these and other self-regarding constraints on its policies and put into practice its declared intentions, it will make a clear step towards a more balanced neighbourhood policy in which 'values' and 'security' complement each other as objectives and driving forces. So far, it has only affirmed in rhetoric that the security of the Mediterranean region and *inter alia* the EU's security can only be achieved through establishing plural and accountable political regimes in the Arab world and supporting the democratic aspirations of the Arab societies, i.e. that the normative and strategic dimensions of its policies are mutually reinforcing ('values as part of security' and 'security as a value').

A new EU neighbourhood strategy?

Does the EU's new approach amount to a 'grand strategy' for the European neighbourhood? Michael E. Smith (2011) has identified three components of 'grand strategy' – physical security, economic prosperity and value projection – and has claimed that the EU is implicitly developing 'a liberal grand strategy', especially visible in the European neighbourhood where geographical proximity and historical links make it a key player. Yet a few elements of the revamped ENP suggest that 'strategic Europe' is still in the making, if not entirely absent from the neighbourhood.

First, the way in which the changes to the policy were brought about indicate a reactive rather than a proactive approach to interest identification, goal setting and resource allocation, processes associated with grand strategy-making (Smith 2011: 145). This is true for both neighbourhoods. The Eastern Partnership was launched in May 2009 after the Georgia–Russia military confrontation of August 2008 that revealed the inadequacies of the previous weak EU attempts to engage the eastern neighbours. Similarly, the Partnership for Democracy and Shared Prosperity with the Southern Mediterranean was initiated after a widely perceived EU policy failure exposed by the popular uprisings in the Arab world. Rushing to correct past policy mistakes with half-thought measures that need further elaboration and specification in the aftermath has so far been the main *modus operandi* of the EU in the neighbourhood.

Second, while the ENP policy documents abound in declarations about the EU's pivotal role in resolving protracted conflicts in the neighbourhood, in reality, the EU has not been a powerful security provider in the neighbourhood (see chapters by Simão and Baracani in this volume). It has been involved to varying degrees in the resolution of the regional conflicts on its periphery, often preferring the status quo to a more robust action that it is capable of mastering as a result of progressive strengthening of its capacities and institutional structures of the CFSP and CSDP (Popescu 2011). The ENP review of May 2011 continues the rhetorical commitment to EU security provision in the neighbourhood and makes reference to the new opportunities in that domain thanks to the new foreign policy instruments introduced by the Lisbon Treaty (Commission 2011b: 5). How exactly the EU plans to fulfil that objective and whether it operates with an inclusive vision of physical security encompassing both its internal security and that of its neighbours is not clear. In fact, EU inaction on security questions in the past can be interpreted as prioritising its own security at the expense of the security of its neighbours, discussed at length in this volume through the 'security versus security' prism. The divisiveness among the EU member states uncovered in the volume suggests that a common vision on neighbourhood security and how to achieve it has not guided the EU policy in the past and the new ENP documents do not seem to fill in the gaps in strategic thinking on this issue. In the absence of a clear master plan on neighbourhood security, the credibility of the EU as a security provider remains at risk.

Third, the EU has emphasised the economic benefits of its neighbourhood policy through giving neighbours the possibility of a 'stake in the internal market' and thus boosting their economic prosperity alongside its own economic well-being. The main tool for delivering on these promises is the establishment of a Deep and Comprehensive Free Trade Area (DCFTA) with neighbouring economies premised on the regulatory convergence of partner states with the EU's single market model. First estimates of the possible impact of this instrument on the eastern neighbours' economies have pointed to the high costs of the convergence process for the eastern countries (Messerlin *et al.* 2011). Unlike in Central and Eastern Europe where both the EU membership prospect and the generous EU financial assistance offered in the pre-accession process were able to offset the short-term costs of adaptation, in the neighbourhood the EU rewards both in terms of market opening and institutional inclusion, as well as financial flows, are much weaker compensatory mechanisms for the scale of domestic change expected from the neighbours. This calls into question the wealth-generating effect of the proposed DCFTA for the neighbours, at least in the short run. If the EU is to make the ENP offer economically attractive, it has to get serious about giving neighbours market access to the singe market in sectors where it matters most to them, including agriculture. It is not clear yet whether the new approach to the neighbourhood will conform to a comprehensive vision of economic prosperity in the EU and the neighbourhood or relations with the neighbours will be defined by economic protectionism captured by the 'security versus security' lens. The revamped ENP has so far not been able to fill in the void in strategic reflection on this issue even though promises for greater market access for neighbours are not lacking.

Finally, the normative language of the ENP review and the rhetorical commitment to strictly applying political conditionality to neighbours suggests that the process of EU value projection may well be under way in the neighbourhood. What is striking again is the hastiness with which 'deep democracy' is being proposed as the cornerstone of the EU's relations with its neighbours without much internal reflection about what the term entails, without forging an internal agreement on the substance of the term among the various EU actors concerned and without consultation with the neighbours as to whether they share in the EU's normative vision for the neighbourhood. In fact, one of the widely acknowledged lessons of the Arab Spring is that the Arab societies do not want Western help in building their new polities and insist on establishing themselves the foundations of more plural and accountable regimes (Khalaf 2011). That democracy is homegrown and cannot be imposed from outside is a non-disputable fact. The question is in how far the promotion of democracy by external actors is compatible with an endogenous process of democratisation? The ENP policy documents do not provide much insight into how the EU plans to address this dilemma and whether this is a concern for the EU at all. In other words, the 'values versus values' tension discussed in this volume may continue to be a relevant prism for examining the EU policies in the neighbourhood, notwithstanding the EU references to universal values as a justification for its normative stance.

On the whole, the book paints a picture of ENP as a policy with complex motives and unclear goals. It is hard to pin down in any of the chapters the notion of a well-defined strategy, which would encompass both security and normative dimensions. Instead, we face an on-going tension, which is reflected in the internal debate among the EU member states (according to the authors between those more security oriented, usually in the South, and those more interested in promoting fundamental values, in the North) and between the member states and the EU institutions, bringing their own agendas to the table. The strategic ENP review does not appear to have changed much in this respect.

BIBLIOGRAPHY

Adamkus, V. (2008), *Completing Europe: Integration with Neighbours and Engagement with Russia*, Speech delivered by the President of the Republic of Lithuania at the London School of Economics and Political Science, London, 14 February.

Adler, E. (2007), 'Seizing the Middle Ground: Constructivism in World Politics', *European Journal of International Relations*, 3:3, 319–63.

Adler, E. (1998), 'Seeds of Peaceful Change: The OSCE's Security Community-building Model', in E. Adler and M. Barnett (eds), *Security Communities* (Cambridge: Cambridge University Press), pp. 119–60.

Adler, E. and M. Barnett (eds) (1998), *Security Communities* (Cambridge: Cambridge University Press).

Aggestam, L. (2008), 'Introduction: Ethical Power Europe?' *International Affairs*, 84:1, 1–11.

Aliboni, R. (1997), 'Change and Continuity in Western Policies towards the Middle East', in L. Guazzone (ed.), *The Middle East in Global Change* (Basingtoke: Macmillan).

Alieva, L. (2006), *EU and the South Caucasus*, CAP Discussions Paper, December. www.cap.lmu.de/download/2006/2006_Alieva.pdf (accessed 8 June 2007).

Alpher, J. (2000), 'The Political Role of the EU in the Middle East: Israeli Aspirations', in S. Behrendt and C.P. Hanelt (eds), *Bound to Cooperate: Europe and the Middle East* (Guetersloh: Bertelsmann Foundation), pp. 193–208.

Amnesty International (2009), Amnesty International Report 2009. State of the World's Human Rights (Russia: Amnesty International). http://report2009.amnesty.org/en/regions/europe-central-asia/russia (accessed 18 May 2012).

Anderson, J. (2007), 'Singular Europe: An Empire Once Again?', in W. Armstrong and J. Anderson (eds), *The Geopolitics of European Union Enlargement* (London: Routledge), pp. 9–29.

Anderson, J. (1996), 'The Shifting Stage of Politics: New Medieval and Post-modern Territorialities', *Environment and Planning D: Society and Space*, 14, 133–55.

Anderson, M. and E. Bort (eds) (1998), *The Frontiers of the European Union* (London: Pinter).

Anderson, P. (2007), 'Depicting Europe', *London Review of Books*, 29:18, 13–21.

Antonescu, M.V. (2008), *The EU, Ancient and Medieval Empires* (Bucharest: Cartea Universtitara).

Ashton, C. High Representative (2011), 'Remarks by EU High Representative Catherine Ashton on Arrival to the Extraordinary European Council', A 102/11, 11 March.

Axelrode, R. and R. Keohane (1985), 'Achieving Cooperation under Anarchy: Strategies and Institutions', *World Politics*, 38, 226–54.

Balfour, R. (2012), *Human Rights and Democracy in EU Foreign Policy. The Cases of Ukraine and Egypt* (London: Routledge).

Balfour, R. (2007), 'Promoting Human Rights and Democracy in the EU's Neighbourhood: Tools, Strategies and Dilemmas', in R. Balfour and A. Missiroli, *Reassessing the European Neighbourhood Policy*, Brussels: European Policy Centre, Issue Paper No. 54, pp. 8–24.

Balfour, R. (2006), 'Principles of Democracy and Human Rights. A Review of the European Union's Strategies Towards its Neighbours', in S. Lucarelli and I. Manners

(eds), *Values and Principles in European Union Foreign Policy* (London and New York: Routledge), pp. 114–29.
Balfour, R. and B. Cugusi (2010), 'EU Policy and Islamist Movements: Constructive Ambiguities or Alibis?', in R. Balfour and D. Pioppi (eds), *Islamist Mass Movements, External Actors and Political Change in the Arab World* (Stockholm: IDEA).
Balzacq, T. (2008), *The Implications of European Neighbourhood Policy in the Context of Border Controls (Readmission Agreements, Visa Policy, Human Rights)*. Ad-Hoc Briefing Paper for the European Parliament (Brussels: Directorate-General Internal Policies).
Balzacq, T. (ed.) (2009), *The External Dimension of EU Justice and Home Affairs: Governance, Neighbours, Security* (Houndmills: Palgrave).
Baracani, E. (2010), 'EU Democratic Anchoring', in E. Baracani (ed.), *Democratization and Hybrid Regimes. International Anchoring and Domestic Dynamics in European Post-Soviet States* (Florence: European Press Academic Publishing), pp. 111–34.
Barbé, E. (1998), 'Balancing Europe's Eastern and Southern Dimensions', in J. Zielonka (ed.), *Paradoxes of European Foreign Policy* (The Hague: Kluwer Law International), pp. 117–29.
Barbé, E. and E. Johansson-Nogués (2008), 'The EU as a Modest "Force for Good": The European Neighbourhood Policy', *International Affairs*, 84:1, 81–96.
Barbé, E. O., Costa, A. Herranz Surralles and M. Natorski (2009), 'Which Rules Shape EU External Governance? Patterns of Rule Selection in Foreign and Security Policies', *Journal of European Public Policy*, 16:6, 834–52.
Barkin, J.S. (2010), *Realist Constructivism: Rethinking International Relations Theory* (Cambridge: Cambridge University Press).
Bastian, K. (2006), *Die Europäische Union und Russland. Multilaterale und bilaterale Dimensionen in der europäischen Außenpolitik* (Wiesbaden: VS Verlag für Sozialwissenschaften).
BBC News Europe (2011), 'Russia Election: Medvedev Facebook Promise Draws Ire', *BBC News Europe* (12 December). www.bbc.co.uk/news/world-europe-16132607 (accessed 6 January 2012).
Bebel, A. (2005) *Hz. Prophet Mohamed and Arab–Islam Culture Period*, translated by V. Atayman (Istanbul: Bordo Siyah).
Bechev, D. (2011), *Constructing South East Europe: The Politics of Balkan Regional Cooperation* (Basingstoke: Palgrave Macmillan).
Bechev, D. (2009), 'From Policy-Takers to Policy-Makers? Observations on Bulgarian and Romanian Foreign Policy Before and After EU Accession', *Perspectives on European Politics and Society*, 10:2, 210–24.
Bechev, D. (2006), *Constructing South East Europe: The Politics of Regional Identity in the Balkans*, RAMSES Series on Europe and the Mediterranean, Working Paper 1/06/2006. www.sant.ox.ac.uk/esc/bechev (accessed 3 March 2006).
Bechev, D. and K. Nicolaidis (2010), 'From Policy to Polity: Can the EU's Special Relations with Its "Neighbourhood" Be Decentred?', *Journal of Common Market Studies*, 48:3, 475–500.
BelTA (2009a), 'Sergei Martynov: Eastern Partnership Needs to be More Dynamic', *Belarusian Telegraph Agency* (9 December). http://news.belta.by/en/news/politics/?id=460566 (accessed 26 June 2010)
BelTA (2009a), 'Belarus' Border Committee to Partake in EU Integrated Border Management Program', Belarusian Telegraph Agency (21 October). http://news.belta.by/en/news/politics/?id=437239 (accessed 26 June 2010)
Berg, E. (2008), 'The Baltic Gateway: A Corridor Leading Towards Three Different Directions', in P. Aalto (ed.), *The EU-Russia Energy Dialogue: Securing Europe's Future Energy Supply* (Aldershot: Ashgate), pp. 145–62.
Berger, H., G. Kopits and I. Szekely (2007), 'Fiscal Indulgence in Central Europe: Loss of

the External Anchor', *Scottish Journal of Political Economy*, 54:1, 116–35.
Berglof, E. and G. Roland (1998), *The EU as an 'Outside Anchor' for Transition Reforms* (Stockholm: Stockholm Institute of Transition Economics and East European Economies, Working Paper No. 132).
Bicchi, F. (2011), 'The Union for the Mediterranean, or the Changing Context of Euro-Mediterranean relations', *Mediterranean Politics*, 16:1, 3–19.
Bicchi, F. (2007) *European Foreign Policy Making Toward the Mediterranean* (New York/Basingstoke: Palgrave MacMillan).
Bicchi, F. (2006), 'Our Size Fits All: Normative Power Europe and the Mediterranean', *Journal of European Public Policy*, 13:2, 286–303.
Bicchi, F. (2004), 'L'Unione europea e la promozione della Democrazia', in F. Bicchi, L. Guazzone and D. Pioppi (eds), *La Questione della Democrazia nel Mondo Arabo* (Monza: Polimetrica), pp. 143–70.
Bidder, B. (2010), 'Kreml gegen Lukaschenko: Diktator in der Klemme', *Spiegel Online* (18 August). www.spiegel.de/politik/ausland/0,1518,druck-712295,00.html (accessed 7 September 2010).
Bigo, D. and E. Guild, 'Introduction: Policing in the Name of Freedom', in D. Bigo and E. Guild (eds), *Controlling Frontiers. Free Movement Into and Within Europe* (Aldershot: Ashgate Publishing Limited), pp. 1–14.
Biscop, S. (2006), 'From Reflections to Power: Implementing the European Security Strategy', in G. Hauser and F. Kernic (eds), *European Security in Transition* (Aldershot: Ashgate), pp. 87–101.
Biscop, S. and V. Arnould (2004) ,'Global Public Goods: An Integrative Agenda for the EU External Action', in E.B. Eide (ed.), *Global Europe Report 1. 'Effective Multilateralism': Europe, Regional Security and a Revitalised UN* (London: Foreign Policy Centre).
Blockmans, S. (2008), 'EU-Russia Relations Through the Prism of the European Neighbourhood and Partnership Instrument', *European Foreign Affairs Review*, 13, 167–87.
Boatca, M. (2008), 'The Epistemology of Frontiers and the Frontiers of Epistemology', Nijmegen Centre for Borders Research, Seminar Bordering Europe: The Frontier, 26–27 September.
Bogutcaia, G., G. Bosse and A. Schmidt-Felzmann (2006), 'Lost in Translation? Political Elites and the Interpretative Values Gap in the EU's Neighbourhood Policies', *Contemporary Politics*, 12:2, 117–37.
Böröcz, J. (2002), 'The Fox and the Raven: The European Union and Hungary Renegotiate the Margins of Europe', *Comparative Studies in Society and History*, 42:4, 847–75.
Böröcz, J. and M. Sarkar (2005), 'What is the EU?', *International Sociology*, 20:2, 153–73.
Bosse, G. (2012a), 'A Partnership with Dictatorship: Explaining the Paradigm Shift in European Union Policy Towards Belarus', *Journal of Common Market Studies*, 50:3, 367–84.
Bosse, G. (2012b), 'Quo-Vadis Belarus?' Policy Brief (Brussels: European Policy Centre).
Bosse, G. (2010), 'The EU's Relations with Moldova: Governance, Partnership or Ignorance', *Europe-Asia Studies*, 62:8, 1291–309.
Bosse, G. (2008), 'Justifying the European Neighbourhood Policy Based on "Shared Values": Can Rhetoric Match Reality?', in E. Tulmets and L. Delcour (eds), *Pioneer Europe? EU Foreign Policy in the Neighbourhood* (Baden-Baden: Nomos), pp. 43–54.
Bosse, G. (2007), 'Values in the EU's Neighbourhood: Political Rhetoric or Reflection of a Coherent Policy', *European Political Economy Review*, 7, 38–62.
Bosse G., and E. Korosteleva (2009), 'Changing Belarus? The Limits of EU Governance in Eastern Europe', *Cooperation and Conflict*, 44:2, 143–65.
Boswell, C. (2003), 'The "External Dimension" of EU Immigration and Asylum Policy', *International Affairs*, 79:3, 619–38.

Boulden, J. (2002), 'The Responsibility to Protect', *Journal of Refugee Studies*, 15:4, 428–9.
Bouzarovski, S. and M. Konieczny (2010), 'Landscapes of Paradox: Public Discourses and Policies in Poland's Relationship with the Nord Stream Pipeline', *Geopolitics*, 15:1, 1–21.
Bretherton, C. and J. Vogler (2006), *The European Union as a Global Actor* (New York: Routledge, 2nd edn).
Browning, C. (2005), 'Westphalian, Imperial, Neo-Medieval: The Geopolitics of Europe and the Role of the North', in C.S. Browning (ed.), *Remaking Europe in the Margins: Northern Europe after the Enlargements* (Aldershot: Ashgate), pp. 85–101.
Browning, C.S. (2003), 'The Region-Building Approach Revisited: The Continued Othering of Russia in Discourses of Region-Building in the European North', *Geopolitics*, 8:1, 45–71.
Browning, C. and P. Joenniemi (2008), 'Geostrategies of the European Neighbourhood Policy', *European Journal of International Relations*, 14:3, 519–51.
Brynen, R. et al. (1995), 'Theoretical Perspectives on Arab Liberalisation and Democracy', in R. Bryner, B. Korany and P. Noble (eds), *Political Liberalisation and Democratisation in the Arab World* (Colorado: Lynne Riener Publishers), pp. 3–29.
Bull, H. (1977), *The Anarchical Society: A Study of Order in World Politics* (London: Macmillan).
Bull, H. (1966), 'International Theory: The Case for the Classical Approach', *World Politics*, 38, 361–77.
Bundesamt für Migration und Flüchtlinge (2011), *Migrationsbericht des Bundesamtes für Migration und Flüchtlinge im Auftrage der Bundesregierung: Migrationsbericht 2009* (Berlin).
Bundesamt für Migration und Flüchtlinge (2008), *Migrationsbericht des Bundesamtes für Migration und Flüchtlinge im Auftrag der Bundesregierung: Migrationsbericht 2007* (Berlin).
Burant, S.R. (1995), 'Foreign Policy and National Identity: A Comparison of Ukraine and Belarus', *Europe-Asia Studies*, 47:7, 1125–44.
Carothers, T. (2002), 'The End of the Transition Paradigm', *Journal of Democracy*, 13:1, 5–21.
Carrapico, H. and F. Trauner (2012), 'The External Dimension of EU Justice and Home Affairs: Post-Lisbon Governance Dynamics', *European Foreign Affairs Review*, Issue 17, Special Issue.
Carrera, S. (2007), *The EU Border Management Strategy FRONTEX and the Challenges of Irregular Immigration in the Canary Islands*. CEPS Working Document No. 261 (Brussels: Centre for European Policy Studies).
Cassarino, J.-P. (2007), 'Informalising Readmission Agreements in the EU Neighbourhood', *The International Inspector*, 42:2, 179–96.
Central Intelligence Agency, *The World Fact Book*. www.cia.gov/library/publications/the-world-factbook/ (accessed 30 April 2012).
Charillon, F. (2005), 'The EU as a Security Regime', *European Foreign Affairs Review*, 10, 517–33.
Checkel, J. (2010), *Theoretical Synthesis in IR: Possibilities and Limits*, Vancouver: School of International Studies, Simons Papers in Security and Development N 6/2010.
Checkel, J. (2005), 'International Institutions and Socialization in Europe: Introduction and Framework', *International Organization*, 59:4, 801–26.
Checkel, J. (2001), 'Why Comply? Social Learning and European Identity Change', *International Organization*, 55:3, 553–88.
Checkel, J. (1998), 'The Constructivist Turn in International Relations Theory', *World Politics*, 50:2, 324–48.
Chong, D. (1996), 'Values Versus Interests in the Explanation of the Social Conflict',

University of Pennsylvania Law Review, 144, 2079–134.
Collina, C. (2008), 'A Bridge in Times of Confrontation: Italy and Russia in the Context of EU and NATO Enlargements', *Journal of Modern Italian Studies*, 13:1, 25–40.
Commission of the European Communities (2011a), 'A Partnership for Democracy and Shared Prosperity with the Southern Mediterranean', COM (2011) 200 final, 8 March.
Commission of the European Communities (2011b), 'A New Response to a Changing Neighbourhood', COM (2011) 303, 25 May.
Commission of the European Communities (2009a), Progress Report, 'EU–Russia Common Spaces, March 2008'.
Commission of the European Communities (2009b), 'Gas Coordination Group: Solidarity Works and the EU's Gas Market Adapts to Challenges of Gas Crisis', RAPID Press Release IP/09/75.
Commission of the European Communities (2009c), 'Measures Discussed at the Gas Coordination Group', RAPID Press Release MEMO/09/4.
Commission of the European Communities (2009d), 'Member State General Situation According the Significance of Impact', RAPID Press Release MEMO/09/3.
Commission of the European Communities (2009e), Progress Report Ukraine, SEC (2009) 515/2.
Commission of the European Communities (2008a), Communication from the Commission to the European Parliament and the Council, 'Barcelona Process: Union for the Mediterranean', COM (2008) 319/3.
Commission of the European Communities (2008b), 'Belarus: Commission Experts in Minsk for Technical Talks on Energy, Transport and Environment', Press Release IP/08/95, 28 January 2008.
Commission of the European Communities (2008c), Communication from the Commission to the Council and the European Parliament, 'Eastern Partnership', COM (2008) 823 final.
Commission of the European Communities (2008d), EuropeAid, 'Project Database'. http://ec.europa.eu/europeaid/cgi/frame12.pl (accessed 15 March 2008).
Commission of the European Communities (2008e), Progress Report Ukraine, SEC (2008) 402.
Commission of the European Communities (2008f), Communication from the Commission to the Council, 'Review of EU–Russia Relations', COM (2008) 740 final/(SEC (2008) 2786).
Commission of the European Communities (2008g), 'Second Energy Review', COM (2008) 744, 13 November.
Commission of the European Communities (2009f), 'The Gas Coordination Group Evaluates the Current Gas Crisis and Confirms Measures to Assist Countries in Need', RAPID Press Release IP/09/30.
Commission of the European Communities (2007a), Communication From The Commission to The European Council and The European Parliament, 'An Energy Policy for Europe', COM (2007) 1 final.
Commission of the European Communities (2007b), 'A Strong European Neighbourhood Policy', COM (2007) 774.
Commission of the European Communities (2007c), Communication from the Commission to the Council and to the European Parliament, 'Black Sea Synergy – a new regional cooperation initiative', COM (2007) 160 final.
Commission of the European Communities (2007d), Country Strategy Paper 2007–2013: Russian Federation.
Commission of the European Communities (2007e), EU/Egypt Action Plan. http://ec.europa.eu/world/enp/pdf/action_plans/egypt_enp_ap_final_en.pdf (accessed 11 October 2010).

Commission of the European Communities (2006a), Communication from the Commission to the Council and the European Parliament on Strengthening the European Neighbourhood Policy, COM (2006) 726 final.
Commission of the European Communities (2006b), ENP Progress Report Ukraine, SEC (2006) 1505/2.
Commission of the European Communities (2006c), 'A European Strategy for Sustainable, Competitive and Secure Energy', COM (2006) 105 final.
Commission of the European Communities (2006d), EU/Georgia Action Plan. http://ec.europa.eu/world/enp/pdf/action_plans/georgia_enp_ap_final_en.pdf (accessed November 2010).
Commission of the European Communities (2006e), EU/Palestinian Authority Action Plan. http://ec.europa.eu/world/enp/pdf/action_plans/pa_enp_ap_final_en.pdf (accessed November 2010).
Commission of the European Communities (2006f), 'Europe in the World: Some Practical Proposals for Greater Coherence, Effectiveness and Visibility', COM (2006) 278.
Commission of the European Communities (2006g), 'On the General Approach to Enable ENP Partner Countries to Participate in Community Agencies and Community Programmes', COM (2006) 724.
Commission of the European Communities (2006h), Non-Paper, 'What the European Union Could Bring to Belarus', December 2006.
Commission of the European Communities (2006i), Country Strategy Paper/National Indicative Programme (Belarus) 2007–2013 – European Neighbourhood and Partnership Instrument.
Commission of the European Communities (2006j), Strategy Paper for the Thematic Programme of Cooperation with Third Countries in the Areas of Migration and Asylum 2007–2010.
Commission of the European Communities (2005a), EU/Israel Action Plan. http://ec.europa.eu/world/enp/pdf/action_plans/israel_enp_ap_final_en.pdf (accessed November 2010).
Commission of the European Communities (2005b), EU/Jordan Action Plan. http://ec.europa.eu/world/enp/pdf/action_plans/jordan_enp_ap_final_en.pdf (accessed 11 October 2010).
Commission of the European Communities (2004a), European Neighbourhood Policy: Country Report Ukraine, SEC (2004) 566.
Commission of the European Communities (2004b), European Neighbourhood Policy: Strategy Paper, COM (2004) 373 final.
Commission of the European Communities (2004c), Communication from the Commission on Relations with Russia, COM (2004) 106.
Commission of the European Communities (2004d), Country Strategy Paper/National Indicative Programme (Belarus) 2005–2006, 28 May.
Commission of the European Communities (2003a), Communication on Reinvigorating EU Actions, Human Rights and Democratisation with Mediterranean Partners, COM (2003) 294 final.
Commission of the European Communities (2003b), Communication from the Commission, 'Wider Europe – Neighbourhood: A New Framework for Relations with our Eastern and Southern Neighbours', COM (2003) 104 final, 11 March.
Commission of the European Communities (2002), Green Paper on the Conversion of the Rome Convention of 1980 on the Law Applicable to Contractual Obligations into a Community Instrument and its Modernisation, COM (2002) 654 final.
Commission of the European Communities (2001), Country Strategy Paper: Ukraine 2002–2006.
Commission of the European Communities (2000), Communication from the

Commission to the Council and the European Parliament on a Community Immigration Policy.
Commission of the European Communities (1998), 'European Union Statement on Human Rights', *EU Bulletin*, no. 12.
Commission of the European Communities (1996), 'Action Plan for Ukraine', COM (96) 593.
Commission of the European Communities (1995), Communication from the Commission, 'The European Union and Russia: The Future Relationship', COM (95) 223 final.
Commission of the European Communities (1991), Declaration of the European Union on the Occasion of the 50th Anniversary of the Universal Declaration on Human Rights', 1991.
Conclusion of the Luxembourg European Council (1991), Declaration on Human Rights (28–29 June). http://centrodirittiumani.unipd.it/a_temi/normedu/003_ue/1_2/1_2_3_en.pdf (acceessed 22 January 2011).
Cooper, R. (2004), *The Breaking of Nations: Order and Chaos in the Twenty-First Century* (London: Atlantic Books).
Cooper, R. (2003), *The Breaking of Nations: Order and Chaos in the Twenty-First Century* (London: Atlantic Books).
The Cooperation Council (2005), *Partnership Between the European Union and Ukraine, Ukraine Action Plan*, UE-UA 1051/05. http://register.consilium.eu.int/pdf/en/05/st01/st01051.en05.pdf (accessed 22 January 2012).
Coppieters, B. (1996), 'The Caucasus as a Security Complex', in B. Coppieters (ed.), *Contested Borders in the Caucasus* (Brussels: VUB, 1996), pp. 193–204.
Coppieters, B., M Emerson, M. Huysseune, T. Kovziridze, G. Noutcheva, N. Tocci and M. Vahl (2004), 'Europeanization and Conflict Resolution: Case Studies from the European Periphery', *Journal on Ethnopolitics and Minority Issues in Europe*, 1. www.ecmi.de/jemie/special_1_2004.html (accessed 29 August 2007).
Copsey, N. and K. Pomorska (2010), 'Poland's Power and Influence in the European Union: The Case of its Eastern Policy', *Comparative European Politics*, 8:2.
Coricelli, F. (2007), 'Democracy in the Post Communist World: Unfinished Business', *East European Politics and Society*, 21:1, 82–90.
Cornell, S. and A. Jonsson (2008), 'Expanding the European Area of Stability and Democracy to the Wider Black Sea region', in D. Hamilton and G. Mangott (eds), *The Wider Black Sea Region in the 21st Century. Strategic, Economic and Energy Perspectives* (Washington D.C.: Center for Transatlantic Relations), pp. 225–50.
Cornell, S.E. and S.F. Starr (2006), 'The Caucasus: A Challenge for Europe', *Silk Road Paper*. www.silkroadstudies.org/new/docs/Silkroadpapers/0606Caucasus.pdf (accessed 23 April 2007).
Council of the European Union (2011), 'Council Conclusions Defining the EU Strategy on Readmission', 9/10 June 2011.
Council of the European Union (2009a), 'Council Conclusions on Belarus', 2974th External Relations Council Meeting, 17 November 2009.
Council of the European Union (2009b), 'Joint Declaration of the Prague Eastern Partnership Summit', 8435/09 Press 78.
Council of the European Union (2009c), 'Note: Relations with Israel. Adoption of the European Union's position for the Association Council's Ninth meeting', 11057/09 LIMITE.
Council of the European Union (2008a), 'EU–Ukraine Summit, Paris, 9 September 2008', 12812/08.
Council of the European Union (2008b), Extraordinary Meeting of General Affairs and External Relations, 12453/08 Press 236.

Council of the European Union (2007a), Declaration by the Presidency on Behalf of the European Union on the Constitutional Reform Process in Egypt, CFSP 8205/07, Presse 73.
Council of the European Union (2007b), 'EU–Ukraine Summit, Kiev, Joint Statement', 12927/07 Presse 199, 14 September 2007.
Council of the European Union (2007c), '17th GCC–EU Joint Council And Ministerial Meeting Joint Communiqué', 8 May 2007. www.consilium.europa.eu/uedocs /cms_data/docs/pressdata/en/er/94036.pdf (accessed 10 October 2010).
Council of the European Union (2007d), 'Council Decision Concerning the Signing of the Agreement between the European Community and the Russian Federation on Readmission', 17 May.
Council of the European Union (2006a), 'EU–Ukraine Summit, Helsinki, 27 October 2006, Joint Press Statement', 14604/06 Presse 297.
Council of the European Union (2006b), 'Joint Action 2006/121/CFSP', *Official Journal of the European Union*, 49, 14–16.
Council of the European Union (2006c), 'Presidency Statement on Behalf of the European Union on PLC elections', CFSP 5738/06 Presse 28.
Council of the European Union (2005a), 'EU–Ukraine Summit, Kiev, 1 December 2005, Joint Statement', 15222/05 Presse 337.
Council of the European Union (2005b), 'Follow-up to the GAERC Conclusions 21 February – Alignment of Ukraine with EU Declarations, Demarches and Common Positions in the Area of CFSP', 8754/05.
Council of the European Union (2005c), Press Release, '2641st Council meeting. General Affairs and External relations', 6420/05 Presse 34.
Council of the European Union (2005d), '15th EU–Russia Summit Moscow, Press Release', 11 May.
Council of the European Union (2005e), '15th EU–Russia Summit Moscow: Road Map for the Common Space of Freedom, Security and Justice', 11 May.
Council of the European Union (2005f), 'Council Decision on the Signing of the Agreement Between the European Community and the Republic of Albania on the Readmission of Persons Residing Without Authorisation', 15 February.
Council of the European Union (2004), '2559th Council meeting – External Relations', 5519/04 Presse 26.
Council of the European Union (2003), 'European Security Strategy – A Secure Europe in a Secure World', 12 December.
Council of the European Union (2002), 'Council Decision Concerning the Conclusion of the Agreement Between the European Community and the Government of the Hong Kong Special Administrative Region of the People's Republic of China on the Readmission of Persons Residing Without Authorisation', 8 November.
Council of the European Union (2001a), 'Relations with Ukraine – Council Report to the European Council on the Implementation of the Common Strategy of the European Union on Ukraine', 15195/01.
Council of the European Union (2001b), 'Catalogue of Recommendations for the Proper Application of the Schengen Acquis and of Best Practices – Removal and Readmission', 16 November.
Council of the European Union (2000a), 'Conclusions of the Feira European Council', 19–20 June.
Council of the European Union (2000b), 'Relations with Ukraine – Information on the Presidency's Work Plan on the Implementation of the Common Strategy', 5434/00.
Council of the European Union (2000c), 'Relations with Ukraine – Information on the Presidency's Work Plan on the Implementation of the Common Strategy', 10018/00.
Council of the European Union (1999a), 'Common Strategies', 10053/99.

Council of the European Union (1999b), 'Tampere European Council Presidency Conclusions', 15/16 October.
Council of the European Union (1998),' Strategy Paper on Immigration and Asylum Policy', 1 July.
Crawford, B. (2004), 'Why the Euro-Med Partnership? Explaining the EU's Strategies in the Mediterranean Region', in V.K. Aggarwal and E.A. Fogarty (eds), *Between Regionalism and Globalism: European Union Interregional and Transregional Trade Strategies* (New York: Palgrave), pp. 93–117.
Dagens Nyheter (2011a), 'Valet I Ryssland 2012. Nej till 00–talets Putinism', *Dagens Nyheter* (13 December). www.dn.se/ledare/huvudledare/nej-till-00–talets-putinism (accessed 6 January 2012).
Dagens Nyheter (2011b), 'Valet I Ryssland 2012. Nätilskan växer i Ryssland', *Dagens Nyheter* (7 December). www.dn.se/nyheter/varlden/natilskan-vaxer-i-ryssland (accessed 6 January 2012).
Dagens Nyheter (2011c), 'Valet i Ryssland 2012. Nya protester i Ryssland', 18 December. www.dn.se/nyheter/varlden/nya-protester-i-ryssland (accessed 6 January 2012).
Dalacoura, K. (1998), *Islam, Liberalism and Human Rights* (New York: IB Tauris).
D'Anieri, P.J. (1999), *Economic Interdependence in Ukrainian–Russian Relations* (Albany: State University of New York Press).
D'Anieri, P.J. (1997), 'Nationalism and International Politics: Identity and Sovereignty in the Russian–Ukrainian Conflict', *Nationalism and Ethnic Politics*, 3:2, 1–28.
Dannreuther, R. (2006), 'Developing the Alternative to Enlargement: The European Neighbourhood Policy', *European Foreign Affairs Review*, 11:2, 183–201.
Debardeleben, J. (2008), 'Public Attitudes toward EU–Russian Relations: Knowledge, Values, and Interests', in J. Debardeleben (ed.), *The Boundaries of EU Enlargement: Finding a Place for Neighbours* (Houndmills: Palgrave), pp. 70–92.
Del Sarto, R.A. and T. Schumacher (2005), 'From EMP to ENP: What's at Stake with the European Neighbourhood Policy towards the Southern Mediterranean?', *European Foreign Affairs Review*, 10, 17–38.
Delanty, G. (2006), 'The Cosmopolitan Imagination: Critic Critical Cosmopolitanism and Social Theory', *The British Journal of Sociology*, 57:1, 25–47.
Delanty, G. and C. Rumford (2005), *Rethinking Europe: Social Theory and the Implications of Europeanization* (London: Routledge).
Dempsey, J. (2010), 'European Engagement with Belarus Takes a Blow', *The New York Times* (22 December 2010). www.nytimes.com/2010/12/23/world/europe/23iht-letter23.html (accessed 22 December 2010).
Der Spiegel (2005), 'Interview with Vladislav Surkov, The West Doesn't Have to Love Us', *Spiegel Online*, 20 June. www.spiegel.de/international/spiegel/0,1518,361236,00.html (accessed 30 April 2012).
Deutsch, K. et al. (1957) *Political Community and the North Atlantic Area* (Princeton, NJ: Princeton University Press).
DG Trade (2010), *Russia. Main Economic Indicators. EU Bilateral Trade and Trade with the World*, Factsheet, Brussels, 25 May.
DG Trade (2007), *Russia. Main Economic Indicators. EU Bilateral Trade and Trade with the World*, Factsheet, Brussels.
DG Trade (2005), *Russia. EU–Bilateral Trade and Trade with the World*, Factsheet, Brussels, 30 March.
Di Tommaso, M.L., M. Raiser and M. Weeks (2007), 'Home Grown or Imported? Initial Conditions, External Anchors and the Determinants of Institutional Reform in the Transition Economies', *The Economic Journal*, 117:520, 858–81.
Diamond, L. (2010), 'Why Are There No Arab Democracies?', *Journal of Democracy*, 21:1, 93–104.

Diez, T. (2005), 'Constructing the Self and Changing Others: Reconsidering "Normative Power" Europe', *Millennium: Journal of International Studies*, 33:3, 613–36.

Diez, T. (2004), 'Europe's Others and the Return of Geopolitics', *Cambridge Review of International Affairs*, 17:2, 319–35.

Diez, T., M. Albert and S. Stetter (2008), *The European Union and Border Conflicts. The Power of Integration and Association* (Cambridge: Cambridge University Press), pp. 173–202.

Dingley, J. (1994), 'Belarus: A Lost Country?', *Journal of Contemporary European Studies*, 2:4, 71–8.

Dodini, M. and M. Fantini (2006), 'The EU Neighbourhood Policy: Implications for Economic Growth and Stability', *Journal of Common Market Studies*, 44:3, 507–32.

Dorraj, M. (2000), 'Islam, Governance and Democracy', in P. Magnarella (ed.), *Middle East and North Africa: Governance, Democratisation, Human Rights* (Aldershot: Ashgate), pp. 11–35.

Duchêne, F. (1973), 'The European Community and the Uncertainties of Interdependence', in M. Kohnstamm and W. Hager (eds), *A Nation Writ Large? Foreign-Policy Problems Before the European Community* (London: Macmillan).

Duchêne, F. (1972), 'Europe's Role in World Peace', in R. Maine (ed.), *Europe Tomorrow: Sixteen Europeans Look Ahead* (London: Fontana).

Dura, G. (2008), CEPS Foreign Policy Brief, 'The EU's Limited Response to Belarus' Pseudo "New Foreign Policy"', No. 151, February 2008.

Durac, V. and Cavatorta, F. (2009), 'Strenghtening Authoritarian Rule through Democracy Promotion? Examining the Paradox of the US and EU Security Strategies: The Case of Bin Ali's Tunisia', *British Journal of Middle Eastern Studies*, 36:1, 3–19.

Elgström, O. and M. Smith (2006), 'Conclusions', in O. Elgström and M. Smith (eds), *The European Union's Roles in International Politics. Concepts and Analysis* (London: Routledge).

Ellner, A. (2008), 'Regional Security in a Global Context: A Critical Appraisal of European Approaches to Security', *European Security*, 17:1, 9–31.

Elster, J. (1989), *Nuts and Bolts for the Social Sciences* (Cambridge: Cambridge University Press).

Emerson, M. (2008), *Making Sense of Sarkozy's Union of the Mediterranean*, Brussels: Centre for European Policy Studies, CEPS Policy Brief 155.

Emerson, M. (2004a), *European Neighbourhood Policy: Strategy or Placebo?*, Brussels: Centre for European Policy Studies, CEPS Working Document 215.

Emerson, M. (2004b), *The Wider Europe Matrix*, Brussels: Centre for European Policy Studies.

Emerson, M. (2002), *The Wider Europe as the European Union's Friendly Monroe Doctrine*, Brussels: Centre for European Policy Studies, CEPS Policy Brief 27.

Emerson, M., G. Noutcheva and N. Popescu (2007), *European Neighbourhood Policy Two Years on: Time Indeed for an 'ENP Plus'*, Brussels: Centre for European Policy Studies, CEPS Policy Brief 126.

Esposito, J. and J. Piscatori (1991), 'Democratisation and Islam', *Middle East Journal*, 45:3, 427–40.

European Commission Officials (2006), Personal Interview, Tbilisi, May 2006.

European Council (2003), 'A Secure Europe in a Better World: European Security Strategy', www.consilium.europa.eu/uedocs/cmsUpload/78367.pdf (accessed 21 January 2012).

European Council (1999), Common Strategy of 11 December 1999 on Ukraine, 1999/877/CFSP, 23 December.

European Council (1980). 'Declaration by the European Council on the Situation in the Middle East', reproduced in C. Hill and K. Smith (2000), *European Foreign Policy: Key Documents* (London: Routledge).

European Council (1977). 'Statement by the European Council on the Middle East', reproduced in C. Hill and K. Smith (2000), *European Foreign Policy: Key Documents* (London: Routledge).
European Council (1973). 'Statement of the Nine Foreign Ministers on the Situation in the Middle East', reproduced in C. Hill and K. Smith (2000), *European Foreign Policy: Key Documents* (London: Routledge).
European Parliament (2007a), Report by the Committee on Foreign Affairs, 'Strengthening the European Neighbourhood Policy', Rapporteur: Charles Tannock and Raimon Obiols, Brussels, A6–0414–2007, 15 November.
European Parliament (2007b), Report on the Proposal for a Council Decision Concerning the Conclusion of the Agreement between the European Community and the Russian Federation on Readmission, A6–0028/2007, 5 February.
European Parliament (2006a), 'European Parliament Resolution on the European Neighbourhood Policy', P6_TA-PROV (2006) 0028, Strasbourg.
European Parliament (2006b), Draft Report on the Proposal of a Council Decision on the Conclusion of the Agreement between the European Community and the Russian Federation on the Facilitation of Issuance of Short-stay Visas, 2006/0062 (CNS) (Brussels: Committee on Civil Liberties, Justice and Home Affairs).
European Parliament (2005), Report on EU–Russia Relations, Rapporteur: C. Malmström, Brussels, European Parliament Committee on Foreign Affairs, 2004/2170 (INI), 4 May.
European Parliament (2004), Report with a proposal for a European Parliament recommendation to the Council on EU-Russia relations, Rapporteur: Bastiaan Belder, Brussels, European Parliament Committee on Foreign Affairs, A5–0053/2004, 2 February.
European Security Strategy (2003), 'A Secure Europe in a Better World', 2 December 2003, www.consilium.europa.eu/uedocs/cmsUpload/78367.pdf (accessed 30 April 2012).
European Union–Palestine Authority (2005), 'European Neighbourhood Policy Action Plan'. http://trade.ec.europa.eu/doclib/docs/2010/junc/tradoc_146237.pdf (accessed 29 April 2012).
Eurostat (2010), *EU–Russia Summit. EU27 Deficit in Trade in Goods with Russia of 50bn euro in 2009. Russia Third Trading Partner of EU27*, STAT/10/76, 28 May.
Eurostat (2009), *EU–Russia Summit. EU27 Deficit in Trade in Goods with Russia of 70bn euro in 2008. Russia Third Trading Partner of EU27*, STAT/09/74, 19 May.
Eurostat (2006), *EU–Russia Summit – An EU25 Trade Deficit of more than 50bn euro with Russia in 2005*, STAT/06/68, 24 May.
Eurostat (2001), *Increasing deficit in EU Trade with Russia*, STAT/01/99, 27 September.
Evans, G. and M. Sahnoun (2002), 'The Responsibility to Protect', *Foreign Affairs*, 81:6, 99–110.
Featherstone, K. (2004), 'The Political Dynamics of External Empowerment: The Emergence of EMU and the Challenge to the European Social Model', in A. Martin and G. Ross (eds), *Euros and Europeans: Monetary Integration and the European Model of Society* (Cambridge: Cambridge University Press), pp. 226–47.
Feklyunina, V. (2008), 'Battle for Perceptions: Projecting Russia in the West', *Europe-Asia Studies*. 60:4, 607–31.
Ferrero-Waldner, B. (2006a), *The European Union and Russia – Developing our Shared European Continent*, Speech delivered at the European Studies Institute, Moscow, 23 June.
Ferrero-Waldner, B. (2006b), *The European Neighbourhood Policy: Bringing our Neighbours Closer*, Speech delivered at the 10th Euro-Mediterranean Economic Transition Conference, Brussels, SPEECH/06/346, 6 June.
Ferrero-Waldner, B. (2006c), *Clash of Civilizations or Dialogue of Cultures: Building Bridges Across the Mediterranean*, Speech delivered during Bibliotheca Alexandrina and Anna

Lindh Foundation Lecture, Alexandria, SPEECH/06/279, 6 May.
Ferrero-Waldner, B. (2006d), *Dialogue of Cultures – Clash of Civilizations or Clash of Ignorance*, Speech delivered during the Euro-Mediterranean Parliamentary Assembly, Plenary Session, Brussels, SPEECH/06/198, 27 March.
Ferrero-Waldner, B. (2005a). *Quo vadis Europa*, Speech delivered at EPP Paneuropa Group, Strasbourg, Speech/05/797, 14 December.
Ferrero-Waldner, B. (2005b), Press Release, *European Neighbourhood Policy: A year of Progress*, IP/05/1467, 24 November.
Ferrero-Waldner, B. (2005c), *Europe's Neighbours – Towards Closer Integration*, Speech delivered at the Brussels Economic Forum, 22 April.
Fierke, K.M. and A. Wiener (2001), 'Constructing Institutional Interest: EU and NATO Enlargement', in T. Christiansen, K.E. Jørgensen and A. Wiener (eds), *The Social Construction of Europe* (London: Sage Publications), pp. 121–39.
Fish, M.S. (2005), *Democracy Derailed in Russia: The Failure of Open Politics* (Cambridge: Cambridge University Press).
Fisher Onar, N. (2009), 'Neo-Ottomanism, Historical Legacies and Turkish Foreign Policy', EDAM Discussion Paper Series, 2009/03.
Fisher Onar, N. (2007), 'Kemalists, Islamists, and Liberals: Shifting Patterns of Confrontation and Consensus, 2002–06', *Turkish Studies*, 8:2, 273–88.
Flautre, H. (2005), 'Interview by S. Carrara, S. Wolff, and S. Witkowski, 'Cafebabel: The EU is not the Teacher in Terms of Democracy', *European Current Affairs Magazine*. www.cafebabel.co.uk/article/15315/the-eu-is-not-the-teacher-in-terms-of-democracy.html (accessed 7 December 2010).
Flockhart, T. (2006), 'Similar and Yet so Different: The Socialization of Democratic Norms in Post-war Germany and Present Day Iraq', *International Politics*, 43:5, 596–619.
Focus Online (2011), 'Putin: Schröder bleibt bei, lupenreiner Demokrat', *Focus Online*, 11 December. www.focus.de/politik/ausland/putin_aid_120847.html (accessed 21 January 2011).
Forbrig, J. (2010), 'The EU's Policy Toward Belarus is in Complete Shatters', German Marshall Fund, quoted in J. Dempsey, 'European Engagement with Belarus Takes a Blow', *New York Times*, 22 December. www.nytimes.com/2010/12/23/world/europe/23iht-letter23.html (accessed 22 December 2010).
Forsberg, T. and A. Seppo (2009), 'Power Without Influence? The EU and Trade Disputes with Russia', *Europe-Asia Studies*, 61:10, 1805–23.
Francois, J.F. (1997), 'External Bindings and the Credibility of Reform', in A. Galal and B. Hoekman (eds), *Regional Partners in Global Markets: Limits and Possibilities of the Euro-Med Agreements* (London: Centre for Economic Policy Research), pp. 35–48.
Freedom House (2010), *Freedom in the World 2010* (Washington D.C.: Freedom House). www.freedomhouse.org/template.cfm?page=15 (accessed October 2010).
Freedom House (2008), *Freedom in the World 2008: Global Freedom in Retreat* (Washington D.C.: Freedom House). www.freedomhouse.org/template.cfm?page=70&release=612 (accessed October 2010).
Freire, M.R. and L. Simão (2007), *The Armenian Road to Democracy. Dimensions of a Tortuous Process*, Centre for European Policy Studies, Working Document 267. http://shop.ceps.eu/BookDetail.php?item_id=1492 (accessed 16 May 2007).
Freire, M.R. and L. Simão (2006), 'The EU's Neighbourhood Policy Towards the Southern Caucasus: Searching for Commonalty in a Patchy Scenario', *Comparative Constitutional Review Journal*, 4:57, 136–44 (in Russian).
Frellesen, T. and C. Rontoyanni (2007), 'EU-Russia Political Relations: Negotiating the Common Spaces', in J. Gower and G. Timmins (eds), *Russia and Europe: An Uneasy Partnership* (London: Anthem Press), pp. 229–46.
Freyburg, T., S. Lavenex, F. Schimmelfennig, T. Skripka and A. Wetzel, 'EU Promotion of

Democratic Governance in the Neighbourhood', *Journal of European Public Policy*, 16:6, 916–34.
Fukuyama, F. (2004), 'The Imperative of State-building', *Journal of Democracy*, 15:2, 17–31.
Füle, Š. (2011), *European Commissioner for Enlargement and Neighbourhood Policy*, Speech on the Recent Events in North Africa delivered at the Committee on Foreign Affairs (AFET), European Parliament, Brussels, SPEECH/11/130, 28 February.
Fuller, G.E. (2004), *Islamists in the Arab World: The Dance around Democracy*, Massachusetts: Carnegie Endowment for International Peace Carnegie Papers.
Gänzle, S. (2008), 'The EU's Policy towards Russia: Extending Governance beyond Borders?', in J. Debardeleben (ed.), *The Boundaries of EU Enlargement: Finding a Place for Neighbours* (Houndsmills: Palgrave), pp. 53–70.
Gathmann, F. and S. Fischer (2007), 'Kanzlerstreit. Eppler und Bahr verteidigen Schröder', *Spiegel Online*, 20 November.
Gavin, B. (2005), 'The Euro-Mediterranean Partnership: An Experiment in North–South–South Integration', *Intereconomics*, 40:6, 353–60.
Gelb, L.H. and J.A. Rosenthal (2003), 'The Rise of Ethics in Foreign Policy', *Foreign Affairs*, 82:3, 2–7.
General Affairs and External Relations Council (GAERC) (2007), Strengthening the European Neighbourhood Policy, Presidency Progress Report 18/19 June.
General Affairs and External Relations Council (GAERC) (2002), *Council Conclusions*, Brussels, October.
German, T. (2007), 'Visibly Invisible: EU Engagement in Conflict Resolution in the South Caucasus', *European Security*, 16:3, 357–74.
Germany's Presidency of the EU (2007), 'Statement on the Shura Council elections in Egypt', 22 June. www.eu2007.de/en/News/CFSP_Statements/index.html (accessed June 2007).
Ginsberg, R.H. (2001), *The European Union in International Politics: Baptism by Fire* (Lanham, MD: Rowman and Littlefield Publishers).
Ginsberg, R.H. (1999), 'Conceptualizing the European Union as an International Actor: Narrowing the Theoretical Capability-Expectations Gap', *Journal of Common Market Studies*, 37: 3, 429–54.
Goldstein, J. and R.O. Keohane (1993), 'Ideas and Foreign Policy. An Analytical Framework', in J. Goldstein and R.O. Keohane (eds), *Ideas and Foreign Policy. Beliefs, Institutions and Political Change* (Ithaca and London: Cornell University Press), pp. 3–30.
Goldthau, A. (2008), 'Rhetoric Versus Reality: Russian Threats to European Energy Supply', *Energy Policy*, 36, 686–92.
Götz, R. (2004), *Schweigen für Gas? Deutschlands Abhängigkeit von Rußlands Energielieferungen*, Berlin: Stiftung Wissenschaft und Politik, SWP-Aktuell 43.
Gower, J. (2007), 'The European Union's Policy on Russia: Rhetoric or Reality?', in J. Gower and G. Timmins (eds), *Russia and Europe: an Uneasy Partnership* (London: Anthem Press), pp. 111–32.
Grabbe, H. (2006), *The EU's Transformative Power: Europeanization through Conditionality in Central and Eastern Europe* (Basingstoke: Palgrave Macmillan).
Grabbe, H. (2001), 'How Does Europeanization Affect CEE Governance? Conditionality, Diffusion and Diversity', *Journal of European Public Policy*, 8:6, 1013–31.
Grevi, G. (2007), *Pioneering Foreign Policy: The EU Special Representatives*, European Union Institute for Security Studies, Chaillot Paper 106.
Gros, D. (2001), *Who Needs an External Anchor?*, Centre for European Policy Studies, Working Document 161.
Gross, E. (2009), *The Europeanization of National Foreign Policy: Continuity and Change in European Crisis Management* (Basingstoke: Palgrave Macmillan).

Guardian, The (2011), 'Tunisia's Election Winners form Interim Government after Uprising', 22 November. www.guardian.co.uk/world/2011/nov/22/tunisia-election-winners-ennahda-ettakatol (accessed 6 December 2011).
Guild, E. and J. Niessen (1996), *The Developing Immigration and Asylum Policies of the European Union* (The Hague: Kluwer Law International).
Gurr, T.R. (2000), *People Versus States. Minorities at Risk in the New Century* (Washington D.C.: United States Institute of Peace Press).
Gustafsson, P. and M. Kott (2011),' Putins gökungar söndrar inifrån', *SVD Opinion Svenska Dagbladet*, (23 December. www.svd.se/opinion/brannpunkt/putins-gokungar-sondrar-inifran_6729131.svd (accessed 6 January 2012).
Hamburger Abendblatt (2004), 'Schröder: "Putin ist lupenreiner Demokrat"', *Hamburger Abendblatt*, 23 November.
Handke, S. and J.J. de Jong (2007), *Energy as a Bond: Relations with Russia in the European and Dutch Context*, The Hague: Clingendael International Energy Programme, CIEP Energy Paper, 02/2007.
Hansen, L. (2006), *Security as Practice: Discourse Analysis and the Bosnian War* (London: Routledge).
Hassner, P. (2002), 'Fixed Borders or Moving Borderlands?: A New Type of Border for a New Type of Entity', in J. Zielonka (ed.), *Europe Unbound: Enlarging and Reshaping the Boundaries of the European Union* (London: Routledge), pp. 38–51.
Hassner, P. (1997), 'Obstinate and Obsolete: Non-territorial Transnational Forces versus the European Territorial State', in O. Tunander, P. Baev and V.I. Einagel (eds), *Geopolitics in Post-Wall Europe. Security, Territory and Identity* (London: Sage), pp. 45–59.
Hauser, G. (2006), 'Regional Approaches to Comprehensive Security in Europe', in G. Hauser and F. Kernic (eds), *European Security in Transition* (Aldershot: Ashgate), pp. 135–44.
Headley, J.M. (2008), *The Europeanization of the World: On the Origins of Human Rights and Democracy* (Princeton and Oxford: Princeton University Press).
Heinrich, A. (2004), 'Globalisierung und Corporate Governance. Russlands Erdöl- und Erdgassektor', *OSTEUROPA*, 54:9–10, 355–65.
Henderson, S. (2007), 'Energy Security and Iran: Assessing the Transatlantic Divide', *Euractiv EU News, Policy Positions & EU Action Online 2007*. www.euractiv.com/en/energy/energy-security-iran-assessing-transatlantic-divide/article-164681 (accessed October 2010).
Hernández i Sagrera, R. (2010), 'The EU–Russia Readmission-visa Facilitation Nexus: An Exportable Migration Model for Eastern Europe?', *European Security*, 19:4, 569–84.
Hettne, B. and F. Soderbaum (2005), 'Civilian Power or Soft Imperialism?: The EU as a Global Actor and the Role of Interregionalism', *European Foreign Affairs Review*, 10:4, 535–52.
Hill, C. (2001), 'The EU's Capacity for Conflict Prevention', *European Foreign Affairs Review*, 6:3, 315–33.
Hill, C. (1998), 'Closing the Capabilities-Expectations Gap?', in J. Peterson and H. Sjursen (eds), *A Common Foreign Policy for Europe? Competing Visions of the CFSP* (London and New York: Routledge), pp. 18–38.
Hill, C. (1993), 'The Capabilities-Expectations Gap, or Conceptualizing Europe's International Role', *Journal of Common Market Studies*, 31:3, 305–28.
Hill, C. and M. Smith (eds) (2005), *The EU and International Relations* (Oxford: Oxford University Press).
Hoffman, S. (2000), 'Towards a Common Foreign and Security Policy?', *Journal of Common Market Studies*, 38:2, 189–98.
Hoffman, S. (1995), 'The Crisis of Liberal Internationalism', *Foreign Policy*, 98, 159–71.

Holm, U. (2008), *North Africa: A Security Problem for Themselves, for the EU and for the US*, Copenhagen: Danish Institute for International Studies, DIIS Report 2.

Holm, U. (2005), *EU's Neighbourhood Policy: A Question of Space and Security*, Copenhagen: Danish Institute for International Studies, DIIS Working Paper 2005/22.

Holm, U. (2004), *The EU's Security Policy Towards the Mediterranean: An (Im)possible Combination of Export of European Political Values and Anti-Terror Measures?*, Copenhagen: Danish Institute for International Studies, DIIS Working Paper 2004/13.

House of Commons (2009), Common Debates, Hansard Written Answers, 4 March. www.publications.parliament.uk/pa/cm200809/cmhansrd/cm090304/text/90304w0018.htm#09030493001266 (accessed 6 January 2012).

Howorth, J. (2007), *Security and Defence Policy in the European Union* (London/New York: Palgrave).

Howorth, J. (2005), 'From Security to Defence: The Evolution of the Common Foreign and Security Policy', in C. Hill and M. Smith (eds), *International Relations and the European Union* (Oxford: Oxford University Press), pp. 179–204.

Hudson, M.C. (1995), 'The Political Culture Approach to Arab Democratisation: The Case for Bringing Back', in R. Bryner, B. Korany and P. Noble (eds), *Political Liberalisation and Democratisation in the Arab World* (Colorado: Lynne Riener Publishers).

Hughes, J. (2007), 'EU Relations with Russia: Partnership or Asymmetric Interdependency?', in N. Casarini and C. Musu (eds), *European Foreign Policy in an Evolving International System. The Road Towards Convergence* (Basingstoke/New York: Palgrave Macmillan), pp. 76–94.

Huntington, S. (1992), *The Third Wave Democratization in the Late Twentieth Century* (Norman: University of Oklahoma Press).

Hyde-Price, A. (2008a) 'A "Tragic Actor"? A Realist Perspective on "Ethical Power Europe"', *International Affairs*, 84:1, 29–44.

Hyde-Price, A. (2008b), 'A Neurotic "Centaur". The Limitations of the EU as a Strategic Actor', in K. Engelbrekt and J. Hallenberg (eds), *The European Union and Strategy. An Emerging Actor* (London: Routledge), pp. 153–66.

Hyde-Price, A. (2006), 'Normative Power Europe: A Realist Critique', *Journal of European Public Policy*, 13:2, 217–34.

Hyde-Price, A. (2004), *The EU, Power and Coercion: From 'Civilian' to 'Civilising' Power*, Oslo: CIDEL, Paper presented at the CIDEL Workshop, 22–23 October 2004.

Interfax (2005), 'Russia Proposes Removing Politics from Human Rights Sphere', 13 March.

International Commission of Jurists (2009), 'Human Rights Committee Consideration of the 6th Periodic Report of the Russian Federation. Submission on the Lists of Issues' (Geneva).

International Crisis Group (2009), 'Georgia–Russia: Still Insecure and Dangerous', Europe Policy Briefing, Europe Briefing 53, 22 June. www.crisisgroup.org/~/media/Files/europe/B53%20Georgia-Russia%20-%20Still%20Insecure%20and%20Dangerous.pdf (accessed 17 January 2012).

International Crisis Group (2006), 'Conflict Resolution in the South Caucasus: The EU's Role', *Europe Report* 173, 20 March. www.crisisgroup.org/~/media/Files/europe/173_conflict_resolution_south_caucasus.pdf (accessed 30 April 2012).

International Organization for Migration (2008), 'Migration in the Russian Federation: A Country Profile' (Geneva).

Ismail, S. (1995), 'Democracy in Contemporary Arab Intellectual Discourse', in R. Bryner, B. Korany and P. Noble (eds), *Political Liberalisation and Democratisation in the Arab World* (Colorado: Lynne Riener Publishers).

Ivanov, S. (2008), *Where is Russia Heading? New Vision of Pan-European Security*, Speech delivered at the Munich Security Conference, 10 February.

Ivanov, S. (2006), Speech at the 42nd Munich Security Conference, 5 February.
Jackson, R.H. (2000), *The Global Convenant: Human Conduct in a World of States* (Oxford: Oxford University Press).
Jeandesboz, J. (2007), 'Labelling the Neighbourhood: Towards a Genesis of the European Neighbourhood Policy', *Journal of International Relations and Development*, 10:4, 387–416.
Jesuit Refugee Service (2009), 'Press Statement: For Immediate Release' (JRS Italy, JHR Malta and JRS Europe), 7 May.
Joenniemi, P. (2005), *The EU's New Neighbourhood Policy: Probing the Impact in Europe's North and South*, Copenhagen: Danish Institute for International Studies, unpublished manuscript.
Joffé, G. (2008),'The European Union, Democracy and Counter-Terrorism in the Maghreb', *Journal of Common Market Studies*, 46:1, 147–71.
Jørgensen, K.E. (2006), 'Theoretical Perspectives on the Role of Values, Images and Principles in Foreign Policy', in S. Lucarelli and I. Manners (eds), *Values in EU Global Action* (London: Routledge), pp. 42–58.
Jorry, H. (2007), *Construction of a European Institutional Model for Managing Operational Cooperation at the EU's External Borders: Is the FRONTEX Agency a Decisive Step Forward?*, CEPS Research Paper, No. 6 (Brussels).
Jünemann, A. (2003), 'Euro-Mediterranean Relations after September 11', in A Jünemann, *Euro-Mediterranean Relations After September 11. International, Regional and Domestic Dynamics* (London: Frank Cass), pp. 1–20.
Jurado, E. (2006), 'Assigning Duties in the Global System of Human Rights: The Role of the European Union', in H. Mayer and H. Vogt (eds), *A Responsible Europe? The Ethical Foundations of EU External Affairs* (Basingstoke: Palgrave Macmillan), pp. 119–39.
Kagarlitsky, B. (1994), *Square Wheels: How Russian Democracy Got Derailed* (New York: Monthly Review Press).
Kaldor, M., M. Martin and S. Selchow (2007), 'Human Security: A New Strategic Narrative for Europe', *International Affairs*, 83:2, 273–88.
Kalniete, S. (2005), 'EU Relations with Russia must Focus on Values, not Trade', *Europe's World*, 1 (Autumn).
Kamov, G. (2006), *EU's Role in Conflict Resolution: The Case of the Eastern Enlargement and Neighbourhood Policy Areas* (Institute Européen des Hautes Etudes Internationales).
Karlekar, K.D. (2008), *Press Freedom in 2007: A Year of Global Decline* (Washington D.C.: Freedom House).
Kausch, K., (2007), *Europe and Russia, Beyond Energy*, Madrid: FRIDE, Working Paper 33.
Kausch, K. and R. Youngs (2009), 'The End of the "Euro-Mediterranean Vision"', *International Affairs*, 85:5, 963–75.
Kelley, J. (2006), 'New Wine in Old Wineskins: Policy Learning and Adaption in The New European Neighborhood Policy', *Journal of Common Market Studies*, 44:1, 29–55.
Kelley, J.G. (2004), 'International Actors on the Domestic Scene: Membership Conditionality and Socialization by International Institutions', *International Organization*, 58:3, 425–57.
Keohane, R. (1989), *International Institutions and State Power. Essays in International Relations Theory* (Boulder, CO: Westview Press).
Keohane, R. and J. Nye (2001), *Power and Interdependence* (New York: Longman).
Keohane, R. and J. Nye (1997), *Power and Interdependence: World Politics in Transition* (Boston: Little, Brown and Co.).
Keohane, R. and J. Nye (1977), *Power and Interdependence. World Politics in Transition* (Boston: Little, Brown).
Keukeleire, S. (2004), 'Structural Foreign Policy and Structural Conflict Prevention', in J. Wouters and V. Kronenberger (eds), *The European Union and Conflict Prevention: Legal*

and Political Aspects (The Hague: T.M.C. Asser Press), pp. 151–72.

Keukeleire, S. (2002), 'Reconceptualizing (European) Foreign Policy: Structural Foreign Policy', Paper presented at the First Pan-European Conference on European Union Politics, 26–28 September). www.wmin.ac.uk/csd/rw/TMP1005915395.htm (accessed 21 January 2012).

Keukeleire, S. (2001), 'Au-delà de la PESC. La politique étrangère structurelle de l'Union Européenne', *Annuaire Français de Relations Internationales*, 2.

Keukeleire, S. and J. MacNaughtan (2008), *The Foreign Policy of the European Union* (Basingstoke/New York: Palgrave Macmillan).

Khalaf, R. (2011), 'Eight Lessons of the Arab Spring', *Financial Times*, 28 July.

Kobrinskaya, I. (2005), 'Russia and the West: A Russian Perspective', in M. Emerson (ed.), *Democratisation in the European Neighbourhood* (Brussels: Centre for European Policy Studies).

Korduban, P. (2009), 'European Union's Eastern Partnership Plan Disappoints Ukraine', *Eurasia Daily Monitor*, 6:64.

Kovács, M. (2001), 'The EU's Discursive Strategies in the 1998 and the 1999 Follow-up Reports', in J. Böröcz and M. Kovács (eds), *Empire's New Clothes: Unveiling EU Enlargement* (Holly Cottage: Central European Review), pp.196– 235.

Kramer, G. (1993), 'Islamist Notions of Democracy', *Middle East Report*, 183, 2–8.

Krastev, I. (2007), 'Where Next or What Next?', in J. Forbrig and P. Demeš (eds), *Reclaiming Democracy. Civil Society and Electoral Change in Central and Eastern Europe* (Washington: The German Marshall Fund of the United States), pp. 235–44.

Krastev, I. and M. Leonard (2010), *The Spectre of a Multipolar Europe*, London: European Council on Foreign Relations, Policy Report.

Kruse, I. (2006), 'EU Readmission Policy and its Effect on Transit Countries: The Case of Albania', *European Journal of Migration and Law*, 8:2, 115–42.

Kruse, I. (2005), *EU Readmission Policy and Its Implications for Non-Member States* (Berlin: Freie Universität Berlin).

Kubicek, P. (2005), 'The European Union and Democratization in Ukraine', *Communist and Post-Communist Studies*, 38, 269–92.

Kuzio, T. (2007), 'Comparative Perspectives on the Fourth Wave of Democracy', in J. Forbrig and P. Demeš (eds), *Reclaiming Democracy. Civil Society and Electoral Change in Central and Eastern Europe* (Washington: The German Marshall Fund of the United States), pp. 217–34.

Laatikainen, K.V. and K.E. Smith (2006), 'Introduction – The European Union at the United Nations: Leader, Partner or Failure?', in K.V. Laatikainen and K.E. Smith (eds), *The European Union at the United Nations. Intersecting Multilateralism* (Houndmills and New York: Palgrave Macmillan), pp. 1–24.

Laïdi, Z. (2008), *Norms over Force: The Enigma of European Power* (Basingstoke: Palgrave Macmillan).

Landaburu, E. (2009), 'It's Time for Hard Choices on EU–Russia Relations', *Europe's World*, 11 (Spring).

Landsbergis, V. (2008), 'Why we Must Learn to say No to Russia', *Europe's World*, 9 (Summer).

Lappin, R. (2010), 'What We Talk About When We Talk About Democracy Assistance: The Problem of Definition in Post-Conflict Approaches to Democratisation', *Central European Journal of International and Security Studies*, 4:1, 183–98.

Larsson, R.L. (2007), *Nord Stream, Sweden and Baltic Sea Security*, FOI Swedish Defence Research Agency, March.

Lavenex, S. (2006), 'Shifting Up and Out: The Foreign Policy of European Immigration Control', *West European Politics*, 29:2, 329–51.

Lavenex, S. (2004), 'EU External Governance in "Wider Europe"', *Journal of European*

Public Policy, 11:4, 680–700.

Lavenex, S. (2001), 'Migration and the EU's New Eastern Border: Between Realism and Liberalism', *Journal of European Public Policy*, 8:1, 24–42.

Lavenex, S. and F. Schimmelfennig (2009), 'EU Rules beyond EU Borders: Theorizing External Governance in European Politics', *Journal of European Public Policy*, 16:6, 791–812.

Lavenex, S. and F. Schimmelfennig (2007), 'Relations with the Wider Europe', *Journal of Common Market Studies*, 45, 143–64.

Lavenex, S. and F. Schimmelfening (2006), 'Relations with the Wider Europe', *Journal of Common Market Studies*, 44, 137–54.

Lavrov, S. (2005), 'Democracy, International Governance, and the Future World Order', *Russia in Global Affairs*, 1.

Le Gloannec, A.-M. and J. Rupnik (2008), 'Democratization by Extension. Seeking Reinsurance', in Z. Laïdi (ed.), *EU Foreign Policy in a Globalized World. Normative Power and Social Preferences* (London and New York: Routledge), pp. 51–67.

Leonard, M. (2005), *Why Europe Will Run the 21st Century* (London: Fourth Estate).

Leonard, M. and N. Popescu (2008), 'A Five-point Strategy for EU–Russia Relations', *Europe's World*, 8, Spring, 20–30.

Leonard, M. and N. Popescu (2007), *A Power Audit of EU–Russia Relations*, London: European Council on Foreign Relations Policy Paper. http://ecfr.eu/page/-/documents/ECFR-EU-Russia-power-audit.pdf (accessed 10 October 2010).

Leshukov, I. (1998), *Beyond Satisfaction: Russia's Perspectives on European Integration*, Bonn: Center for European Integration Studies (ZEI), Discussion Paper C26.

Levitsky, S. and L.A. Way (2007), 'Linkage, Leverage, and the Post-Communist Divide', *East European Politics and Society*, 21:1, 48–66.

Levitsky, S. and L.A. Way (2006), 'Linkage and Leverage: How do International Factors Change Domestic Balances of Power?', in A. Schedler (ed.), *Electoral Authoritarianism: The Dynamics of Unfree Competition* (Boulder, Lynne Rienner), pp. 199–216.

Levitsky, S. and L.A. Way (2005), 'International Linkage and Democratization', *Journal of Democracy*, 16:3, 20–34.

Light, M. (2009), 'Russia and Europe and the Process of EU Enlargement', in E. Wilson Rowe and S. Torjesen (eds), *The Multilateral Dimension in Russian Foreign Policy* (London and New York: Routledge), pp. 83–96.

Light, M. (2008), 'Keynote Article: Russia and the EU: Strategic Partners or Strategic Rivals?', *Journal of Common Market Studies*, Annual Review 46, 7–27.

Linklater, A. (2005), 'A European Civilising Process?', in C. Hill and M. Smith (eds), *The EU and International Relations* (Oxford: Oxford University Press), pp. 367–87.

Lobjakas, A. (2006), 'Azerbaijan: EU Taking Note of Baku's Strength', *Radio Free Europe/Radio Liberty*, November. www.rferl.org/content/article/1072568.html (accessed: 11 January 2008).

Lucarelli, S. (2006), 'Introduction. Values, Principles, Identity and European Union Foreign Policy', in S. Lucarelli and I. Manners (eds), *Values and Principles in European Union Foreign Policy* (London and New York: Routledge), pp. 1–18.

Lucarelli, S. (2011), and L. Fioramonti (eds) (2010), *External Perceptions of the European Union as a Global Actor* (London: Routledge).

Lucas, E. (2011), 'Goodbye to All That: "The West" is No Longer a Template for the Ex-Communist Countries', *The Economist*, November 17. www.economist.com/node/21537019 (accessed 5 January 2012).

Lynch, D. (2003), 'The EU: Towards a Strategy', in D. Lynch (ed.), *South Caucasus: A Challenge for the EU*, Chaillot Papers 65, 171–96.

Magen, A. and L. Morlino (2008), *International Actors, Democratization and the Rule of Law. Anchoring Democracy?* (London: Routledge).

Mandelson, P. (2007), *The EU and Russia: Our Joint Political Challenge*, Speech delivered in Bologna, 20 April, SPEECH/07/242.

Mandil, C. (2008), 'Energy Security and the European Union. Proposals for the French Presidency', Report to the Prime Minister, 21 April. www.premier-ministre.gouv.fr/IMG/pdf/08–1005_Rapport_au_Premier_ministre_final_ENG.pdf (accessed 30 November 2008).

Manners, I. (2006), 'Normative Power Europe Reconsidered: Beyond the Crossroads', *Journal of European Public Policy*, 13:2, 182–99.

Manners, I. (2002), 'Normative Power Europe: A Contradiction in Terms?', *Journal of Common Market Studies*, 40:2, 235–58.

Manners, I. and R. Whitman (2000), *The Foreign Policies of European Union Member States* (Manchester: Manchester University Press).

Marin, A. (2011), 'Divided we Fail: Time for the EU to Speak with One Voice to Belarus', FIIA Briefing paper, No. 85, 1 June, Finnish Institute of International Affairs, Helsinki.

Markell, P. (2006), 'Recognition and Redistribution', in J.S. Dryzek, B. Honig and A. Phillips (eds), *The Oxford Handbook of Political Theory* (Oxford: Oxford University Press).

Marples, D. (2005), 'Europe's Last Dictatorship: The Roots and Perspectives of Authoritarianism in "White Russia"', *Europe-Asia Studies*, 57:6, 895–908.

Mayer, H. and H. Vogt (eds) (2006), *A Responsible Europe? Ethical Foundations of EU External Affairs* (Basingstoke: Palgrave Macmillan).

McCormick, J. (2007), *The European Superpower* (Basingstoke: Palgrave Macmillan).

McFaul, M. (2005), 'Transitions from Postcommunism', *Journal of Democracy*, 16:3, 5–19.

Medvedev, D. (2009) , 'Go Russia!', Article by the President of Russia, *RT*, 11 September. http://rt.com/politics/official-word/dmitry-medvedev-program-document (accessed 22 January 2012).

Medvedev, D. (2008a), 'Poslanie Prezidenta RF Federal'nomu Sobraniyu', Annual Address to the Federal Assembly of the Russian Federation, *Rossiskaya Gazeta*, 6 November.

Medvedev, D. (2008b), Speech at Meeting with German Political, Parliamentary and Civic Leaders, Berlin, Ministry of Foreign Affairs of the Russian Federation, Information and Press Department, 5 June.

Messerlin, P., M. Emerson, G. Jandieri and A. Le Vernoy (2011), *An Appraisal of the EU's Trade Policy Towards Its Eastern Neighbours: The Case of Georgia* (Paris, Groupe d'Economie Mondiale and Brussels: Centre for European Policy Studies).

Meunier, S. and K. Nicolaidis (2011), 'The European Union as a Trade Power', in C. Hill and M. Smith (eds), *The International Relations of the European Union* (Oxford: Oxford University Press, 2nd edn.), pp. 275–98.

Ministry of Foreign Affairs of Georgia (2006), *National Security Concept of Georgia*. www.mfa.gov.ge/index.php?lang_id=ENG&sec_id=12&info_id=9052 (accessed 19 April 2006).

Missiroli, A. (2003), 'The EU and its Changing Neighbourhood. Stabilization, Integration and Partnership', in R. Dannreuther (ed.), *European Union Foreign and Security Policy. Towards a Neighbourhood Strategy* (London/New York: Routledge,), pp. 12–26.

Moldova.com (2009), 'Voronin: Eastern Partnership is Encircling Russia like a Ring', *Moldova.com*, February 27. http://moldova.com (accessed 21 April 2009).

Møller, J. (2005), 'The Travails of Liberal Democracy in the Post-Soviet Setting. Fiscal Incentives and Societal Constraints', in R. Di Quirico (ed.), *Europeanisation and Democratisation: Institutional Adaption, Conditionality and Democratisation in EU's Neighbour Countries* (Florence: European Press Academic Publishing), pp. 217–26.

Moravcsik, A. (1997), 'Taking Preferences Seriously: A Liberal Theory of International Politics', *International Organization*, 51:4, 513–53.

Moreno, L. (2006), 'The Genesis of the European Union's Relations with Ukraine and

Belarus. Fredo Arias-King Interview with Luis Moreno', *Demokratizatsiya. The Journal of Post-Soviet Democratization*, 14:4, 535–44.

Morgenthau, H. (1973), *Politics Among Nations* (New York: Alfred A. Knopf).

Morgenthau, H. (1948), *Politics Among Nations: The Struggle for Power and Peace* (New York: A. Knopf).

Morini, M., R. Peruzzi and A. Poletti (2010), 'Eastern Giants. The EU in the Eyes of Russia and China', in S. Lucarelli and L. Fioramonti (eds), *External Perceptions of the European Union as a Global Actor* (London: Routledge).

Neumann, I.B. (1998), 'European Identity, EU Expansion, and the Integration/Exclusion Nexus', *Alternatives: Global, Local, Political*, 23:3.

Newton, J.M. (2003), *Russia, France, and the Idea of Europe* (Basingstoke: Palgrave Macmillan).

Nodia, G. (2008), 'Reviving Georgia's Western Dream', *Project Syndicate*, 1 January. www.project-syndicate.org/commentary/nodia1 (accessed 15 November 2008).

Noël, P. (2008), Policy Brief, 'Beyond Dependence: How to Deal with Russian Gas', European Council on Foreign Relations.

Nonneman, G. (2006), 'Political Reform in the Gulf Monarchies: From Liberalisation to Democratisation? A Comparative Perspective', *Durham Middle East Papers*, 8.

Norton, A.R. (1999), *Hizballah of Lebanon: Extremist Ideals vs. Mundane Politics* (New York: Council of Foreign Relations).

Nygren, B. (2008), 'The EU's Democratic Norm Project for Eurasia. Will the Beauty Tame the Beast?', in K. Engelbrekt and J. Hallenberg (eds), *The European Union and Strategy. An Emerging Actor* (London: Routledge), pp. 111–29.

Olsen, G.R. (2000), 'Promotion of Democracy as a Foreign Policy Instrument of Europe: Limits to International Idealism', *Democratization*, 7, 142–67.

Olson, R.K. (1997), 'Partners in Peace Process: The United States and Europe', *Journal of Palestine Studies*, 26:4, 78–89.

Önis, Z. and C. Bakir (2007), 'Turkey's Political Economy in the Age of Financial Globalization: The Significance of the EU Anchor', *South European Society and Politics*, 12:2 (2007), 147–64.

Paasi, A. (2005), 'Generations and the Development of Border Studies', *Geopolitics*, 10, 1–9.

Pace, M. (2007), 'Norm Shifting from EMP to ENP: The EU as a Norm Entrepreneur in the South?', *Cambridge Review of International Affairs*, 20:4, 659–75.

Pace, M. (2006), 'The EU Surrounded by a "Ring of Friends": The Impact of the ENP on Europe's South'. Paper presented at the BRIT VIII conference on *Neighbours, Citizens and Borders. The Making of Geo-Political Relations and Communities*, 21–25 September.

Pace, M., and S. Stetter (2003), *A Literature Review on the Study of Border conflicts and Their Transformation in the Social Sciences* (Birmingham: University of Birmingham). www.euborderconf.bham.ac.uk/publications/files/stateoftheartreport.pdf (accessed 26 August 2007).

Parker, C. (2006), 'Inside Myanmar's Secret Capital', *Asia Times Online*. www.atimes.com/atimes/Southeast_Asia/HJ28Ae01.html (accessed 15 May 2009).

Patten, C. and J. Solana (2002), 'Letter to the Danish Presidency', Brussels, 7 August.

Perthes, V. (2004), 'America's Greater Middle East and Europe: Key Issues for Dialogue', *Middle East Policy*, 11:3, 85–97.

Peters, J. (1996a), *Pathways to Peace: The Multilateral Arab-Israeli Talks* (London: Royal Institute of International Affairs).

Peters, J. (1996b), 'The Emergence of Regional Cooperation in the Middle East', *The Middle East in the Post Peace Process: The Emerging Regional Order and its International Implications* (Tokyo: Institute of Developing Economies), pp. 75–117.

Petersen, M.J. (2008), *Social Welfare Activism in Jordan: Democratisation in Disguise?*,

Copenhagen: Danish Institute for International Affairs, DIIS Brief.
Pevehouse, J.C. (2002), 'Democracy from Outside-In? International Organisations and Democratisation', *International Organisation*, 56:3, 515–49.
Popescu, N. (2011), *EU Foreign Policy and Post-Soviet Conflicts: Stealth Intervention* (New York and Basingstoke: Routledge).
Popescu, N. (2007), *Europe's Unrecognised Neighbours: The EU in Abkhazia and South Ossetia*, Brussels: Centre for European Policy Studies, Working Document No. 260.
Popescu, N. and A. Wilson (2009), *The Limits of Enlargement-Lite: European and Russian Power in the Troubled Neighbourhood*, London: Council on Foreign Relations, Policy Report.
Portela, C. (2008), 'Sanctions against Belarus: Normative Unintended', in N. Tocci (ed.), *The European Union as a Normative Policy Actor*, Brussels: Centre for European Policy Studies, Working Document No. 281, pp. 5–9.
Potemkina, O. (2004), 'Ramification of Enlargement for EU–Russia Relations and the Schengen Regime', in J. Apap (ed.), *Justice and Home Affairs in the EU: Liberty and Security Issues after Enlargement* (Cheltenham: Edward Elgar Publishing).
Pravda.ru (2006), 'Russia pays off USSR's Entire Debt, Sets to Become Crediting Country', *Pravda*, 22 August. http://english.pravda.ru/russia/economics/84038–paris-club-0 (accessed 20 April 2009).
President of Ukraine (1998), Decree on Strategy of Ukraine's Integration to the European Union, 615/98, Kiev, 11 June.
Pridham, G. (2009), 'Securing the Only Game in Town: The EU's Political Conditionality and Democratic Consolidation in Post-Soviet Latvia', *Europe-Asia Studies*, 61:1, 51–84.
Pridham, G. (2006), 'European Union Accession Dynamics and Democratization in Central and Eastern Europe: Past and Future Perspectives', *Government and Opposition*, 41:3, 373–400.
Prizel, I. (1998), *National Identity and Foreign Policy. Nationalism and Leadership in Poland, Russia and Ukraine* (Cambridge: Cambridge University Press).
Prodi, R. (2000), *An Enlarged and More United Europe, A Global Payer – Challenges and Opportunities in the New Century*, Speech delivered by the President of the European Commission at the College of Europe, Bruges, 12 November, Speech/01/528.
Prodi, R. (2001), *Ukraine and Europe Moving Forward Together*, Speech delivered by the President of the European Commission at the National Academy of Science, Kiev, 10 November, Speech/00/429.
Putin, V. (2010), Putin: Plädoyer für Wirtschaftsgemeinschaft (guest contribution), 'Von Lissabon bis Wladiwostok', *Süddeutsche Zeitung* online edition, 25 November.
Putin, V. (2007a) 'Poslanie Federal'nomu Sobraniyu Rossiiskoi Federatsii', Annual Address to the Federal Assembly of the Russian Federation, *Rossiskaya Gazeta*, 11 May, pp. 1–3.
Putin, V. (2007b), 'Poslanie Federal'nomu Sobraniyu Rossiiskoi Federatsii Prezidenta Rossii Vladimira Putina', Annual Address to the Federal Assembly of the Russian Federation, *Rossiskaya Gazeta*, 27 April, pp. 3–5.
Putin, V. (2007c), Speech at the 43rd Munich Conference on Security Policy 10 February.
Putin, V. (2005), Poslanie Federal'nomu Sobraniyu Rossiiskoi Federatsii (Annual Address to the Federal Assembly of the Russian Federation), *Rossiskaya Gazeta*, 26 April, 3–4.
Putin, V. (2004a), 'Poslanie Federal'nomu Sobraniyu Rossiiskoi Federatsii', Annual Address to the Federal Assembly of the Russian Federation, *Rossiskaya Gazeta*, 27 May, pp. 3–4.
Putin, V. (2004b), 'Poslanie Prezidenta Rossii Vladimira Putina Federal'nomu Sobraniyu RF', Annual Address to the Federal Assembly of the Russian Federation, *Rossiskaya Gazeta*, 17 May), p. 3.
Putin, V. (2004c), 'Statement and Answers to Media Questions at the Joint Press

Conference Following Tripartite Talks with FRG Federal Chancellor Gerhard Schröder and French President Jacques Chirac', 11 April, St. Petersburg.
Putin, V. (2003a), Poslanie Prezidenta Rossii Vladimira Putina Federal'nomu Sobraniyu RF (Annual Address to the Federal Assembly of the Russian Federation) *Rossiskaya Gazeta*, 17 May, 4.
Putin, V. (2003b), Statement and Answers to Media Questions at the Joint Press Conference Following Tripartite Talks with FRG Federal Chancellor Gerhard Schröder and French President Jacques Chirac, 11 April, St Petersburg.
Putin, V. (2002), 'Rossii nado byt' sil'noi i konkurentnosposobnoi', Annual Address to the Federal Assembly of the Russian Federation, *Rossiskaya Gazeta*, 19 April, pp. 4–7.
Putin, V. (2001), 'Ne budet ni revolutsii, ni kontrrevolyutsii', Annual Address to the Federal Assembly of the Russian Federation, *Rossiskaya Gazeta*, 14 April, pp. 3–4.
Putin, V. (2000), 'Kakuyu Rossiyu my stroem', Annual Address to the Federal Assembly of the Russian Federation, *Rossiskaya Gazeta*, 11 July, pp. 1–3.
Radio Free Europe/Radio Liberty (2009), 'Moldova unhappy with EU's Eastern Partnership Offer', *RFE/RL*, 25 March, www.rferl.org (accessed 21 April 2009).
Raik, K. (2006), 'The EU as a Regional Power: Extended Governance and Historical Responsibility', in H. Meyer and H. Vogt (eds), *A Responsible Europe? Ethical Foundations of EU External Affairs* (Basingstoke: Palgrave Macmillan).
Raik, K. (2005), 'EU Accession of Central and Eastern European Countries: Democracy and Integration as Conflicting Logics', *East European Politics and Societies*, 18:4, 567–94.
Ria Novosti (2009a), 'Russia-Azerbaijan Gas Deal Would Boost Energy Security – Medvedev', *Ria Novsoti*, 17 April. http://en.rian.ru/russia/20090417/121182922.html (accessed 29 May 2009).
Ria Novosti (2009b), 'EU excludes Nabucco Gas Pipeline Project from Priority List', *Ria Novosti*, 17 March. http://en.rian.ru/world/20090317/120598679.html (accessed 17 March 2009).
Rijpma, J. and M. Cremona (2007), 'The Extra-Territorialisation of EU Migration Policies and the Rule of Law', *EUI Working Paper Law 2007/01* (Florence: European University Institute).
Risse, T. (2004), 'Social Constructivism and European Integration', in A. Wiener and T. Dietz (eds), *European Integration Theory* (Oxford: Oxford University Press), pp. 159–76.
Risse, T. (2000), '"Let's argue!": Communicative Action in World Politics', *International Organization*, 54:1, 1–39.
Risse-Kappen, T. (1994), 'The Long-term Future of European Security: Perpetual Anarchy or Community of Democracies?', in W. Carlsnaes and S. Smith (eds), *European Foreign Policy. The EC and Changing Perspectives in Europe* (London: Sage/ECPR), pp. 45–60.
Roberson, B. (1998), 'Islam and Europe: An Enigma or a Myth?', in B. Roberson (ed.), *The Middle East and Europe: the Power Deficit* (London: Routledge), pp. 288–308.
Robins, P. (2006), 'The 2005 BRISMES Lecture: a Double Gravity State: Turkish Foreign Policy Reconsidered', *British Journal of Middle Eastern Studies*, 33:2, 199–211.
Roig, A. and T. Huddelston (2007), 'EC Readmission Agreements: A Re-evaluation of the Political Impasse', *European Journal of Migration and Law*, 9, 363–87.
Rosamond, B. (2000), *Theories of European Integration* (New York: Palgrave Macmillan).
Roth, M. (2011), 'Poland as Policy Entrepreneur in European External Energy Policy: Towards Greater Energy Solidarity vis-à-vis Russia?', *Geopolitics*, 16:3, 600–25.
Roth, M. (2009), *Bilateral Disputes between EU Member States and Russia*, Centre for European Policy Studies, CEPS Working Document No. 319.
Ruggie, J.G. (1993), 'Territoriality and Beyond: Problematising Modernity in International Relations', *International Organization*, 47:1 1993, 139–74.
Rumelili, B. (2004), 'Constructing Identity and Relating to Difference: Understanding the EU's Mode of Differentiation', *Review of International Studies*, 30:1, 27–47.

Rumford, C. (2008), *Cosmopolitan Spaces: Europe, Globalization, Theory* (London: Routledge).
Rushd, I. (2001), *Basics of Political Thought*, trans. M.H. Ozev (Istanbul: Bordo Siyah).
Ryzhkov, V. (2005a), 'Sovereignty Versus Democracy', *Russia in Global Affairs*, 4 (October–December), 101–13.
Ryzhkov, V. (2005b), 'Sovereign Democracy and the Usurper State', *Moscow Times* (16 August).
Saari, S. (2009), 'European Democracy Promotion in Russia Before and After the "Colour" Revolutions', *Democratization*, 16:4, 732–55.
Said, E.W. (1978), *Orientalism* (New York: Vintage Books).
Sakwa, R. (2008), 'Putin's Leadership: Character and Consequences', *Europe-Asia Studies*, 60:6, 879–97.
Sánchez Andrés A., (2007), *Russia and Europe: Mutual Dependence in the Energy Sector*, Madrid: Real Instituto Elcano, Working Paper 25.
Sasse, G. (2008), 'The European Neighbourhood Policy: Conditionality Revisited for the EU's Eastern Neighbours', *Europe-Asia Studies*, 60:2, 295–316.
Saurugger, S. (2009), 'Sociological Approaches in EU Studies', *Journal of European Public Policy*, 16:6, 935–49.
Schieffer, M. (2003), 'Community Readmission Agreements with Third Countries: Objectives, Substances and Current State of Negotiation', *European Journal of Migration and Law*, 5:14, 343–57.
Schimmelfennig, F. (2008), 'EU Political Accession Conditionality After the 2004 Enlargement: Consistency and Effectiveness', *Journal of European Public Policy*, 15:6, 918–37.
Schimmelfennig, F. (2005a), 'The Community Trap. Liberal Norms, Rhetorical Action and the Eastern Enlargement of the European Union', in F. Schimmelfennig and U. Sedelmeier (eds), *The Politics of European Union Enlargement. Theoretical Approaches* (London and New York: Routledge), pp. 142–71.
Schimmelfennig, F. (2005b), 'European Neighborhood Policy: Political Conditionality and its Impact on Democracy in Non-Candidate Neighboring Countries', Paper prepared for the EUSA Ninth Biennial International Conference, Austin, 31 March–2 April.
Schimmelfennig, F. (2003), *The EU, NATO and the Integration of Europe: Rhetoric and Rules* (Cambridge: Cambridge University Press).
Schimmelfennig, F. (2001), 'The Community Trap: Liberal Norms, Rhetorical Action and the Eastern Enlargement of the European Union', *International Organization* 55:1, 47–80.
Schimmelfennig, F. (2000), 'International Socialization in the New Europe: Rational Action in an Institutional Environment', *European Journal of International Relations*, 6:1, 109–39.
Schimmelfennig, F. and U. Sedelmeier (eds) (2005), *The Europeanization of Central and Eastern Europe* (Ithaca, NY: Cornell University Press).
Schimmelfennig, F. and U. Sedelmeier (2004), 'Governance by Conditionality: EU Rule Transfer to the Candidate Countries of Central and Eastern Europe', *Journal of European Public Policy* 11:4, 661–79.
Schmidt, D. (2005), 'Eine Wertelücke zwischen Rußland und dem Westen? Vorläufige Anmerkungen zu einem schwierigen Diskurs', in 'Rußland und der Westen', *Rußland Analysen*, 70.
Schmidt-Felzmann, A. (2011), 'EU Member States' Energy Relations with Russia: Conflicting Approaches to Securing Natural Gas Supplies', *Geopolitics*, 16:3, 574–99.
Schütte, R. (2004), *E.U.–Russia Relations: Interests and Values – A European Perspective*, Carnegie Moscow Centre, Carnegie Papers No. 54.
Secrieru, S. (2009), *Russian Foreign Policy in Times of Crisis: Greater Compliance or Resilient Self-confidence?*, Centre for European Policy Studies, CEPS Policy Brief No. 192.

Sedelmeier, U. (2006a), 'Europeanisation in New Member and Candidate States', *Living Reviews in European Governance* 1:3. www.livingreviews.org/lreg-2006-3 (accessed 14 May 2008).
Sedelmeier, U. (2006b), 'Pre-accession Conditionality and Post-accession Compliance in the New Member States: A Research Note', in W. Sadurski, J. Ziller and K. Zurek (eds), *Après Enlargement. Legal and Political Responses in Central and Eastern Europe* (Florence: Robert Schuman Centre for Advanced Studies, European University Institute), pp. 145–60.
Sedelmeier, U. (2005), 'Eastern Enlargement. Risk, Rationality and Role-compliance', in F. Schimmelfennig and U. Sedelmeier (eds), *The Politics of European Union Enlargement. Theoretical Approaches* (London and New York: Routledge), pp. 120–41.
Seminatore, I. (2006), *L'Europe et la grande stratégie. Pacte de stabilité du Caucase du sud et de la grande Mer Noire*, Presentation delivered at the European Parliament Committee on Foreign Affairs Delegation to the Parliamentary Cooperation Committees EU-Armenia, EU-Azerbaijan and EU-Georgia as speaker of the Institut européen des relations internationals, Brussels, 22 February.
Sil, R. and P. Katzenstein (2010), 'Analytic Eclecticism in the Study of World Politics: Reconfiguring Problems and Mechanisms across Research Traditions', *Perspectives on Politics* 8:2, 411–31.
Simão, L. (2010), *Engaging Civil Society in the Nagorno Karabakh Conflict: What Role for the EU and its Neighbourhood Policy?*, Brighton: MICROCON, MICROCON Policy Working Paper 11.
Simão, L. and M.R. Freire (2008), 'The EU's Neighbourhood Policy and the South Caucasus: Unfolding New Patterns of Cooperation', *Caucasian Review of International Affairs*, 2:4, 47–61.
Sjursen, H. (2006), 'The EU as a "Normative" Power: How Can This Be?', *Journal of European Public Policy*, 13:2, 235–51.
Sjursen, H. (2002), 'Why Expand? The Question of Legitimacy and Justification in the EU's Enlargement Policy', *Journal of Common Market Studies*, 40:3, 491–513.
Skinner, Q. (2001), *Machiavelli: A Very Short Introduction* (Oxford: Oxford University Press).
Smith, K. (2005a), 'The Outsiders: The European Neighbourhood Policy', *International Affairs*, 81:4, 757–73.
Smith, K. (2005b), 'Engagement and Conditionality: Incompatible or Mutually Reinforcing?', in R. Youngs (ed.), *Global Europe: New Terms of Engagement* (London: The Foreign Policy Centre and The British Council Brussels), pp. 23–30.
Smith, K. (2004), *The Making of EU Foreign Policy. The Case of Eastern Europe* (New York: Palgrave Macmillan, 2nd edn).
Smith, M.E. (2011), 'A Liberal Grand Strategy in a Realist World? Power, Purpose and the EU's Changing Global Role', *Journal of European Public Policy*, 18:2, 144–63.
Solana, J. (2009), *We Tend to Believe That Security Inside Europe is Largely 'Completed'*, Speech delivered at the 45h Munich Security Conference, 2 June.
Solana, J. (2000), 'EU and Ukraine – Evolving Strategic Partnership', *Zerkalo Nedeli*, 19 September.
Solchanyk, R. (2001), *Ukraine and Russia. The Post-Soviet Transition* (United States: Rowman and Littlefield Publishers).
Sparre, S.L. (2008), *Muslim Youth Organisations in Egypt: Actors of Reform and Development?*, Copenhagen: Danish Institute for International Affairs, DIIS Brief.
Spruds, A. (2002), 'Perceptions and Interests in Russian-Baltic Relations', in H. Hubel *et al.* (eds), *EU Enlargement and Beyond: The Baltic States and Russia*, vol. 18, Nordeuropäische Studien (Berlin: BERLIN VERLAG, Arno Spitz GmbH).
Stefanova, B. (2005), 'The European Union as a Security Actor: Security Provision Through Enlargement', *The Brown Journal of World Affairs*, 168:2, 51–66.
Steinmeier, F.-W. (2007), 'Verflechtung und Integration. Eine neue Phase der Ostpolitik

der EU: Nicht Abgrenzung, sondern Vernetzung lautet das Gebot der Globalisierung', *Internationale Politik*, 62:3, 6–11.

Stern, J. (2005), *The Future of Russian Gas and Gazprom* (Oxford: Oxford University Press for the Oxford Institute for Energy).

Sushko, O. (2007), 'Ukraine and the EU de facto Came Close to the Associative Type of Relations', in Ukrainian Centre for Economic and Political Studies (Razumkov Centre) and Europa Institut at the University of Zurich, *Ukraine – EU: from the Action Plan to an Enhanced Agreement* (Kiev: Razumkov Centre and 'Zapovit' Publishing House).

Sutela, P. (2005), *EU, Russia and Common Economic Space*, Helsinki: Bank of Finland Institute for Economies in Transition Online, No. 3.

Tarasyuk, B. (2008), *Ukraine's Relations with NATO/Europe. His Excellency Borys Tarasyuk, Foreign Minister of Ukraine*, Speech delivered at 17th International Workshop on Global Security, Berlin, 2–5 June.

Tarasyuk, B. (2006), *Ukraine Working for Peace, Freedom and Democracy*, Speech delivered by H.E. Mr. Borys Tarasyuk, Minister for Foreign Affairs of Ukraine, at the Society and Defense Annual National Conference, Sälen, 16 January.

Tarasyuk, B. (2000), *Ukraine's Relations with NATO/Europe. His Excellency Borys Tarasyuk, Foreign Minister of Ukraine*, 17th International Workshop on Global Security, Berlin, 2–5 June 2000. www.csdr.org/2000Book/tarasyuk.htm (accessed 23 May 2008).

Tarasyuk, B. (1998), *Ukraine's Contributions to European Capabilities in Response to Security Challenges to the New NATO*, Speech delivered at 15th International Workshop on Global Security, Vienna, 19–23 June.

Tassinari, F. (2006), *A Synergy for Black Sea Regional Cooperation: Guidelines for an EU initiative*, Brussels: Centre for European Policy Studies, CEPS Policy Brief No. 105.

Tassinari, F. (2005*), Security and Integration in the EU Neighbourhood – The Case for Regionalism*, Brussels: Centre for European Policy Studies, CEPS Working Document No. 226.

Timmins, G. (2007), 'German–Russian Bilateral Relations and EU Policy On Russia: Reconciling the Two-Level Game?', in J. Gower and G. Timmins (eds), *Russia and Europe: An Uneasy Partnership* (London: Anthem Press), pp. 169–84.

Timmins, G. (2006a), 'Bilateral Relations in the Russia–EU Relationship: The British View', in H. Smith (ed.), *Two Levels of Cooperation: Russia, the EU, Great Britain and Finland* (Helsinki: Kikimora Publications), pp. 49–65.

Timmins, G. (2006b), 'German Ostpolitik Under the Red–Green Coalition and EU–Russia Relations', *Debatte – Journal of Contemporary Central and Eastern Europe*, 14:3, 301–14.

Tkachenko, S.L. (2008), 'Actors in Russia's Energy Policy towards the EU', in P. Aalto (ed.), *The EU–Russia Energy Dialogue: Securing Europe's Future Energy Supply* (Aldershot: Ashgate), pp. 163–92.

Tocci, N. (ed.) (2008), *Who is a Normative Foreign Policy Actor? The European Union and Its Global Partners* (Brussels: Centre for European Policy Studies).

Tocci, N. (2007a), 'Can the EU Promote Democracy and Human Rights through the ENP? The Case for Refocusing on the Rule of Law', in M. Cremona and G. Meloni (eds), *The European Neighbourhood Policy: A Framework for Modernisation?*, Brussels: European University Institute, Working Paper Law 2007/21.

Tocci, N. (2007b), *The EU and Conflict Resolution. Promoting Peace in the Backyard* (London: Routledge, 2007).

Tocci, N. *et al.* (2007), 'The Closed Armenia–Turkey Border: Economic and Social Effects, Including Those on the People; and Implications for the Overall Situation in the Region', in a study made under the framework contract with Trans European Policy Studies Association for the Foreign Affairs Committee of the European Parliament (Brussels: European Parliament).

Toje, A. (2008), 'The European Union as a Small Power, or Conceptualizing Europe's Strategic Actorness', *Journal of European Integration*, 30:2, 199–215.

Tonra, B. (2001), *Europeanisation of National Foreign Policy: Dutch, Danish and Irish Foreign Policy in the European Union* (Aldershot: Ashgate).

Tovias, U. and M. Ugur (2004), 'Can the EU Anchor Policy Reform in Third Countries?', *European Union Politics*, 5:4, 395–418.

Trauner, F. and I. Kruse (2008), 'EC Visa Facilitation and Readmission Agreements: A New Standard EU Foreign Policy Tool?', European Journal of Migration and Law, 10:4, 411–38.

Treaty Establishing the European Economic Community as Amended by Subsequent Treaties (1957). Rome, 25 March.

Tretyakov, V. (2003), 'The Putin Imperatives: Managed Democracy and Unmanaged Authoritarianism – How the Oligarchs Helped Create Russia's Managed Democracy and Learned to Regret It', *Literaturnaya Gazeta*, 5–11 November.

Tsygankov, A.P. (2010), 'Russia's Power and Alliances in the Twenty-First Century', *Politics*, 30:1, 43–51.

Tunander,O. (1997), 'Post-Cold War Europe: Synthesis of a Bipolar Friend–Foe Structure and a Hierarchic Cosmos–Chaos Structure?', in O. Tunander, P. Baev and V.I. Einagel (eds), *Geopolitics in Post-Wall Europe. Security, Territory and Identity* (Oslo/London: PRIO/ SAGE=), pp. 17–44.

Udovenko, H. (1997), *NATO Enlargement, Ukraine and European Security*, Speech delivered at 14th International Workshop on Global Security, Prague, 21–25 June.

Udovenko, H. (1996), *European Security: A Ukrainian View*, Speech delivered at 13th NATO Workshop on Political Military Decision Making, Warsaw, 19–23 June.

Udovenko, H. (1995), 'European Stability and NATO Enlargement: Ukraine's Perspective', *NATO Review*, 43:6, 15–18.

Ugur, M. (1999), *The European Union and Turkey: An Anchor/Credibility Dilemma* (Aldershot: Ashgate).

Ukrainian Centre for Economic and Political Studies (2007), 'Public Monitoring of the Ukraine–EU Action Plan Implementation: Preliminary Assessments', *National Security and Defence*, 86:2, 2–12.

UNHCR (2004), *The European Union, Asylum and the International Refugee Protection Regime: The New Multiannual Programme in the Area of Freedom, Security and Justice* (Geneva).

United Nations (1992), General Assembly Forty-seventh session. Provisional verbatim record of the 16th meeting, A/47/PV.16, 29 September.

United Nations Development Program (1994), *Human Development Report 1994* (Oxford and London: Oxford University Press. http://hdr.undp.org/en/reports/global/hdr1994/ (accessed 2 October 2010).

Uppsala University (2010), *Uppsala Conflict Data Program* 10/12/20, UCDP Conflict Encyclopedia. www.ucdp.uu.se/database (accessed 17 May 2012).

Uppsala University (2009), *Uppsala Conflict Data Program* 09/06/24, UCDP Database, Uppsala. www.ucdp.uu.se/database (accessed 29 September 2010).

USA Today (2011), 'Muslim Broherhood Top Winner in Egyptian Elections', 5 December. www.usatoday.com/news/world/story/2011-12-04/israel-egypt-elections/51641978/1 (accessed 6 December 2011).

Ušackas, V. (2008), *The Impact of Lithuania's EU membership for Lithuania–Russia Relationship*, Lecture delivered at the Jean Monnet Symposium by the Lithuanian Ambassador to the UK, Wolverhampton University, 10 March.

Vachudova, M. (2005), *Europe Undivided: Democracy, Leverage and Integration after Communism* (Oxford: Oxford University Press).

Vahl, M. (2007), 'EU–Russia Relations in EU Neighbourhood Policies', in K. Malfliet, L. Verpoest and E. Vinokurov (eds), *The CIS, the EU and Russia. The Challenges of Integration* (Houndmills/Basingstoke: Palgrave Macmillan), pp. 121–220.

Vieira, A. and L. Simão (2008), 'The European Neighbourhood Policy Viewed from

Belarus and Georgia', *CFSP Forum*, 6:6, 1–6.
Vizoso, J.C. (2008), 'Lebanon', in R. Youngs (ed.), *Is the European Union Supporting Democracy in its Neighbourhood?* (Madrid: FRIDE), pp. 55–78.
Waever, O. (1998), 'Insecurity, Security, and Asecurity in the West European Non-war Community', in E. Adler and M. Barnett (eds), *Security Communities* (Cambridge: Cambridge University Press), pp. 69–118.
Waever, O. (1997), 'Imperial Metaphors: Emerging European Analogies to Pre-Nation State Imperial Systems', in O. Tunander, P. Baev and V.I. Einagel (eds), *Geopolitics in Post-Wall Europe. Security, Territory and Identity* (London: Sage and Oslo: International Peace Research Institute), pp. 59–93.
Wallace, W. (2003), *Looking After the Neighbourhood: Responsibilities for the EU-25*, Notre Europe, Policy Paper No. 4.
Wallace, W. (2002), 'Where does Europe End? Dilemmas of Inclusion and Exclusion', in J. Zielonka (ed.), *Europe Unbound: Enlarging and Reshaping the Boundaries of the European Union* (London: Routledge), pp. 78–95.
Waltz, K. (1979), *Theory of International Politics* (Reading MA: Addison-Wesley).
Wagner, R.H. (1988), 'Economic Interdependence, Bargaining Power, and Political Influence', *International Organization*, 42:3, 461–83.
Wagnsson, C. (2010), 'Divided Power Europe: Normative Divergences among the EU "Big Three"', *Journal of European Public Policy*, 17:8, 1089–105.
Walters, W. (2004), 'The Frontiers of the European Union: A Geostrategic Perspective', *Geopolitics*, 9:3, 674–98.
Wasilewski, A. (2004), 'Natural Gas in Russia's Foreign Policy', *The Polish Quarterly of International Affairs*, 13:10, 89–113.
Weber, K., M.E. Smith and M. Baun (eds) (2007), *Governing Europe's Neighbourhood: Partners or Periphery?* (Manchester: Manchester University Press).
Wendt, A. (1999), *Social Theory of International Politics* (Cambridge: Cambridge University Press).
Westphal, K. (2008), 'Germany and the EU-Russia Energy Dialogue', in P. Aalto (ed.), *The EU–Russia Energy Dialogue: Securing Europe's Future Energy Supply* (Aldershot: Ashgate), pp. 93–118.
Wheatley, J. (2010), 'Georgia's Democratic Veneer: Scraping the Surface', in E. Baracani (ed.), *Democratization and Hybrid Regimes. International Anchoring and Domestic Dynamics in European Post-Soviet States* (Florence: European Press Academic Publishing) pp. 351–80.
Whist, B.S. (2009), 'Nord Stream: A Litmus Test for Intra-EU Solidarity', in A. Kasekamp (ed.), *Estonian Foreign Policy Yearbook 2009* (Tallinn: Eesti Välispoliitika Instituut), pp. 75–122.
White, B. (2001), *Understanding European Foreign Policy* (Basingstoke: Palgrave Macmillan).
Whitman, R. (2010), 'The EU: Standing Aside from the Changing Global Balance of Power?', *Politics*, 30:1, 24–32.
Whitman, R. (2005), 'Winning Hearts and Minds', in R. Youngs (ed.), *New Terms of Engagement* (London: The Foreign Policy Centre), pp. 30–7.
Whitman, R. (1998), *From Civilian Power to Superpower? The International Identity of the European Union* (Basingstoke: Palgrave).
Whitman, R. and S. Wolff (2010), *The European Neighbourhood Policy in Perspective. Context, Implementation and Impact* (Basingstoke: Palgave Macmillan).
Willis, A. (2009), 'EU Not Getting "One Drop" of Russian gas', *EUObserver*, 13 January.
Wolczuk, W. (2000), 'History, Europe and the "National Idea": the "Official" Narrative of National Identity in Ukraine', *Nationalities Papers*, 28:4, 671–94.
Wolfers, A. (1962), *Discord and Collaboration: Essays on International Politics* (Baltimore,

MD: Johns Hopkins University Press).
Wolff, S., N. Wichmann and G. Mournier (eds) (2009), 'The External Dimension of Justice and Home Affairs? A Different Security Agenda for the EU', *Journal of European Integration*, Special Issue, 31:1, 9–23.
Wong, R. (2007), 'Foreign Policy', in P. Graziano and M. Vink (eds), *Europeanization: New Research Agendas* (Basingstoke: Palgrave Macmillan), pp. 321–34.
Wong, R. (2005), 'The Europeanization of Foreign Policy', in C. Hill and M. Smith (eds), *International Relations and the European Union* (Oxford: Oxford University Press), pp. 134–53.
Wong, R. and C. Hill (2011), *National and European Foreign Policies – Towards Europeanisation* (New York and Basingstoke: Routledge).
World Bank (2010), *Russian Federation. Indicators since 1960*, WDI 2010, last updated 23 September 2010. http://go.worldbank.org/N1PG9OQ8C0 (permanent URL).
World Bank (2006), *Doing Business 2006 Country Profile Georgia*. Washington: The International Bank for Reconstruction and Development.
Yacoby, H. and D. Newmann (2008), 'The EU and the Israel–Palestine conflict', in T. Diez, M. Albert and S. Stetter (eds), *The European Union and Border Conflicts. The Power of Integration and Association* (Cambridge: Cambridge University Press), pp. 173–202.
Yesilyurt-Gunduz, Z. (2009), 'The Euro-Mediterranean Partnership: On Good Intentions, Shopping Lists and à la carte Menus', in B. Balamir Coskun and B. Demirtas-Coskun (eds), *Neighbourhood Challenge: The EU and Its Neighbours* (Boca Raton: Universal Publisher), pp. 145–64.
Youngs, R. (ed.) (2010), *The European Union and Democracy Promotion: A Critical Global Assessment* (Baltimore: Johns Hopkins University Press).
Youngs, R. (2009), 'Democracy Promotion as External Governance?', *Journal of European Public Policy*, 16:6, 895–915.
Youngs, R. (2008), 'Assessing European Democracy Support in the Neighbourhood,' in R. Youngs (ed.), *Is the European Union Supporting Democracy in its Neighbourhood?* (Madrid: FRIDE), pp. 1–7.
Youngs, R. (2007), 'The European Union and Palestine: A New Engagement?', *Open Democracy*, 28 March. www.opendemocracy.net/trackback/4485 (accessed 13 October 2007).
Youngs, R. (2006), *Europe and the Middle East: In the Shadow of September 11* (Boulder: Lynne Rienner).
Youngs, R. (2004), 'Normative Dynamics and Strategic Interests in the EU's External Identity', *Journal of Common Market Studies*, 42:2, 415–35.
Youngs, R. (2001), *The European Union and the Promotion of Democracy* (Oxford: Oxford University Press).
Zagorski, A. (2004), 'Policies Towards Russia, Ukraine, Moldova and Belarus', in R. Dannreuther (ed.), *European Union Foreign and Security Policy. Towards a Neighbourhood Strategy* (London: Routledge).
Zagorski, A. (2002), *EU Policies Towards Russia, Ukraine, Moldova and Belarus*, Geneva: Centre for Security Policy, Occasional Paper, No. 35.
Zaiotti, R. (2007), 'Of Friends and Fences: Europe's Neighbourhood Policy and the "Gated Community Syndrome"', *Journal of European Integration*, 29:2, 143–62.
Zakaria, F. (1997), 'The Rise of Illiberal Democracy', *Foreign Affairs*, 76: November–December, 22–43.
Zielonka, J. (2006), *Europe as Empire* (Oxford: Oxford University Press).
Zisenwine, D. (2004), 'Tunisia's Elections: The Long Road to Democracy', *Tel-Aviv Notes*, 113.
Zürn, M. and J. Checkel (2005), 'Getting Socialized to Build Bridges: Constructivism and Rationalism, Europe and the Nation-State', *International Organization*, 59:4, 1045–79.

Index

Abant Platform 96
Abbas, Mahmoud 97
Abduh, Muhammad 95
Abkhazia 118
accession to the EU, process of 33
acquis communautaire 30, 32, 36, 185
Action Plans for the ENP 39, 48–9, 60, 73, 87–9, 114–16, 153–4, 164
Adamkus, Valdas 194
Adler, E. 111
Agadir Process 31
Albania 36, 205
Algeria 31, 41–2, 74, 76, 81
Amnesty International 213–14
Amsterdam Treaty (1997) 117, 201, 204
analytical eclecticism 221
Anderson, M. 50
Anderson, Perry 44
Annual Reports on Human Rights 73
Arab Spring (2011) 3, 6, 13–14, 67–9, 74–7, 81, 86–7, 92–6, 102, 229, 233
Arafat, Yasser 143
Area of Freedom, Security and Justice (AFSJ) 201
Armenia 104, 112–13, 118, 120
Ashton, Catherine 230
Association Agreements 35, 40, 75–6, 144, 150
asymmetric relationships 30–1
authoritarian regimes 11, 14, 22, 32, 93–4, 99, 183, 193–4
Azerbaijan 31, 39, 104, 112–13, 120

Balzacq, T. 208
Barcelona Declaration (1995) 87, 150
Barcelona Process 69, 72, 75, 78, 83, 87–90, 149
  see also European Mediterranean Partnership
Barnett, M. 111
Beck, Ulrich 28
Belarus 12, 40, 122–35, 177
Ben Ali, Zine el Abidine 74, 93–4
Berlin Declaration (1999) 144
Berlusconi, Silvio 184
bilateralism 5–7, 83, 193, 195
Black Sea Synergy 6
Boatca, Manuela 59
Bologna Process 48
border controls 201–3, 215
borders of Europe, ambiguities in definition of 54–6
  see also re-bordering, cultural
Böröcz, J. 51, 53
Bort, E. 50
Bosnia 30–1, 35–6, 40
'bridge-building' between research traditions 224–5
British Council 182
Browning, C.S. 52
Bulgaria 6, 34
Bush, George W. 82

capabilities–expectations gap 29, 226
Carothers, Thomas 114
centre–periphery relationships 25, 34, 42–3

Checkel, J. 107
Chernobyl disaster 128–9, 161
Chong, D. 17
civil society 182, 198
Civil Society Forum 7, 133
Civil Society Neighbourhood Facility 230
'civilising mission' 50–1, 61
Cold War, ending of 43, 71, 124, 126, 129, 185
colonialism 95
Common Foreign and Security Policy (CFSP) 12, 18, 26, 40, 69, 73, 75, 79–80, 83, 86, 106–7, 155, 157–60, 163–70, 172, 226, 231
Common Security and Defence Policy (CSDP) 27, 40–1, 106–7, 118, 155, 231
Common Space on Freedom, Security and Justice (CSFSJ) 205–6
common values 19, 47–51, 57, 61–3, 206, 230
conditionality 3–4, 11, 30, 33–6, 39, 51–2, 62, 75–6, 81, 86, 99, 107, 110, 119, 134, 180
'conditioned anchoring' 140, 148–9, 155
conflict resolution 117–20
Constitutional Treaty of the EU (2005) 26
constructivism in International Relations theory 8–10, 16–17
see also social constructivism
convergence with and within the EU 4, 160, 165–6, 226
Cooper, Robert 36, 44
Copenhagen criteria (1993) 32–3, 57
Cornell, S.E. 114
Council for Mutual Economic Assistance (COMECON) 33
Council of Europe 105, 111, 114–15
Cremona, M. 201
Croatia 35–6
cultural differences 46, 58–9
cultural relativism 94
Cyprus 41, 87

Czech Republic 115

Dalacoura, Katerina 94
Dayton Peace Accords (1995) 35
deep and comprehensive free trade areas (DCFTAs) 76, 150, 232
'deep democracy' 230
democracy, definition of 20
democratisation 3, 125, 176–84, 193, 197, 230
  in the Middle East 84–102
deportation 213
Derrida, Jacques 28
Deutsch, Karl 103, 106
differentiation between countries 56, 77
diffusion of norms and values 32, 80
discourse analysis 221
Djukanović, Milo 36
Dura, George 127

Eastern Partnership (EaP) 7, 19, 31, 39, 109, 123, 131–4, 150, 175, 231
Economic and Monetary Union (EMU) 34
Egypt 30, 40, 42, 68, 79–80, 90, 94
Elgström, Ole 226
Emerson, M. 52
energy resources 13, 98, 120, 187–90, 196
energy security 130–1, 139
English School of International Relations theory 16
Enlargement Policy of the EU 3, 32–3
Enlightenment thinking 94
Estonia 34
ethno-political conflicts 155
  listing of 141–2
Euro-Mediterranean Association Agreements (EMAAs) 144
Euro-Mediterranean Partnership (EMP) 73–9, 83, 87, 150
European Agency for the Management of Operational Cooperation at External Borders (FRONTEX) 27, 210, 214

INDEX

European Coal and Steel Community (ECSC) 43
European Commission 55–9, 81, 87–8, 124, 127–31, 134, 164, 167, 176, 181, 187, 203
European Council 86, 122–3, 126, 147, 161–5, 168
European Economic Area (EEA) 30
European Endowment for Democracy 230
European External Action Service 36, 82
European Instrument for Democracy and Human Rights (EIDHR) 88–9, 128–9
European Law Enforcement Organisation (EUROPOL) 210
European Neighbourhood Investment Facility 4
European Neighbourhood Partnership Instrument (ENPI) 48, 88–9, 128–9, 210
European Neighbourhood Policy (ENP) 39–40, 46–7, 69–70, 73, 75, 76, 79, 83, 87–8, 110–11, 116, 119–20, 122–3, 127, 162, 175, 212, 225
  'common values' dimension of 19
  dilemmas of 2–8
  strategic review of 229, 231–2
  tensions within 1–2, 233
  transformative potential of 227
European Neighbourhood Strategy Paper (2004) 47–8
European Parliament 56, 116, 176, 183, 204–5, 211–15
European Security Strategy 9, 13, 31–2, 70, 72, 96, 162
European Year of Intellectual Dialogue (2008) 60
'Europeanisation' of national foreign policy 226
'Europeanness' 42–3, 55, 159
extradition 214

Feira Headline Goals 117

Ferro-Waldner, Benita 48–50
Fierke, K.M. 109
Flautre, Hélène 100
foreign policy of the EU 16, 107, 155, 219–20
  'actorness' in 225–8
  dilemmas of 67–83
France 26, 80, 83
free movement of people 40
Freedom House 89–93
Freyburg, T. 213
'frozen conflicts' 15, 140
Fukuyama, F. 114
Füle, Štefan 135
Fuller, Graham E. 93

Gaddafi, Muammar 41, 81
Gamsakhurdia, Zviad 145
gate-keeping 33, 36
Georgia 41–2, 104, 107, 112, 115, 117, 120, 141, 145–54, 182
Germany 42, 79–80, 206
Goldstein, J. 70–1
Gorbachev, Mikhail 33
governance, 'external' 27
Governance Facility of the ENP 4, 75, 114
governance standards 113–14
'grand strategy', components of 231
Greece 35
Gulf Cooperation Council (GCC) 90–2

Habermas, Jürgen 28
Hamas 74–5, 79–80, 97, 141, 143
'hard power' 29
Hassner, P. 55
Headley, J.M. 84–5
hegemonic order, features of 30
hegemony 25, 28–9, 39–44
  of Europeanness 42–3
  limits to 40–3
Helsinki Headline Goals 117
Henderson, Simon 98
High Representative for the CFSP 117
Hill, Christopher 226

Hong Kong 204
hub-and-spoke structures 31
Huddelston, T.H. 209
Hughes, J. 194
human rights 59, 73, 77, 80–1, 85–91, 94–5, 99, 124, 176–81, 196–7, 204–6, 211–16
human security doctrine 9
Huntington, S. 93
Hyde-Price, A. 8, 125, 195

Iceland 30
idealist values 124–6, 134
incentives for reform 4, 75–6, 160, 187, 220
individualism 94–5
integration, European 28–9, 119
inter-cultural dialogue 58–62
intergovernmentalism 68–9
'interlacing' 193–4
International Criminal Court 73
International Criminal Tribunal for Former Yugoslavia (ICTY) 36
International Organisation for Migration (IOM) 210–11
Iran 98
Iraq 12, 28, 91
Islam and Islamism 60, 63, 93–5
Israel 3, 6, 19, 31, 75–7, 141–5, 149–54
Italy 83

Jackson, R.H. 16
'joint ownership' principle 4
Jordan 77
Jurado, Elena 179, 192, 197
Justice and Home Affairs (JHA) Council 205

Kagan, Robert 28
Katzenstein, P. 219, 221–2
Kelley, J. 160
Keohane, R. 16, 70–1
Keukeleire, S. 107, 195
Kosovo 30–6, 40–1
Kovács, M. 59

Kuchma, Leonid 164
Kuzio, Taras 115

Laïdi, Z. 10
Lampedusa 99, 212
Landsbergis, Vytautas 194
Larsson, R.L. 196
Lavrov, Sergey 209
Lebanon 3, 76, 90
liberalisation, economic 36, 40, 91
liberalism in International Relations theory 8
Libya 31, 41, 75–7, 81
Lichtenstein 30
Light, Margot 177
Lisbon Treaty (2007) 26, 69, 82, 117, 155, 157, 176, 231–2
Lithuania 115
Locke, John 85
'logic of diversity' regarding foreign policy 82–3
Lucarelli, S. 157
Lukashenko, Alexander 122, 126–7, 130, 134–5

Maastricht Treaty (1992) 86, 124, 176
Macao 204
Macedonia 35–6
McFaul, Michael 115
Machiavelli, Niccolò 28, 125
MacNaughton, J. 195
Malta 87
Mandelson, Peter 193
Manners, I. 8, 14
Markell, P. 159
market access 11, 30, 40
Mediterranean European Development Action (MEDA) 88–9
Medvedev, Dmitri 182
methodological pluralism 220–1
migration flows and migration control policy 97, 201–4
milieu goals 10
Milošević, Slobodan 35
Mohamed the Prophet 95

Moldova 2, 39, 41, 55, 57, 62, 109, 127
Montenegro 36
Moratinos, Miguel Ángel 144
Morgenthau, Hans 27
Morocco 41, 56–7, 57, 75–6, 79
Mubarak, Hosni 74
multilateralism 71–2, 81

nation-states 27
natural gas supplies 187–8
natural law 85, 94
Neighbourhood East Parliamentary Assembly 133–4
Netherlands, the 26
non-refoulement principle 208
North Atlantic Treaty Organisation (NATO) 13, 35, 40–1, 76
North–South divide in the EU 78, 80–1
Norway 30

official development assistance (ODA) 151–3
Organisation for Security and Cooperation in Europe (OSCE) 105, 111, 114–15, 147, 170–1
Oslo Peace Accords (1993 and 1995) 143
Otte, Marc 144

Pace, M. 52
Palestine 3, 6, 19, 74–5, 90, 97, 141–5, 149–55
Partnership and Cooperation Agreements 38, 176
Partnership for Democracy and Shared Prosperity with the Southern Mediterranean 229, 231
partnership principle 4
peace promotion 139
peacekeeping operations 13
Poland 34, 115
police missions 13
Policy IV 90, 92
positivist epistemology 220
poverty 34
power politics 20, 29

power without politics 26–9
protectionism 40
'pull' effect of the EU 31
Putin, Vladimir 177, 182–5, 192–3, 198

Raik, Kristi 179
raison d'état 28
rapprochement 4
rational choice theory 178–9
rationalism in International Relations theory 8–9, 16
readmission agreements 19, 201–16
  implementation process 207–11
realism in International Relations theory 8
realpolitik 19, 125
re-bordering, cultural 46–51, 58–63
refugee protection 211–13, 216
'regatta principle' 31
regionalism 5–7, 116–17
Rehn, Ollie 27
religious differences 60
Renaissance thinking 84
rendition 77
'repertoire of integration' and 'repertoire of differences' 19, 54–62
research questions 219–20
'return to Europe' narrative 42
Rijpma, J. 201
'ring of friends' concept 48–9, 79
Roig, A. 209
Romania 6, 34
Rome Statute 73
rules of engagement 30
Rumelili, B. 159
Russia 6–7, 12–15, 20, 31, 41–2, 57, 62–3, 98, 107, 118–20, 130–1, 139, 146–7, 161–2, 175–99, 202–16
  GDP in 186
  obstacles to EU's influence on 181–92

Saakashvili, Mikhail 118, 145–6
Said, Edward 95
Sakwa, Richard 177
sanctions 71, 75–6, 134–5, 195–6

Sarkar, M. 53
Sarkozy, Nicolas 88, 147
Sasse, G. 4
Schengen agreements 34, 201, 215
Schimmelfennig, Frank 32–3, 110, 180
Schmidt, D. 183
Schröder, Gerhard 184, 193
security: definition of 119
  development of EU role as a provider of 105–8
  differences in the concept of 15, 20, 157–8
  in relation to values 1, 8–18, 25, 28–9, 63, 67–8, 72, 82–3, 85, 99, 124, 178, 192, 197, 202, 222, 229
  types of 13
  as a value in itself 19, 104, 109, 158, 172
Sedelmeier, Ulrich 180
Semneby, Peter 147
September 11th 2001 attacks 67–8, 72–3, 82
Serbia 41
Seventh Framework Programme (2007–13) 26
Sikorski, Radoslaw 5
Sil, R. 219, 221–2
Single Market, European 41, 44
Sjursen, H. 14, 110
Slovakia 34
Slovenia 34–5
'smart power' 27
Smith, Karen 5
Smith, Michael E. 226, 231
social constructivism 179
socialisation promoting change 4, 10, 80, 107, 110–11, 119, 193, 197–8
'soft' policy instruments 11, 29, 32, 53, 85, 99, 120, 161–2
Solana, Javier 107, 161
South Caucasus 19, 104–20
  expansion of European security community in 111–12
  see also Armenia; Azerbaijan; Georgia
South Ossetia 7, 118, 139, 141, 145–9, 155
sovereignty 27, 111
Soviet Union 30
  dissolution of 3
  see also Russia
Spain 83
Stabilisation and Association Process (SAP) 35
stability, pursuit of 31–2
Stability Pact for South East Europe 117
Starr, S.F. 114
state-building 30–1
Steinmeier, F.-W. 193–4
'structural conflict prevention' 140, 156
supranational institutions 44
Sushko, O. 167
Switzerland 30
synthesis of different theoretical schools 221
Syria 75, 90

Talvitie, Heikki 146–7
Tarasyuk, B. 163, 168
Technical Assistance to the Commonwealth of Independent States (TACIS) 128–9, 210
trade relations 36, 39–40
'transformative power' 51
transition from centrally planned to market economies 3
transition periods for elements of the *acquis* 34
Tunisia 68, 74–7, 90, 93–4
Turkey 30, 37–9, 42–3, 87, 107, 118

Ukraine 2, 20, 30–1, 39–42, 55, 57, 62, 107, 109, 115, 127, 157–73, 182
  alignment with CFSP acts, declarations and common positions 165–70, 172
  alignment with OSCE and UN 170–2
  institutionalisation of cooperation on CFSP 163
  recognition of the country's European character 162–3

role within European security
architecture 161–2
Union for the Mediterranean (UfM)
6–7, 69, 75, 83, 150
United Nations General Assembly
171–2
United States (US) 41, 71
universal values 58, 230
Uzbekistan 214

Vahl, M. 150
values: definition of 157
differences in the concept of 13–14,
46, 20, 184
European 4–5, 52–3, 100, 122–3, 176
islamic and *Western* 94–6, 102
universal application of 58, 230
see also common values; security in
relation to values
visa regimes 11, 40

Visegrad Cooperation 31

Waever, O. 105
Wallace, W. 53
Walters, W. 50–1
'Wider Europe' document 29, 108
Wiener, A. 109
Wolfers, A. 10
Wong, R. 226
World Trade Organisation (WTO)
191–2, 198

Yanukovych, Viktor 157
Yeltsin, Boris 182–3
Yesilyurt-Gunduz, Z. 100
Youngs, Richard 87, 124–5

Zakaria, Fareed 114
Zielonka, Jan 27

EU authorised representative for GPSR:
Easy Access System Europe, Mustamäe tee 50,
10621 Tallinn, Estonia
gpsr.requests@easproject.com

www.ingramcontent.com/pod-product-compliance
Ingram Content Group UK Ltd.
Pitfield, Milton Keynes, MK11 3LW, UK
UKHW021836140426
5217IPUK00021B/1483